JAZZ

JAZZ

JOHN FORDHAM

BARNES
&NOBLE
BOOKS
NEW YORK

Project Editor
Susannah Marriott

Design
Jane Bull Shobha Mucha Hazel Taylor

Senior Art Editor
Tracy Timson

Managing Art Editor
Carole Ash

Deputy Editorial Director
Daphne Razazan

Photography
The Dorling Kindersley studio
Dave King

Production
Antony Heller

U.S. Editor
Charles A. Wills

Respect to players here and gone — and especially to Monk,
who said "Play your own way."

This edition published by Barnes & Noble, Inc., by arrangement
with Dorling Kindersley, Inc.
1999 Barnes & Noble Books
M 10 9 8 7 6 5 4 3 2 1
ISBN 0-7607-1566-1
Copyright © 1993
Dorling Kindersley Limited, London
Text copyright © 1993 John Fordham
Foreword copyright © 1993 Sonny Rollins

Library of Congress Cataloging-in-Publication Data

Fordham, John.
Jazz / by John Fordham.--1st American ed.
p. cm.
Includes index.
ISBN 0-7607-1566-1
1. Jazz--History and criticism. 1. Title.
ML3506.F67 1993
781.65--dc20   93-850
CIP
MN

Reproduced in Singapore by Colourscan
Printed and bound in Slovakia

Contents

INTRODUCTION
Foreword by Sonny Rollins **6**

THE HISTORY OF JAZZ 8

The sources of jazz **10** • New beginnings **12**
1900-1920 timechart **14** • New Orleans **16**
1920s timechart **18** • Chicago **20** • 1930s timechart **22**
New York **24** • Swing **26** • 1940s timechart **28**
Bebop **30** • 1950s timechart **34** • Cool jazz **36**
Hard bop **38** • 1960s timechart **40** • Free jazz **42**
Fusion **44** • 1970-1990 timechart **46** • Jazz today **48**

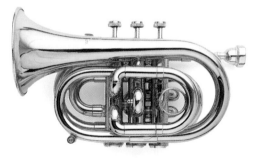

AN ANATOMY OF INSTRUMENTS 52

The voice **54** • Trumpet **56** • Trombone **60**
Clarinet **62** • Saxophone **64** • Woodwind **68**
Drums **70** • Percussion **74** • Vibraphone **78**
Keyboards **80** • Strings **84** • Guitar **86**
Bass **88** • Sampling **91**

JAZZ GIANTS 92

Scott Joplin **94** • Jelly Roll Morton **95**
Louis Armstrong **96** • Bix Beiderbecke **98**
Sidney Bechet **99** • Duke Ellington **100**
Coleman Hawkins **102** • Billie Holiday **104**
Lester Young **106** • Count Basie **108**
Charles Mingus **109** • Charlie Parker **110**
Dizzy Gillespie **112** • Miles Davis **114**
Thelonious Monk **116** • Art Blakey **117**
Sonny Rollins **118** • John Coltrane **120**
Ornette Coleman **122** • Keith Jarrett **123**

A GALLERY OF CLASSIC RECORDINGS 148

Blues & roots **150** • Ragtime & stride **152**
New Orleans style **154**
Chicago & New York **158** • Early singers **160**
Swing **162** • Bebop **166** • Cool jazz **170**
Hard bop **174** • Early funk **178** • Mainstream **180**
Postwar singers **182** • Free jazz **184**
Postbop big bands **188**
Modal jazz **190** • Latin jazz **192** • Fusion **194**
In the tradition **196** • Club jazz **200**
Freebop & funk **202** • Worldbeat **206**

TECHNIQUES 124

Musical roots **126** • Melody **128** • Rhythm **130**
Harmony **132** • Improvisation **134**
Composing & arranging **137**
The recording **140** • Dance roots **142**
Jazz dance today **144** • Club dance **146**

INDEX **212**
ACKNOWLEDGMENTS **216**

Foreword

It was a pleasure to be asked to write the foreword to this most comprehensive and substantial book about my favorite subject: jazz. Indeed, it is past time that the misconceptions which abound about this most singular form of music are explored and put to rest. This, John Fordham has admirably done with his scholarly, informative, and eminently readable text.

Here, for the first time, the reader will be able to see demonstrated many of the unique techniques employed in the creation of this magical music. There is something here for everyone, newcomer to connoisseur. Those new to the music will be captivated even as I was by the incredible folklore that surrounds it. Seasoned fans will be able to further their involvement by cross-referencing techniques and recordings to gain new insights into their favorite performers. Students will be immeasurably served.

Nothing like this was available for my generation when we were growing up. We had to pick up what we could when we could and where we could. It was mainly recordings in those days until we were old enough to be admitted to nightclubs, which, unlike today, were the only places the music was being played. But even before I was old enough to have like-minded friends, as a young boy growing up in New York's Harlem, jazz had become part of my life. It wasn't just the music, as great as it was, it was the sense of truth and goodness that it embodied — a way of bringing smiles to people's faces and warmth to the spirit. A way of honoring skill while validating intuition. A way of realizing that yes, there is a difference between right and wrong, honesty and dishonesty, good and bad. Make no mistake, jazz music is a tremendous force for peace and understanding between nations and peoples, and our world would be a far grimmer place without it.

I wish I could describe to you what it actually feels like to play jazz. Suffice it to say, there is nothing like the exhilaration which the challenge of improvisation invites. Sometimes when I am in the midst of a really good performance my mind will imperceptibly switch to automatic pilot and I find myself just standing there while the spirit of jazz, as it were, occupies my body, choosing for me just the correct note, the correct phrase, the correct idea, and when to play it. It is a profound spiritual experience!

Today it is a matter of no small significance that we are seeing ever-increasing numbers of young people drawn to jazz. I have been observing this most encouraging trend for over a decade now. As the world prepares to enter the new century, it is heartening to hope that some of the leaders of tomorrow will have known and experienced the spiritual certitude of jazz.

Finally, I should like to take the liberty of speaking for some of my colleagues, past and present, who in many cases endured severe hardship and deprivation to bring this music to us. I am sure they would be pleased, as I am, with John Fordham's book.
For them, and the list is long, I say thank you for giving us
jazz — the universal music.

Sonny Rollins

Introduction

There's a moment on Miles Davis's classic recording *Kind of Blue* that sprang at least one fine musician I know into the choice that shaped his life. There are many such moments in jazz, but this one says more about perfect timing than any book, nor could its essence be captured in any form of notation I know of. It is the sound of the skipped heartbeat, the caught breath, the sudden smile.

It comes deceptively after a soft, padding double-bass statement of the theme "So What." As it ends, Miles Davis's trumpet solo begins, with only two notes, the second an octave below the first. The first haunting sound hangs on its own in an otherwise empty space for a second that seems to go on forever. As it dips, the drummer suddenly hits his cymbal with a single reverberating blow that erupts like a flare over a twilit scene, and the jangling rivets sizzle on as Davis's horn eases nonchalantly into swing. It sounds both inevitable and astonishing at every new hearing.

It is the sound of jazz.

It is a sound that has transcended differences of age, culture, language, and musical history all over the world throughout this century. It is an amalgam of African and European music that could not have taken place, or taken so many enthralling forms, except in the "New World." It has changed the way we hear music, the way we dance, the way we talk. And though it has taken a painfully long time (too painful for some major artists of the past to bear) for jazz to be accepted as one of the most inventive and inspirational developments of our century, it is increasingly accepted and loved today for its spirit of change. The work of Charlie Parker or Thelonious Monk, rejected or belittled by many in its time, is now reinterpreted as classic music by performers as far apart as Prince and the Kronos String Quartet. When the great drummer Art Blakey, in his 70s and in his last years on the road, found listeners young enough to be his grand-children improvising new dance steps to music he had been playing for 40 years, it bore out a dictum he had repeated most of his life: "From the Creator, to the artist, direct to the audience, split-second timing, ain't no other music like that."

Jazz cannot, of course, be discovered by reading a book. It has to be listened to, in performance and on record, for its exuberance, defiance, wit, and energy to reach you where it counts. But it has a history, and its history and the unique methods evolved from it are the subjects of *Jazz*. This book is not an explanation, but perhaps a guide to some landmarks. It is also a tribute, and a gesture of thanks — both to the countless musicians who inspired it, and to the many people who helped bring it to life.

John Fordham

1

THE HISTORY OF JAZZ

Although not yet a century old, jazz has passed through
so many changes that admirers of one face of it
frequently fail to recognize the others as relatives.
Yet from rugged, ironic rural blues to breathtaking turn-
on-a-dime swing orchestras, from romantic
balladeers to willful, wailing free improvisers, from its
roots in the American South to branches in Rio,
Bombay, Cape Town, Melbourne, and even Azerbaijan,
jazz has been the modern world's soundtrack of surprise,
spontaneity, frailty, honesty, and strength.
Jazz has grown up alongside dance crazes, the movies,
record industry, and worldwide broadcasting — and it
has changed forever the way we hear tonality and
rhythm. Although often sidelined by establishment arts,
the history of jazz and blues is the hottest story
in 20th-century music.

The sources of jazz

Work songs, with their compelling rhythms and call-and-response patterns, provided vital ingredients for the structures of early jazz.

WHEN THE WRITER F. Scott Fitzgerald declared the arrival of "The Jazz Age" in the 1920s, he meant the word "jazz" to describe an attitude. You didn't have to know the music to understand the feeling, because it was about the changing mood of the 1920s. The most destructive war in history had ended. The automobile, the phonograph record, and network radio were transforming notions of distance, leisure, community — and "freedom." And three years before the decade began, a group of enthusiastic white musicians unexpectedly sold out Reisenweber's fashionable restaurant on New York's Columbus Circle and cut the first raucous, uneven, but spirited jazz record, "Livery Stable Blues" and "Original Dixieland One-Step." The sound was so strange at first that the customers had to be told they could dance to it. Two weeks later, they couldn't be stopped. The record sold a million copies, and the Original Dixieland Jazz Band put the word *jazz* into the vocabularies of street corners and royal palaces via Harlem rent parties and elegant Edwardian parlors. The message hummed around the world.

But the members of the Original Dixieland Jazz Band did not invent jazz.

Blues was flexible in form in the late 19th century but by about 1915, when these blues were published, it had become harmonically formalized. Its timbres, however, were still African.

They had heard it in New Orleans. In the red-light district of Storyville, in the street parades and the funeral marches, they had listened in astonishment to this unfamiliar, discordant, bittersweet sound. It seemed to mingle military music, vaudeville songs, religious pieces, rural blues, celebration, labor, and regret. It was not like anything they had heard before.

In the Place to Be

Jazz may not have entered public currency until the O.D.J.B. hit the jackpot in 1917, but a lot of Americans had been hearing fragments of it for years before the parts came together and gained a name. The music had not made the headlines then because the ingredients were scattered unrecognizably all over the States, and there had previously been no single moment when the right place, the right time, and the right name were ready to coincide. It was also unheralded because most of the people who had an inkling of this music were the southern black population, not the white bourgeoisie who thought good music was made in recital halls, not bordellos. Jazz

had been blooming in the secret gardens of the "New World" for a long time. Although the blooms had burst open in New Orleans, this was not its only home.

But if jazz didn't begin at Reisenweber's restaurant on Columbus Circle in 1917, where did it begin? Take a choice from any of the following: the "ring shouts" of camp meetings and religious gatherings from the late 1700s; the segregated churches of the post–Civil War era; the demobilization of Civil War armies and the cheap availability of their cast-off instruments; work songs on the railroads, in the cotton fields, or in the seaports; traveling minstrel shows; the rondo form of European music translated into ragtime. Or to go even further back: the circle dances, forerunners of the ring shouts, where the dancers became possessed, protected by friends and family in the ring; drum choirs, in which a number of drummers play several different rhythms simultaneously; ancestor worship, secret societies, and religious ceremonies.

Exodus

Much of this was not American culture but West African. When slavery brutally spliced a dispossessed African civilization into a mixed and transplanted European one, a resounding result was jazz — a hybrid formed out of two old civilizations transformed by coexistence in a New World struggling to invent itself.

The slave trade forcibly brought hundreds of thousands of Senegalese, Yorubas, Dahomeans, and Ashantis, each group with its own unique traditions — and dropped them into the tobacco and cotton industries of the Caribbean and the Americas. If the traditions of the slaves were not all alike, neither were those of the slave owners. The Catholics — Portuguese, Spanish and French — left West African culture more intact than did British Protestantism with its bans on dancing and drumming. All these conflicts flowed into jazz. Mingled African and Catholic ritual, shorn of "disrespectful" movement by Protestantism, spawned the vocally rhythmic preaching of revivalism. The rituals of Catholicism and those of West Africa sometimes overlapped

to the extent that some slaves would play drums for St. Patrick's Day, disguising one religion with the ritual of another.

In prerevolutionary Cuba, African dance survived well: the rhumba, conga, mambo, and cha-cha were mainly African. Trinidad's calypso is West African in origin. The blend of French and West African culture in Martinique, with its similarities to the makeup of New Orleans, produced an independently evolved music rather similar to early jazz.

African Rhythm

For all the differences among the African peoples chained and hauled to the New World, there were common strands, too. In West African music, rhythm had a pre-eminence over melody and harmony, which dominated European music. However, the principles of melody in African and European music were close enough for an assimilation to take place in song. Spoken

languages dependent on pitch and intonation as much as vocabulary for meaning introduced subtleties of sound that had no part in the European musical traditions — singing in falsetto, for instance, and bending and eliding notes rather than trying to hit them with a chorister's purity. And the significance of drum choirs and percussion music in African religious ceremonies had, over the centuries, resulted in a sophistication of rhythm — often with sounds grouped in triplets, set slightly out of phase and overlaid on each other — which would have been unthinkable in the West.

None of these elements on their own made jazz the music it came to be. But had their coincidental chemistry not been the way it was, jazz would never have been born.

If resources are scarce, singing, stamping, and clapping make music. In the South, the voice, banjo, and "percussion" of the body kept African musical traditions alive.

New beginnings

THERE WERE FOUR MILLION black slaves in North America by the middle of the 19th century, when the chains were finally unlocked. But though slaves had been without rights or choices, three hundred years of an inexorable flow of rituals, passions, and ideas across the Atlantic had not left the New World unmarked. And while white tolerance of African customs was usually limited to what would oil the wheels of business, and racial discrimination often did the work of the old overseers once slavery had been abolished, black and white people were living too close together not to change each other.

A convenient white justification for slavery was that it was an opportunity to reveal the true faith to a heathen, so much contact came through religion. As early as the 18th century, white preachers would enlist the help of black partners, engaged to provide theatrical performances that would swell the crowd at large outdoor meetings, but as slavery developed, black assistants became thought of as troublemakers and were discouraged. In the 1770s, a parson known popularly as Black Harry became celebrated for the fire of his rhythmic sermonizing, rejuvenating standard psalms with spine-chilling sliding-pitch African intonation, a compelling beat, and a technique called "lining out," whereby the congregation would rhythmically repeat the preacher's words every two or three lines. Inherited from British church practice to cope with congregations who could not read the prayer book, lining out echoed the African "call and response" interplay that runs right through gospel music, through the exchange of riffs between the sections in big band jazz, and in the swapping of instrumental choruses against drum breaks that frequently winds up a theme in smallgroup bebop music.

Work songs, built on rhythms suited to the job, were among the ingredients of jazz, as were sea chanteys, adapted from African origins by the black sailors of Savannah and New Orleans.

European and West African music came together in church and at work. Overseers did not often interfere with African work songs because they improved the output and the mood of the captive laborers. "Art music" had no meaning in Africa. Music was in all things: there were songs for courtship, for gossip and abuse, songs with rhythms suited to particular tasks, songs of seamanship, worship, and war. Now the work song found its rhythmic parallel in the clang of the hammer and the pickax, and odd hybrids of melody and lyrics came together, like those of the black sailors operating out of Savannah or New Orleans, whose chanteys mingled African themes and even elements from the English music hall.

Blues — the Soulful Truth
One of the fundamentals of almost all types of jazz, and of much Western popular music, derives from the blues. But blues in the twelve-bar, three-chord form that every earnest

When the Fisk Jubilee Singers began touring the United States and beyond in 1871, they brought African-American music to a wider public and deepened white understanding of what life meant for black people in America.

teenage guitarist learns today is a relatively late development, mixing African-American rural music and the harmonies of European church song. Before 1900, a traveling solo blues musician with a guitar or banjo would be offhand about how many beats a chord change should last. To such a musician, harmony was considered to be less important than the song and its unique sound — that sliding, emotional, and elusive swerving and soaring of pitch, the falsetto cry or holler (a plantation greeting), and the pragmatic, shorthand lyric with its ironies, casual tragedies, and mocking punch lines.

After 1900, more orderly blues in written form became popular hits (W. C. Handy's "St Louis Blues" was one of the most famous of these), and there was a brief boom for the idiom in the 1920s and early 1930s, when the burgeoning record industry found a market for its "race" labels in black neighborhoods across America. The Depression finally drove blues music to the margin until its eventual development into rock and roll in the 1950s.

Minstrelsy

As the 20th century dawned, other equally volatile ingredients dropped into the caldron from which jazz music was to erupt, and these elements included minstrelsy, spirituals, and ragtime. Minstrel shows, which dominated American entertainment from the middle to the end of the 19th century, had their roots in white sentimentalizing of "the noble savage," and the early white minstrel performers played in "blackface" makeup caricaturing what they assumed to be black life. One of the most famous routines of minstrelsy, a hit both in the United States and Britain, was "Jumpin' Jim Crow," white minstrel Tom Rice's representation of a hopping dance he watched a

The professional lives of many of jazz and blues stars of the 1920s and 1930s began in the minstrel shows. Minstrelsy originated popular dance hits like the cakewalk and produced many astonishing singers and dancers. But its underlying racism, which shouts from these song covers, led many black musicians to look hard at stage presentation from the late 1930s.

disabled black slave called Crow perform in the southern town of Louisville.

Minstrelsy was not a big influence on jazz, but with the rise of black minstrel shows in the later 19th century, early jazz and blues musicians like Ma Rainey, Jelly Roll Morton, and Clarence Williams found work in the tent shows and on the vaudeville circuit. The cakewalk — originally a mockery of the deportment of white aristocrats — was the finale of many minstrel shows, and it became a dance hit of the Jazz Age. Furthermore, minstrels acquainted a growing white public with musical

The musical complexity of some of the ingredients of jazz were drawn from European formal practice. But the unique flavor of the music came from its oral inheritance – from blues musicians who traveled the South in the late 19th and early 20th centuries, exchanging songs and using extensive improvisations.

ideas that prepared it for jazz. So did spirituals — contemplative, slow variations on African-American religious music that came closest to the precepts of European music in form and were the first type of black American music to make it into the world's concert halls on a regular basis.

Ragtime

Last came ragtime, another craze that took a firm hold in Europe as well as in America in the final decade of the 19th century. The expression literally means "ragged time." A technically complex piano music adapting European light classics, it depended on a steady, marchlike, two-beat left hand, given rhythmic charge by the right hand, which doubled the tempo and placed emphatic accents between the strong beats of the left hand rather than on top of them. Although this cross-rhythmic approach had black echoes in ceremonial and voodoo music, it could be traced in Western classical music, usually only as a passing effect. Ragtime was generally an amiable and optimistic music and lacked the expressive power of blues, but virtuosos like Tom Turpin gave the idiom immense fire and punch. Its jaunty, chugging beat, mingled with straight march time, became an important undertow to the music of early jazz bands and to the dynamic 1920s and 1930s jazz piano style known as "stride."

1900 – 1920

IN THE FIRST TWO DECADES of the 20th century a new sound emerged in America that made the world hear music afresh. Its rhythms and the expressiveness of its phrasing went back to Africa, its feel was fresh, dynamic, and urgent. The world woke up to "jazz" in 1917, when the Original Dixieland Jazz Band's first records were released, but the music had been simmering for a long time. In the rural blues and field

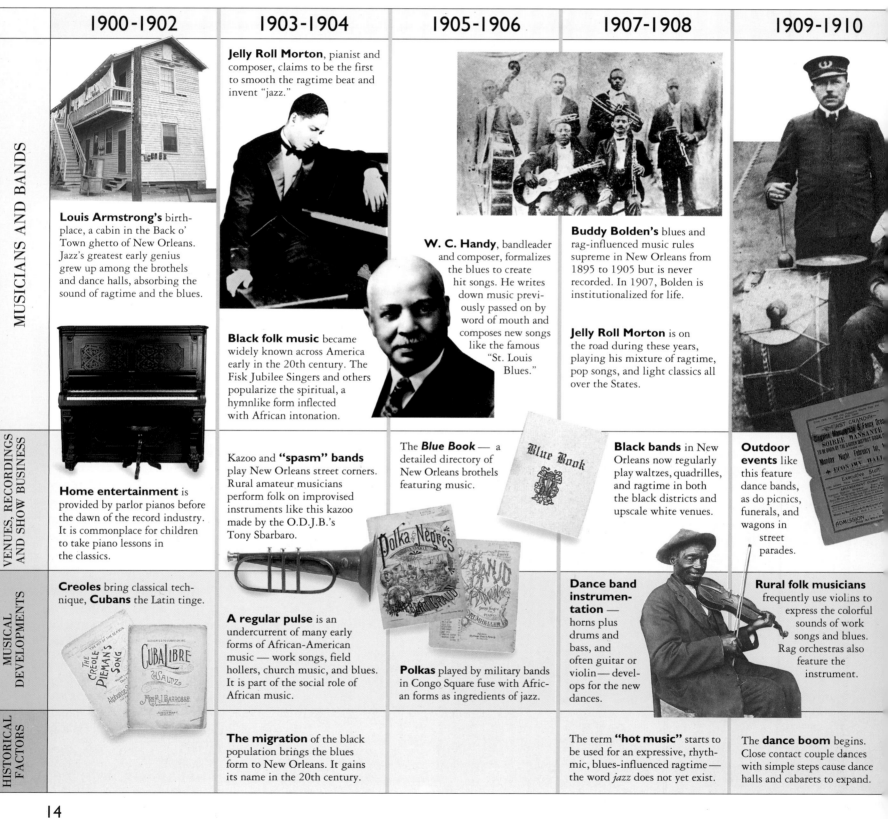

	1900-1902	1903-1904	1905-1906	1907-1908	1909-1910
MUSICIANS AND BANDS	**Louis Armstrong's** birthplace, a cabin in the Back o' Town ghetto of New Orleans. Jazz's greatest early genius grew up among the brothels and dance halls, absorbing the sound of ragtime and the blues.	**Jelly Roll Morton**, pianist and composer, claims to be the first to smooth the ragtime beat and invent "jazz." **Black folk music** became widely known across America early in the 20th century. The Fisk Jubilee Singers and others popularize the spiritual, a hymnlike form inflected with African intonation.	**W. C. Handy**, bandleader and composer, formalizes the blues to create hit songs. He writes down music previously passed on by word of mouth and composes new songs like the famous "St. Louis Blues."	**Buddy Bolden's** blues and rag-influenced music rules supreme in New Orleans from 1895 to 1905 but is never recorded. In 1907, Bolden is institutionalized for life. **Jelly Roll Morton** is on the road during these years, playing his mixture of ragtime, pop songs, and light classics all over the States.	
VENUES, RECORDINGS AND SHOW BUSINESS	**Home entertainment** is provided by parlor pianos before the dawn of the record industry. It is commonplace for children to take piano lessons in the classics.	Kazoo and **"spasm" bands** play New Orleans street corners. Rural amateur musicians perform folk on improvised instruments like this kazoo made by the O.D.J.B.'s Tony Sbarbaro.	The **Blue Book** — a detailed directory of New Orleans brothels featuring music.	**Black bands** in New Orleans now regularly play waltzes, quadrilles, and ragtime in both the black districts and upscale white venues.	**Outdoor events** like this feature dance bands, as do picnics, funerals, and wagons in street parades.
MUSICAL DEVELOPMENTS	**Creoles** bring classical technique, **Cubans** the Latin tinge.	**A regular pulse** is an undercurrent of many early forms of African-American music — work songs, field hollers, church music, and blues. It is part of the social role of African music.	**Polkas** played by military bands in Congo Square fuse with African forms as ingredients of jazz.	**Dance band instrumentation** — horns plus drums and bass, and often guitar or violin — develops for the new dances.	**Rural folk musicians** frequently use violins to express the colorful sounds of work songs and blues. Rag orchestras also feature the instrument.
HISTORICAL FACTORS		**The migration** of the black population brings the blues form to New Orleans. It gains its name in the 20th century.		The term **"hot music"** starts to be used for an expressive, rhythmic, blues-influenced ragtime — the word *jazz* does not yet exist.	The **dance boom** begins. Close contact couple dances with simple steps cause dance halls and cabarets to expand.

music of the South, in the boogie piano sounds of the railheads and saloons, in the mingled rhythmic energy and parlor piano elegance of ragtime, in marching bands, funeral bands, and brothel piano "professors," lay the cells from which the embryo formed. These elements existed in many parts of the States, not just New Orleans, but the unique makeup of that city made it the hothouse where they grew strong.

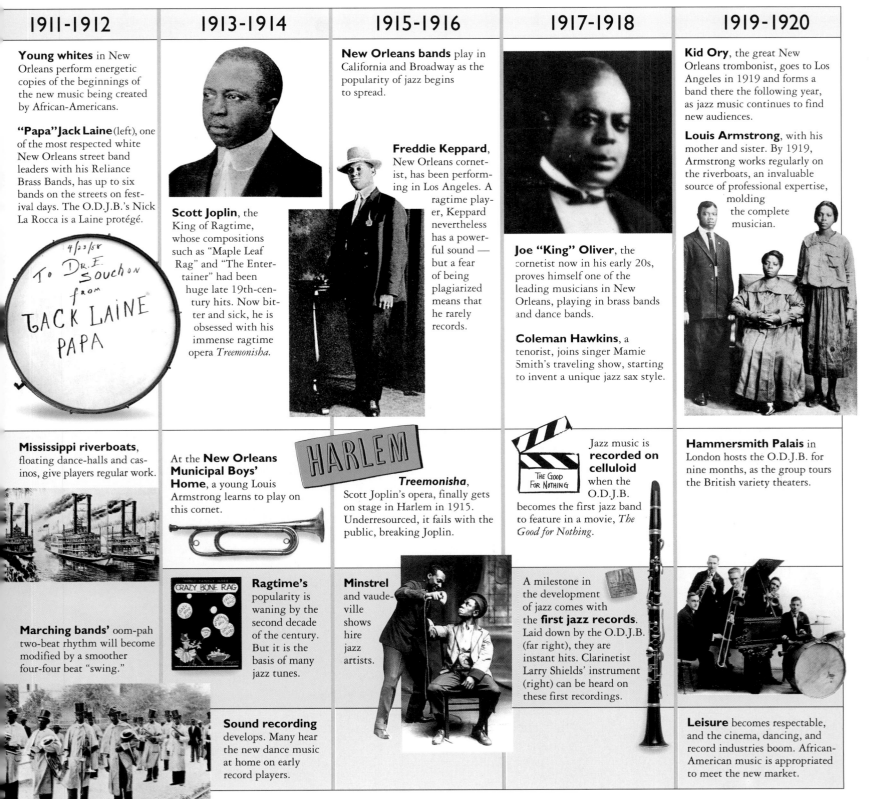

1911-1912

Young whites in New Orleans perform energetic copies of the beginnings of the new music being created by African-Americans.

"Papa" Jack Laine (left), one of the most respected white New Orleans street band leaders with his Reliance Brass Bands, has up to six bands on the streets on festival days. The O.D.J.B.'s Nick La Rocca is a Laine protégé.

4/23/58 To Dr. E. Souchon from JACK LAINE PAPA

Mississippi riverboats, floating dance-halls and casinos, give players regular work.

Marching bands' oom-pah two-beat rhythm will become modified by a smoother four-four beat "swing."

1913-1914

Scott Joplin, the King of Ragtime, whose compositions such as "Maple Leaf Rag" and "The Entertainer" had been huge late 19th-century hits. Now bitter and sick, he is obsessed with his immense ragtime opera *Treemonisha.*

At the **New Orleans Municipal Boys' Home,** a young Louis Armstrong learns to play on this cornet.

CRAZY BONE RAG

Ragtime's popularity is waning by the second decade of the century. But it is the basis of many jazz tunes.

Sound recording develops. Many hear the new dance music at home on early record players.

1915-1916

New Orleans bands play in California and Broadway as the popularity of jazz begins to spread.

Freddie Keppard, New Orleans cornetist, has been performing in Los Angeles. A ragtime player, Keppard nevertheless has a powerful sound — but a fear of being plagiarized means that he rarely records.

HARLEM

Treemonisha, Scott Joplin's opera, finally gets on stage in Harlem in 1915. Underresourced, it fails with the public, breaking Joplin.

Minstrel and vaudeville shows hire jazz artists.

1917-1918

Joe "King" Oliver, the cornetist now in his early 20s, proves himself one of the leading musicians in New Orleans, playing in brass bands and dance bands.

Coleman Hawkins, a tenorist, joins singer Mamie Smith's traveling show, starting to invent a unique jazz sax style.

THE GOOD FOR NOTHING

Jazz music is **recorded on celluloid** when the O.D.J.B. becomes the first jazz band to feature in a movie, *The Good for Nothing.*

A milestone in the development of jazz comes with the **first jazz records.** Laid down by the O.D.J.B. (far right), they are instant hits. Clarinetist Larry Shields' instrument (right) can be heard on these first recordings.

1919-1920

Kid Ory, the great New Orleans trombonist, goes to Los Angeles in 1919 and forms a band there the following year, as jazz music continues to find new audiences.

Louis Armstrong, with his mother and sister. By 1919, Armstrong works regularly on the riverboats, an invaluable source of professional expertise, molding the complete musician.

Hammersmith Palais in London hosts the O.D.J.B. for nine months, as the group tours the British variety theaters.

Leisure becomes respectable, and the cinema, dancing, and record industries boom. African-American music is appropriated to meet the new market.

New Orleans

JELLY ROLL MORTON, sometime pimp, gambler, boxing manager, and fulltime jazz genius, called trumpeter Buddy Bolden "the blowingest man ever lived since Gabriel." But it is only in the work of aging New Orleans musicians who committed their memories to print or record that Bolden's big sound and remolding of the components of prejazz survived. The first jazz brass hero, he was spending the tenth of his last twenty-four years in a mental institution in Jackson, Louisiana, when the first jazz records were made in 1917.

Yet by 1905, Bolden's example had already done its work. His band had played a mixture of popular dances, a rough-and-ready ensemble version of ragtime, and the blues. Featuring cornet, clarinet, valve trombone, guitar, double bass, and drums, its repertoire evolved in uptown New Orleans in the last decades of the 19th century. It was a music commonly performed by working-class black musicians who improvised and played by ear. It did not make much sense to the city's white bourgeoisie, nor to the French-educated class of black Creoles, the mixed-race descendants of French and Spanish settlers, who enjoyed a virtually middle-class status in the city and whose schooling meant that many read music and played the classics.

Creoles Meet the Blues

After decades of cosmopolitan, boomtown coexistence, racial discrimination began to intensify in New Orleans in the 1890s. As whites poured into the South, black people moved out of the smart districts and out of

New Orleans's Congo Square was the scene of thrilling re-creations of African music and dance.

the jobs. Sophisticated Creole musicians moved uptown to what was becoming a ghetto. They found themselves alongside players who made up much of the music as they went along. Recollections of the tremendous power of Buddy Bolden may have had as much to do with the startling sound — to Europeanized ears — of his "impure" pitching as to his sheer volume. But the technical skills of the Creole players, mingling with the bluesier, earthier music they found themselves confronted with, brought the simmering emergence of a new music closer to a boil.

New Orleans is usually thought of as the birthplace of jazz, although it is now known to be far from its only early home. The city had some unique qualifications for the role, however. At the beginning of the 1800s, the population of New Orleans was roughly half black and half white. After the United States acquired New Orleans in the Louisiana Purchase of 1803, American settlers came south in increasing numbers. More slaves were brought, too, bringing fresh injections of traditional African culture. Jelly Roll Morton was a devout believer in voodoo throughout his life because he grew up in a city in which the practice permeated the uptown black areas and brought with it music of such eloquent rhythms that they kept disrupting the obedient, orderly tread of military music. In Congo Square in New Orleans, formerly an authorized music and dance venue for slaves, musicians had, by the 1880s, started to mingle European instruments with African ones and to sing call-and-response patterns in Creole patois.

Marching On

The music of late 19th-century New Orleans was dominated by brass bands, as was true almost everywhere in the States. A plentiful supply of cheap military band instruments after the Civil War and demobilization provided the means, and the prosperity and swelling population of New Orleans provided the demand. Brass bands

played for parades, dances, riverboat trips, and funerals. For the recent descendants of West African societies, devoting music and energy to respect for the dead was an important reminder of home. African cult groups and secret societies resurfaced in New Orleans, operating like Masonic lodges or friendly societies. If payments were kept up, they guaranteed a decent send-off when the time came, with as many musicians, as loud a noise, and as lengthy a wake as the installments allowed. As in Dahomey, Africa, where funerals were seen as a celebration, an impassioned ceremonial at the graveside was followed by a raucous journey back into town, and favorites of later New Orleans jazz like "Didn't He Ramble" and "When the Saints Go Marching In" were homecoming funeral band tunes.

In 1897, alderman Sidney Story officiated over the creation of the city's legal red-light district at South Rampart and Perdido streets. It bore the name Storyville until 1917, when it was closed down for being detrimental to morale during World War I. The sporting houses were a lucrative source of work for resourceful young

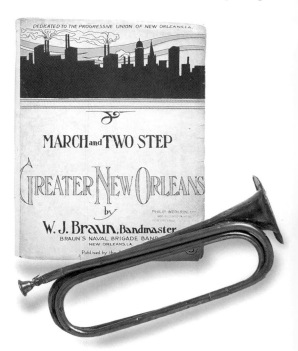

Early jazz instrumentation reflected that of military bands, although the bugle was soon replaced by the more flexible cornet. This Civil War bugle, used in the Confederate Army, was later reappropriated to play jazz.

At open-air events in the city, like this opening of a park, minstrel shows and brass bands provided the entertainment.

Louis Armstrong was a genius, but he needed a little theory to be a professional. Riverboat work with the Fate Marable band was an invaluable apprenticeship.

pianists like Jelly Roll Morton, on the run from declining Creole prosperity. Pianists played in the perfumed, scarlet velvet and candelabra-strewn interiors of the brothels, and brass bands played in the streets or on the backs of carts. Europe and America mingled further. The Original Dixieland Jazz Band's "Tiger Rag" was the same piece, several different titles removed, from an old French quadrille.

The classic New Orleans instrumentation thus proved eclectic in its evolution: brass and drums descended from military bands, clarinet came from the educated but downwardly mobile Creole musicians, and banjo or guitar derived from minstrelsy and blues. The frontline instruments interleaved in a general approximation of European conservatory counterpoint, but the constant spontaneous reworking of the lines was African in origin, where no one melody was so sacrosanct as to be beyond improvement in the next performance. "Jazz" was the name sticking to this new sound, with a meaning more sexual than musical. But in New Orleans, those meanings were in close embrace anyway.

By 1910, Buddy Bolden had been locked up for three years after running amok in the streets, but plenty of powerful players had learned by his example and were ready to take his place. Joe "King" Oliver had worked the best brass bands and dance ensembles in town by 1910. Louis Daniel Armstrong, son of a part-time prostitute and servant in the uptown ghetto, knew how to sing close harmony for nickels by the same date and learned cornet in a home for delinquent black boys not long afterwards. The prestigious Creole clarinet teacher Lorenzo Tio had a star pupil, Sidney Bechet, who was similarly holding down any job in the New Orleans music market when barely into his teens. Jelly Roll Morton was evolving his own versions of ragtime piano from around 1904. Cornet players Freddie Keppard and Bunk Johnson were respected inheritors of Bolden's methods — and although neither recorded until much later, Keppard had toured both coasts long before the emigration from New Orleans began. But as the new music of the South first matured, it was already time to move.

1920s

Novelist F. Scott Fitzgerald called the 1920s "The Jazz Age." The spirit of jazz, its exuberance, honesty, spontaneity, and directness, reflected a young nation's growing self-confidence. A new phenomenon, the leisure industry, developed on both side of the Atlantic with breakthroughs in recording, cinema and radio. And New Orleans jazz, which had erupted in 1917, put fire into urbane 1920s dance music. Louis

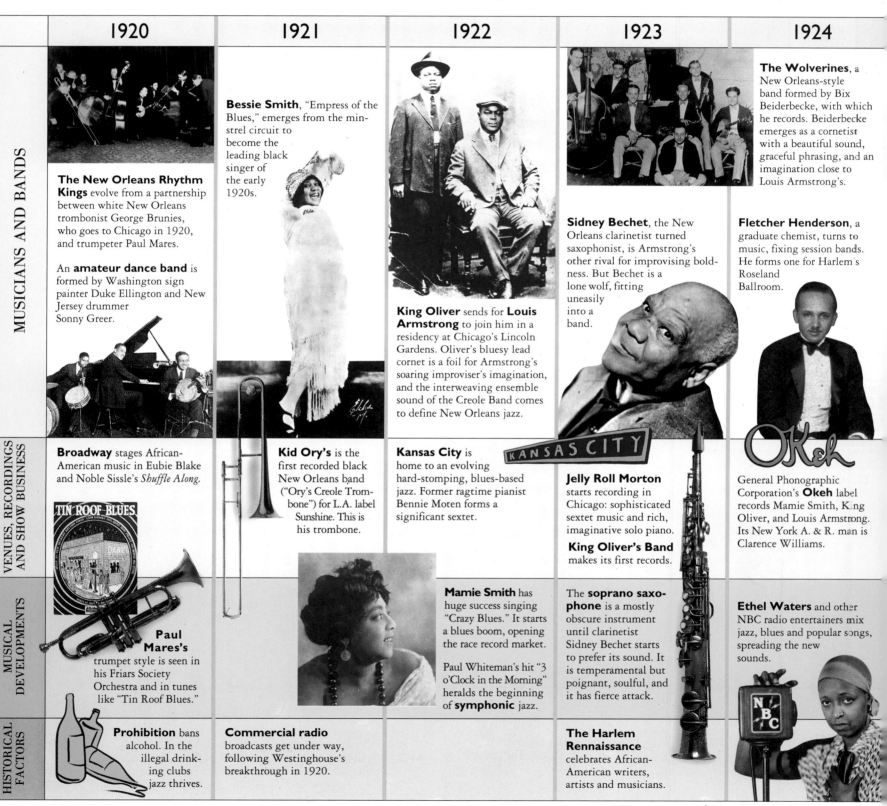

	1920	1921	1922	1923	1924
MUSICIANS AND BANDS	**The New Orleans Rhythm Kings** evolve from a partnership between white New Orleans trombonist George Brunies, who goes to Chicago in 1920, and trumpeter Paul Mares. An **amateur dance band** is formed by Washington sign painter Duke Ellington and New Jersey drummer Sonny Greer.	**Bessie Smith**, "Empress of the Blues," emerges from the minstrel circuit to become the leading black singer of the early 1920s.	**King Oliver** sends for **Louis Armstrong** to join him in a residency at Chicago's Lincoln Gardens. Oliver's bluesy lead cornet is a foil for Armstrong's soaring improviser's imagination, and the interweaving ensemble sound of the Creole Band comes to define New Orleans jazz.	**Sidney Bechet**, the New Orleans clarinetist turned saxophonist, is Armstrong's other rival for improvising boldness. But Bechet is a lone wolf, fitting uneasily into a band.	**The Wolverines**, a New Orleans-style band formed by Bix Beiderbecke, with which he records. Beiderbecke emerges as a cornetist with a beautiful sound, graceful phrasing, and an imagination close to Louis Armstrong's. **Fletcher Henderson**, a graduate chemist, turns to music, fixing session bands. He forms one for Harlem's Roseland Ballroom.
VENUES, RECORDINGS AND SHOW BUSINESS	**Broadway** stages African-American music in Eubie Blake and Noble Sissle's *Shuffle Along*.	**Kid Ory's** is the first recorded black New Orleans band ("Ory's Creole Trombone") for L.A. label Sunshine. This is his trombone.	**Kansas City** is home to an evolving hard-stomping, blues-based jazz. Former ragtime pianist Bennie Moten forms a significant sextet.	**Jelly Roll Morton** starts recording in Chicago: sophisticated sextet music and rich, imaginative solo piano. **King Oliver's Band** makes its first records.	General Phonographic Corporation's **Okeh** label records Mamie Smith, King Oliver, and Louis Armstrong. Its New York A. & R. man is Clarence Williams.
MUSICAL DEVELOPMENTS	**Paul Mares's** trumpet style is seen in his Friars Society Orchestra and in tunes like "Tin Roof Blues."		**Mamie Smith** has huge success singing "Crazy Blues." It starts a blues boom, opening the race record market. Paul Whiteman's hit "3 o'Clock in the Morning" heralds the beginning of **symphonic** jazz.	The **soprano saxophone** is a mostly obscure instrument until clarinetist Sidney Bechet starts to prefer its sound. It is temperamental but poignant, soulful, and it has fierce attack.	**Ethel Waters** and other NBC radio entertainers mix jazz, blues and popular songs, spreading the new sounds.
HISTORICAL FACTORS	**Prohibition** bans alcohol. In the illegal drinking clubs jazz thrives.	**Commercial radio** broadcasts get under way, following Westinghouse's breakthrough in 1920.		**The Harlem Rennaissance** celebrates African-American writers, artists and musicians.	

Armstrong launched out of the early collective ensemble sound and turned jazz into a soloist's art, with virtuosos like Earl Hines, Coleman Hawkins and Sidney Bechet in his wake. Blues singers briefly grew rich on record sales. Musicians migrated from Chicago to New York, and although a semiclassical symphonic jazz was briefly popular, Ellington's blues-influenced orchestral music pointed to the future.

1925

Louis Armstrong works with the **Hot Fives** and starts some recordings that are among a handful of the leading classics of jazz. Showcasing him as a soloist, the Hot Fives work makes his phrasing and timing models for all jazz musicians.

The last lineup of **N.O.R.K. disbands** shortly after this concert. Unable to take New Orleans jazz further, the band fails to adapt to looser swing.

AT THE
ITALIAN HALL · 1020 ESPLANADE AVENUE
SATURDAY, APRIL 18, 1925, 8 P.M.
MUSIC BY THE FAMOUS
NEW ORLEANS RHYTHM KINGS
Played successfully for big audiences in New York and Chicago for the last three years. You have heard their delightful music on OKEH and GENNETT records.

Electrical recording starts. Past musicians played into an acoustic horn fixed to a stylus that cut the wax disk. Mikes now take signals to the stylus for better sound.

Louis Armstrong echoes his trumpet with a gravelly, rhythmically unpredictable singing. "Heebie Jeebies" features an early version of this wordless **"scat."**

The Great Gatsby, F. Scott Fitzgerald's famous novel of the Roaring Twenties, is published. He christens the decade "The Jazz Age."

1926

Earl Hines is the first great jazz piano virtuoso, changing the formal ragtime right hand to resemble horn-solo phrasing. A remarkable technician and willing ensemble player, he helps to galvanize many Chicago bands.

Bix Beiderbecke and saxophonist partner **Frankie Trumbauer** join Jean Goldkette's sophisticated popular Detroit dance orchestra.

Chicago jazz, as it will be dubbed, develops in the hands of young white musicians. It is a fast, energetic brand of New Orleans music.

Serious jazz criticism flows from the pens of Britain's Spike Hughes and Hugues Panassie in France, while European New Orleans-style bands form.

National Broadcasting Company (NBC) sets up a network of radio stations, transmitting nationally.

1927

Duke Ellington opens at the Cotton Club in Harlem and rapidly moves to a prominent position in the jazz world. Influential soloists like saxophonist Harry Carney and clarinetist Barney Bigard join the orchestra.

Paul Whiteman has dubbed himself the King of Jazz but realizes that symphonic jazz is too demure for a changing public. He hires a group of leading white "hot" soloists including Beiderbecke and Trumbauer.

On Hot Fives and early **Hot Sevens** sets Armstrong is audacious, his horn independent of the original material.

Jelly Roll Morton records with his classic Red Hot Peppers.

"Black and Tan Fantasy" reflects Ellington's move from smooth dance music to a sound influenced by New Orleans. Cowritten with Bubber Miley, it is a masterpiece.

1928

The New Orleans style is already dying out. The most **progressive bands** are using more complex arrangements and adding saxophones.

The **stride piano** style, derived from ragtime, is by now a self-contained jazz piano technique, with its own virtuosos like James P. Johnson and Luckyeth Roberts.

Luis Russell, the Panamanian bandleader, develops a vigorous ensemble style starring brilliant trumpeter, Henry "Red" Allen. The band accompanies Louis Armstrong in 1929, and in the 1930s becomes his backing band.

Johnny St. Cyr's banjo had a key rhythmic input on Armstrong's early classics and the Red Hot Peppers sessions.

Chicago's booming **nightlife declines** when the city cracks down on the mobsters — a blow for jazz musicians' job prospects.

1929

Morton's **Red Hot Peppers** provide new ideas for musicians everywhere, using subtle ensemble harmonies and counter-melodies. However, they are reluctant to abandon New Orleans ideas at a time when Ellington and Fletcher Henderson are moving away from collective improvisation.

A **movie** dramatization of the blues, featuring Fletcher Henderson's musicians, sees Bessie Smith play the wronged wife.

ST LOUIS BLUES

Jazz critic Robert Donaldson Darrell, writing in *Phonograph Monthly Review* and *Disques*, develops a style of extended analysis of jazz pieces, notably Duke Ellington's "Black and Tan Fantasy."

The **Wall Street Crash** begins a major depression in the U.S. economy. It contributes to changes in musical tastes, and a rejection of the blues.

Chicago

THE INDESTRUCTIBLE CLASSICS of jazz recorded in the 1920s by King Oliver, Louis Armstrong, Jelly Roll Morton, and Sidney Bechet are generally known as New Orleans jazz. The name now suggests a rugged, informal, small-group music for brass instruments, woodwind, piano, and percussion, dancing breezily down the decades and heard through the crackle of an old record. Yet the mature years of the style were not spent in the Crescent City, and none of the early key recordings was made there. New Orleans jazz reached full flower in the cold and grime of Chicago, eight hundred miles north, rather than in the Mississippi Delta's subtropical climate.

In 1900, three-quarters of America's black population lived in the rural South; barely a fifth of that number lived there less than fifty years later. These teeming migrations from the fields, cotton industry, and gathering racism of Louisiana to the blast furnaces, lumber industry, and factories of the North followed the summons of young America's thundering economy.

Although jazz was a word on everybody's lips after 1917, it did not necessarily mean the kind of jazz that made sense to King Oliver or Jelly Roll Morton. An expanding leisure market meant a demand for light, modern dance music with enough of an earthy tang to give law students and the prospective inheritors of thriving businesses the impression of needling their respectable parents and putting a toe in the dirt. But it also meant that five years after its smash hit "Livery Stable Blues," the Original Dixieland Jazz Band was playing foxtrots more often than hot jazz.

Heading North

If a predominantly black music leaned more toward ecstatic rhythms and the loaded, sensuous inflections of the slow

Chicago in the 1920s meant the promise of a new life — especially for the southern black population, drawn to the city's expanding industries.

Joe "King" Oliver's Creole band drew the crowds to Chicago's Lincoln Gardens. Its rhythm and bluesy sound exuded a new excitement.

blues dancing that put Storyville customers in the mood, the only place for its players to go when Storyville closed down was to a town just as acquainted with human frailty. Chicago was in the hands of the gangsters in the 1920s, harboring as many cabarets and dance joints as there had ever been down South and more, and the cash was better even if the bosses were volatile. New Orleans jazz found a new academy in such venues as the Lincoln Gardens on Chicago's South Side, the Plantation, the Sunset, and the Nest. Not long after the migrants arrived, Prohibition came in. The legislation that banned alcohol triggered an explosion in bootleg liquor crime and gave rise to a twilight network of speakeasies. People looking for a drink wanted music to accompany it.

The Original Dixieland Jazz Band had gone to Chicago from New Orleans in 1916. Joe "King" Oliver followed two years later and formed his famous ensemble, the Creole Band, there. Oliver regularly worked at the Lincoln Gardens, and in 1922 he sent for Louis Armstrong, the gifted young trumpeter he had taught in New Orleans ragtime bands. Armstrong had come a long way in the four years since his mentor had left the South. He had replaced Oliver in the prestigious outfit led by trombonist Kid Ory and had worked the Mississippi riverboats playing for dances, molding his raw talent into a professional expertise. More tellingly, Louis Armstrong now had a melodic imagination extending beyond that of his teenage heroes, and one which could not be precisely tracked to any single influence more explicable than his own genius.

Inventions and Dimensions

Jazz was still largely an ensemble music, with improvisation being mostly a matter of texture and embroidery rather than the streams of spontaneous new melody that were to characterize it later. But Oliver's disciplinarian approach ensured that the parts meshed, and his band had a taut, muscular energy. When he brought Armstrong in, he broke the rules, giving the group a two-cornet front line. The result was simply devastating. Oliver was a

fine trumpeter, but he kept close to the melody and explicit beat, producing variations through timbre and an imaginative use of mutes. Armstrong was already doubling the number of notes he would squeeze into a bar and sounding them at unequal lengths and with unpredictable emphasis. The music began to take on a tidal ebb and swell rather than the raglike rocking time that had gone before. He also seemed to build his improvisations over longer stretches, like miniature narratives, and his trumpet sound shone.

Out of the Ghetto

The sound carried a long way outside the ghetto. Young middle-class whites were coming to black neighborhoods to hear the new music. At first this audience swelled the crowds mostly on weekends, but the King Oliver band became so popular that the proprietors of the Lincoln Gardens staged "midnight rambles" on Wednesday nights specifically for white fans like Benny Goodman, Bix Beiderbecke, and Gene Krupa. Whites had role models closer to home, too, like the New Orleans Rhythm Kings, a white band influenced by both the Original Dixieland Jazz Band and the growing rhythmic looseness of the Oliver band with Armstrong. Musicians like Beiderbecke already had a more polished, less bluesy sound, and the "Austin High

Smashing the barrels – the authorities' attempt to keep the city dry. Prohibition brought gangsters, mob-run drinking clubs and speakeasies, all work opportunities for jazz musicians.

School gang" (associated with Benny, trumpeter Jimmy McPartland, saxophone player Bud Freeman, and guitarist Eddie Condon) developed a crisp, light, swinging jazz rather misleadingly labeled Chicago style, which influenced swing and the mainstream movement to come.

Chicago's role in jazz history was not to endure; nor was the New Orleans music that the city helped introduce to the world. Jazz news was spreading much faster than ever before. The first commercial radio broadcasts had drifted over the rooftops in 1920, and within two years more than five hundred stations had signed up. All over the States, budding musicians latched on to the sounds produced in the North. A new Chicago administration came to power and hit the gangsters hard, closing down the dives. And America was tuning in to a cooler, hipper rhythm, the four even beats over the bar that Jelly Roll Morton swore he had imagined twenty years before, leaving the dated oom-cha ragtime bounce behind. New York was becoming the center of America's entertainment business. It was time to move again.

1930s

THE 1930S BEGAN WITH THE WORD JAZZ, so dominant in the decade before, all but buried by the Wall Street crash and the economic slump that followed. The audience had not gone away, but the record industry almost capsized, and the rise of network radio hit it even harder. When recovery came, a new audience demanding a new music arrived, too. The New Orleans notion of jazz or a simple, unvarnished

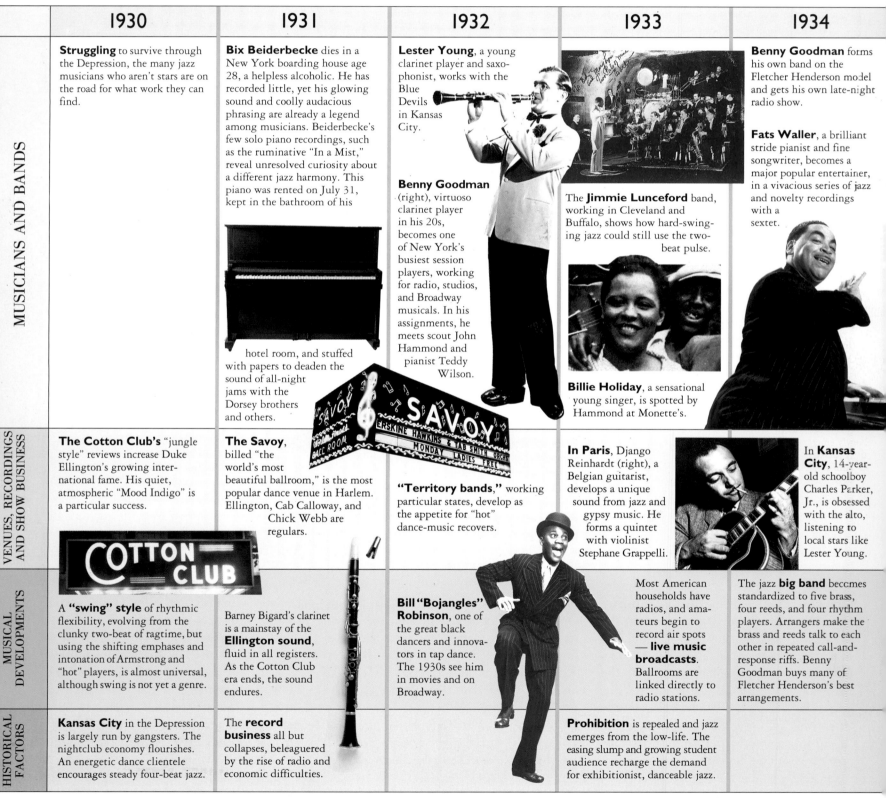

	1930	1931	1932	1933	1934
MUSICIANS AND BANDS	**Struggling** to survive through the Depression, the many jazz musicians who aren't stars are on the road for what work they can find.	**Bix Beiderbecke** dies in a New York boarding house age 28, a helpless alcoholic. He has recorded little, yet his glowing sound and coolly audacious phrasing are already a legend among musicians. Beiderbecke's few solo piano recordings, such as the ruminative "In a Mist," reveal unresolved curiosity about a different jazz harmony. This piano was rented on July 31, kept in the bathroom of his hotel room, and stuffed with papers to deaden the sound of all-night jams with the Dorsey brothers and others.	**Lester Young**, a young clarinet player and saxophonist, works with the Blue Devils in Kansas City. **Benny Goodman** (right), virtuoso clarinet player in his 20s, becomes one of New York's busiest session players, working for radio, studios, and Broadway musicals. In his assignments, he meets scout John Hammond and pianist Teddy Wilson.	The **Jimmie Lunceford** band, working in Cleveland and Buffalo, shows how hard-swinging jazz could still use the two-beat pulse. **Billie Holiday**, a sensational young singer, is spotted by Hammond at Monette's.	**Benny Goodman** forms his own band on the Fletcher Henderson model and gets his own late-night radio show. **Fats Waller**, a brilliant stride pianist and fine songwriter, becomes a major popular entertainer, in a vivacious series of jazz and novelty recordings with a sextet.
VENUES, RECORDINGS AND SHOW BUSINESS	**The Cotton Club's** "jungle style" reviews increase Duke Ellington's growing international fame. His quiet, atmospheric "Mood Indigo" is a particular success.	**The Savoy**, billed "the world's most beautiful ballroom," is the most popular dance venue in Harlem. Ellington, Cab Calloway, and Chick Webb are regulars.	**"Territory bands,"** working particular states, develop as the appetite for "hot" dance-music recovers.	**In Paris**, Django Reinhardt (right), a Belgian guitarist, develops a unique sound from jazz and gypsy music. He forms a quintet with violinist Stephane Grappelli.	In **Kansas City**, 14-year-old schoolboy Charles Parker, Jr., is obsessed with the alto, listening to local stars like Lester Young.
MUSICAL DEVELOPMENTS	A **"swing"** style of rhythmic flexibility, evolving from the clunky two-beat of ragtime, but using the shifting emphases and intonation of Armstrong and "hot" players, is almost universal, although swing is not yet a genre.	Barney Bigard's clarinet is a mainstay of the **Ellington sound**, fluid in all registers. As the Cotton Club era ends, the sound endures.	**Bill "Bojangles" Robinson**, one of the great black dancers and innovators in tap dance. The 1930s see him in movies and on Broadway.	Most American households have radios, and amateurs begin to record air spots — **live music broadcasts**. Ballrooms are linked directly to radio stations.	The jazz **big band** becomes standardized to five brass, four reeds, and four rhythm players. Arrangers make the brass and reeds talk to each other in repeated call-and-response riffs. Benny Goodman buys many of Fletcher Henderson's best arrangements.
HISTORICAL FACTORS	**Kansas City** in the Depression is largely run by gangsters. The nightclub economy flourishes. An energetic dance clientele encourages steady four-beat jazz.	The **record business** all but collapses, beleaguered by the rise of radio and economic difficulties.		**Prohibition** is repealed and jazz emerges from the low-life. The easing slump and growing student audience recharge the demand for exhibitionist, danceable jazz.	

idiom like the blues seemed somewhat dated and unsophisticated. A faster, smoother, more powerful music emerged for a mass market of young dancers — big band swing. From 1935, swing bands domin-ated popular entertainment. With them came a crop of brilliant instrumental soloists, able to tell increasingly fast and complex spontaneous stories over the smoothly charging rhythms of the orchestras.

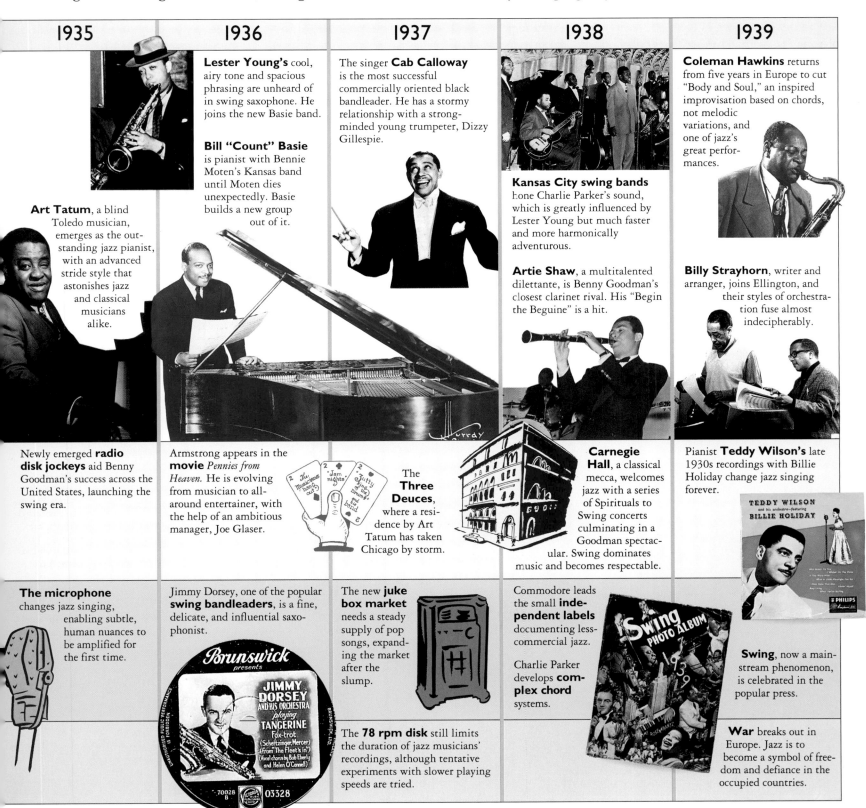

1935

Art Tatum, a blind Toledo musician, emerges as the outstanding jazz pianist, with an advanced stride style that astonishes jazz and classical musicians alike.

Newly emerged **radio disk jockeys** aid Benny Goodman's success across the United States, launching the swing era.

The microphone changes jazz singing, enabling subtle, human nuances to be amplified for the first time.

1936

Lester Young's cool, airy tone and spacious phrasing are unheard of in swing saxophone. He joins the new Basie band.

Bill "Count" Basie is pianist with Bennie Moten's Kansas band until Moten dies unexpectedly. Basie builds a new group out of it.

Armstrong appears in the **movie** *Pennies from Heaven.* He is evolving from musician to all-around entertainer, with the help of an ambitious manager, Joe Glaser.

Jimmy Dorsey, one of the popular **swing bandleaders**, is a fine, delicate, and influential saxophonist.

Brunswick presents
JIMMY DORSEY AND HIS ORCHESTRA *playing* TANGERINE Fox-trot (Schertzinger, Mercer) (from *The Fleet's In*) (Vocal chorus by Bob Eberly and Helen O'Connell)

70028 B   03328

1937

The singer **Cab Calloway** is the most successful commercially oriented black bandleader. He has a stormy relationship with a strong-minded young trumpeter, Dizzy Gillespie.

The **Three Deuces**, where a residence by Art Tatum has taken Chicago by storm.

The new **juke box market** needs a steady supply of pop songs, expanding the market after the slump.

The **78 rpm disk** still limits the duration of jazz musicians' recordings, although tentative experiments with slower playing speeds are tried.

1938

Kansas City swing bands hone Charlie Parker's sound, which is greatly influenced by Lester Young but much faster and more harmonically adventurous.

Artie Shaw, a multitalented dilettante, is Benny Goodman's closest clarinet rival. His "Begin the Beguine" is a hit.

Carnegie Hall, a classical mecca, welcomes jazz with a series of Spirituals to Swing concerts culminating in a Goodman spectacular. Swing dominates music and becomes respectable.

Commodore leads the small **independent labels** documenting less-commercial jazz.

Charlie Parker develops **complex chord** systems.

1939

Coleman Hawkins returns from five years in Europe to cut "Body and Soul," an inspired improvisation based on chords, not melodic variations, and one of jazz's great performances.

Billy Strayhorn, writer and arranger, joins Ellington, and their styles of orchestration fuse almost indecipherably.

Pianist **Teddy Wilson's** late 1930s recordings with Billie Holiday change jazz singing forever.

TEDDY WILSON and his orchestra—featuring BILLIE HOLIDAY

PHILIPS

Swing, now a mainstream phenomenon, is celebrated in the popular press.

War breaks out in Europe. Jazz is to become a symbol of freedom and defiance in the occupied countries.

23

New York

WHEN THE ORIGINAL Dixieland Jazz Band played Broadway, the world noticed. What happened in New York was news, for as the entertainment industry grew to reward a population that wanted to play as hard as it was working, New York became its natural center. New York was home to most of the new phonograph industry and many of the new radio stations. Tin Pan Alley, the song publishing industry that had boomed at the end of the previous century, was the nickname for the area around 32nd Street and Broadway.

Yet the black South had given jazz a unique pungency that show business entrepreneurs could not. The New Orleans ensemble sound and the blues were the sources of this dynamism. Although a move toward more intimate, couple-centered "social dancing" was under way, the sharp end of New Orleans music was still too insistent, too raucous, too choppy for a mass market, and its upfront, raunchy sound made the connection between dance and sex a little too explicit for some.

The music industry's problem had been first addressed on the West Coast around 1915. A white arranger and pianist, Ferde Grofé, familiar with both European classical music and low-life dance venues, was experimenting with symphonic techniques for a dance band, using saxophones (not generally taken seriously outside vaudeville) to carry a harmonized theme and creating contrasting written parts for instruments. Paul Whiteman, an ambitious young bandleader with a background similar to Grofé's, augmented his already popular dance band with Grofé's imaginative arrangements. Whiteman's symphonic jazz was an immediate hit (he sold over three million copies of his first disk in 1922) and on the strength of it, the bandleader billed himself as the King of Jazz.

There was little jazz in the New Orleans sense in Whiteman's orchestra, and its musicians had neither the inclination nor the skill to improvise much, but it sounded like jazz with the rough edges polished off. This was the basis on which Whiteman

marketed himself. He staged a famous concert in an upmarket venue, New York's Aeolian Hall, in February 1924, specifically to demonstrate how far things had moved from "discordant early jazz to the melodious form of the present." George Gershwin introduced his *Rhapsody in Blue* on the same show.

Paul Whiteman did not improve jazz, but his music was classy and elegant and close enough to jazz to widen the taste for it. His influence on dance music in New York was so persuasive that all musicians in the dance business tried to emulate him. Fletcher Henderson, a shy but talented college graduate, was finding around 1920 that a chemistry degree did not help a young black man become a chemist. He first worked demonstrating sheet music, then acted virtually as a house pianist for the first black record company, Black Swan. Hauling together freelance musicians for recording projects with the label eventually made a reluctant bandleader of Henderson, but his early exploits followed Whiteman's example — smooth, gliding, saxophone choir music, often with a ragged edge.

Raising the Temperature

Henderson and his chief arranger Don Redman improved on Whiteman's interplay of brass and reeds and the use of contrasting voicings, one section behind another. Henderson also realized, as did Duke Ellington and Whiteman himself, that the dancing public was not as solidly sold on refinement and restraint as was thought. Bandleaders began to hire jazz improvisers to raise the temperature, although in such short bursts at first that soloists had to seek out after-hours jamming sessions to play for pleasure.

Fletcher Henderson brought Louis Armstrong to New York in 1924 for just that reason, and this revolutionized the jazz of the next decade. Duke Ellington, begin-

In the 1920s, reluctant bandleader Fletcher Henderson realized that a powerful brew could be made by mixing smooth New York dance music with the rougher New Orleans sound. Louis Armstrong (third from left) was the spark.

Formerly owned by boxer Jack Johnson, Harlem's Cotton Club was one of the most famous nightspots in 1920s New York. Its revues were both theatrical and musical, often caricatures of traditional African life — but the jazz was hot.

Duke Ellington's residency at the Cotton Club (1927 to 1931) was its most celebrated period, followed by Cab Calloway. When these bands played the club, some of America's most famous musicians appeared.

ning to dominate what had once been a collectively run dance band called The Washingtonians, hired Oliver-influenced "Bubber" Miley to do the same thing. Falling into line, and starting to change his mind about "discordant early jazz," Whiteman hired Bix Beiderbecke and the saxophonist Frankie Trumbauer.

Harlem Renaissance

As New York's music scene changed on the upmarket dance floors, its subculture altered, too. The city's Harlem Renaissance began in the 1920s. Black poetry, art, music, literature, and philosophy flowered, partly encouraged by the optimism about the perfectability of the human spirit that had fueled the religious revivalism of the previous century and the Prohibition laws. For a while, the white intelligentsia saw black people as privy to the secret of a life more spiritual and enlightened than their own. Harlem night spots became magnets for a white audience, and the Duke Ellington band's residence at the Kentucky Club and then the Cotton Club thrived on

a frequently caricatured image of African life. "Black and Tan Fantasy," a famous Ellington piece, was composed for just such a music theater celebration of the notion of "the noble savage."

Harlem did not just buzz in the night spots. Rent parties and parlor socials, where tenants engaged musicians in their own homes and charged a modest fee to cover the week's rent, created open houses for musicians. Both the boogie-woogie pianists, whose ancestry lay in the frontier saloons, and the classy stride masters with immense technique, like Luckyeth Roberts, James P. Johnson, and Fats Waller, made a circuit out of them. In 1925, guitarist and blues singer Huddie "Leadbelly" Leadbetter came out of prison and frequently took his guitar around the Harlem parlors, too, singing the music he had learned from rural musicians who knew little of jazz but a lot about the blues, ring shout, and holler.

The music industry's hunger for new markets identified sales potential in black neighborhoods and developed "race" labels

specifically for the black shops. This fueled a blues boom that thrived until the Wall Street crash and the Depression. The majestic, operatic blues artist Bessie Smith brought a fortune to troubled Columbia Records, and Leadbelly heard her records and marveled. Louis Armstrong, King Oliver, and Sidney Bechet were among many young black jazz musicians accompanying blues sessions, learning ever more about phrasing, timing, and emotion. A new lifeblood was flowing into dance music, changing it forever. By the early 1930s, Duke Ellington's blues-steeped version of symphonic jazz had displaced Whiteman in the popularity polls. The Jazz Age died with the economic slump, but the swing age was about to be born.

Swing

A FREEWHEELING American economy finally spun off the road in 1929. Jazz spent the years until 1935 trying to hitch a ride back. The ambitious and enthusiastic Austin High band lived on baked beans. Sidney Bechet took up shoeshining and helped trumpeter friend Tommy Ladnier with his struggling tailoring business. In the Midwest and Southwest, "territory bands" in battered buses lived on the road and played for peanuts. Some prominent black musicians, like Louis Armstrong and Duke Ellington, went to Europe to play. Not long after Coleman Hawkins did the same in 1934, the Fletcher Henderson band, which had done so much to make a big jazz ensemble swing like Louis Armstrong, fell apart.

Henderson had relied on his arranger, Don Redman, to do much of the groundwork by expanding the voicing for that elusive concept, swing. What Armstrong's trumpet did was to suggest rhythms on rhythms, the beat of an improvised melody line whirling away from the chug of an underlying rhythm but snapping back to it when it counted. Using a bigger band, divided into brass, reeds, and rhythm sections, Don Redman developed ensemble playing that sounded like an Armstrong solo and set the brass and reeds exchanging colorfully harmonized riffs. This gave the whole outfit a shouting, crackling energy that was intensified when the soloists blew. It was the diametric opposite of the discreet, nonimprovisational coasting through off-the-shelf arrangements that most bands went in for, although white bands like those of Jean Goldkette and Red Nichols came close to Henderson's sound.

Redman and Henderson had this style working by 1931, but for the most part only the Harlem audiences knew it. Duke Ellington, Chick Webb, Earl Hines, Luis Russell, and William McKinney had not been far behind. Henderson absorbed the method from Redman, who had derived it from a mixture of Armstrong's improvising

Basie's orchestra had the best soloists and the fiercest attack of the genre, and if Goodman seemed to be the King of Swing, Basie was always waiting in the wings.

and an understanding of the orchestral methods of Paul Whiteman and Ferde Grofé. Henderson improved on it himself once there were no sidekicks to call on.

Stompin' at the Savoy

But the Depression and his own casualness left Henderson in difficulties. A way out came when the shrewd impresario and record company scout John Hammond set him up to provide charts for Benny Goodman, a young, classically schooled white bandleader and clarinetist. Goodman was one of twelve children from an Eastern European Jewish family, whose prodigious clarinet talents were seen by his father as the way out of the ghetto. The boy was a full-time pro by the age of 14 and became the family breadwinner not long after. Goodman's models were the highly creative Dorsey brothers, and a white Detroit band that mingled New York subtleties with midwestern bluesy directness, the Casa Loma Orchestra. Despite the Depression, Casa Loma was big on college campuses, and the long-range implications were not lost on Goodman's manager.

Swing and dance were inseparable. At the Savoy Ballroom in Harlem, lindy-hoppers developed the style to early swing, encouraging the transition to an even four-four beat to accompany a fluid, flowing dance idiom.

In August 1935, Goodman's band, including powerful performers in trumpeter Bunny Berigan and drummer Gene Krupa, played the Palomar Ballroom in Los Angeles after a desultory coast-to-coast tour. Goodman began the gig performing soft dance music to an unimpressed audience of college students. As a sink-or-swim gesture, he launched into Fletcher Henderson's arrangement of Jelly Roll Morton's "King Porter Stomp" — New Orleans and Harlem united via the Jewish ghetto. The audience roared, the commercial breakthrough for a hot, vigorous, up-tempo, big band jazz in the black style had come, and Goodman was on the way to being dubbed the King of Swing.

The spread of radio was crucial to this boom in swing, as were the end of the Depression, growing sales of "hot" black music like Armstrong's to an expanding white student audience, and Goodman's age, race, and talent. He was younger than all the jazz pioneers whose music seemed rooted in the Roaring Twenties, he resembled the boys in college campus audiences, and he played with a mixture of improvisational attack and European scrupulousness of intonation that rang bells with a young educated audience all over the States.

The King of Swing

Five years after the California success, Goodman was an international star who brought jazz even to the world of classical concert halls with the famous 1938 Carnegie Hall "Spirituals to Swing" show. He was also instrumental in bringing about mixed-race bands when he hired pianist Teddy Wilson, vibraharpist Lionel Hampton, and guitarist Charlie Christian. This open-mindedness had developed by listening to the New Orleans pioneers in Chicago and hiring musicians such as Coleman Hawkins and Billie Holiday for John Hammond's 1933 recording projects.

Benny Goodman and Gene Krupa, stars of swing. Krupa pioneered the virtuosic solo based on drum rudiments played at furious speed. His sticks bear witness to this.

White bandleaders like Jimmy and Tommy Dorsey, Bob Crosby, and Glenn Miller succeeded with this new wider audience; so did exciting bands like Jimmie Lunceford's and Andy Kirk's. Nor was the Goodman model of smoothly driving, flawlessly played, tightly disciplined jazz the only music benefiting from the swing boom. Duke Ellington's impressionistic, rich, painterly music was also being unfurled over a compelling pulse learned in the competitive atmosphere of ballrooms. The Ellington band would eventually make its most subtle, arousing, and focused music just when wartime economics and the rise of bebop in the 1940s were making most other jazz orchestras unfashionable.

Swing, Brother, Swing

In Kansas City, a simpler, riskier, bluesier, more riff-centered music had been flourishing since the 1920s, notably the Bennie Moten outfit, which included saxophonist Ben Webster and pianist William "Count" Basie. Basie incorporated many of the personnel, and the approach, into a band of his own after Moten's death in a tonsillectomy operation. When the band came to New York, it became nearly as popular a swing band as Benny Goodman's was, with a relaxed, flowing rhythm and sublime soloing strength from the likes of Buck Clayton, Herschel Evans, and Lester Young. It even began to influence the repertoire and approach of the King of Swing himself.

Goodman's music wasn't all it influenced. Basie's drummer, Jo Jones, with his looser, floating time, lovely cymbal sound, and lighter bass drum technique, pointed toward a new route for percussion and rhythm playing. The graceful, dancing four-four beat made room for an improvised music of intensity without bluster, and Count Basie's own dabbing left hand and quietly eloquent right became a model for a more restrained way of playing piano.

There were many ingredients that led to the rise of the bebop movement that followed, not least of which was impatience with the rituals of swing. But the inspiration of Count Basie was acknowledged by musicians of every generation and taste.

1940s

Swing seemed indomitable as the 1930s ended, with even Carnegie Hall won over. But the style was such a hot ticket it was bound to become repetitive. A group of bored young big band players including trumpeter Dizzy Gillespie, saxophonist Charlie Parker, and guitarist Charlie Christian turned the page. They expanded harmonies and disrupted the steady swing pulse to create a tense, fragmented, ambiguous music that revolu-

	1940	1941	1942	1943	1944
MUSICIANS AND BANDS	Drummer **Kenny Clarke** switches the beat from bass drum to cymbals, with a light and looser rhythm and more unpredictable accents. **Ben Webster**, the lustrous-toned Kansas tenorist, joins Duke Ellington's Orchestra at the beginning of its most creative phase in the 1940s.	**Charlie Christian**, Benny Goodman's guitar star, founder of bop guitar and an important developer of amplification, has a key role in the new movement, experimenting with unusual harmonies. He dies young.	**Charlie Parker's** solos swing from whispers to cries, yearning blues to breakneck speed, spikiness to grace in the space of a few choruses. **Lionel Hampton**, exhibitionist drummer and vibraharpist, is one of the swing musicians who still flourish.	Virtuoso **Bud Powell** is the most influential early bop pianist. His right hand melodies resemble horn lines. **Earl Hines**, swing piano star and bandleader, hires Gillespie and Parker.	Drummer **Max Roach** performs with uncanny empathy on some of Charlie Parker's most crucial sessions. **Thelonious Monk's** jerky, percussive technique and acerbic compositions are later seen as 20th-century classics.
VENUES, RECORDINGS AND SHOW BUSINESS		**Minton's**, a 108th Street club where the swing stars let their hair down, and where Kenny Clarke is invited to form a house band. He brings together several of the frustrated young musicians who transform jazz.	**The Onyx**, where Dizzy Gillespie takes a band with Max Roach in one of the first bebop gigs.	At the end of the year **Coleman Hawkins records** again. No bebopper, he is nonetheless intrigued by the new music.	Hawkins makes the **first bop recordings** after the ban.
MUSICAL DEVELOPMENTS	**Jimmy Blanton**, Ellington's young bassist, transforms the accompanying role of the bass, playing fast, guitarlike counter-melodies against soloists.	The boppers **augment** basic chords and improvise on the upper notes — Charlie Parker's biographer Ross Russell later calls it "skimming along the very tops of the chords."	Bop's **uncommerciality** is written off by many major stars, but it spreads among adventurous players and open-minded fans. With America on a war footing, a new **cabaret tax** makes promoters favor smaller bands, an encouragement to the small-group music of bebop.	**Bop drummers** have simpler kits with a lighter, crisp sound, using the bass drum for offbeats ("bombs"), not timekeeping.	Bop creates a backlash, a revival of the amiable, melodic sound of New Orleans. The veteran cornetist **Bunk Johnson** makes his first recordings.
HISTORICAL FACTORS		More political young African-American musicians begin to **reject racist** stereotypes in show business.	A **recording ban** is enforced by the American Federation of Musicians, seeking a percentage of record sales. As a result, bop develops almost underground.		

28

tionized composition and solo styles on all instruments. Parker was its high priest and erratically enlightened visionary, but the new bebop burst from a chemistry of musical and socioeconomic changes during World War II. African-American entertainers grew more impatient with their roles. Big bands collapsed. Jazz briefly became more insular, but its origins in blues and African rhythms had been reinforced, not rejected.

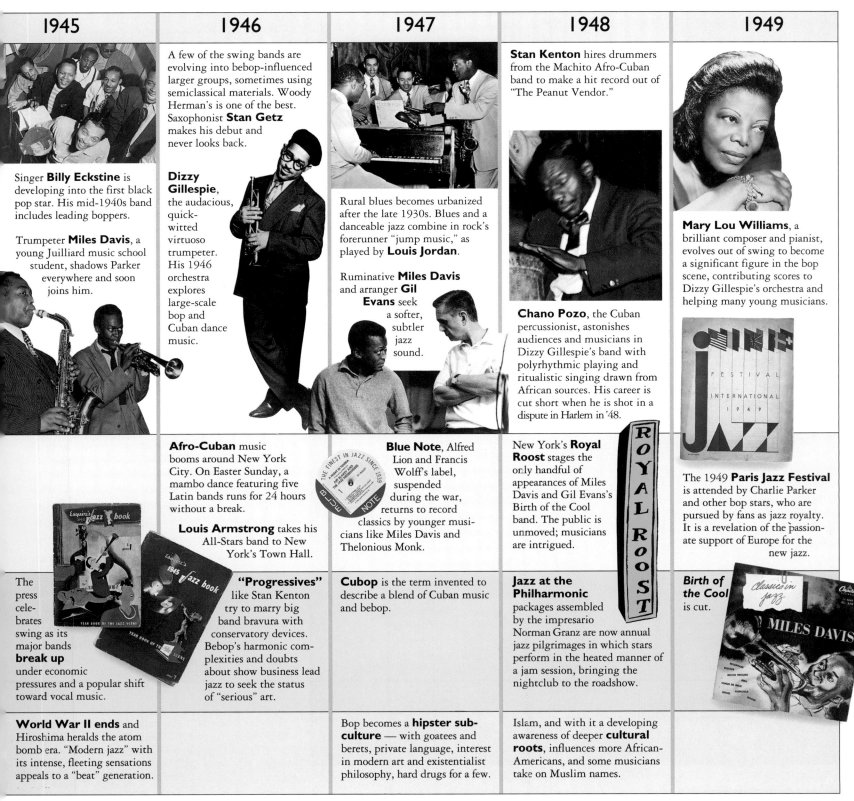

1945

Singer **Billy Eckstine** is developing into the first black pop star. His mid-1940s band includes leading boppers.

Trumpeter **Miles Davis**, a young Juilliard music school student, shadows Parker everywhere and soon joins him.

The press celebrates swing as its major bands **break up** under economic pressures and a popular shift toward vocal music.

World War II ends and Hiroshima heralds the atom bomb era. "Modern jazz" with its intense, fleeting sensations appeals to a "beat" generation.

1946

A few of the swing bands are evolving into bebop-influenced larger groups, sometimes using semiclassical materials. Woody Herman's is one of the best. Saxophonist **Stan Getz** makes his debut and never looks back.

Dizzy Gillespie, the audacious, quick-witted virtuoso trumpeter. His 1946 orchestra explores large-scale bop and Cuban dance music.

Afro-Cuban music booms around New York City. On Easter Sunday, a mambo dance featuring five Latin bands runs for 24 hours without a break.

Louis Armstrong takes his All-Stars band to New York's Town Hall.

"Progressives" like Stan Kenton try to marry big band bravura with conservatory devices. Bebop's harmonic complexities and doubts about show business lead jazz to seek the status of "serious" art.

1947

Rural blues becomes urbanized after the late 1930s. Blues and a danceable jazz combine in rock's forerunner "jump music," as played by **Louis Jordan**.

Ruminative **Miles Davis** and arranger **Gil Evans** seek a softer, subtler jazz sound.

Blue Note, Alfred Lion and Francis Wolff's label, suspended during the war, returns to record classics by younger musicians like Miles Davis and Thelonious Monk.

Cubop is the term invented to describe a blend of Cuban music and bebop.

Bop becomes a **hipster subculture** — with goatees and berets, private language, interest in modern art and existentialist philosophy, hard drugs for a few.

1948

Stan Kenton hires drummers from the Machito Afro-Cuban band to make a hit record out of "The Peanut Vendor."

Chano Pozo, the Cuban percussionist, astonishes audiences and musicians in Dizzy Gillespie's band with polyrhythmic playing and ritualistic singing drawn from African sources. His career is cut short when he is shot in a dispute in Harlem in '48.

New York's **Royal Roost** stages the only handful of appearances of Miles Davis and Gil Evans's Birth of the Cool band. The public is unmoved; musicians are intrigued.

Jazz at the Philharmonic packages assembled by the impresario Norman Granz are now annual jazz pilgrimages in which stars perform in the heated manner of a jam session, bringing the nightclub to the roadshow.

Islam, and with it a developing awareness of deeper **cultural roots**, influences more African-Americans, and some musicians take on Muslim names.

1949

Mary Lou Williams, a brilliant composer and pianist, evolves out of swing to become a significant figure in the bop scene, contributing scores to Dizzy Gillespie's orchestra and helping many young musicians.

The 1949 **Paris Jazz Festival** is attended by Charlie Parker and other bop stars, who are pursued by fans as jazz royalty. It is a revelation of the passionate support of Europe for the new jazz.

Birth of the Cool is cut.

Bebop

IF SWING WAS JAZZ that went to the public with open arms, bebop was jazz that seemed to have turned its back on its audience. Many of the leading swing musicians of the 1940s felt personally insulted. Tommy Dorsey told *Down Beat* magazine that "bebop has set music back 20 years." Even the genial Louis Armstrong broke into rare reproof when he talked about those "weird chords which don't mean nothing . . . you got no melody to remember and no beat to dance to."

After the dust settled, musicians and the public perceived that bebop did not really sound so different. And nearly fifty years after it settled, Charlie Parker's saxophone solos swirl behind restaurant conversations, and Thelonious Monk's "Round Midnight" is heard anywhere from the supermarket to a classical pianist's recordings of great 20th-century compositions.

For all its apparent dislocation from the past, bebop's arrival made sense. It mostly operated over swing's fast four-four beat,

but with the accents more unpredictably scattered and without that steady thump of the bass drum. It involved improvisation over chords, but these chords were modified from simple Tin Pan Alley roots by extra notes to enrich the voicings, and they changed far more often — flickering past like subliminal images linking the principal changes to each other. Pianist Art Tatum and swing saxophonist Coleman Hawkins had long been doing something similar, and modern European classical concert music was full of such devices.

Bebop's favorite chord vehicles were the blues and the harmonic progressions of a thirty-two bar pop song with an eight-bar countermelody — like "I Got Rhythm." But part of the fun for the pioneering boppers was to disguise the songs so that even their most loyal fans would not recognize them. If splicing the theme chords from "I Got Rhythm" with the middle-eight passage from a completely different song tripped up a famous swing star who was

trying to jam on it or infuriated the now aging bobbysoxers who had made the swing stars in the first place, so much the better.

While advanced musicians like Art Tatum and Coleman Hawkins understood the fundamentals of bebop, and others like Lester Young, the trumpeter Roy Eldridge, pianists Count Basie and Clyde Hart, and drummer Jo Jones were barely a step away from playing it, that step was the hardest to take. In the end, it needed the fresh energy of newcomers, with reputations yet to invent, and less to lose. This was the coterie of young swing sidemen who met in after-hours joints in New York. No single one of them, not even Charlie "Yardbird" Parker himself, had imagined the future architecture of bebop whole and perfect. They were bored, talented and rebellious — and they lived for playing. Each one of them heard a fragment of the future. It was when they came together that "modern jazz" was really born.

Straight No Chaser

Bebop's presiding genius was Charlie Parker, although many other musicians played their own crucial, distinctive roles. Parker was already established as an alto saxophone master, performing in a fast, harmonically advanced style derived from Lester Young in the blues-oriented swing orchestra of Jay McShann. Parker was self-taught but obsessively had learned to play his saxophone in every key and with bewildering speed by the time he had reached his midteens. When he joined Jay McShann's band, Parker was already hearing an elusive but gradually coalescing new way of improvising, one that released the harmonic potential in the chords of songs and thus gained more notes to juggle with in solos. The harmonic changes made bebop ostensibly a more Europeanized music — as Bach might have sounded if he had been acquainted with the blues and African time.

"The Street": 52nd Street in New York, between 5th Avenue and Broadway, was bursting with jazz in the 1940s, in basement clubs like the Onyx, the Famous Door, and the Three Deuces.

But, like all previous breakthroughs in jazz, bebop's contribution lay in its rhythm. Although New Orleans music and swing used rhythmic ideas previously unknown in the West, they were a partial rediscovery of African ancestry and nowhere near as eloquent as an African drum choir. As bop developed as a movement, the style of its drumming went closer to recapturing the mysterious, talkative polycurrents swirling beneath jazz. The man who pushed the new music hardest toward a more multilayered pulse was drummer Kenny Clarke.

Clarke was drumming with the Teddy Hill swing band. Also in the lineup was a young trumpeter called John Birks "Dizzy" Gillespie — a willful and anarchic schooled musician who was already experimenting with swing harmony. Inspired by the work of Count Basie's Jo Jones, Clarke wanted to make the drum sound lighter and create more interesting tension — as pioneering jazz musicians had been doing since the birth of the music — by setting contrasting rhythmic ideas to pull and push each other. He had acquired the nickname "Klook" or "Klook-a-mop" in imitation of the sound of his snare and bass drum accents, which prodded and elbowed the regular beat in a manner distinctly different from the steady pump of swing.

Clarke's boss, Teddy Hill, eventually fired him for musical disruption in 1940, but remembered the stubborn young drummer a year later when hired to put together a small-group house band for a new venue, Minton's Playhouse on 108th Street in Harlem. Hill asked Clarke to gather some cheap musicians who could play well enough to back star visitors and attract a sizeable crowd. Clarke took this opportunity to search out like-minded players. As well as Gillespie, he found Thelonious Monk, a vague but inventive pianist influenced by stride piano and the Baptist Church, who used odd, dissonant chords and left unexpected cliff-hanging spaces in his music.

Arriba!

Meanwhile, at another Harlem jamming joint called Monroe's Uptown House, alto saxophonist Charlie Parker was eking a thin living from a cut of the door money. When Kenny Clarke heard him perform, as he told Parker's biographer Ross Russell, he found that "he was twice as fast as Lester Young and into harmony Lester hadn't touched." Parker was brought to Minton's and a new repertoire began to develop. Although established jazz stars like Coleman Hawkins, Duke Ellington,

Count Basie, and even Fats Waller came to Minton's to let off steam in the small hours after the grind of the popular swing circuit, the house band Clarke had assembled had its collective mind elsewhere.

A name began to stick for what they did (not that the musicians initially liked it). "Bebop," or its forerunner "rebop," are usually taken as vocal mimicry of the darting, offbeat accents of this new music — although jazz critic Marshall Stearns has suggested that the Spanish *arriba* might also have been the source. Its English translation ("go!") was often shouted at bop soloists by fans to push an improvisation ever faster and higher.

To swing musicians trying to sit in, let alone to unfamiliar audiences, bebop sounded at first as if the soloists entered too early or too late, left phrases hanging unresolved, or were unaware of the bar lines or parent key. In swing, the moment of a chord change or the important notes in phrases usually coincided with the traditional strong beat. Bebop perversely reversed these musical signposts to hit weak or offbeats instead.

Charlie Parker's saxophone improvisations are among the most dazzling examples of spontaneous composition in 20th-century music. Impulsive and unpredictable, Parker was a visionary who overturned conventions of timing and phrasing.

Charlie Parker's sense of time and location in the structure of a tune was so secure that he could abandon the framework for long improvised stretches, tantalizingly skydiving into distant keys, always landing on his feet. Bebop's horn players were encouraged to take risks with the accents and rhythm by fronting active, needling rhythm sections like those featuring new drummers Kenny Clarke and Max Roach.

The Sound of Rebellion

Bebop was a release for musicians, opening up a new vocabulary to jazz improvisation. It was also being forged by a generation of black performers very different in experience and outlook from the New Orleans pioneers. Swing had not simply been a way of making music, it had eventually

Dizzy Gillespie, if not bop's presiding genius, influenced its development and growing popularity. His ebullience endeared him to successive generations of fans, as reflected in a riotous welcome home to New York in 1948 (right) from a two-month tour of European concert halls.

The Paris jazz festival of 1949, featuring Charlie Parker and Miles Davis, showed the Americans that a knowledgeable audience for the new music existed outside the States.

become an industry — the biggest, brashest, and most profitable the popular music business had experienced until then. Black bands, however, had regularly earned half the amount of their white contemporaries in the 1930s. The slow shift toward mixed-race bands deepened discontent as well as relieved it: while black soloists like Roy Eldridge made more money in a white band, they still could not eat in the same diner in the South. Growing fury and political enlightenment about racism among African-Americans led, especially in Harlem, to a renewed interest in Islam and in African history. Some musicians took Muslim names and began to wear robes during stage performances.

Another problem with swing was a musical one that frustrated younger black and white musicians alike. Fan clubs had sprung up all over the country in the wake of swing. Artie Shaw's gliding "Begin the Beguine," Benny Goodman's "Stompin' at the Savoy," Glenn Miller's "Moonlight Serenade" were signature tunes, and audiences insisted on them. But that success became a pressure for repetition — and what was repeated quickly became cliché.

Many of the new generation would not go along with it. They were aware of the respect accorded to other major figures of modern art and music — Stravinsky, Schönberg, Picasso, Kandinsky — and felt that a unique and vibrant music largely created by African-Americans deserved to be given the same serious attention. World War II had also fostered a new sense of

frustration and pessimism among artists and intellectuals in the United States and Europe. Bebop's mercurial fleeting-moment sound and the indifference of its practitioners to show business suited the prevailing ethos of the artist as untouchable witness to humanity's mistakes, an outsider rejecting old values that had taken the world to the brink. The hipster generation's sense of operating in a moral universe of its own, coupled with the pressures of racism, rejection by the respectable, and the intense moment-by-moment demands of improvisation, led increasingly to escape through drink and narcotics as well as music. Heroin became a treacherous crutch for many of the first bebop generation — white and black.

At first, the beboppers enjoyed their underground cult status. Although musicians and a small enthusiastic following in New York knew about bebop at the start, few others did. Radio deejays were still selling swing, and between 1942 and 1944 the American Federation of Musicians shut down the record business in pursuit of better rates. Bebop musicians honed the music almost in secret as far as the mainstream record-buying public was

show biz–conscious performer, helped a new public find a new music, and at the end of the 1940s, he formed a dramatic big band that embraced Latin-American dance music, further reuniting jazz with its rhythmic ancestry. The luminous inspiration of Parker, Gillespie, and their contemporaries encouraged many brilliant young musicians to follow in their wake, such as trumpeters Fats Navarro and Clifford Brown, and saxophonists Dexter Gordon, Sonny Rollins, and Sonny Stitt.

Enlightened swing bandleaders like pianist Earl Hines, singer-trumpeter Billy Eckstine, and subsequently the adaptable Woody Herman, sensed the new mood and encouraged the bebop players, as did saxo-

phonist Coleman Hawkins, who played with almost the same harmonic sense as the new generation and who encouraged bop to enter the studio.

There were two fascinating counter reactions to this revolution. Bebop's labyrinthine melodies, breathless tempos, and complexity led to a revival of interest in the genial, conversational styles of early jazz, and a New Orleans renaissance occurred that brought even the legendary cornetist Bunk Johnson out of retirement to record for the first time. It also led to a music that used many of the innovations of bebop, but caressed the audience with a softer sound instead of shaking it until its teeth rattled. That was "cool" jazz.

aware. When the ban ended and bebop finally emerged, full-fledged and wailing, the shock wave was all the more dramatic.

Revolutionary Classics

The recordings from that first wave are now classics of jazz music. A band that included Charlie Parker and Max Roach played New York's Three Deuces in 1944, and a Coleman Hawkins-led band including Dizzy Gillespie made the first bebop recordings when the union ban lifted. Polls began to acknowledge the ascendancy of the new musicians, and in 1945 Parker and Gillespie began the sensational succession of small-group recordings that produced "Groovin' High," "Billie's Bounce," "Now's the Time" and "Ko-Ko."

Bebop became both a musical and a social revolution, changing the sound of jazz, along with the vocabulary and fashion sense of the young. Dizzy Gillespie, always the most

Cuban percussionist Machito (right) and his orchestra lit up the 1940s and 1950s Cubop craze, when bebop musicians recognized that African polyrhythms had come to the Americas in many guises.

1950s

JAZZ FRAGMENTED IN THE 1950S. Where swing had dominated the 1930s, and bebop the following decade, the 1950s saw swing first capsize, then re-surface as mainstream, while bebop turned funkier as hard bop or softer as cool jazz, then evolved into less formalized modalism. It also saw some of the earthi-est origins of African-American music celebrated, at one extreme in the vocalized sounds and rejection of

	1950	1951	1952	1953	1954
MUSICIANS AND BANDS	**Stan Kenton's** 43-piece semi-symphonic Innovations in Modern Music Orchestra tours the States. **Frank Sinatra** overtakes Bing Crosby as the highest-paid singer in the United States, signing a multi-million dollar radio contract.	Pianist **Lennie Tristano's** linear, low-key improvising methods inspire the emerging cool school.	The **Modern Jazz Quartet** is presaged by a quartet offshoot of Dizzy Gillespie's band, led by vibra-harpist Milt Jackson and including pianist John Lewis. A **jazz school** is founded in New York by cool guru Lennie Tristano, using sympathizers like Lee Konitz and Warne Marsh to teach his methods. **Chet Baker**, a soft-toned, romantic trumpeter.	**Gerry Mulligan**, baritonist and arranger, joins Chet Baker in a delicate, contrapuntal, piano-less band. A commercial hit, it is dubbed the West Coast sound. **Horace Silver**, pianist/com-poser, records, heralding a new movement — hard bop, fusing bebop, r & b and gospel.	**Ella Fitzgerald's** swing and range has a big following. With Norman Granz she plans a series on U.S. songwriters. **The Jazz Messengers**, a hard bop co-operative, forms with Horace Silver and explo-sive drummer Art Blakey.
VENUES, RECORDINGS AND SHOW BUSINESS	**Louis Armstrong's 50th year** is celebrated by *Down Beat*. Armstrong is back on the road with a band recall-ing his youth, the All-Stars.	America's **West Coast** becomes a focus for a softer, white-dominated version of bebop. The region gives the style a name that comes to be linked with all cool jazz.	**Ellington** takes to composing suites in several movements, encouraged by the development of the long-playing record.	An **all-star bop** group forms for a Canadian tour. Bird, Dizzy, Mingus, Bud Powell and Max Roach record live at Toronto's Massey Hall.	**Bill Haley**, a pop singer, covers "Shake Rattle and Roll," written by the Basieite blues singer Big Joe Turner. *Rock Around the Clock*, the first rock and roll album is released in the following year.
MUSICAL DEVELOPMENTS	Count Basie's Orchestra, which has dominated swing since the mid-1930s, **disbands**. Benny Goodman's band has stopped touring, reforming only for specific projects.	**Rock and roll** comes out of boogie woogie, rhythm and blues, country music, and late-1940s jump music. Direct, emo-tional, and danceable, it has the effect on 1950s youth that swing had on the bobby-soxers and quickly dominates the music business.	**George Russell**, bop drummer turned composer and theoreti-cian, publishes his *Lydian Chromatic Concept of Tonal Organization*, a complex study of scales and modes. It becomes the basis of a new, non chordal way of improvising.	Not all young 1950s musi-cians play bop or cool. Melodic cornettist **Ruby Braff** stays with a small-group swing, at the beginning of "mainstream."	The first **jazz history** in musi-cians' own words, *Hear Me Talkin' to Ya*, is compiled by Nat Hentoff and Nat Shapiro, highlighting the neglect of African-American music.
HISTORICAL FACTORS	Recording expands. PVC or "vinyl" records are cheap, and the fine-grain structure ushers in **"microgroove"** LPs to doc-ument extended improvisers.	The first **H-bomb** is tested on an atoll in the Pacific — declared to be hundreds of times more powerful than the bombs used on Hiroshima and Nagasaki.			

structure in the beginnings of free-form jazz, at the other in a mingling of white country music and urban rhythm and blues in rock and roll. All these developments happened in parallel and made the jazz world more divided and sectarian in some respects, richer and more resourceful in others. A mix of affluence and rebelliousness among the young made bop culture central to the beat generation.

1955

Clifford Brown, a lyrical, inventive trumpeter, plays in one of the finest hard-bop bands with Max Roach and Sonny Rollins. His death in a road accident in the following year is a major blow.

Max Roach, a brilliant exponent of multilayered, tonally subtle drumming, and a vigorous campaigner for black rights and culture.

Newport, one of the longest-running jazz festivals, expands under director George Wain's guidance at Newport, Rhode Island. Duke Ellington's spectacular performance there the following year brings the band back to prominence.

The **Harmon mute** is taken up by Miles Davis.

Charlie Parker dies at 35, a week after a show at Birdland.

Elvis Presley, the Memphis ex-truck driver turned rock and roll singer, is almost a millionaire at 20.

1956

Bassist and composer **Charles Mingus's** Jazz Workshop is developing powerful jazz by oral as much as notated methods.

Miles Davis, after his Newport comeback, moves to the front rank of hard bop with the classic albums *Workin'* and *Steamin'*.

Dizzy Gillespie's band tours Iran, Syria, Greece, Pakistan, and Turkey, then South America. It works under the auspices of the State Department and establishes Gillespie as a **musical ambassador**, like Armstrong before him.

Louis Armstrong records a set of new versions of his great performances on *Satchmo: A Musical Autobiography* and some of them are equals of the originals.

Eisenhower's administration is marked by action for **civil rights**, such as despatching troops to safeguard black access to schools in Little Rock, Arkansas.

1957

Thelonious Monk, after some lean years, becomes one of the most respected musicians in jazz with a series of great recordings starting in 1957.

Organist **Jimmy Smith's** New York debut is followed by a triumph at Newport that establishes him as a major figure in blues and gospel-influenced soul jazz.

Cecil Taylor's recording career (started in 1956) marks him as the emerging avant-garde's foremost pianist. He absorbs himself in musicians as varied as Ellington, Monk, Brubeck, and Stravinsky, producing percussive, dense, sometimes atonal music.

Jimmy Smith's acclaim makes the **Hammond organ**, previously a novelty instrument occasionally played by Count Basie and Fats Waller, into a powerful improviser's tool.

1958

Sonny Rollins, a willful, witty, unpredictable improviser, makes some of his finest albums.

Trumpeter **Lee Morgan**, influenced by Clifford Brown, develops into a bold and vivid instrumentalist, and joins the Jazz Messengers for a formative three-year stay.

Ornette Coleman, heralded by some as a genius, by some as an imposter, emerges as the most revolutionary saxophonist since Charlie Parker.

Jack Kerouac's *On the Road* is the bible of the beats, with its rejection of materialism, empathy with bop, and search for the quintessentially hip.

1959

Bill Evans is a much-imitated pianist after his delicate work on *Kind of Blue* and a series of fine recordings.

Count Basie is a large figure in the new mainstream picture, but his sometime swing partners of the 1930s, Lester Young and Billie Holiday, die prematurely.

Jackie McLean, a searing hard bop altoist, also distinguishes himself as an actor, appearing in Jack Gelber's drugs drama *The Connection*.

The most harmonically complex and the most structurally simplified **evolutions from bebop** are recorded in the same year and are destined for classic status — Coltrane's hurtling and convoluted *Giant Steps*, and Miles Davis's contemplative *Kind of Blue*.

Stereo reproduction, creating a broader "sound stage" between two speakers, gains popularity.

Cool jazz

IN THE LATE 1940s, boppers wore out the grooves listening to Charlie Parker's records. Young jazz musicians from Los Angeles to London, Lyons, and Leningrad wanted to sound like him. Parker was the Messiah, and to be hip you had to know it. But by the early 1950s, hipness meant you danced — or more likely nodded your head, or just raised an eyebrow — to a very different kind of jazz.

In 1948, trumpeter Miles Davis had assembled a nine-piece band for a handful of gigs in New York, recording in the following year. This was not fast, explosive, and bluesy like Parker's bop. It was an ethereal, drifting cloud music that used French horns as well as regular jazz instruments, highly wrought arrangements, and rich tone colors, through which the soloists played in a measured, walking-on-eggshells manner. Parker's idea of an arrangement, after all, was usually little more than could be scribbled on a scrap of paper before the tapes rolled. The tracks that this subtle, spacious band cut in 1949 and 1950

became known as the Birth of the Cool. Davis had partly taken this course because his own trumpet technique, stronger on timbre than fusillades of sixteenth notes, didn't suit bop. He had also, like Charlie Parker in his last years, come to feel that improvisation based on pop song chords straitjacketed jazz into a shorthand, haikulike form in which you either had to put up fast or shut up.

Davis pulled in the young Canadian arranger, Gil Evans, who had studied European classics and Duke Ellington, and worked out many of the subtler shades of a new tonal palette in a classy, underrated dance orchestra led by Claude Thornhill. Some adventurous big bands, like Woody Herman's and Stan Kenton's, also leaned toward a Europeanized jazz with longer, suitelike pieces and devices as likely to be drawn from Debussy as Charlie Parker.

Davis also wanted soloists more like himself, who didn't play everything as if they had heard someone fire a starting pistol. The soloists he found included two

white saxophonists, baritonist and composer Gerry Mulligan and altoist Lee Konitz from the Thornhill band. It was clear that Konitz had been influenced by Parker but, under the guidance of a tough, single-minded teacher, the blind Chicago pianist Lennie Tristano, he edited Bird in his own way. Gerry Mulligan's sound was affected by the only other saxophonist whose influence on horn players still rivaled Parker's — the poetic, rhapsodic Lester Young.

Way Out West

"Cool" jazz arrived, ironically sidelining Parker and Young. Both were becoming increasingly sick and erratic by the early 1950s, and it pained Parker to find that fashion was moving toward the kind of elegant jazz chamber music he had come to dream of playing himself. Young heard a raft of successful young saxophonists leading the cool school (Konitz and Mulligan, Brew Moore, Art Pepper, Warne Marsh, Paul Desmond, Stan Getz), whose sounds seemed clones of his. But the true representations of cool were the unforgiving Tristano strand and the velvety, sensuous Miles Davis line.

Tristano, a merciless taskmaster, resembled Davis only in that he disliked Tin Pan Alley chords as a basis for improvisation. He valued the melody line above all and was puritanical about flashy effects, blues clichés, striving for freak notes, and other safe bets that infested swing and some variations of bop. As younger instrumentalists in jazz had tried to emulate Parker's saxophone, Tristano's disciples tried to sound like pianists, even if they were saxophonists, spinning long, impassive lines way out over the old bar line breaks, twisting, weaving and doubling back, but rarely shifting in volume above a steady murmur. Drummers and bassists were timekeepers only — there was none of the clattering intervention of Max Roach or Kenny Clarke. Tristano's music was too cerebral for some, but in moving away from song forms, the pianist anticipated a free jazz movement that would not become public knowledge for another decade.

Tristano's subdued melodic ingenuity and the Miles Davis mini-orchestra's gleam-

The famous 1949 *Birth of the Cool* recording sessions. Young guru Miles Davis is on the left. Lee Konitz (center) and Gerry Mulligan (right) brought a lighter, more considered sound than regular bop, influenced by Lester Young and Claude Thornhill's urbane dance band.

COOL JAZZ

Chicago pianist/composer Lennie Tristano was the focus of cool's most fascinatingly formal experiment. He changed the shape, balance, and intensity of bop-derived improvising and avoided crowd-baiting clichés.

the Modern Jazz Quartet was creating a similar intimate atmosphere but with a unique combination of baroque European music (its classically trained pianist John Lewis was fond of rondos and Bach-like fugues) and blues from superb bop vibes improviser, Milt Jackson.

Mucho Calor

Not all the jazz musicians working in the California sunshine were cool players in the sense of Baker and Mulligan. There were fiery white performers like altoist Art Pepper and fiery black ones like Frank Morgan, whose careers were interrupted by narcotics problems but who could, at times, sound almost as impassioned as Parker, although their phrasing was more fragmented. There was also a variety of bands led by trumpeter Shorty Rogers with sidemen (including Pepper) from the

Stan Kenton orchestras, often playing a robust, purposeful, boppish music midway between the Parker bands and the Birth of the Cool sessions. There was the group led by pianist Hampton Hawes, with saxophonist Harold Land, which played bebop as fierce as any on 52nd Street. And California also boasted Dexter Gordon, one of the hottest, bluesiest players in jazz.

Yet the fulcrum was still Miles Davis, as he was to be for the next two decades. Davis always blended hot and cool, both in his own playing and with his bands. Although he had done much to launch the fashion for cool music, he was in the thick of the reaction that followed — hard bop.

Trumpeter Chet Baker epitomized the West Coast in his youth — sun, sea, a dream of freedom. Even into broken middle-age, he played as if it were still real.

ing harmonies were the essence of the cool school — a more Europeanized music that some saw as an appropriate score for the chastened era of the atom bomb and the Cold War. But the cool sound is usually identified with the music on America's West Coast in the same period — much of which wasn't cool at all, even when it revealed a scholarly interest in formal musical experiments and conservatoire devices.

The Dave Brubeck group, which became one of the most bankable bands in jazz by the early 1960s, made fascinating experiments with European classical forms and time signatures complex even by jazz standards, but Brubeck hit the piano with an earthy, two-fisted vigor, and his drummer Joe Morello was certainly no metronome. Gerry Mulligan, with trumpeter Chet Baker, performed a quietly conversational kind of bebop without a piano, which became commercially very successful, not least because Baker — who resembled James Dean and played deadpan, romantic trumpet like a less baleful Miles Davis — was a popular crooner, too. The Mulligan-Baker band's balletic, airy jazz became the sound most often associated with cool. But the fashion also encouraged one of the most long-lived and popular of all jazz groups on the opposite coast. Here,

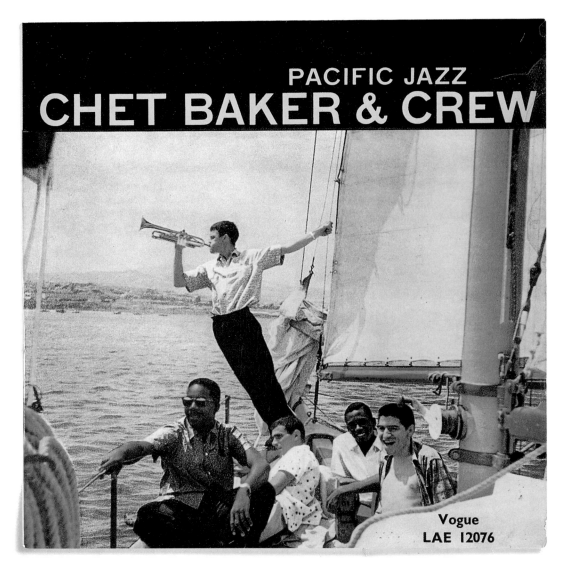

PACIFIC JAZZ
CHET BAKER & CREW
Vogue
LAE 12076

37

Hard bop

Blue Note records' cofounder Alfred Lion (left) ponders a playback with Jazz Messengers Lee Morgan (seated) and Bobby Timmons (standing).

EVERY TIME enough people do the same thing at the same time for long enough to have the uniform of a "movement" stretched over them, the movement itching to throw it all out is already at the door. In the 1950s, cool jazz was first seen as the chic and elegantly lyrical jazz that flattered postwar youth, then it began to be viewed as a repressed and emotionally disengaged form of music that seemed to portray uptightness rather than poise.

The reason was rock and roll, which had swept away the sentimentality, cosy emotions, repressed sexuality, and blandness that a pop music delivered by crooners born of the dance-band era had turned into. When radio deejays in the southlands had started playing Elvis Presley's "That's All Right Mama," switchboards jammed with requests to hear it again and again. The rhythmic drive of long-gone boogie pianists and the emotive intonations of the fields and the railheads had come down the decades to a Memphis white boy with talent and a guitar, and the result was a change in music that dislodged jazz from its pivotal role in pop. However cool it was, jazz could not keep from blinking in the fires lit by rock and roll. Rock made some of the routinely fashionable jazz of the early 1950s sound not just cool, but inert.

Hard bop's popular performances restored verve to jazz. Musicians after the first wave of bop — Lee Morgan, Max Roach, Freddie Hubbard, Milt Jackson — simplified its harmonies to make more direct music.

For many jazz musicians, cool had never seemed like the way to play anyway. Among the followers of Charlie Parker and the bebop movement were players whose lives had been transformed forever — like West Coast bop pianist Hampton Hawes, who recalled a night hearing Parker in California: "Bird played an eight-bar channel [middle section] on 'Salt Peanuts' that was so strong, so revealing that I was molded on the spot, like a piece of clay, stamped out."

This was the way Clarence Williams had felt when he ran away from home at the age of 13 to go to New Orleans because he had just heard Buddy Bolden.

Feelin' the Spirit

The bop influence did not shrivel up when cool's modulated tones drifted over the jazz circuit; indeed, bop's disciples continued to learn, develop, and flourish. Bass virtuoso Charles Mingus had set up his own record company with Max Roach to specialize in tougher new music. In the mid-1950s, he formed a loose workshop organization to explore bebop, gospel, and blues-influenced music and find a form of composing and arranging appropriate to them all. Saxophonist Sonny Rollins, a powerful, craggy-toned performer who had blended the lessons of Coleman Hawkins, Lester Young, and Charlie Parker, was working with Miles Davis and Thelonious Monk, then with Max Roach and the dazzling young Gillespie-disciple Clifford Brown to deliver a crisp and pungent kind of bebop. Dexter Gordon had formed a thrilling boppish two-tenor partnership with Wardell Gray. The young drummer Art Blakey, a man with a snare roll like a skyrocket, formed a group influenced by bop and by the ideas of its bluesy, gospel-inflected pianist Horace Silver. Under the name of the Jazz Messengers, and eventually Blakey's exclusive leadership, the group performed more or less the same repertoire until Blakey's death in 1990.

None of these musicians wanted to sound like cool players; they wanted to retain the vocal tones, hot vibrato, urgent ensemble sounds, and punchy rhythm sections of earlier jazz and of the sanctified church. They were too dispersed to amount to anything deserving the title of a movement in the beginning, but eventually the style acquired the name "hard bop." Although some fine hard bop players were white musicians (notably saxophonist Joe Farrell and the pianist Joe Zawinul, eventually a cofounder of the fusion band Weather Report), most were black and working on the East Coast or in tough industrial towns like Chicago and Detroit.

Sweet Soul Music

By the mid-1950s, these developments were acquiring some general coherence, and the band Miles Davis formed after a comeback from heroin addiction in 1955 featured two Philadelphia players (tenor saxophonist John Coltrane and drummer Philly Joe Jones), one from Detroit (bassist Paul Chambers), and Texan pianist Red Garland. The band played with a collective urgency Davis's music had not shown for years, and Coltrane, the trumpeter's diametric opposite, combined soulfulness with a single-mindedness about extending bop harmony that made him one of the most innovative improvisers of the era.

Bandleader and composer George Russell was influential in Coltrane's researches, having written an exhaustive harmony study, the *Lydian Chromatic Concept of Tonal Organization* in the early 1950s, and the arrangers' workshops of Russell and Charles Mingus developed increasingly flexible ensemble frameworks for the expressive hard bop solo styles that opened the doors to free jazz.

Always There

Hard bop surged back in popularity in the 1980s when old jazz recordings returned to the clubs in the hands of young deejays, such as Paul Murphy and Gilles Peterson in London, as music for a new generation of dancers inspired by their high-voltage rhythmic input. "Funk" was a word used by Horace Silver as far back as the mid-

1950s, and out of hard bop had grown soul jazz, with even more emphasis on repeated bluesy motifs, churchy ensemble sounds, and a rousing, relentless beat.

Bop musicians such as the saxophonist Julian "Cannonball" Adderley (composer of "Sack o' Woe"), and the pianists Horace Silver ("Song for My Father"), Bobby Timmons ("Moanin'"), and Joe Zawinul ("Mercy, Mercy, Mercy") with deep roots or a powerful affection for rhythm and blues and the black church accelerated this movement. Riding the crest of a subsequent wave came the virtuoso pianist Herbie Hancock, who had a pop hit with the jazz-funk song "Watermelon Man" in 1962, and the trumpeter Lee Morgan, whose attractive mid-tempo dance blues "The Sidewinder" was a smash 45 r.p.m. single in the 1960s and then claimed success again twenty years later. Other musicians closer to pop music have made creative use of hard bop styles — such as the 1960s orchestras of Ray Charles, the

organists Jimmy Smith and Richard "Groove" Holmes, and pianists Ramsey Lewis and Les McCann.

The hard bop movement has sometimes come under the gun for overindulgence in road-weary blues devices hung on skeletal or repetitive small-band ensemble clichés. Its tendency toward extended solos — which helped mold the astonishing improvising facility of musicians like Sonny Rollins and John Coltrane — might never have developed as far as it did without the invention of the microgroove long-playing record. However, the best hard bop effuses an immediacy and shoulder-charging force that came as a welcome antidote to cool jazz. Its renewed popularity is enduring evidence of its vitality and the expressiveness of its roots in the church and the blues.

Hard bop was rarely far from blues and gospel, and the Hammond organ evoked the preaching link. Jimmy Smith is one of the most dramatic Hammond players in jazz.

1960s

AT THE BEGINNING OF THE 1960s, free music or the New Thing set the agenda — musicians were either playing it or reacting against it. Ornette Coleman's album, simply entitled *Free Jazz*, bore an abstract painting on its cover to reinforce the point. Even Miles Davis, who disliked the new style, let his bands grow looser and more reflexive between 1960 and 1965. The civil rights struggle in the States grew

1960

MUSICIANS AND BANDS

John Coltrane's playing by 1960 is equally affecting on a ballad like "Naima" or a storming uptempo piece. He begins experimenting with split notes (harmonics) and the little-used soprano sax, the latter on the great *My Favorite Things*.

VENUES, RECORDINGS AND SHOW BUSINESS

Sketches of Spain, a selection of Spanish themes, sees Miles Davis and Gil Evans's adventurousness turn to making the trumpeter the only soloist against an orchestra.

MUSICAL DEVELOPMENTS

Jazz with an **explicit civil rights** message is made, like this Max Roach suite with a still imperious Coleman Hawkins.

HISTORICAL FACTORS

New art is linked with Ornette Coleman's: he uses abstract expressionist painter Jackson Pollock's *White Light* on *Free Jazz*.

1961

Michigan-born **Elvin Jones** becomes the most admired drummer of the era for his work with the classic John Coltrane Quartet, formed in 1960.

McCoy Tyner, from Benny Golson's Jazztet, is another powerhouse of Coltrane's Quartet. With drumlike force and density, he sustains the torrential impact of Coltrane.

In places, notably Britain, a **Dixieland revival** gets underway, using a modified New Orleans/Chicago style.

Elvin Jones rewrites drumming, overlaying pulses for a looser feel.

Musicians improvise on scales, **modes**, over simple repeated vamps.

Club business **declines** as a younger public finds rock and roll.

FREE JAZZ
A COLLECTIVE
IMPROVISATION
BY THE
ORNETTE
COLEMAN
DOUBLE
QUARTET

1962

Stan Getz, the tenorist, has always hushed rooms with his soft, glancing phrasing and fragile tone. But he makes a commercial breakthrough with *Jazz Samba*, quiet variations on Latin dance grooves that become perennial nightclub favorites.

The Beatles, a young Liverpool rhythm and blues band, are turned down by Britain's Decca Records, despite the group's success with audiences in the Merseyside clubs. They consider self-producing a first album.

The **jazz samba** boom is underway with its first chart hit, the breezy sway of "Desafinado," followed by "Girl from Ipanema."

Russia and America back off from cataclysmic confrontation over **Cuba**. The world has come near nuclear war. Protest music develops in folk and some jazz.

1963

Yusef Lateef, saxophonist and flutist, mystic, composer, and artist, shows that Asian and Middle Eastern instruments and techniques can greatly extend jazz timbres.

Charles Mingus, the gifted bassist/composer, fronts musician-led attempts to control business opportunities. He hits financial trouble.

James Brown sells out Harlem's **Apollo**, long-time home of black dance, as African-American music dominates the world's pop scene.

A **future for jazz** even more uncompromising and shorn of scales and chords than Coleman's style begins to be perceived by saxophonist Albert Ayler.

Dr. Martin Luther King tells Washington "I have a dream" in August. In September, four black girls are killed in an Alabama church bombing.

1964

Eric Dolphy, virtuoso altoist, architect of new sophistication for flute, bass clarinet pioneer and avant-garde visionary, dies age 36 after the all-time classic *Out to Lunch*.

Herbie Hancock, classical prodigy turned jazz pianist, and drummer Tony Williams provide Miles Davis with unprecedented upfront accompaniment, making the band Davis's most alert and controversial.

John Coltrane's **A Love Supreme**, a mix of unparalleled saxophone virtuosity, gradual rejection of his early structural preoccupations, and black sermonizing, inspires rock and jazz musicians.

The Jazz Composers Guild forms in New York. A free-jazz cooperative, it later becomes the **Jazz Composers Orchestra Association** under Carla Bley and Mike Mantler.

more inflamed, and the social tensions caused by the prolonged war in Vietnam intensified a feeling that music could represent protest, shared convictions, ecstasy, and solace. Although free jazz developed the vocabularies of fine musicians — notably Ornette Coleman and John Coltrane — it was mostly uncommercial. The young turned to rock and soul, musicians followed and the late 1960s heralded the arrival of fusion.

1965

Avant-garde bandleader **Sun Ra's** self-produced albums become a cult.

Albert Ayler's search for a way forward draws on the past, mingling fierce atonal playing with the street sounds of old New Orleans.

Ornette Coleman, on hearing Ayler's frenzy, creates atonal textural and rhythmic roles using the violin.

Coltrane also thought Ayler influenced his playing on **Ascension**, a free-session with added horns playing at the wailing extremes of their registers.

Ascension
John Coltrane

Chicago's Association for the Advancement of Creative Musicians (**A.A.C.M.**) forms. Free jazz is not popular, but the musicians are on a creative roll.

AACM 10th ANNIVERSARY

Association for the Advancement of Creative Musicians
Past, Present and Future Liberation

Malcolm X, black rights leader, is shot. Race riots in Watts, Los Angeles, claim 34 lives.

1966

Saxophonist **Cannonball Adderley's** hit "Mercy, Mercy, Mercy," written by young Austrian pianist Joe Zawinul, strengthens the soul-jazz movement.

Lee Morgan develops into a distinctive trumpet soloist, often in company with the fine saxophonist Hank Mobley.

THE SIDEWINDER
LEE MORGAN

On the back of **soul jazz**, Lee Morgan has a dance hit — a funky mid-tempo blues "The Sidewinder."

The **Black Power** slogan is front-page news. Huey Newton and Bobby Seale form the **Black Panther Party**.

1967

Multi-instrumentalist **Rahsaan Roland Kirk** plays several horns at once to crowds even in a low era for straight jazz.

Pharoah Sanders, Coltrane's new saxophonist, occupies the abstract, high-energy territory of Ayler. He continues in Alice Coltrane's group after the leader's death.

Majestic gospel-influenced **Aretha Franklin** tops the U.S. charts with "Respect" as President Johnson orders a commission to report on continuing racial violence. **Sly Stone's** "Dance to the Music" hits the charts.

Miles Davis listens to Sly Stone and Hendrix and works on a **jazz rock** band, as do other musicians. *Down Beat* says "jazz as we know it is dead."

Mike Westbrook attracts British attention, mingling **Ellington and free jazz**.

Racial tension increases in America, inflamed by the casualty level among black draftees in Vietnam.

1968

Archie Shepp, saxophonist, playwright, actor, and academic, campaigns for the acceptance of jazz as "black classical music" and regards free music as synonymous with political protest.

Cecil Taylor gives one of his finest displays of avant-garde piano virtuosity as principal soloist on the Jazz Composers Orchestra Association's recording of Mike Mantler's pieces.

Eubie Blake, the ragtime pianist, comes back in his 80s, demonstrating the music of the prejazz era.

U.S. free players work in **Europe**. The French government almost falls to student and labor protest.

BLACK MASS

LeRoi Jones
Le SUN RA

LeRoi Jones, later the radical black writer Amiri Baraka, sets his political poetry in a musical context with Sun Ra.

Dr. Martin Luther King is killed in Memphis, and rioting increases in American cities.

Vietnam peace moves begin.

1969

Charlie Haden, ex-Coleman bassist, gives revolutionary songs a jazz context with a poll-winning *Liberation Music*.

The **Art Ensemble of Chicago** records six albums within two months of moving to France and gains a reputation there as one of the most inventive and visually theatrical of all free jazz groups.

Miles Davis's **Bitches Brew**, setting jazz solos against rock rhythm patterns and electronic textures, becomes his best-selling album and helps open up the work of jazz musicians to a younger audience. Some Davis musicians set up their own fusion bands.

Jimi Hendrix, ex-U.S. serviceman based in Britain, **revolutionizes guitar** improvisation with a blues-based music as wild and abstract as free jazz. Jazz guitarists absorb his sound effects.

Rock's **Frank Zappa** works with violinist Jean-Luc Ponty on underrated, influential *Hot Rats*.

Free jazz

IN THE LATE 1950s, saxophonist Ornette Coleman was quoted by the writer Nat Hentoff on the liner notes to his first album: "I think one day that music will be a lot freer. The creation of music is just as natural as the air we breathe."

Coleman broke over the jazz horizon in 1959, like a comet to some, like an unguided missile to others. But he arrived just as one of the most compelling pieces of evidence that there was life after bebop was being put together. Miles Davis had collaborated with the soulful tenorist John Coltrane and the lyrical pianist Bill Evans on *Kind of Blue*, a series of all but trance-like ruminations over modes rather than chords which had a rippling, reflective quality quite unlike the breathless surge of bop. Davis followed this classic with sophisticated partnerships with Gil Evans and an orchestra on *Porgy and Bess*, *Sketches of Spain*, and other ventures in which the trumpet was displayed like a solo voice over lustrous ensemble textures.

The Shape of Jazz to Come
Coltrane took the *Kind of Blue* approach much further, exploring modes with such intensity that the flurries of notes became so molten as to be dubbed "sheets of sound." Composer/arrangers like George Russell and Charles Mingus were also making a new ensemble music that used modal playing, impressionistic sound effects, blues and gospel, and free improvising. In doing so, they partially solved some difficult questions about how to take a larger modern ensemble back to the organizational notions that predated the military discipline of swing. Adventurous musicians knew by the late 1950s that simplifying the underlying structure somehow had to be the answer. But nobody thought of going as far as Ornette Coleman.

As a young man, Coleman played Texas blues, honky tonk, and church music. Yet within a few years, he moved from the role of a rhythm and blues saxophonist in Fort Worth dance halls, to an *enfant terrible*

who split jazz allegiances down the middle. He was quickly heralded by academic and establishment figures such as composer-conductors Gunther Schuller and Leonard Bernstein, and by Modern Jazz Quartet maestro John Lewis, as a new force in 20th-century music. Coleman was just as briskly rejected by many critics and jazz fans at the time as being deaf to lyricism, out-of-tune, and indifferent or even downright aggressive to his audiences.

But, as had happened with bebop after its first wave almost two decades before, Coleman's work eventually came to be recognized as an earthy, impulsive style that had much of the directness and emotional candor of early blues musicians — with just as idiosyncratic a palette of squawks, cackles, anguished vibrato, and falsetto hoots. Together with a strident beat, it offered a

Archie Shepp's apartment with tribute to Langston Hughes. In the 1960s, the civil rights movement and free jazz developed together. Many African-American musicians looked to their African heritage as a source of liberating renewal in all the American arts.

Synth pioneer Sun Ra landed in the outer reaches of 1960s new music. His band was an idiosyncratic creative community, typified in this poetry and Saturn label literature.

genuine expansion on a style of saxophone phrasing that had seemed beyond reconsideration — Charlie Parker's. What unsettled listeners was the way Coleman ditched chords (after his first album in 1959, he did not hire a piano player for thirty years) and pursued a reflexive, immediate, small-group jazz in which the melody line with its key and harmony shifts, rhythm, and intensity all evolved organically, one performer picking up the ideas of another. With *Something Else!* and *Tomorrow Is the Question* Coleman became the first prophet of the 1960s movement known as free jazz. Some of the results were sublime. Some of it substituted outpourings of volume, ferocity, and bluster for structure, alienating many jazz lovers and scaring away the record business in the process.

Freedom Time
Free jazz in America coincided with the rise of the civil rights movement — 1957 was the year in which the U.S. government sent in the army to escort black students into formerly segregated Southern schools. It was a period in which many African-American jazz musicians saw the purpose of their work as being no different from that of James Baldwin or Malcolm X: a declaration of independence and rejection of the values of a largely white-run

entertainment business. The saxophonist Archie Shepp, a writer and polemicist as well as a musician, frequently said as much. Nor were all the committed jazz musicians free players — bop drum star Max Roach made *We Insist! — Freedom Now Suite* (which featured a revitalized Coleman Hawkins), and Sonny Rollins made *The Freedom Suite.*

These statements saw artistic boldness running parallel to political affirmation — Ornette Coleman put Jackson Pollock's abstract painting *White Light* on the cover of his influential 1960 *Free Jazz.* The Coltrane quartet that included pianist McCoy Tyner, bassist Jimmy Garrison, and drummer Elvin Jones, developed an elementally energetic quality that still influences younger jazz musicians around the world.

Fire Music

Although the free musicians of the 1960s were ostensibly loosening jazz improvisation from bop's relentless system, they weren't necessarily doing it by indifference to European music, however much they might veil it. Virtuoso pianist Cecil Taylor, the Art Tatum of the avant-garde scene, intimately intertwined jazz and contemporary classical devices at such a whirlwind pace that the links were disguised. The influences on multireed player/composer Anthony Braxton were not only Coltrane and Coleman, but modern straight-music gurus like John Cage and Karlheinz Stockhausen, and he often gave compositions abstract titles that looked like algebra.

In its first phase, free music fell between the arts funding establishments and the commercial music industry and had to fend for itself. The Association for the Advancement of Creative Musicians (A.A.C.M.) in Chicago, with pianist Muhal Richard Abrams among its leading figures, and the Jazz Composers Orchestra Association (J.C.O.A.) in New York (with Cecil Taylor, Carla Bley, Don Cherry, and Mike Mantler among its associates) took wing; comparable cooperatives began in Europe. In Britain, the West Indian saxophonist Joe Harriott had already been exploring looser, nonbop structures, and the generation that followed him mingled increasingly with musicians from the Scandinavian countries, Germany, Italy, and Eastern Europe to take the ideas of Ornette Coleman, Coltrane, and the others further, sometimes uniting them with folk roots of their own. Jan Garbarek was inspired by Coltrane but developed an authentically Norwegian music, while German Peter Brotzmann concentrated on the style's firm, assertive intensity. In Britain, John Surman adapted Coltrane's off-the-register techniques to the baritone saxophone as well as the soprano, to play music evocative of rural England. Briton Evan Parker took Coltrane's technical advances ever further, into methods of playing separate lines simultaneously which produced chords and harmonic effects previously considered impossible.

Some inventive players made progress without either diving back into the past or wholeheartedly grasping the future. Miles Davis intensely disliked free music, but the work of his brilliant mid 1960s band (with saxophonist Wayne Shorter, pianist Herbie Hancock, bassist Ron Carter, and drummer Tony Williams) produced some of the most loose and explicitly emotional, yet emphatically shapely music he had ever recorded. Sonny Rollins, a man always more inclined to making an untrammeled, unpremeditated story out of a solo than to following a chord pattern, worked with Ornette Coleman's trumpeter Don Cherry. And the Art Ensemble of Chicago, which grew out of the A.A.C.M., made theatrical, collagelike events out of its live performances, shifting through many jazz idioms and making the continuity of the music's restless development graphically explicit.

Free jazz never won a big public. In some hands, it was an artistic dead end, too, its freedoms legitimizing the dependence on faked "emotion," by a handful of repeated figures, as pervasively as had happened in bebop. But, through its boldness, free jazz kicked open doors that have never completely closed, familiarizing audiences, even those who were initially reluctant, to a wealth of new sounds. It has massively extended contemporary jazz.

The most intuitive jazz of Ornette Coleman (center right) depended on a repertory group of regular partners. Here it features New Orleans drummer Ed Blackwell, swing arranger Don Redman's tenorist son Dewey, and bassist Charlie Haden.

Fusion

THE EXTREMES OF JAZZ in the 1950s and early 1960s were the cool school with its tricky time signatures and melodic intrigue, and the beginnings of a new, hot free music that seemed at first to have no rules at all. But if both approaches seemed closer to art music than show business, the historical connection between jazz and dance had not withered away in the 1950s. It just did not make the newspapers.

Nor had the prophets of the New Thing arrived from another galaxy. Ornette Coleman and John Coltrane had learned their craft in blues bands, playing dance halls and bars. Ray Charles's clamorous, gospelly big bands of the 1950s showed the tight relationship of blues and hard bop, as did pianist Horace Silver. The modern descendants of the boogie woogie pianists arrived, Hammond organists like Jimmy Smith and Jimmy McGriff, halfway between jazz and rhythm and blues, and saxophonist Eddie "Cleanhead" Vinson was still as bluesy as a guitar player.

Funky jazz was not just an American phenomenon. Late 1950s Britain spawned skilled blues musicians from the skiffle "jug band" boom, who frequently drew on jazz for inspiration. John McLaughlin made his breakthrough in the driving rhythm and blues band led by the late Graham Bond, and 1960s British r & b stars like Cream's Jack Bruce and Ginger Baker cut their teeth on the London jazz scene.

Jazz Carnival

Even cool jazz had flirtatious fusions with dance, although they took an appropriately languid form. Stan Getz, the graceful saxophonist close to the cool school, collaborated with a group of Brazilian musicians to spark off the seductive bossa nova craze. Fusion existed long before it became a genre and gained a capital letter.

By 1965 a mass movement of young rock fans heard jazz as the bearer of a dated message. Their parents had jazz record collections. It was time for something new — in music, fashion, personal politics, and ethics. A more complex, extended, instrumental, and improvisational rock music (often using modal methods) was uniting tens of thousands of entranced listeners. Massive outdoor festivals seemed to sustain the dream of a community of youth with its own values and language and without frontiers, that could inhabit a world of its own. In the States, disaffection with an older generation's legacy intensified with racial tension and the war in Vietnam.

Miles Davis dominated the first fusion era, as he had earlier periods in jazz: by listening to black American soul and electronic music such as Stockhausen's, he helped redirect jazz.

Box office and record sales declined for jazz. Even Miles Davis started to notice the difference — and if he did, every other jazz musician would have been noticing it more. It was not just expediency that moved jazz musicians toward the new rock, even if Columbia's executives began dropping hints to Davis that he might broaden his listening habits. Not every young musician wanted to be a rock and roll star. Many still loved jazz and learned its craft, but the sound palette was now far more colorful. The Moog synthesizer was used by improvisers from the mid-1960s. Ray Charles had played an electric piano in 1959, and its glittering sound appealed to jazz keyboardists like Herbie Hancock. Guitarists would no longer simply dream of cloning the soft, deft, rounded sound of Wes Montgomery or Jim Hall, but mixed it with the howl of Jimi Hendrix. Double bass players learned to double on bass guitar.

Funky Drummer

Jazz rock, or fusion — mingling bop, r & b, and fatback funk devices lifted from Motown, Stax, James Brown, and from bands like Sly Stone's — grew by the day. The word *jazz* was often dropped from marketing as bad for business. Bigger bluesy bands like Blood, Sweat and Tears and Chicago featured horn lineups with jazzy licks. Vibes player Gary Burton pioneered the remarkable technique of bending notes like a blues guitarist and began to play a mix of jazz and country blues in the later 1960s, introducing young guitarists Larry Coryell, Pat Metheny, and John Scofield. Another vibist, Roy Ayers, fused catchy songwriting with Afrocentric funk. Saxophonist Yusef Lateef, a broad-minded artist who had long drawn on music from other cultures, explored jazz funk, as did the trumpeter Randy Brecker and his virtuoso saxophonist brother Mike. Professor Donald Byrd at the University of Southern California, formerly a Blue Note trumpet star, collaborated with students like brother producers Larry and Fonce Mizell, taking jazzy street funk to the discos with the best-selling *Black Byrd* and now collectible *Places and Spaces*. He forged a market for younger musicians like pianist Patrice Rushen and his students, the Blackbyrds, who took the sound onto 45 rpm format with singles such as "Do It Fluid."

But, not for the first time, the convert who became the most charismatic preacher of a new gospel to jazz musicians in this period was Miles Davis. The band he had been leading, which included Herbie Hancock, Wayne Shorter, Tony Williams, and Ron Carter, had stretched jazz improvisation to the limits of freedom compatible with maintaining a structure and a pulse. Now Davis steeped himself in the music of Sly Stone and Jimi Hendrix. With all his old audacity, he spliced the solo resources of a sensational band into an electric music that still had space, drama, and surprise but increasingly used electronic effects to paint active backdrops as haunting and suggestive as Gil Evans had produced with a conventional orchestra. *In a Silent Way* and *Filles de Kilimanjaro* began a change for him that passed through a big-selling classic of fusion atmospherics, *Bitches Brew*. This was followed by less distinct phases bordering on disco — electronics made his trumpet sound more impersonally guitarlike — and on to the hip hop and rap sounds of the 1980s and 1990s.

Armando "Chick" Corea
brought the vivacity of Latin-American music to his brand of fusion and successfully combined the careers of acoustic jazz player, original composer, and funk star through the 1970s and 1980s.

Survival of the Fittest

Davis's sidemen branched into fusion experiments of their own. Wayne Shorter and keyboardist Joe Zawinul formed Weather Report, a fusion band performing exhilarating original compositions. Pianist Chick Corea set up Return to Forever, an exuberant Latin-influenced band that started light and delicate but grew closer to hard rock in the 1970s. Miles Davis's sensational young drummer Tony Williams put together the raucous but more abstract Lifetime with guitarist John McLaughlin and Cream's Jack Bruce. A cooler, and more romantic fusion came with Pat Metheny, who not only proved that a guitar synthesizer could genuinely extend the eloquence of the instrument, but whose music never stopped suggesting a tousle-haired kid hitching a ride with a guitar on his back. Gil Evans, the painterly genius of jazz instrumentation who master-

minded *Birth of the Cool* in the 1950s, produced some uneven but often thrilling fusion sessions, even arranging some of Jimi Hendrix's songs for a full-scale orchestra.

Some jazz players stayed on the fusion road until it wound all the way into pop — like guitarist George Benson, one of the finest improvisers since Wes Montgomery. Benson restricted his jazz playing to after-hours sessions once the soft funk and Nat King Cole-influenced vocals of his 1976 album *Breezin'* changed his life.

Fusion eventually suffered from its own self-importance, dependence on technical bravura, and repetitive formulas that cramped improvisation. But at its best, fusion permanently transformed jazz, and in the 1980s, all inhibitions about what jazz could appropriate as its own disappeared.

Founded on the collaboration of keyboardist Joe Zawinul and saxophonist Wayne Shorter, Weather Report was popular and musically challenging. For 15 years it produced classics of funk and Latin drive colored by collective improvising.

1970 — 1990

Rock went through such a creative surge in the 1960s and 1970s that most of the world's music was affected by it — including jazz, which had the same roots. Synthesizers, electric bass and keyboards, and massive amplification became regular features of the countless rock-oriented jazz bands in the early 1970s, on a roll not unlike that of swing 40 years earlier. Yet many musicians, disliking the repetitiveness

	1970-1971	1972-1973	1974-1975	1976-1977	1978-1979
MUSICIANS AND BANDS	Pianist **Chick Corea** leaves Miles Davis with bassist Dave Holland and forms the free jazz group named Circle, featuring the multi-instrumentalist Anthony Braxton. **Louis Armstrong** dies in New York on July 6, 1971. He is mourned worldwide, both as a popular entertainer, and as a giant of jazz.	British guitarist **John McLaughlin's** Mahavishnu Orchestra mixes racing rock rhythms, headlong improvising, dramatic themes, and Indian music. **Freddie Hubbard**, a graceful bop trumpeter, shows fusion's commerciality.	**Keith Jarrett**, another ex-Miles Davis sideman, rejects electric music and explores delicate solo piano, drawing on classical music, country music, and Bill Evans. A group sound reveals his developing composition skills. **Miles Davis quits** music because of ill-health and creative exhaustion. **Wayne Shorter**, a great saxophonist, is modest in Weather Report, but its Latin excursions affect his samba-inflected *Native Dancer*.	**Betty Carter**, the highly creative bop-based vocalist, avoids commercial projects in the 1960s and 1970s. An appearance in the musical *Don't Call Me Man* puts her back on the road.	**Scott Hamilton**, a swing-style tenorist, works with Benny Goodman and begins a run of fine recordings that put him at the forefront of mainstream. **Herbie Hancock** in the same year, 1978, performs subtle acoustic piano duets with Chick Corea, and uses the voice-synth Vocoder in a massive pop hit "I Thought It Was You."
VENUES, RECORDINGS AND SHOW BUSINESS	Small labels like **Black Jazz** and **Strata East** document fusion and political jazz with awareness of black social issues.	The Scott Joplin **movie soundtrack** for *The Sting,* starring Paul Newman and Robert Redford, revives a popular taste for ragtime music.	Keith Jarrett cuts the unaccompanied **The Köln Concert**, the best-selling piano disk ever. His refined jazz makes him an international star, and boosts his German label ECM.	Guitarist **George Benson's** hit soul jazz disk *Breezin'* features his Nat Cole-like voice. It defines middle of the road jazz, and downplays his improvising.	**Pat Metheny's** 1978, *Pat Metheny Group* is a best-seller. On it, the Missouri-born guitar prodigy, who graduated to Berklee's staff soon after joining as a student, shows that fusion can be romantic, subtle, improvisational, and have lasting themes.
MUSICAL DEVELOPMENTS		The musicians who have worked with **Miles Davis** (left) extend his influence on jazz rock: in Joe Zawinul and Wayne Shorter's Weather Report, Tony Williams's Lifetime, and the Mahavishnu Orchestra.	A revived interest in **classic bop** is signaled with West Coast altoist Art Pepper's dramatic comeback after narcotics difficulties.	**Disco** music dominates the dance floors of the West. Rugged, hard bop tenorist Dexter Gordon (left) **returns to New York** after 13 years in Europe, packing the Village Vanguard.	**Gil Scott-Heron**, a godfather of rap, outspoken jazz poet and songwriter. His hardhitting storytelling deals with racism, drug abuse, and the pursuit of justice.
HISTORICAL FACTORS		**U.S. involvement in Vietnam ends.** The damage to Western confidence is immense. Many musicians are cynical about the system in which they are entertainers.		**Elvis Presley**, king of rock and roll, dies aged 42. His life earnings are estimated to have been $1 billion.	

of commercial music or fusion's unsuitability for nuances, explored other jazz forms, including swing, bop, and free. Their time returned when younger musicians, developing subtler blends of jazz, funk, and Latin, made earlier fusion sound overweight and pretentious. Bop's agility brought it back into favor, and "world music" — sharing ideas between jazz and non-jazz cultures — enriched the soundscape.

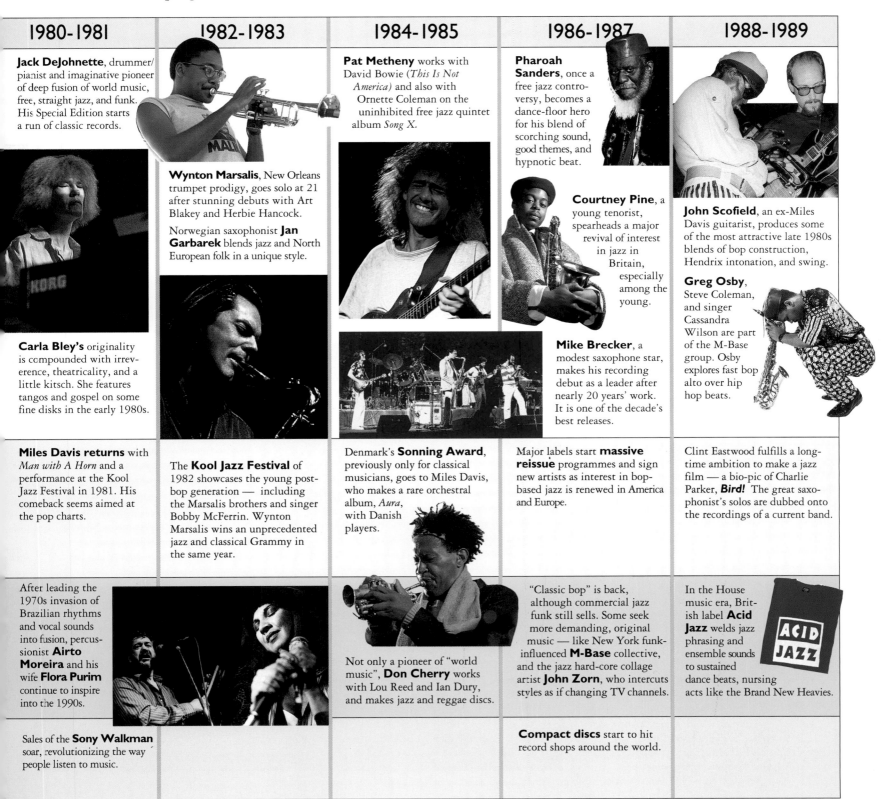

1980-1981

Jack DeJohnette, drummer/pianist and imaginative pioneer of deep fusion of world music, free, straight jazz, and funk. His Special Edition starts a run of classic records.

Carla Bley's originality is compounded with irreverence, theatricality, and a little kitsch. She features tangos and gospel on some fine disks in the early 1980s.

Miles Davis returns with *Man with A Horn* and a performance at the Kool Jazz Festival in 1981. His comeback seems aimed at the pop charts.

After leading the 1970s invasion of Brazilian rhythms and vocal sounds into fusion, percussionist **Airto Moreira** and his wife **Flora Purim** continue to inspire into the 1990s.

Sales of the **Sony Walkman** soar, revolutionizing the way people listen to music.

1982-1983

Wynton Marsalis, New Orleans trumpet prodigy, goes solo at 21 after stunning debuts with Art Blakey and Herbie Hancock.

Norwegian saxophonist **Jan Garbarek** blends jazz and North European folk in a unique style.

The **Kool Jazz Festival** of 1982 showcases the young postbop generation — including the Marsalis brothers and singer Bobby McFerrin. Wynton Marsalis wins an unprecedented jazz and classical Grammy in the same year.

1984-1985

Pat Metheny works with David Bowie (*This Is Not America*) and also with Ornette Coleman on the uninhibited free jazz quintet album *Song X*.

Denmark's **Sonning Award**, previously only for classical musicians, goes to Miles Davis, who makes a rare orchestral album, *Aura*, with Danish players.

Not only a pioneer of "world music", **Don Cherry** works with Lou Reed and Ian Dury, and makes jazz and reggae discs.

1986-1987

Pharoah Sanders, once a free jazz controversy, becomes a dance-floor hero for his blend of scorching sound, good themes, and hypnotic beat.

Courtney Pine, a young tenorist, spearheads a major revival of interest in jazz in Britain, especially among the young.

Mike Brecker, a modest saxophone star, makes his recording debut as a leader after nearly 20 years' work. It is one of the decade's best releases.

Major labels start **massive reissue** programmes and sign new artists as interest in bop-based jazz is renewed in America and Europe.

"Classic bop" is back, although commercial jazz funk still sells. Some seek more demanding, original music — like New York funk-influenced **M-Base** collective, and the jazz hard-core collage artist **John Zorn**, who intercuts styles as if changing TV channels.

Compact discs start to hit record shops around the world.

1988-1989

John Scofield, an ex-Miles Davis guitarist, produces some of the most attractive late 1980s blends of bop construction, Hendrix intonation, and swing.

Greg Osby, Steve Coleman, and singer Cassandra Wilson are part of the M-Base group. Osby explores fast bop alto over hip hop beats.

Clint Eastwood fulfills a longtime ambition to make a jazz film — a bio-pic of Charlie Parker, *Bird!* The great saxophonist's solos are dubbed onto the recordings of a current band.

In the House music era, British label **Acid Jazz** welds jazz phrasing and ensemble sounds to sustained dance beats, nursing acts like the Brand New Heavies.

ACID JAZZ

Jazz today

IN 1990, *TIME* MAGAZINE ran a cover picture of young trumpeter Wynton Marsalis. The words heralded "The New Jazz Age." They were late catching up with this story: the signs had been there since the early 1980s — some would even say 1976, when the Village Vanguard club was unexpectedly overrun with fans of emigré bop saxophonist Dexter Gordon on his return to New York. But a jazz renaissance still came as news to many. After being all but unmentionable for almost a decade, jazz had risen from the grave.

Time magazine could hardly contend that jazz was enjoying a public status it hadn't known since the last "Jazz Age" — no jazz artists were doing enough business to cause Madonna or Michael Jackson to lose sleep, nor were they having the kind of popular appeal that gained Paul Whiteman his King of Jazz title sixty years before. But jazz had undoubtedly acquired an influence outside music again, although maybe not in the way F. Scott Fitzgerald had meant it. The word, particularly in Europe, could be found adorning cars, perfume, and clothes. Jazz seemed chic and, by implication, people who bought a package bearing its name were either heading upmarket or already there.

The Revival

Although many suspected the sincerity of this unaccustomed embrace, international appreciation of the music was expanding fast. People bought more jazz records, those who had put their jazz collections in the attic brought them down again, and younger listeners sought role models in a flood of talented, technically astonishing newcomers emerging from a strengthened jazz college system. This new enthusiasm

not only put neon-lit names to new faces, but rejuvenated the careers of veteran players like Dexter Gordon, Art Blakey, Horace Silver, and Johnny Griffin.

This renewal was happening against the background of a rapidly evolving international music community. The 1980s was the decade of "world music," in which

faster communications further shrank the globe, growing understanding between Western and non-Western cultures accelerated the sharing of musical languages, and traditional frontiers between "high" and "popular" art relaxed. For the first time, jazz became a truly international language without old pecking orders of nations that could and couldn't swing. Russian jazz musicians toured the States; American jazz musicians collaborated with Europeans; Australians, Japanese, South Africans, and

Joe Henderson reminded the 1980s that playing "classic" jazz was more than a matter of running down the notes. A highly personal improviser, he is given to unpredictable slews in phrase length and dynamics and his solos reject jazz clichés.

At clubs such as New York's Giant Step, deejays mixed modal jazz with hot Latin, rap, and live shows that revived artists like Roy Ayers and Mark Murphy, and fed new talent.

Bulgarians were increasingly at ease with vocabularies coined in Harlem and Kansas City and were even enthusiastically inventing new ones of their own. Scandinavian saxophonist Jan Garbarek spine-tinglingly mixed Coltrane's tenor sound with northern European folk music including elements such as the cattle calls of Norway. Ever more technically skilled newcomers could treat Parker's and Coltrane's innovations as invaluable preparation, but as a starting point rather than an ultimate destination.

Back on the Scene

The heartbeat of the comeback was bebop. Dismissed by many as antijazz or even antimusic in the early 1940s, four decades later it became the gracefully swinging idiom that most casual listeners identified as the sound of jazz. The world of 52nd Street clubs and the spreading bohemianism of "modern jazz" in the postwar era was far enough in the past to be reinvented in semifictional feature films like Clint Eastwood's *Bird!* (devoted to Charlie Parker) and Bertrand Tavernier's *Round Midnight*. The latter movie even turned Dexter Gordon into more of a celebrity as an actor than he had been as a player when he portrayed a central figure modeled on Lester Young.

New interest in the era that spawned bop brought back some of its most powerful, experienced practitioners, showing that in the years when their styles were supposed to be dead they had been making

fine music. Among the most powerful was Joe Henderson, one of the few saxophonists in jazz with an approach similar to that of Sonny Rollins. Trumpeter Woody Shaw was an older bop-oriented master, who had worked in Paris with one of the idiom's founders, drummer Kenny Clarke. Like fellow trumpeter Freddie Hubbard, who swung back from mostly routine fusion to some inspired straight-ahead playing, Shaw had brilliant technique, a warm tone, and an improviser's imagination that could hear beyond the next four bars. Something of Shaw's desire to extend the regular bounds of bop was long a feature of the group led by tenorist George Adams and pianist Don Pullen, prolific ex-Mingus sidemen who ran the same band from 1979 to 1989 with the rhythmic propulsion of another Mingus legend, drummer Dannie Richmond, driving it on. The Adams-Pullen group unfailingly delivered thrilling blends of free music, blues, bop, and down-the-line swing, which were only silenced by Richmond's death.

After years of adding his own inimitable flourishes to others' records, saxophonist Mike Brecker waited until he was 38 to make a superb debut album, in 1987, which mixed bop and bursts of Coltranish fire and featured a spectacular band including guitarist Pat Metheny. For all his lyrical soft-fusion reputation, Metheny was one of the great bop improvisers of his generation, occasionally demonstrated in a powerhouse trio with drummer Roy Haynes and bassist Dave Holland. McCoy Tyner, a strong, committed performer since his days with Coltrane, was also active, occasionally with a hard-swinging, imaginative big band.

Other pianists — Joanne Brackeen, Steve Kuhn, Geri Allen, and Keith Jarrett — hit independent routes. Allen emerged as a virtuoso performer, mingling the rich keyboard voicing of Bill Evans with steely resolve and Monklike truculence. Jarrett continued to be one of the era's most remarkable phenomena. Since the running success of his 1975 *The Köln Concert*, Jarrett had continued to attract

big audiences for an intense, acoustic music. He spent the era in astonishing productivity with solo piano recitals and small-group shows with the Standards Trio.

Destination Out!

But it was not just older listeners and a new cognoscenti that supported the revival. Teenage dancers and deejays around the world discovered the hard bop records of the 1950s and 1960s, and a nightclub scene sprang up that depended heavily on classic jazz records — even rare ones on 1970s labels like Black Jazz, Strata East, and Flying Dutchman. They mixed standards with funk, rap, and Latin grooves. Teenagers learned that Art Blakey not only had a beat that sent the music into orbit but, in the 1980s, was still alive and kicking. Blakey's ardent, bluesy bands were still packed with rising young stars (he had always been a sorcerer with a roster of gifted apprentices). From 1980, his Jazz Messengers included trumpeter Wynton Marsalis and saxophonist brother Branford.

Wynton Marsalis was so influential in the 1980s that the *Time* magazine cover presenting him as the guru of the New Jazz Age came as no surprise.

In the mid-1980s, a young London rehearsal band became the powerful collective orchestra Loose Tubes. Its pieces, often by the original pianist and composer Django Bates, drew on jazz, funk, and European music.

Wynton Marsalis spearheaded a group that came to be bracketed as neo-classicists, and a search for his musical roots obsessed him through the 1980s. A brilliant technician, at home in classical music and jazz, he spent the decade working back from bop-oriented jazz and the influence of Miles Davis's acoustic bands to a sound recalling the ensemble voicings of early New Orleans, with the group approach of Charles Mingus. He began to develop ensemble writing, too.

If Marsalis was investigating virtually all jazz, regardless of the era, to find a voice, others made journeys more limited in focus. The mainstream style, which in the 1950s meant musicians who played like cut-down Basie swing bands, embraced couplings of swing and other idioms. Saxophonist Scott Hamilton and trumpeters Ruby Braff and Warren Vache were lyrical and rhythmically effortless exponents. Some younger players, who were also inspired by the past but who spliced styles together in a less scholarly way, formed highly entertaining, theatrical outfits. One of the most irrepressible was the Louisiana-based Dirty Dozen Brass Band, a fresh, exuberant, young eight-piece that delivered Cajun music, funk, and bop in unpredictable proportions.

Apart from young American virtuosos like the measured, mature trumpet prodigy Roy Hargrove, the Blakey-like Harper brothers, and the hauntingly Miles Davis–like Wallace Roney, vigorous neo-bop developments took place outside the States. Britain produced an evocative, technically remarkable saxophonist in Courtney Pine — whose work drew together Coltrane, African pop music, and reggae from his parents' homeland — and the quirkily melodic Andy Sheppard. There was also London pianist Julian Joseph, an inspired interpreter of a relaxed, Herbie Hancock style. Pine and Sheppard worked in homegrown big bands, too, reflecting creative blends of Charles Mingus's ensemble looseness, elements of free jazz, and local references of their own.

Meanwhile fusion, the triumphant instrumental music of the 1970s, had not gone away. Sometimes criticized for rigidities of structure that cramped improvisation, and for sacrificing the loose, surging rhythms of jazz to a hard, inexorable backbeat, fusion and acoustic jazz techniques increasingly began to meet on equal terms.

Miles Ahead

The big news at the beginning of the 1980s was that Miles Davis was returning after a five-year layoff for illness and creative exhaustion. Davis sounded hesitant, and his music was ostensibly oriented toward winning airplay on black radio stations. Although his power to astonish an audi-

ence with a single note had diminished, Cyndi Lauper's "Time After Time" on 1984's *You're Under Arrest* demonstrated that Davis had recovered much of his old lyricism. On the same record, the guitarist John Scofield combined boplike melodies with a funky beat and bass lines in a promise of a revitalized jazz. Scofield became one of the most interesting guitarist/composers of the era: 1990's *Time on My Hands* was one of the disks of the decade.

Weather Report, the longest lasting and frequently most musical of fusion bands, broke up in 1985, which released its

Miles Davis's album *Doo-Bop*, completed after his death in 1991, was an uneven but intriguing mix of jazz trumpet soloing, samples and hip-hop rhythms.

influential saxophonist Wayne Shorter to recover his trenchant, muscular way of playing and composing with his own bands. Pianist Chick Corea began to divide his time between an acoustic and an electric band, and soul sax star David Sanborn made the jazzy album *Another Hand* in the 1980s as a personal departure from his more pop-oriented style.

All these musicians seemed to have been consolidating music of the 1970s. Miles Davis, although his health was failing, kept looking forward. His posthumously completed last record, *Doo-Bop*, reflected the dance rhythms of hip hop and the insistent, emphatic accents of rap. While some of it was self-congratulatory, Davis's solos were as jazzlike as anything he had recorded in twenty-five years and suggested one way that contemporary jazz might go.

Somethin' Else

Young musicians, like members of New York's M-Base collective, also searched for meeting points between the jazz tradition and new black American dance music. Saxophonist Steve Coleman, a devastating bop player as likely to quote James Brown as Charlie Parker when asked about his influences, formed the Five Elements band and developed a music in which shifting rhythmic patterns drawn from funk seemed to replace older notions of melody. Gary Thomas and Greg Osby, two other M-Base saxophonists, explored similar ground, Osby finding inspiration among the young hip hop and dance jazz musicians developing their own sound in London. Cassandra Wilson, an agile, fierce-toned singer influenced by New York street sounds, funk, and Betty Carter, was a major international talent spawned by the M-Base ethos in the 1980s. And Betty Carter, now the doyenne of jazz vocalists after the death of Sarah Vaughan and the decline in health of Ella Fitzgerald, continued to tour the world with a spine-chillingly dramatic, personal show that recalled Billie Holiday.

Cassandra Wilson is a leading figure in jazz vocals. Influenced by Abbey Lincoln and Betty Carter, she is a singer of strength, character, and swing on standards or funk.

Not all 1980s developments were what most listeners might describe as jazz, yet the sound and approach toward spontaneous music making were sufficiently identifiable as a jazz line for the term to fit. All over the world, the free improvised music that was generated in the 1960s and early 1970s had released jazz-oriented musicians in many cultures to find their own voices. In Europe, a highly sophisticated free scene developed, players from different countries working together in ever-changing bands.

Pianist Cecil Taylor, one of the geniuses of the American avant-garde worked fruitfully in Europe with local players. In New York, the composer John Zorn developed music impossible to categorize but significantly motivated by the European free jazz scene. Zorn depended on improvisers, and his listening habits put Japanese pop next to Bobby McFerrin next to reggae next to hard-core punk. It became obvious from the 1980s on that younger musicians were also listening to music in the same flexible way.

2

AN ANATOMY OF INSTRUMENTS

Where students of Western classical music iron out idiosyncrasies of technique, students of jazz cultivate them — jazz is founded on the notion that a piece is infinitely malleable to a performer's personality. The characteristic sound of a creative jazz player is as personal as a signature or the sound of a voice.

Using instruments originally from military, circus, or vaudeville bands, occasionally from the classical orchestra, and more recently from computer technology, jazz musicians have absorbed traditional techniques and superimposed on them methods of their own making.

In these pages, prominent jazz musicians reveal secrets of their craft and demonstrate that while jazz often sounds as elusive as magic, its techniques are specific, disciplined, and hard-won.

The voice

Cleveland Watkiss

THE OLDEST MUSICAL INSTRUMENT is the "horn" in the throat. For thousands of years, singing has played a part in religious ritual, hunting and work, childcare and play. Many musicians, whatever their instrument, hear the sound of voices as a primary inspiration. And voices – particularly African voices – are at the root of the uniquely eloquent tonalities of jazz. Notes that hang between the "pure" pitches of Western classical music go back to Africa, and the call-and-response of swing band sections echoes work song messages of encouragement and despair exchanged by slaves in the Americas. Because jazz has no fixed methodology, singers have made up their own rules, governed only by their own imagination and anatomy. African-American styles of singing have transformed the music of the 20th century.

Each singer's "inner face," the vocal and nasal tracts, produces a unique sound

STARS AND STYLES

Louis Armstrong's exploration of the drumlike explosive sounds of wordless, improvised scat singing was one of the most influential examples of jazz singers forging their own sound. His gravelly tonality was very different from European standards, but its expressiveness is immense. Key blues singers included the earthy, humorous **"Ma" Rainey** and majestic Empress of the Blues, **Bessie Smith**, whose sound could suggest a Baptist choir or growling gutbucket trumpet. **Ethel Waters** showed how much color and character could be injected into popular songs, but **Billie Holiday** was the quintessential jazz singer. Her small, sensitive voice had a saxophonelike improvisational flexibility, and she could make even the most mundane song seem sublime. Big bands brought the relaxed, infectiously swinging **Ella Fitzgerald** and the assured **Sarah Vaughan** and **Billy Eckstine**; then came the deft, unsentimental, instrumentlike performers of bebop in **Carmen McRae**, **Anita O'Day**, **Betty Carter** (now matured into a vocalist whose impact can border on Holiday's), and the trio **Lambert, Hendricks, and Ross**, whose "vocalese" legacy was continued by **Manhattan Transfer**. **Leon Thomas** and more recently **Al Jarreau** and **Bobby McFerrin** have extended scat, sound effects, and popular song into fusion and funk, as have **Dee Dee Bridgewater**, **Jean Carn**, **Marlena Shaw**, and **Ricky Lee Jones**.

The movement of air

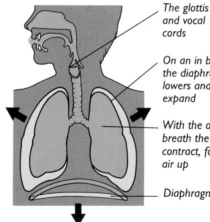

The glottis and vocal cords

On an in breath the diaphragm lowers and lungs expand

With the out breath the lungs contract, forcing air up

Diaphragm

The column of vibrating air that produces sound comes from the chest, pumped by the moving diaphragm below the lungs. Low tones need a longer air column, with vibrations felt in the chest. Higher tones with a shorter air column are felt in the throat and head. From the lungs, the air passes through the cartilage "horn" of the larynx: two vibrating muscular folds, the vocal cords, and the space between them, the glottis. Sound from the throat is subject to varying air pressure by the tongue's position on the palate and teeth, the shape of the lips, and the amount of air emitted through the mouth or nose.

Singers are taught to lower the center of gravity and train the belly to drop. Cleveland Watkiss says he "breathes from the feet."

Shifting sound

A vocal sound is not pure like a tuning fork — it consists of a fundamental tone, determined by the singer's anatomy, with "overtones" on top. Cord size determines the fundamental frequency or range of a voice: an average singer's might be two octaves, a good one's three or more. Varying the degree of tension of the cords, the aperture of the glottis and the air pressure from below shift the musical pitch. Overtones are hard-to-catch faint sounds above the fundamental tone, but they give any musical sound its particular expressive timbre or tone color. Classical singers give overtones that are even multiples of the basic tone. The rougher, more idiosyncratic and speechlike tone color of jazz and blues singers comes from an irregular ratio of harmonic and nonharmonic overtones.

The **"head voice"** — throat constricted, teeth closed to produce a flat, lean sound characteristic of styles as diverse as soul and flamenco. Stevie Wonder sings this way, as do many contemporary vocalists, influenced as much by soul as by the percussive, lips-together style of bop-inspired scat.

Returning to the body as a noise-making device, as in ancient music, singers have rediscovered a range of effects. Bobby McFerrin performs solo concerts mimicking instruments and adding drumlike "percussion" by beating his chest. Yodeling, throat sounds without oral variations, has entered jazz via original singers like Leon Thomas and the Briton Phil Minton.

Projecting the voice, with the mouth open and the sound coming from the chest, was a technique of blues and vaudeville singers before the invention of the microphone. In recent years, voice teachers have concluded that singers' problems often stem from overconcentration on the chest. Notions drawn from sources such as martial arts focus on breathing farther down.

Amplification

Before the microphone, singers in tent shows and traveling variety troupes used volume to communicate. Microphones transformed jazz singing. Nuances lost in acoustic shows could be given such emphasis over a sound system that the redefining of vocal dynamics became virtually a new art. Microphones contain diaphragms that vibrate sympathetically with sound waves, turning them into electrical pulses which are magnified in amplifiers, then converted back to vibrations in loudspeakers. Amplification technology has come far since the 1930s: much of the naturalness and subtlety of timbre of an unamplified singer in a small space can be recaptured in large halls. This sensitivity is essential to jazz performances.

Different microphones offer variations in sensitivity and degree of background ambience reproduced

The microphone in modern singing is as much an instrument as the voice. How far it is held from the mouth and its changing position during the sounding of a note, even whether it is struck on the chest or touched with the lips — all extend a singer's range. Billie Holiday's intimacy could not have been expressed without the microphone. It made audible the subtle nuances in her voice, which transformed jazz singing.

Trumpet

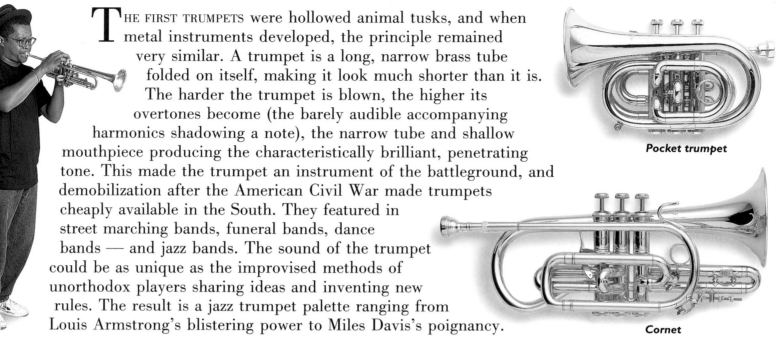

THE FIRST TRUMPETS were hollowed animal tusks, and when metal instruments developed, the principle remained very similar. A trumpet is a long, narrow brass tube folded on itself, making it look much shorter than it is. The harder the trumpet is blown, the higher its overtones become (the barely audible accompanying harmonics shadowing a note), the narrow tube and shallow mouthpiece producing the characteristically brilliant, penetrating tone. This made the trumpet an instrument of the battleground, and demobilization after the American Civil War made trumpets cheaply available in the South. They featured in street marching bands, funeral bands, dance bands — and jazz bands. The sound of the trumpet could be as unique as the improvised methods of unorthodox players sharing ideas and inventing new rules. The result is a jazz trumpet palette ranging from Louis Armstrong's blistering power to Miles Davis's poignancy.

Claude Deppa

Pocket trumpet

Cornet

The trumpet

The standard trumpet used in jazz is the instrument that has a fundamental tone of B flat. The bugle, the trumpet's forerunner, was valveless — the addition of valves and extra tubing extended the range. In early jazz the cornet, which in 19th-century music played parts later taken by the trumpet, was in general use. It is a little easier to blow than the trumpet. The flügelhorn, sometimes dubbed the valved bugle, has a plusher, more mellow sound and is often used as a trumpeter's second instrument, although players such as Art Farmer have specialized in it.

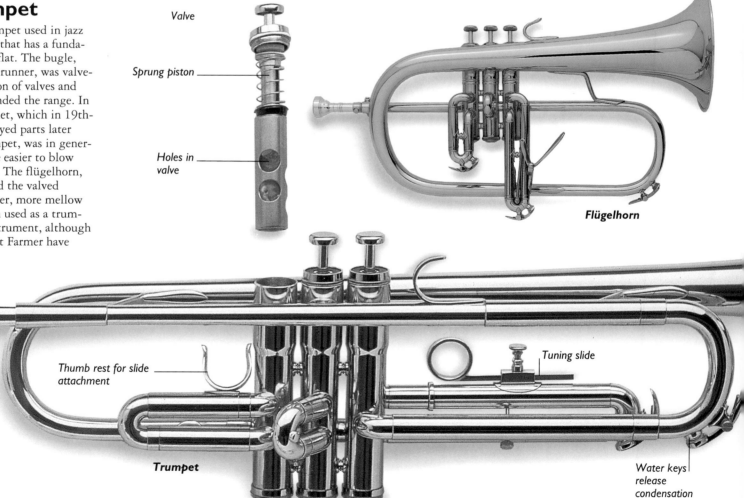

Valve

Sprung piston

Holes in valve

Flügelhorn

Cup-shaped mouthpiece

Thumb rest for slide attachment

Tuning slide

Trumpet

Water keys release condensation

STARS AND STYLES

Cornet-playing first man of jazz **Charles "Buddy" Bolden** had a powerful sound and bluesy tonality that predated recording. Strong New Orleans leader **Joe "King" Oliver** inspired **Louis Armstrong**, who revolutionized the rhythmically stiff, blues-based styles of the early years, making them brighter, more at odds with the beat, and with more sustained narrative logic. **Bix Beiderbecke** developed an elegant, silvery-toned, cooler version in the 1920s, and **Henry "Red" Allen** nearly rivaled Armstrong for technique, plus an extraordinary repertoire of trills, growls, and vocal effects borrowed even by the 1960s avant-garde. **Roy Eldridge** was the fast, spectacular swing trumpeter who influenced **Dizzy Gillespie's** firecracker of a saxophonelike bebop technique. The short-lived **Clifford Brown** was a graceful bebop master, but **Miles Davis's** sensuous, contemplative trumpet dominated postwar jazz. **Wynton Marsalis**, a musician of phenomenal technique, can play comfortably in virtually all trumpet styles today.

Trumpet range The cornet is built to play in the key of B flat, its music written a tone above the actual sound. The range extends from the E below middle C to the second B flat above. The trumpet and pocket trumpet are built to the same pitch.

Extended jazz range

Middle C

Trumpet *Pocket trumpet* *Cornet* *Flügelhorn*

Embouchure

Clarinetists and saxophonists use wooden or plastic reeds to vibrate a column of air, but the brass player's natural double reed is the lips. The muscles around the mouth are trained so that their changing shape produces a wide range of timbres and notes without fatigue or damage. Textbooks advocate central placing of the mouthpiece, covering each lip equally, but different faces lead to differing methods.

Sounding a note

In the playing of all wind instruments, the column of air to be vibrated at the mouthpiece needs to be thought of as continuous — beginning at the bottom of the lungs and extending to the bell of the horn. Good breath control involves strengthening the diaphragm — the wide, flat muscle under the lungs — and expanding the solar plexus to create additional room for the lungs to swell. Steady support for the air column is essential for strong, unfaltering note production. The trumpeter can produce seven basic notes (C-G-C-E-G-B flat-C) simply by embouchure changes, introducing the valves to add the missing notes. Depressing the first valve lowers the fundamental note to B flat. In practice, each successive lowering of the fundamental by depressing a valve distorts the pitch — the trumpeter's embouchure and the tuning slide constantly have to correct it.

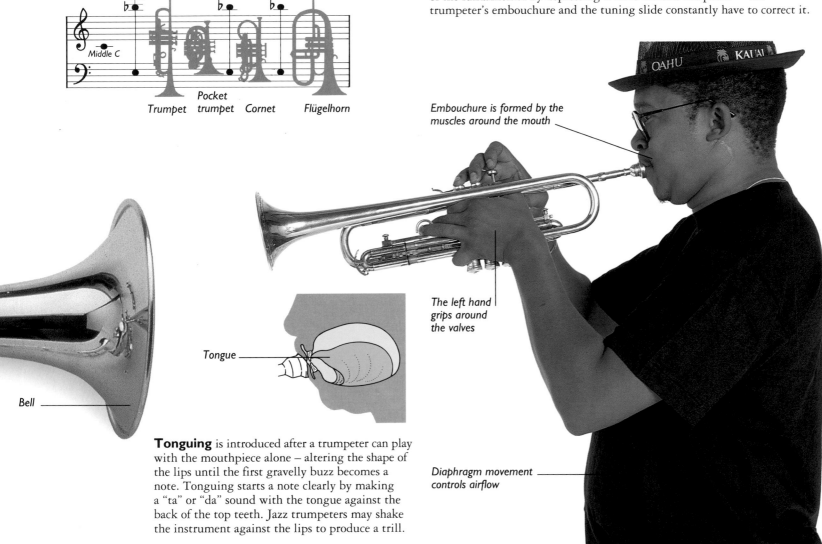

Embouchure is formed by the muscles around the mouth

The left hand grips around the valves

Diaphragm movement controls airflow

Bell

Tongue

Tonguing is introduced after a trumpeter can play with the mouthpiece alone – altering the shape of the lips until the first gravelly buzz becomes a note. Tonguing starts a note clearly by making a "ta" or "da" sound with the tongue against the back of the top teeth. Jazz trumpeters may shake the instrument against the lips to produce a trill.

Using the valves

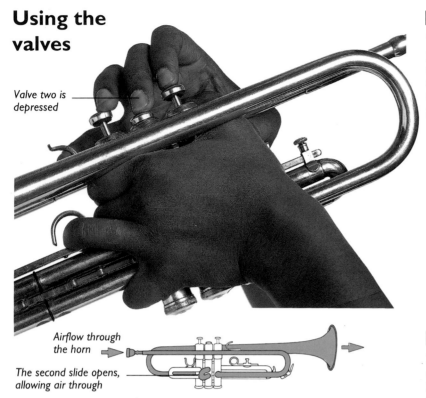

Valve two is depressed

Airflow through the horn →

The second slide opens, allowing air through

An orthodox valve position, depressing valve two here, allows air through the short slide, lowering the basic notes of the instrument by half a tone. Using the lip muscles with this valve position, the trumpet player produces a range that runs: B-F sharp-B-D sharp-F sharp-A-B.

All three valves are depressed, but not fully

The column of air is diffused by partially opening all three valves

In opening the valves partially, jazz players bend the rules. Altering normal embouchure, too, restricts the air column, producing a note of ambiguous or slurred pitch. Coupled with gradual opening to the full extent, this gives special effects like the gliss (pitch slide) and vibrato.

Extending the tube

The trumpet is not a perfect design — each lowering of the fundamental pitch by depressing the valves needs more tubing to make the pitching accurate than is practical. Trumpeters therefore make small pitch adjustments not only with embouchure, but also by slightly altering the length of the first and third slides. This is also the trumpeter's way of adjusting the pitch of the instrument slightly to other horns in the ensemble.

Third finger pulls the tuning slide in slightly

Pocket trumpet

Really a squashed trumpet, the pocket trumpet is pitched in the same range as an early instrument, but its tubing is very tightly coiled. Some musicians like the instrument's portability and its characteristically tight, closeted sound. Adventurous jazz trumpeter and "world" musician Don Cherry, one-time partner of saxophonist Ornette Coleman, has long preferred this smaller horn, and with it he produces an instantly recognizable, bubbly, semiabstract, vocalized sound.

Mutes

Mutes obstruct the movement of sound waves in brass — effectively they amplify certain overtones and reduce others. Jazz musicians have long experimented with their own forms of muting, from inserting a hand into the bell (an orthodox technique on some classical horns) to covering it with a bowler hat or using a beer glass like King Oliver. Oliver pioneered extended mute use, inspiring Duke Ellington's Bubber Miley, one of the most famous of mute specialists. With bebop and its aftermath, mutes were virtually abandoned, except in revivalist music and for special effects in free jazz. Widespread use of the Harmon mute in modern jazz was inspired by the inimitably ambiguous and private sound of Miles Davis.

The plunger mute has given jazz some of its earthiest and most vocal trumpet sounds. Trumpet players borrowed rubber cups from sink plungers to get this effect, giving the device its name. In plunger technique, the cup is held over the bell and the degree of closure is varied to produce a wah-wah effect.

Plunger

Cup mute

Bucket mute

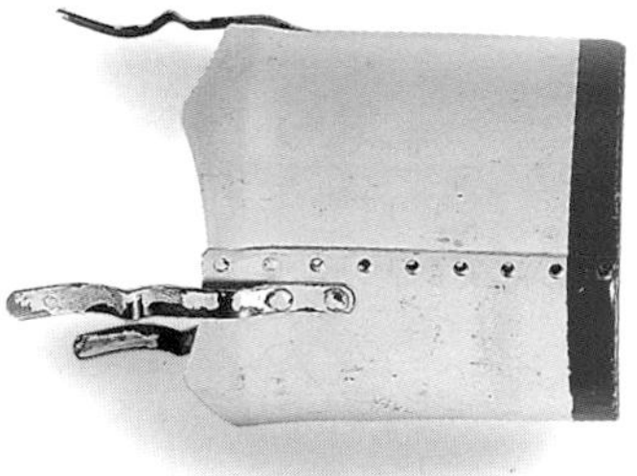

Harmon mute

The cup mute has a conical shape, with a cup shape over its wide end, often felt-lined. This mute reduces the volume and cutting edge of the trumpet's sound, but adds a softer, yielding quality. The position of the cup in relation to the cone part of the mute can be adjusted to alter its distance from the bell of the horn.

Wah-wah technique, as used by King Oliver, did much to found the notion of the vocalized "talking" trumpet

The bucket mute produces the softest and quietest sounds obtainable from a trumpet. Cylindrical, it clips over the bell of the horn. The trumpet is played into the mute's open end, and sound waves pass into a sound-absorbent material filling the cylinder.

Vibrating air can only leave the instrument through a sliding tube in the mute's center

This mute gives the horn a relaxed, sidelong sound

The Harmon mute, invented in 1865, is a metal tube fitting closely into the trumpet bell, sealed with a cork collar. How far in or out the mute is placed affects its characteristically remote and ethereal timbre — Miles Davis was one of its most famous exponents.

Trombone

THE FIRST JAZZ ROLE for the trombone's big, blustery sound and slurred intonation was to lubricate the melody lines of the other brass instruments in New Orleans music and sometimes to double as a bass. With the coming of big bands, the trombone played both a supportive and a solo role, its tonal flexibility inviting vivid special effects. Bebop made the languid horn, like all the other instruments, run to catch up, and trombonists acquired remarkable techniques to mimic saxophones and trumpets. During the free jazz era, some players pursued the pre-bop trombone's tone color and fluidity and even developed multiphonics — singing one note and blowing another — for playing chords. In recent jazz, younger players have combined boppish technical expertise with the timbres of earlier music.

Fayyaz Virgi

STARS AND STYLES

New Orleans musicians **Kid Ory** and **George Brunies** perfected the trombone's underpinning role to corral the lighter horns. 1930s swing gave it a more streamlined manner, brought to the forefront by Fletcher Henderson's **Jimmy Harrison**. **Jack Teagarden** gave it grace and humor and Ellington's **Tricky Sam Nanton** added a bluesy growl. Bandleader **Tommy Dorsey** swung with faultless intonation, and Woody Herman's **Bill Harris** and bebopper **J. J. Johnson** had a saxophonelike clarity at speed. Free music restored an earthier trombone with **Roswell Rudd** and **Grachan Moncur**, while **Albert Mangelsdorff** accompanies himself, harmonizing through multiphonics.

The trombone

Formerly called a sackbut, the trombone is a 15th-century instrument with a straight sliding tube to change the range. Its unwieldy length led to the development of a **U**-shaped slide, halving the demands on the player's reach. The slide acts as valves do on other horns and is ideal for jazz with its bending, indeterminate notes.

The slideless valve trombone is easier to play fast notes on, but gives intonation problems.

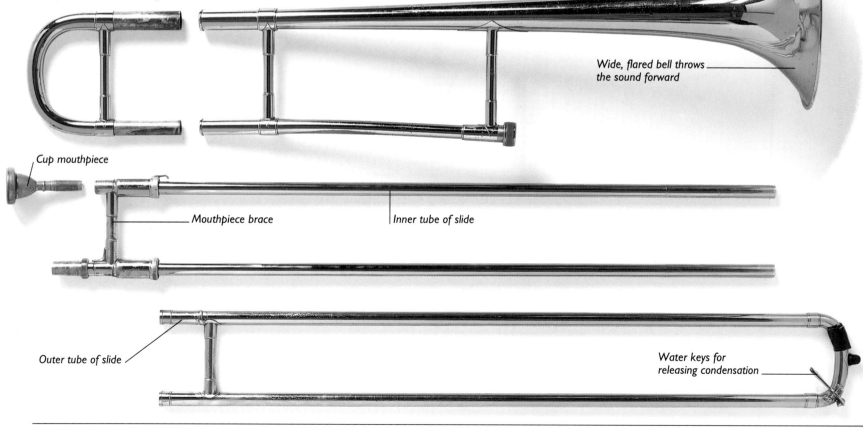

Wide, flared bell throws the sound forward

Cup mouthpiece

Mouthpiece brace

Inner tube of slide

Outer tube of slide

Water keys for releasing condensation

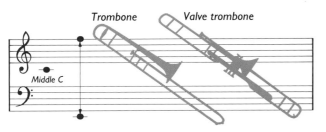

Trombone   Valve trombone

Middle C

Trombone range The most widely used trombones are B-flat tenors, with a basic range sounding from the bottom E of a double bass to F an octave above middle C. The bass trombone has some variations, using valves to supplement pitch changes, and the true bass trombone can comfortably be blown as low as the third C below middle C, with pitches below the F used for sustained sounds.

Making the sound

As with trumpeters, it is the vibration of the lips as the column of air is pushed upward from the lungs through the mouthpiece that makes the sound. Therefore, the disciplined development of the lip muscles is as essential as the training of steady, deep breathing. The trombone mouthpiece has a deeper cup than a trumpet. Slightly differently shaped mouthpieces are produced to suit both anatomical differences and varying musical requirements, with the cup depth, curvature, and taper subject to small but significant alterations.

Embouchure

The positioning of the lips and teeth on the mouthpiece is known as embouchure. An ideal trombone embouchure is formed by projecting the lower jaw to align the teeth. The mouth is pursed in a whistle shape, but the lips are kept close together, sustaining the muscle formation of a slight smile. The aperture is widest and airflow directed straight into the mouthpiece on the lowest notes.

On high notes the aperture is tight and the airflow angled toward the chin, striking the curve of the mouthpiece close to the rim. The mouthpiece should not press hard on the lips. Like a trumpeter, the trombonist makes a "ta" sound with the tongue briefly striking the upper teeth to initiate a note. Faster playing can be achieved by double-tonguing ("ta-ka") or triple tonguing ("ta-ka-ta").

Seven main slide positions are situated roughly three to four inches apart. From the basic tone available at each position, the trombonist can produce seven others related to its upper overtones, taking the range up over two octaves by altering the embouchure. An upright stance prevents the "bellows" of the lungs and diaphragm from becoming cramped, and the grip on the horn is supportive but light. Trombonists practice low-pressure playing by balancing the horn on their fingertips — when blown too hard, the instrument moves away from the lips.

1 2 3 4 5 6 7

Mutes

The plunger mute is a cup held against the bell, giving a voicelike sound of subtle nuances. Ellington's Tricky Sam Nanton would alternate the plunger with a trumpet straight mute.

A cup mute is usually adjusted by trombonists so that it stands about a quarter inch from the bell. Cups soften and fatten the sound, and mutes made from fiber and metal offer further variations of timbre.

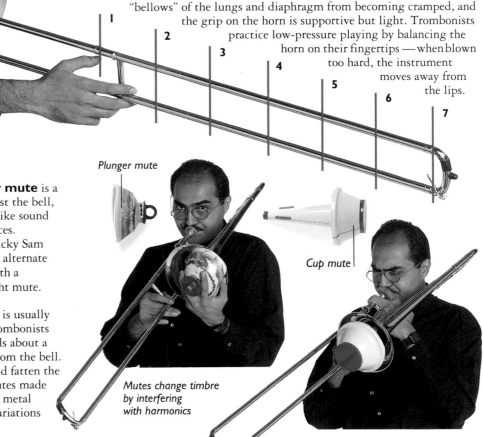

Plunger mute

Cup mute

Mutes change timbre by interfering with harmonics

Clarinet

THE CLARINET largely fell out of use in jazz after the 1940s, when bebop confirmed the saxophone's ascendancy. Until then, its fragile autumnal tone, liquid sound, and capacity for evocative bluesiness or ecstatic upper-register wailing had made the clarinet influential all the way from New Orleans ensembles to those gliding limousines, swing bands. In early jazz, clarinetists were often harmonically advanced Creoles who inherited the French classical tradition, expertly weaving supple, supportive lines around the brass. Others introduced the earthiness of the blues, counterbalancing Creole elegance. The bass clarinet's deep tones became popular in the 1960s.

Jimmy Giuffre

Reed

Soprano clarinet

Bass clarinet

STARS AND STYLES

Legendary New Orleans player **Lorenzo Tio** taught celebrated exponents **Sidney Bechet** and **Barney Bigard**. Other early stars were genial, oblique **Jimmie Noone** and the bluesy, soulful **Johnny Dodds**. **Omer Simeon** and Bigard suited Jelly Roll and Ellington's sophistication. Swing virtuosos **Jimmy Dorsey**, **Benny Goodman**, and **Artie Shaw** had trumpeterlike fame. Mainstream favoured laconic **Pee Wee Russell**, and **Jimmy Giuffre's** low-register deliberations set cool's clarinet voice. **Eric Dolphy** added evocative bass clarinet.

The soprano clarinet in its B-flat form is the most widely used version of the instrument in jazz. A single-reed instrument, the clarinet has a segmented wooden or plastic body and four registers in the widely used Boehm key system, although other systems are also available.

Cork seals the joints

The right little finger works these keys

The bass clarinet has a rich, deep tone and woody sound that has given it a textural role (as played by Harry Carney for Duke Ellington). Eric Dolphy's extraordinary technique liberated its evocative solo use in the 1960s.

Grip

Master clarinetist Jimmy Giuffre believes in holding the instrument with the mouthpiece pushed firmly upward. Giuffre's subtle, sidelong sound is quite different from that of most clarinetists.

Extended jazz range

Middle C

Soprano clarinet   *Bass clarinet*

Clarinet range: on a B-flat soprano, the extreme upper register can be extended by using advanced techniques. The B-flat bass clarinet is pitched an octave lower.

Metal bell

A curved tube is a feature of the deeper-sounding instrument

Embouchure

In single embouchure playing, the lower lip is more tightly curled over the teeth than the upper lip, and this is the most common method of playing. Both the embouchure and type of reed used crucially affect the sound.

The double embouchure: both the upper and lower lip are tightened, the jawline slightly projected. It is a little harder to sound the instrument this way, but soloists find their own preference early and stick to it.

Bass clarinet is played using a double embouchure and a plastic reed. The note sounding here is an E flat in the lower range, so a great deal of air is passing through the instrument.

E flat two octaves higher: when higher notes are played, the airflow has to be restricted and the embouchure is closed down to shrink the aperture. The lips are tighter and the lower jaw juts farther forward.

Sounding a note

The long, narrow column of air in the bass clarinet requires a lot of support, particularly when sustained notes are played at the bottom end of the register. In order to do this, the player keeps the diaphragm tight, and the chest cavity may become distended.

Fingering

E using all the fingers

E with octave key lifted

— Air column

— First open key

— Sound waves

The column of air in the horn starts to vibrate and creates a sound wave when it is first blown. As the air column hits the first open key, the air is dispersed. The length of the column of air indicates the pitch of the note: a shorter column gives a higher tone. Here, John Surman is sounding an open G, the highest note in the register.

Like all reed instruments used in jazz, the soprano clarinet can produce a note with different fingerings and blowing techniques as a way of altering the tone color on the same pitch. Jimmy Giuffre plays an E with conventional fingering (left) and with a form of false fingering (above) that gives the note a more distant, ethereal sound.

An extra key on the bass clarinet, in the cluster of four at the bottom of the tube, allows the instrument to sound its resounding low E flat. The register, down in the range of the double bass, is one of the characteristics of the instrument that has added to its appeal in more impressionistic and experimental areas of jazz.

John Surman sounds the low E flat

Saxophone

ADOLPHE SAX invented the saxophone in 1846 for military bands. In the 1900s it was used as a novelty in vaudeville or as a substitute for violin in dance bands. Then jazz musicians, adapting the attack and phrasing of New Orleans trumpeters, gave the saxophone a forceful solo identity, such that it all but upstaged the trumpet as primary jazz instrument. Alto and tenor dominated 1930s and 1940s music. The delicate alto embraced the romantic tones of Johnny Hodges and Charlie Parker's searing intensity. The heavier tenor imparted a broad swing to big band music, a punchy funk to blues and fusion, and a poignancy to hard bop and the 1960s New Thing.

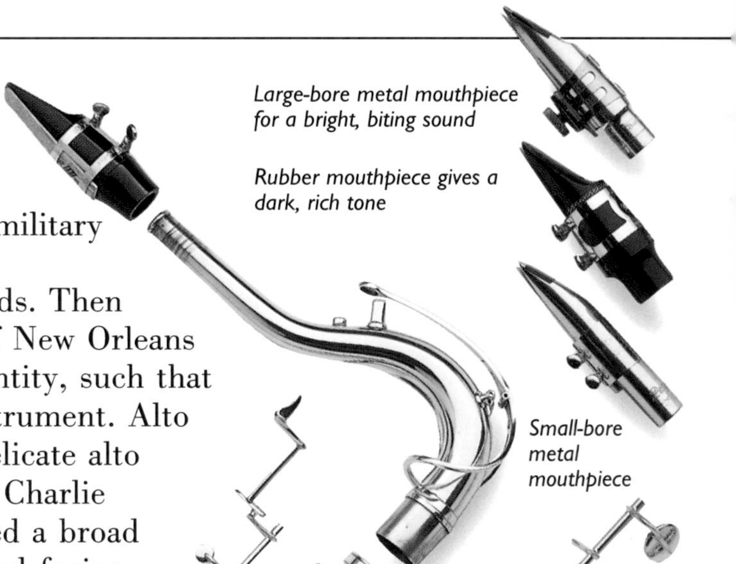

Andy Sheppard

Large-bore metal mouthpiece for a bright, biting sound

Rubber mouthpiece gives a dark, rich tone

Small-bore metal mouthpiece

The tenor saxophone is capable of earthy, dramatic low-register sounds, but extended into the soprano range by post-Coltrane techniques, it is one of the most expressive of all jazz instruments. Evan Parker uses it for astonishing atonal and multiline playing. Despite being an altoist, Ornette Coleman has contended that some of the most honest revelations of African-American soul came through the tenor.

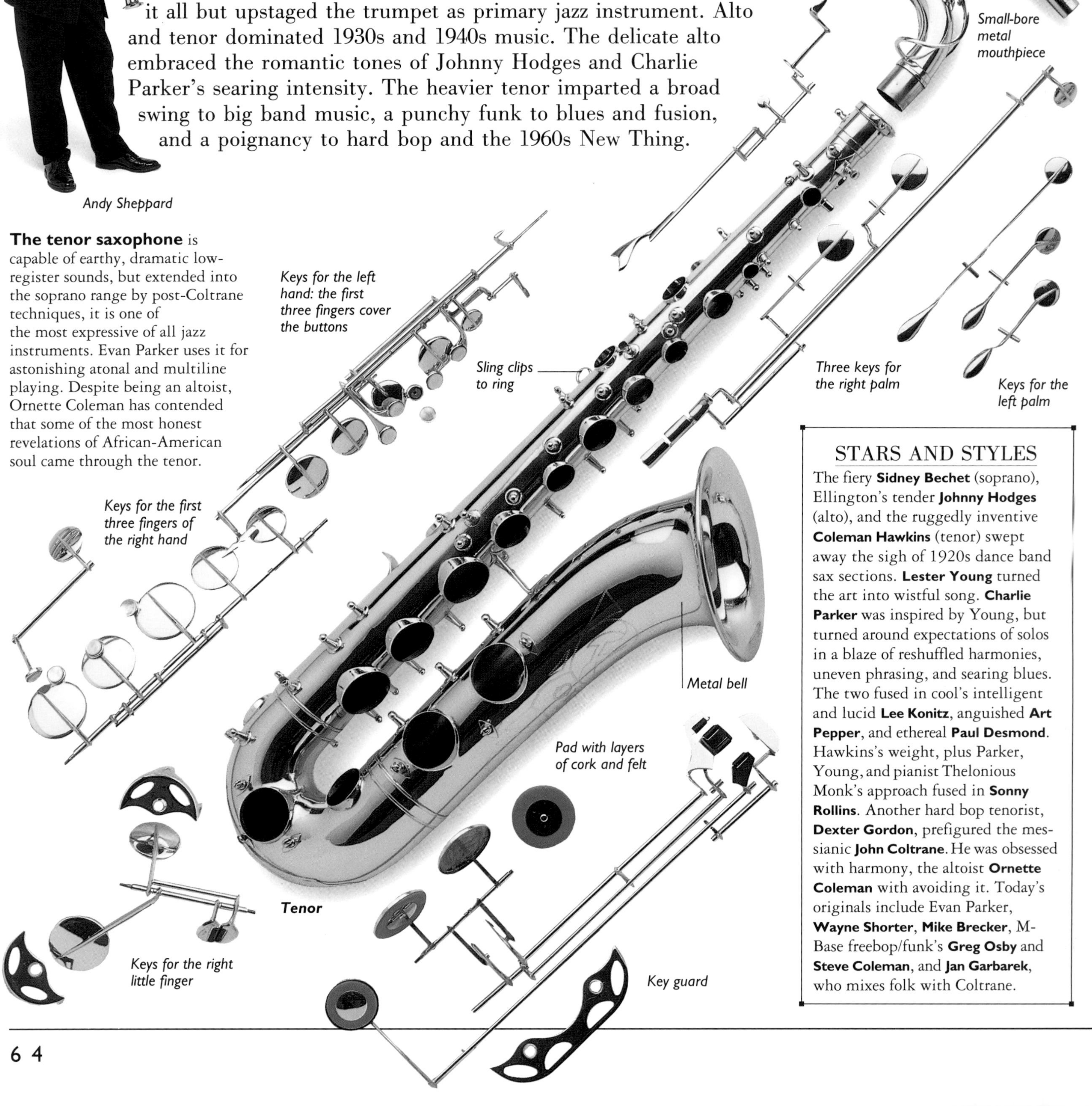

Keys for the left hand: the first three fingers cover the buttons

Sling clips to ring

Three keys for the right palm

Keys for the left palm

Keys for the first three fingers of the right hand

Metal bell

Pad with layers of cork and felt

Tenor

Keys for the right little finger

Key guard

STARS AND STYLES

The fiery **Sidney Bechet** (soprano), Ellington's tender **Johnny Hodges** (alto), and the ruggedly inventive **Coleman Hawkins** (tenor) swept away the sigh of 1920s dance band sax sections. **Lester Young** turned the art into wistful song. **Charlie Parker** was inspired by Young, but turned around expectations of solos in a blaze of reshuffled harmonies, uneven phrasing, and searing blues. The two fused in cool's intelligent and lucid **Lee Konitz**, anguished **Art Pepper**, and ethereal **Paul Desmond**. Hawkins's weight, plus Parker, Young, and pianist Thelonious Monk's approach fused in **Sonny Rollins**. Another hard bop tenorist, **Dexter Gordon**, prefigured the messianic **John Coltrane**. He was obsessed with harmony, the altoist **Ornette Coleman** with avoiding it. Today's originals include Evan Parker, **Wayne Shorter**, **Mike Brecker**, M-Base freebop/funk's **Greg Osby** and **Steve Coleman**, and **Jan Garbarek**, who mixes folk with Coltrane.

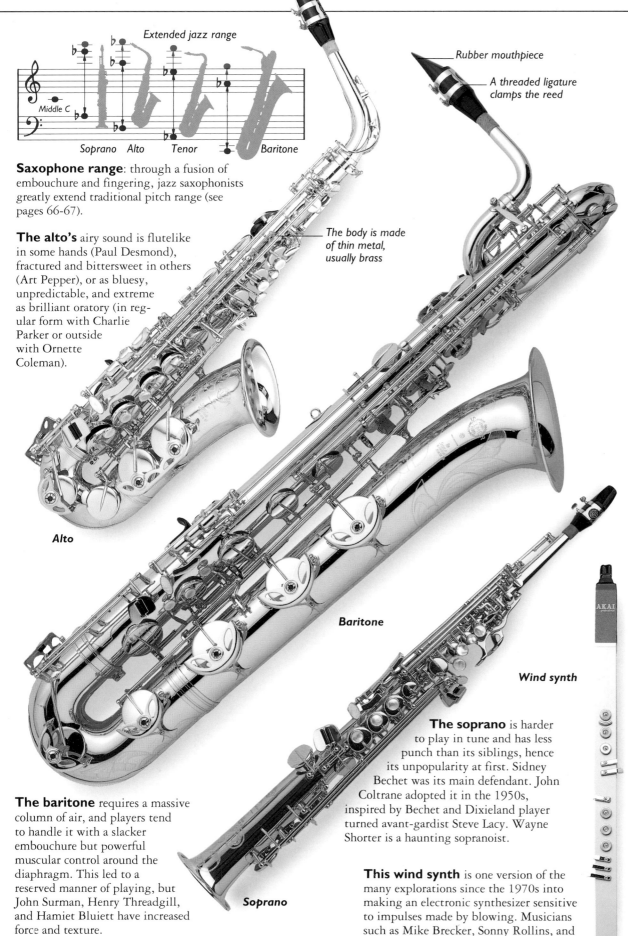

Extended jazz range

Middle C

Soprano Alto Tenor Baritone

Saxophone range: through a fusion of embouchure and fingering, jazz saxophonists greatly extend traditional pitch range (see pages 66-67).

The alto's airy sound is flutelike in some hands (Paul Desmond), fractured and bittersweet in others (Art Pepper), or as bluesy, unpredictable, and extreme as brilliant oratory (in regular form with Charlie Parker or outside with Ornette Coleman).

Alto

— *The body is made of thin metal, usually brass*

Rubber mouthpiece

A threaded ligature clamps the reed

Baritone

The baritone requires a massive column of air, and players tend to handle it with a slacker embouchure but powerful muscular control around the diaphragm. This led to a reserved manner of playing, but John Surman, Henry Threadgill, and Hamiet Bluiett have increased force and texture.

Soprano

Wind synth

The soprano is harder to play in tune and has less punch than its siblings, hence its unpopularity at first. Sidney Bechet was its main defendant. John Coltrane adopted it in the 1950s, inspired by Bechet and Dixieland player turned avant-gardist Steve Lacy. Wayne Shorter is a haunting sopranoist.

This wind synth is one version of the many explorations since the 1970s into making an electronic synthesizer sensitive to impulses made by blowing. Musicians such as Mike Brecker, Sonny Rollins, and Wayne Shorter have experimented with it.

The reed

Reeds can be made of plastic or wood. How much a reed invites or resists vibration (soft or hard) has a crucial effect on volume and tone.

Shaving the reed with a reed knife helps when it is too hard or too thick, which makes the horn tough to blow. Unevenly shaved reeds reduce sound projection.

Cutting the end of the reed helps if it has become too soft or too thin and the gap with the mouthpiece has closed, which reduces the sound of the saxophone.

Moistening the reed stops squeaks and overblows. Presoaking is best: saliva helps in onstage emergencies.

Good reed, shaved evenly, thick part in the middle

Uneven reed, thickest at one side

Embouchure

In double embouchure, here on the tenor, both lips draw back over the teeth. Coltrane favored this old-style clarinet technique. A saxophonist's relatively loose embouchure (see page 57) gives the instrument a wide tonal range.

With single embouchure, the upper lip is drawn back tighter than the lower. It is Sonny Rollins's preference, but the choice of either variation of embouchure is a matter of a horn player's personal taste.

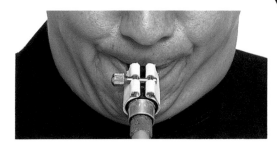

Soprano embouchure needs to be much tighter in the muscles around the mouth than for the alto or tenor horn. Each saxophonist adopts a personal style: here Andy Sheppard demonstrates a mid-range F sharp.

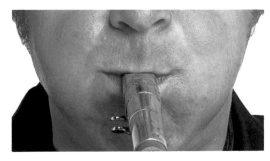

Baritone embouchure is generally slacker than that for the other saxophones. Because the column of air in the instrument is bigger, the aperture and positioning of lips are looser, except when playing very high notes.

Circular breathing

As with a singer, poor breathing on any wind instrument breaks up a solo's shape and flow. Besides diaphragm control, saxophonists have developed circular breathing techniques to produce seamless lines, inhaling through the nose while simultaneously filling the cheeks with air — a demanding exercise.

John Surman imagines breathing into his knees while circular breathing

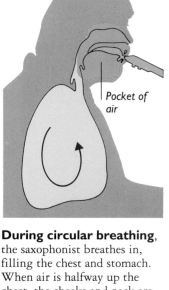

Pocket of air

During circular breathing, the saxophonist breathes in, filling the chest and stomach. When air is halfway up the chest, the cheeks and neck are inflated. The air in this area is forced into the instrument and the player simultaneously breathes in through the nose to the bottom of the stomach. Modern saxophonists Rahsaan Roland Kirk and Pharoah Sanders adopted the style.

Stance

Classical wind players learn how to stand; jazz musicians often find their own style. Andy Sheppard hunches a shoulder for greater expression. But idiosyncrasies in style can bring muscular problems.

Fingering

Jean Toussaint uses standard fingering to produce the note A

The right hand does not touch the keys

As with clarinet and other woodwinds, notes on the saxophone can be played in the "right" and "wrong" way, and the wrong way can produce interesting effects in a music not preoccupied with tonal purity. This is the correct way to sound the note A.

Closing the lower keys gives an overtone

In "false" fingering, by skillful use of embouchure and closing the lower keys, the note A takes on different overtones and a more ambiguous timbre. Alternating the two As produces a wah-wah effect, and the method is also used to extend the upper register.

Harmonics

Conventional embouchure is used to form a note. With an even flow of air and the jaw remaining relatively relaxed, the sound is rounded and stable.

Upper harmonics — a high-pitched, whistle-like sound — are produced with the same fingering but using higher air pressure, tighter embouchure, and a jutting lower jaw. Notes in this range are hard to control, but they are valuable as special effects.

Special effects

Slapping the keys with a wide arc of the fingers produces a bluesy, percussive effect. This is a difficult technique to use well because it usually slows down the fingering. Sonny Rollins favors it and is devastatingly fast, too.

Slap-tonguing, a saxophone effect from vaudeville, is still used. A vacuum is created as the tongue presses hard against the reed and is then withdrawn to produce a percussive sound. Andy Sheppard is fond of it in solos.

Woodwind

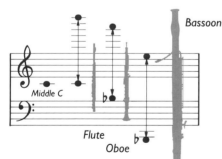

JAZZ BANDS may have expanded in size over the first half of the 20th century, but virtually no new instruments augmented the traditional horns. It was as if some instruments were so linked with European classics that jazz could not adopt them without risking its independent vitality and appetite for breaking rules. In post-World War II jazz, these inhibitions began to fade. Wind instruments such as the oboe and bassoon had lent their musky fragrance to jazz compositions before, but from the 1950s they began to be heard as solo voices. Flutes gained ground in jazz at the same time, usually as a saxophonist's second instrument. In mainstream swing and relaxed West Coast styles, jazz flutists showed they could play with a punchy attack and informal, vocalized candor, as well as with the instrument's traditional modesty.

Lindsay Cooper

STARS AND STYLES

Oboe and bassoon are rare solo instruments, although **Yusef Lateef** used both. Folk jazz's **Paul McCandless** is an expressive oboist, and **Lindsay Cooper** pioneers free improvised music. Flute started jazz solo life with 1950s bop saxophonists **Jerome Richardson** and **Frank Wess**. West Coast altoist **Bud Shank** followed, and **Yusef Lateef** added Middle Eastern flavor. **Herbie Mann** produced the cult fusion disk *Memphis Underground*, **Eric Dolphy** played with a quiet passion, and **Sahib Shihab** pioneered the singing/blowing style played by **Rahsaan Roland Kirk**.

Bassoon

Middle C

Flute

Oboe

Wind range encompasses the concert flute, soprano-voiced oboe, and bass woodwind bassoon, which has a wide-ranging compass starting below the bass staff.

The bassoon uses a double reed with a flattened conical shape and long folded tube. Its timbre varies between its lower and upper ends, rich and woody at the bottom register, wistful at the top.

Bamboo double reed

Oboe

Bassoon

Nagaswaram

The oboe, a double-reed instrument, adapts its name from the French *hautbois* (loud wood), referring to the brilliant, cutting tone. The keywork has increased in number to ten keys, and variations in bore and reed size give instruments that vary in timbre.

The nagaswaram, notably used in jazz by saxophonist Charlie Mariano, shares the double reed. Its fierce sound is central to the South Indian classical repertoire.

The flute is blown sideways and played horizontally. It is built in three parts, and at the final joint of the tube are tone holes, which extend the range downward.

Blowhole

Flute

Tone holes

Using reeds

Oboists and bassoonists believe that saxophonists have an easy life with their single reeds, while they must devote a great deal of care to theirs. The bamboo double reed of the woodwinds is small, delicate, and subject to major changes of sound from tiny adjustments of its aperture. Many players make their own, tailored to their particular sound and type of music. The two halves of the reed are held together with plastic binding, formerly cotton batting coated in shellac.

The bassoon's double reed, like that of all double-reed instruments, also acts as the mouthpiece. Since the teeth cannot come in contact with it as they might in saxophone embouchure, the lips are tight.

In oboe embouchure, the muscles at the sides of the mouth exert more control, and the lips are tighter. The oboe's bright sound requires an embouchure of narrow aperture. It is demanding to play fast and in tune.

Flute sounds, in contrast to those of other woodwind instruments, are formed by one of the most ancient techniques in music — blowing across the sharp edge of a reedless hole to vibrate a column of air.

Making a sound

Coronary thrombosis is sometimes an occupational hazard of oboe players! The narrow column of air and restricted aperture require far more pressure than the bassoon does. The tight airflow nevertheless means that lengthy passages can be played without drawing breath.

The bassoon's sound was described by writer Sacheverell Sitwell as "like a sea-god speaking." The doubled-up wooden tube is more than eight feet long.

To raise a flute's pitch, the air column must be shortened either by opening the tone holes or blowing the instrument harder.

A microphone picks up the sound

Eddie Parker

Singing and blowing was developed simultaneously by flutists like Sahib Shihab and great multi-instrumentalist Rahsaan Roland Kirk. Players sing most frequently an octave away from the sounded note, and the overtones create a gruff sound. Percussive noises made with the lips give the instrument a quality quite different from its usual intonation.

Fingering

When Theobald Boehm, a German flutist, invented a key system in the 1800s, it replaced finger holes with keys, making the flute easier to play and wider in range. Flutes have a breathy fragility of their own, one that can't be successfully mimicked on any other instrument, and the key system retained this haunting sound. The system spread from the flute to the oboe, bassoon, and clarinet, improving them all.

Keys

Oboe fingering in jazz uses the same techniques as regular classical playing. The musician achieves variations in timbre and expression by phrasing.

Button used most often by the thumb

The keywork on the bassoon is complex, and the instrument remains awkward and difficult to play, particularly for fast phrasing. This has restricted its use in jazz. The right thumb has ten keys to choose from at the bottom end of the instrument.

Drums

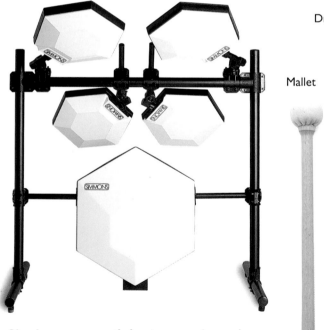

Mark Mondesir

DRUMS HAVE ANCIENT associations with war and dance, and their sound is the heartbeat of jazz. The music brought by Africans to the Americas gave rhythm the dominance that melody and harmony had in the West. Although the subtlety of West African drumming was not recovered in jazz until later, the gap between the expressiveness of African talking drums and the complex, dramatic polyrhythmic playing of Max Roach or Elvin Jones is not wide. A thumping street band bass drum was the underpinning of early jazz and, as the music developed, drummers increasingly enriched their playing behind soloists. The even dance beat of swing evolved into the provocatively emphasized offbeats of bebop. The 1960s avant-garde brought an ebb and flow of percussive texture in place of the clear, driving cymbal beat, and percussionists began appearing alongside drummers. By the 1990s drummers were delivering dazzlingly complex styles merging bop and free approaches, funk, hip hop, and Latin rhythms.

STARS AND STYLES

As jazz evolved from street bands, drummers loosened up to echo the improvised patterns of soloists. **Warren "Baby" Dodds** and **Zutty Singleton** used woodblocks or snare drum for accents, cymbals for emphasis. **Dave Tough**, **Gene Krupa**, **Cozy Cole**, and **Jo Jones** developed swing's even-four beat, Fletcher Henderson's **Walter Johnson** inventing a deft, on-off high-hat style. Tough and Jones lightened the sound, switching the beat to a hissing cymbal flow behind soloists, and Krupa conceived the spectacular featured drum solo, **Buddy Rich** his most celebrated disciple. Bop's **Kenny Clarke**, **Max Roach**, and **Art Blakey** amplified the ride cymbal beat, making other accents irregular, especially the bass drum, dubbed "bomb-dropping." Drummers were moving toward implication rather than statement of tempo. **Elvin Jones**, **Tony Williams**, **Jack DeJohnette**, **Jeff Watts** and **Tony Oxley** have taken this to the point where the beat has no single focus. Cool players **Shelly Manne**, **Joe Morello**, and **Paul Motian** emphasize subtlety and precision.

Drumstick

Mallet

Brush

Simdrums or synthdrums are pads struck by the drummer; they might be used to augment a regular drum kit or sometimes to replace it entirely. Each pad is programmed to produce a preset sound, which can be varied by manipulating a central control unit or dials on the pads. Such effects, which are electronic but activated conventionally by striking a kit with sticks, were introduced into jazz by drummers during the 1970s.

Gripping the sticks

Jazz music's emphasis on fast cymbal patterns led to drumsticks becoming lighter. They are usually made from hardwood — synthetic materials are rarely popular with drummers. Most jazz drumming concentrates on deft, clipped sounds and steady, hissing cymbal rhythms, so light, strong sticks are important, balancing easily between the fingers and palm. For more dramatic effects, the classical tympanist's mallets with their felt, wood, plastic, or packed cotton heads are sometimes used. For quiet accompaniment, a jazz drummer will use wire brushes in a sliding, rather than striking motion, on the drums or as a pattering sound on the cymbals.

A tight grip on the drumsticks gives extra emphasis and greater impact. Grip is a crucial element in producing a good sound, whether the drummer wishes to play in a hard, clattering way or to convey the impression of a loose and floating rhythm.

Light pressure on the sticks using just the first two fingers and the thumb can be enough to create a light and airy beat on the ride cymbal (see opposite page). This technique gives the graceful optical illusion that the drumstick is bending at speed.

The kit

The 19th-century invention of the pedal enabled one player to handle a bass drum, snare, and high hat cymbal. However, early drum kits were groupings of largely unmodified street band instruments, including a large, deep bass drum with a Turkish cymbal clamped to it, woodblocks, cowbells, and often a Chinese tom-tom. As techniques evolved and drumming became faster and lighter, the size of the instruments diminished, and the sound became crisper.

The ride cymbal became prominent in jazz drumming from the swing era onward, conveying the steady, swishing "ten-to-two, ten-to-two" pulse.

Ride cymbal

The ride cymbal is clamped to the bass drum

Tom-tom

High hat

Tom-tom

Snare drum

Stick bag

Floor-mounted cymbal for texture

The bass drum is played by striking the skin at the back with a felt-covered beater operated by a foot pedal. Its deep, thudding sound was a prominent feature of orchestral swing and has played a big role in rock. In recent jazz it has been used more often for variety of accent.

Bass drum

When the pedal is depressed, the cymbals close together

Basic drumming

The fundamentals of drumming developed on the snare drum in the 1930s and are known as the rudiments. They include simple roll figures and combinations played with the two sticks, which can be fused together to create a wide range of effects. Of these rudiments, the most basic figure is the roll, an even-sounding figure, alternating left and right hands that forms a steady *ta-ta-ta-ta* pattern on the drum. It can be difficult to execute fast, although some exceptional players, notably Buddy Rich, have accelerated it into a blur of sound in which the individual strokes become almost impossible to separate.

Variations on the basic roll figure include:

• the double roll, where the drummer creates a *tata-tata-tata-tata* effect by alternating double strokes with first the right, then the left hand.

• the flam, a popular technique in which the drummer strikes one stick lightly before the other so that the shots glide into each other, sounding *tTa, tTa*. The first, very short sound is known as a grace note.

• the paradiddle, which sounds just like its name, four even notes starting with the left hand (L.R.L.L.), followed by the same figure beginning with the right hand (R.L.R.R.): *tatatata, tatatata*.

Posture

A fluent, relaxed, and musical drum sound that will last hour after hour, night after night, needs the relaxed application of energy. Most drummers adopt an upright but relaxed position, sitting at such a distance to the instruments as will permit loose wrist action without effort, or with the arms tucked up at the elbow. But many great jazz drummers have their own variations: Jack DeJohnette often plays cymbals with straight arms, and Buddy Rich used to hunch over his kit as if he were riding a racing bike.

Mark Mondesir keeps an easy, upright stance and groups his instruments to produce any combination of drum sounds without stretching.

Rim shots

Rim shots played a part in jazz with the coming of 1930s swing, when players began to intensify patterns in their accompaniment. Rim shots can be produced either by laying a stick across both the rim and the drumhead and lifting and closing it, or by striking one stick resting on the drumhead with another.

Rim shot with stick hitting the rim of the drum

One stick strikes the other, which rests on the head

Different styles of drumming

An unpredictable mix of a steady beat and a disrupted one gives jazz its sense of unruly, exhilarating energy. The beat is usually divided into brief quavers, or eighth notes, sounded in more or less equal pairs in Latin, soul, funk, jazz rock, and ragtime music, and in uneven triplet figures in New Orleans, swing, bop, and modal jazz.

Bebop style, now often dubbed straight-ahead jazz, frequently uses variations on a triplet cymbal beat "ten-to-two, ten-to-two" with the right hand on the ride cymbal, and contrasting uneven accents on the snare, tom-toms, and bass.

The right hand plays the ride cymbal

Riding on the left allows the drummer freedom to move around the rest of the kit with the right hand

Stick bag

Fusion drumming developed during the 1960s from a complex hybrid of jazz, rock, and Latin rhythms. This type of drumming tends to be more dense, constantly sweeping the full extent of the kit, often with a steady flow of pairs of quavers, or eighth notes, on the cymbals, with the snare highlighting "backbeats," emphasizing what are usually the weak beats in a bar.

The snare accents counts two and four

Motown style drumming and the 1960s and 1970s funk sound have greatly influenced modern jazz, and Mark Mondesir believes that a good drummer has to understand jazz to be able to play funk well. The drummer keeps up a constant beat on the toms and snare drum.

Percussion

Nana Vasconcelos

WHEN CUBAN drummer Chano Pozo joined Dizzy Gillespie's band in 1947, he stunned a New York audience for thirty minutes, chanting in a West African dialect and producing a monsoon of polyrhythms and dazzling colors on a conga drum. Early in the century, Jelly Roll Morton observed how much closer to Africa were Latin rhythms than North American hybrids (he called the characteristic Ba-ba ba-Ba ba-ba Ba-ba the Spanish tinge). Now South American, Caribbean, Asian, and African instruments have joined jazz percussion as musicians search for new sounds.

Curved stick

Strings

The African talking drum has a resonating waisted body, with strings stretched across the narrowed section. A traditional instrument of great tonal variation, it is sounded by striking the head with the curved stick. By squeezing the strings, the player can vary the pitch of the note.

The cuica is a Brazilian friction drum. Attached inside the skin is a reed, which the drummer rubs with a moistened cloth while applying pressure to the drumskin, to create a vocalized moaning sound often featured in fusion.

Stone

Rattle and stick

The Brazilian berimbau, a traditional instrument that sounds just like its name, resembles a bow strung with steel wire, with a resonating gourd at one end, played with a stone or coin, shaker, and stick (see page 77). Airto Moreira popularized its use in jazz and fusion.

Congas are Afro-Cuban drums, played with the fingers and palms of the hands, sometimes singly, often in pairs with variations of tuning. Chano Pozo introduced them to jazz on Dizzy Gillespie's "Cubana Be, Cubana Bop" and their mellow, eager sound has become an essential of Latin jazz.

Canes bound together with tape

The tabla, from Indian classical percussion, is growing in popularity in Western jazz and improvised music. Its hollow, reverberating sound is combined with jazz rhythms in the hands of percussionists like Trilok Gurtu. Hitting the center of the drum creates the sound, which is warped by pressing with the palm. Tablas are often played in pairs.

A Ghanaian uduh borrowed from village domestic use liquifies the more usual clipped sound of percussion, producing a warm, soothing effect.

Woodblocks played by Nana Vasconcelos with mallets or brushes.

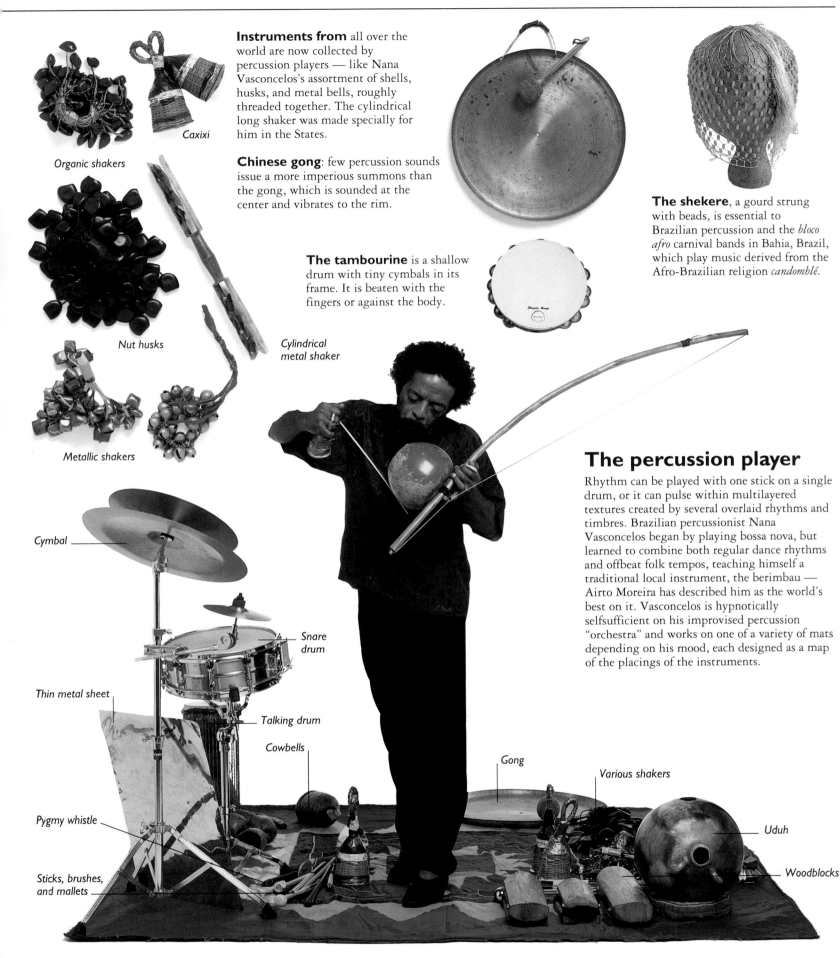

Instruments from all over the world are now collected by percussion players — like Nana Vasconcelos's assortment of shells, husks, and metal bells, roughly threaded together. The cylindrical long shaker was made specially for him in the States.

Chinese gong: few percussion sounds issue a more imperious summons than the gong, which is sounded at the center and vibrates to the rim.

The tambourine is a shallow drum with tiny cymbals in its frame. It is beaten with the fingers or against the body.

The shekere, a gourd strung with beads, is essential to Brazilian percussion and the *bloco afro* carnival bands in Bahia, Brazil, which play music derived from the Afro-Brazilian religion *candomblé*.

Organic shakers

Caxixi

Nut husks

Metallic shakers

Cylindrical metal shaker

The percussion player

Rhythm can be played with one stick on a single drum, or it can pulse within multilayered textures created by several overlaid rhythms and timbres. Brazilian percussionist Nana Vasconcelos began by playing bossa nova, but learned to combine both regular dance rhythms and offbeat folk tempos, teaching himself a traditional local instrument, the berimbau — Airto Moreira has described him as the world's best on it. Vasconcelos is hypnotically selfsufficient on his improvised percussion "orchestra" and works on one of a variety of mats depending on his mood, each designed as a map of the placings of the instruments.

Cymbal

Snare drum

Thin metal sheet

Talking drum

Cowbells

Pygmy whistle

Gong

Various shakers

Uduh

Sticks, brushes, and mallets

Woodblocks

Talking drum

An early message service, talking drums were built on both coasts in Africa and in parts of Southeast Asia to be expressive enough to mimic the rhythms and the rise and fall of sound in spoken language. Squeezing the strings with the fingers and forearm in conjunction with the patterns produced by striking the head produces a wide range of tones and effects.

The hand and arm squeeze the strings

Releasing and catching the drum beneath the arm gives a percussive sound

Wedging the drum between elbow and knee, Nana Vasconcelos is free to play with palm and fingers

Body percussion

The South African pianist Abdullah Ibrahim, once asked to name the first music he heard, said "my heart." The most fundamental of percussion instruments is the human body. The solo performances of Nana Vasconcelos often concentrate on the deepest roots of percussion and song, and are enriched with dance, mime, and music theater. But although Vasconcelos's art is always linked to the traditional music of Brazil, with its mixture of light, flowing rhythms and sonorous, rain forest sounds, he has discovered —

as have several other contemporary vocalists and percussionists — that the feel of the music can be caught without instruments other than the ones he was born with. Hand clapping and foot stamping have supplied the drums for thousands of years of religious rituals and communal dances. Indeed, subtle polyrhythms generated on these "body instruments" were sometimes all that remained to African slaves in the Americas when drums were banned because of their subversive connotations.

Contrasts of pitch and texture, corresponding to the differences between drums, can be established by striking the limbs or the chest, and Nana Vasconcelos couples all this with whistling and singing sounds, while throwing his voice like a ventriloquist.

A sequence might start with a clap

The voice is thrown

A sonorous tap of the ribs and shoulder

A slap against the upper thigh

Mime, sound, and dance are indivisible

Rattles and shakers

In South and Central America, instruments without a specific pitch have resonances as vital to the vibrant energy of the music as instruments that play conventional notes. Percussionists use a wide variety of rattles and shakers, some derived from natural materials (South American maracas were originally hollow gourds containing seeds), some simply shells or husks threaded together, others using steel beads. Although they do not have the capacity for "melody" in the European sense, as wide a range of moods, drama, and contrasts can be established by these percussion instruments as by those capable of playing a scale — from a rustle like a breeze in the trees, or a dramatic crackle like approaching footsteps in dry leaves, to a tumultuous wave-breaking sound.

Gong

Gongs frequently feature in Southeast Asian music and ritual. Because the sound is so emphatic and sonorous, they are more often used as an isolated effect in improvised music, although in some Eastern music, gongs of different timbres are played in groups. Rapid hammering of the gong gives a continuous thunder.

Shakers can sound soft and caressing

Melodic and ethereal bells

Rattles build a gathering drama

A metal shaker makes a gleeful clamor

Humming into the vibrations at the top edge of the gong

Woodblocks

Blowing into the gourd — an improvised technique

Berimbau

The berimbau came to Brazil with Bantu slaves. When the metal string is played, sound resonates into the musician's chest via the hollow gourd pressed to the body. The Brazilian martial arts tradition *capoiera* has developed four specific rhythms for the instrument. Although Nana Vasconcelos is capable of playing all four — originally intended for four berimbau — simultaneously on one instrument, he adds improvised techniques of his own, such as running a stick around the hole in the gourd or blowing into it.

Woodblocks of different thicknesses produce different tones, and the materials used to strike them, whether bunched canes or wound yarn beaters, release other qualities from the instrument. The improvisation above combines the percussive sharpness of the woodblock with the mellow, fluid sound of the uduh, played with the palm of the hand.

Traditional berimbau technique

Moving the stone against the string bends the note

A stick and shaker in the right hand add further rhythms

Vibraphone

Orphy
Robinson

W ITH A SLIGHT silvery tone, fixed pitch, and lush vibrato, the vibraphone hardly seems built for jazz, but as a percussion instrument with pianolike melodic potential, it is more suitable than it looks, and some jazz interpreters have played it with character and feeling. The vibes came to America in 1916, and entered jazz in the 1930s, usually as a second instrument used for the novelty of its sound. Saxophonist Adrian Rollini played it, and Lionel Hampton was a drummer first. But it did not have to be played as if its only virtue was shimmering delicacy. Swing made it a bold, attacking instrument, and several bebop players played powerful blues and created complex lines without losing crispness.

How it works

The vibraphone is a set of metal bars, suspended horizontally on cords, arranged like piano keys to encompass three octaves, and struck by mallets. Each bar is laid over a vertical tube in which the sound produced by striking the bar can resonate like an organ pipe and be subjected to a variable vibrato. There is also a pianolike foot pedal used to sustain sounds.

Different mallets — some rubber, some with wound heads — give various sounds

A revolving vane is fitted close to the top of each resonating tube. The speed at which the vane revolves governs the intensity of the vibraphone's characteristic vibrato effect.

British vibist Orphy Robinson has restored a drummerlike vigor to vibes playing, his influences coming from funk and African music

A fanbelt driven by a silent electric motor rotates the vanes. The musician can vary the speed at which the motor runs or can cut the vibrato by turning it off, leaving the vanes vertical and tubes open.

The foot pedal controls the duration of sound, as it does on a piano

Styles of playing

Although the vibraphone has to be struck to be sounded, musicians can produce very different qualities of timbre, some so light and yielding as to make the percussive principle hard to believe, others continuing the powerful, emphatic swing of performers like Lionel Hampton. As jazz musicians free themselves from dependence on more orthodox brass and reeds, the unique vibes sound makes it increasingly attractive.

Two mallets are most commonly used for fast, boplike improvised lines. The quality of the sound can depend not only on the mallets used and the level of vibrato, but on whether the bars are struck at the extreme ends (a hard, deadened sound) or close to the center (a full, rounded sound).

Chord playing is possible with extra mallets, and good players display astonishing speed in chordal sequences. Chord playing developed as the vibraphone began to play a more prominent part in jazz, enlarging the rather thin, airy tone and extending the range of harmonic subtlety.

Dragging the note, a difficult technique, produces a bluesy, guitarlike slur. Since the 1960s, American Gary Burton has used this technique of holding a small hard mallet against the point where the cord supports the bar, sounding the note and dragging the mallet down it simultaneously.

Marimba

Marimba is an African term for xylophone, but the similarities between the most common marimba designs and the vibraphone are obvious. Marimbas use tubes or gourds to resonate the sound of wooden bars; although their sound cannot be varied as much as the vibes, they have a direct musicality that leads some vibists to prefer their woody tone. Marimbas come in various sizes (some strap to the waist, others are very large), and they are very popular in Central America.

Since the keys are all on the same plane, either single mallets are used, or pairs, usually to play chords

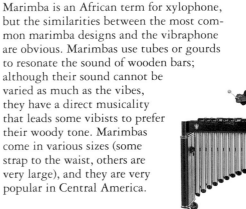

A medium-hard yarn-wound mallet can be used for marimba or vibraphone

The pedal can sustain the flow of a melody line

Playing technique on the marimba and vibraphone is largely similar. A common range for the orchestral marimba is three and a half octaves, and variations of timbre, as with the vibes, are dependent on the material used for the mallet head and the part of the bar that is struck.

Keyboards

A FIXED-PITCH instrument without the haunting cry of a horn, the piano in its role as composer's tool and miniature orchestra has been essential to jazz. At first the piano delivered the raw excitement of the unschooled blues and boogie players and the elegant prance of ragtime. Jazz turned ragtime piano into the pumping stride style of the 1920s, reaching a dazzling zenith with Art Tatum, his left and right hands in storming communion. Then bebop made all instruments hornlike, and the frontline harmonic adventurers induced pianists to echo them with fast right hands while the left sketched sparse, fragmentary chords. Both funk and free jazz brought thicker, more percussive piano styles, and although electronics broadened the range after the 1960s, brilliant acoustic players have continued to appear. Many play bebop, but a renewed sense of the past has recovered many of the orchestral, two-handed keyboard techniques of earlier decades.

Julian Joseph

Concert grand and upright pianos continue to be the main instruments for jazz keyboardists. The range covers seven octaves and the notes are made by rebounding hammers, activated by keys, striking against strings. Able to sound many notes at once, the piano can easily sustain unaccompanied performance.

The Hammond organ was favored by 1950s soul jazz players for its reverberating bass, piercing treble, and wailing sustain. The rotating tone wheel design dates to 1935 (Fats Waller used it in 1939). A spinning reflector in the Leslie speaker (left) imparts vibrato.

Speaker gives the signature sound

Pedals control volume and duration of sound

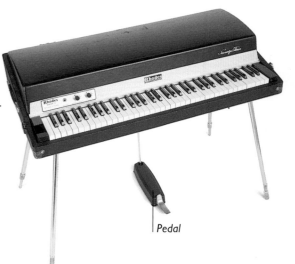

The Fender Rhodes, marketed in 1965, was the first popular electric piano used in jazz. It mimics the workings of an acoustic piano in that wires are sounded by hammers, but each wire is partnered with a resonating tone bar that complements and enriches the vibrations and the hammers are rubber-headed. The design produces a chiming sound that was used by Herbie Hancock, Joe Zawinul, and Chick Corea.

Pedal

Bass strings

The Minimoog synthesizer was used in jazz from the late 1960s. It synthesizes sound electronically and, when coupled with a keyboard, adds a previously inconceivable range of timbres to a melody line. Its wild slews of pitch bending extend one of the fundamentals of jazz tonality. Although the Moog is old, it has a uniquely rich sound and remains popular as the "human" electronic instrument.

Hammers

Polyphonic keyboards such as the D-50 give dazzling tone color to more than one line or to chords, unlike early synthesizers which were monophonic. The computer in the D-50 can store a variety of timbres — even the sound of massed violins — and recall them in various combinations by keypunching the appropriate number.

STARS AND STYLES

The countermelodies of **Jelly Roll Morton**, piano professor of ragtime, early jazz, and blues, prefigured **Earl Hines** and **Art Tatum**. Harlem's stride school's **Luckyeth Roberts, Willie "The Lion" Smith** and **James P. Johnson** blended classical devices with rags, influencing composer-pianists **Duke Ellington** and **Count Basie**. Stride peaked with effervescent **Fats Waller's** displays, swing's light touch and walking left hand with **Teddy Wilson**. Bop saw virtuoso **Bud Powell**, and **Thelonious Monk** spliced bop and stride with wide spaces. **Erroll Garner** merged bop's melodic sense with seamless swing left hand, **Bill Evans** and **Lennie Tristano** added long lines, cool delivery, and odd harmony, influencing **McCoy Tyner, Chick Corea, Herbie Hancock, Keith Jarrett**, and later, **Geri Allen, Michel Petrucianni, Michel Camilo**, and **Julian Joseph**. In free music, **Cecil Taylor** hypnotizes.

Keyboard

Tuning pins

Styles of playing

In stride piano, and until jazz musicians started spinning long chains of notes to echo a horn solo, pianists coupled a repertoire of trills, chords, and brief right hand figures with a powerful left hand that mixed bass notes and chords. In stride, bass notes are played on the strong first and third beats, chords on the weak beats.

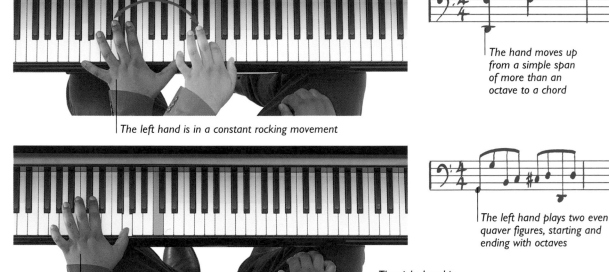

The left-hand stride figure

The left hand is in a constant rocking movement

The hand moves up from a simple span of more than an octave to a chord

Early boogie and blues began with more makeshift methods than ragtime and stride, which required considerable piano skill. The "walk" is a steady, repetitive sequence of short, even notes in the bass. The right hand slides black and white notes into each other to emulate the slur of horns, interspersed with short runs and chords.

The left hand repeats this walk pattern

The right hand is less prominent

The left hand plays two even quaver figures, starting and ending with octaves

Quick chords in the left hand

Constant runs of long melody lines

Bebop soloists liked wandering away from fundamental harmony, so pianists made the left hand less specific to accommodate them. The rise of the timekeeping bass player also liberated the pianist from a steady left hand beat. Bop piano is typified by dabbing left hand chords and a stream of improvised melody in the right.

The part of the melody line being played left

Sparing left hand chords

A more pianistic style, with chordwork and a rich harmonic vocabulary strongly linked to the European classical tradition, is used by pianists like Herbie Hancock. Great virtuosity typifies the style, with both hands equally creative on the keys. A jazz pianist through and through, Hancock has created some of the most influential funk.

A dissonant chord using many notes is typical of this style, which makes full use of both hands

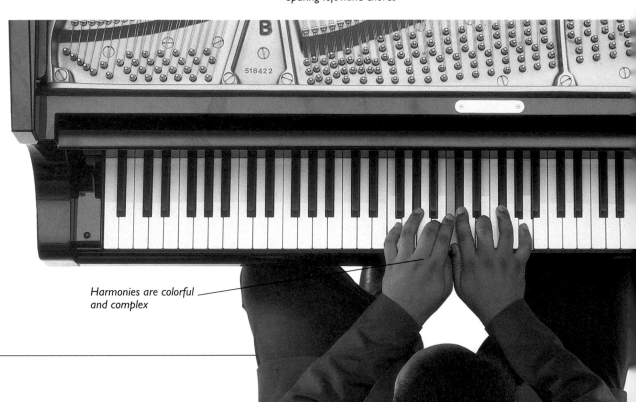

Harmonies are colorful and complex

Using the pedal

Pedal technique enhances the contrasts and subtleties of jazz piano. Here, the sustain pedal is being operated at the instant that the hands are lifted from sounding a chord. The music therefore lingers, even though the duration of the sounded chord is short.

The hands lift after playing a chord

The right pedal is pressed to sustain the sound

Julian Joseph demonstrates a more pianistic style of playing

Electric keyboards

Increasing use of amplification after the 1950s overwhelmed the acoustic piano. And since jazz had second-class citizenship in music for many years, pianists were often expected to play on faulty or out-of-tune instruments. These were circumstances that made the development of portable electric keyboards popular. They have never replaced acoustic pianos but have become valued for unique qualities of their own.

Analog keyboards

Analog technology was popular in the 1970s, but it could not digitize and store sounds. The Moog keyboard, for example, can play just one note at a time, and the player has to manipulate a variety of filters, modulators, and mixers manually to change its sound qualities.

On the Moog, Jason Rebello fattens the sound played by his right hand using one of three oscillators. Because the single sound produced is not perfect, the Moog has a human feel and is good for soloing.

Digital keyboards

Digital technology revolutionized synthesizers in the 1980s, enabling sounds to be broken down into basic components and stored in computer code. Linking them in fast-moving chains produces soundwaves with immense potential. A repertoire of sounds for the D-50 is available in a computer program card inserted in the back. Sounds can also be programmed in, allowing players to carry their unique sounds around on a plastic card.

Jason Rebello

The left hand works the modulator

By programming digital synthesizers, musicians can write qualities onto sounds. Clearly identifiable aspects make up a sound's timbre: volume relative to another sound; emphasis with which it begins (the attack) and decays. Here, Jason Rebello creates a sound and selects a number code to recall it.

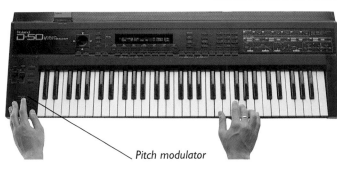

Pitch modulator

A pitch modulator on the synthesizer allows the musician to bend a note. The range of undulation can be as much as an octave, but the sound of the slurring note has already become a musical cliché, particularly in fusion, so contemporary jazz players use the effect carefully.

With the pedal on the D-50, the musician can vary volume and select filters to alter the sound. It can also be used to bend pitch when the musician's hands are occupied soloing on one keyboard and playing chords on another.

Strings

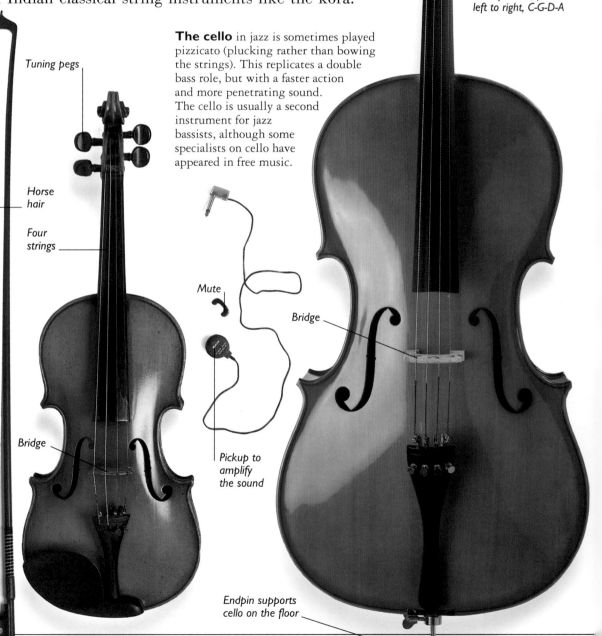

A S CENTERPIECES of the European classical orchestra, and as delicate instruments swamped by brass, strings have stayed on the fringes of jazz. But they have been used by pioneers since the early swing era, and they had an important ensemble role in bigger ragtime and dance bands. In the 1930s, hardswinging, inventive violin soloists appeared (Joe Venuti, Stuff Smith, and Stephane Grappelli), with techniques ranging from classical smoothness to the grittiness of the blues. They pioneered bold styles, even using the bow upside down to extend chords. In fusion music, electronics and amplification reinforced the violin's impact. The cello was briefly popular in bop — a way to play fast bass lines. It is now usually a textural instrument in free improvised music. Open musical frontiers have brought African and Indian classical string instruments like the kora.

Johnny Van Derrick

Gut strings

The cello strings are usually tuned, from left to right, C-G-D-A

STARS AND STYLES

Joe Venuti, **Stuff Smith**, and **Stephane Grappelli** were pioneers, Venuti exuberant and percussive, Grappelli elegant. Smith, wildly adventurous, amplified a violin in the 1930s. In the 1970s **Jean Luc Ponty** took it further. **Zbigniew Seifert** played impassioned Coltrane-like violin; **Didier Lockwood** followed. In free players **Leroy Jenkins**, **Billy Bang**, and **John Blake**, old and new converge. Indian **L. Shankar** fuses East and West, improvising on a ten-string violin.

The cello in jazz is sometimes played pizzicato (plucking rather than bowing the strings). This replicates a double bass role, but with a faster action and more penetrating sound. The cello is usually a second instrument for jazz bassists, although some specialists on cello have appeared in free music.

Tuning pegs

Horse hair

Four strings

Mute

Bridge

Bridge

Pickup to amplify the sound

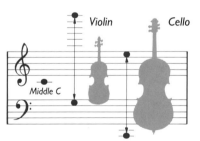

Violin   *Cello*

Middle C

String range Some violinists have extended the downward range with redesigned violins of five or six strings.

The soprano member of the violin family, the violin dominated European orchestral music by the 17th century. Jazz musicians have invented violin techniques inconceivable to traditional tutors. The closest jazz style to an orthodox method has been Stephane Grappelli's. The traditional gut strings and wooden body were augmented when amplification and electronics introduced steel strings and plastic bodies.

Endpin supports cello on the floor

The kora is a lyrical traditional West African instrument used in African classical music. Half a calabash, it has 21 strings, and its melodic sounds have a harplike delicacy. Tunde Jegede studied with one of the last of the Gambian master kora players, Amadu Jobarteh, and brings together the African classical tradition with jazz and Western classical music.

The violin

Starting a note with the end of the bow gives greater attack

Self-taught fingering and bowing positions give more clipped phrases, unusual harmonies, and percussive effects. This muted style uses the end of the bow (left) distanced from the bridge. Stuff Smith's harder sound was played nearer the bridge. Many free improvisers have developed raw, fast bowing styles.

Inverting the bow to draw the hairs over all four strings and produce a more complex chord was an early technique and an idea of Joe Venuti's. The sound it gives is not pure, but it has a driving, unruly excitement.

Tuning strings

21 strings in two rows

Cello

Many jazz bassists have doubled on the smaller, higher pitched cello, whether as a means of playing complex bass parts more easily or to lend contrast to unaccompanied solo recitals. It is still in far less common jazz use than the violin, and new instrument designs (such as Eberhard Weber's electric six-string bass) have offered its range in more adaptable forms. Adventurous blends of jazz and nonjazz styles, particularly in free improvised music, have nevertheless made creative use of the traditional cello.

Kora

The kora is traditionally played seated on the floor, although Tunde Jegede has adapted it for playing with jazz ensembles. It is tuned to other instruments in a group by pushing up the cords to which the strings are attached. The two rows of strings are plucked like a harp. Chords are not part of classical kora music, but Tunde Jegede has evolved a style that includes them.

Strings are plucked with index finger and thumb

Traditional method of sitting to play kora

Calf skin stretched over half a calabash

Guitar

Tony Rémy

THE GUITAR, which superseded the banjo in early jazz bands, was primarily a rhythm instrument for a long time — Count Basie's guitarist Freddie Green did not play a solo in four decades. Amplifiers expanded the guitar's potential in the 1930s, letting it cut through the roar of big band brass, although Belgian gypsy Django Reinhardt still astonished the jazz world with an acoustic instrument. In 1940s bebop, the electric guitar became a frontline contender, a solo instrument played with the phrasing of a saxophone or a bop pianist's garrulous right hand. The jazz guitar became more raucous with the impact of 1960s rock guitarists like Jimi Hendrix.

STARS AND STYLES

Visionary **Charlie Christian** explored the twisting phrasing and harmonies of early electric guitar. The solos of swing lyrical genius **Django Reinhardt** were models of joyous concision. Bop also included **Barney Kessell**, **Tal Farlow**, reserved, poetic **Jim Hall**, and swinging **Wes Montgomery**. The impact of **Jimi Hendrix** led to muscular, jarring **John Scofield**. Pop, bop, and country rock spawned **Pat Metheny**, and free atonality surfaced in **Bill Frisell** and **Sonny Sharrock**.

Twin-neck guitars, one for a twelve-string fingerboard, the other for a six, were popular in the fusion era. John McLaughlin was a notable exponent.

Fretboard

Bridge

The Gibson single cutaway semiacoustic was one of the most popular jazz guitars for its fast, smooth action and rich tone. Wes Montgomery's use of it encouraged many others.

The deep-bodied acoustic gives a sound preferred by many even in an era of highly sophisticated electronic sound generation, and it is often used in electric bands. It can be played with microphones directed at the box or with a clip-on pickup.

Tone hole

Fret markers

Highest frets

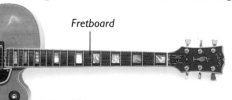

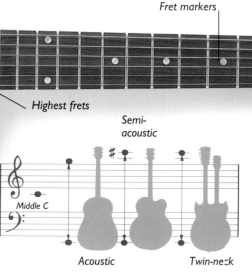

Middle C

Semi-acoustic

Acoustic

Twin-neck

Guitar range The upper range of the guitar can be extended by a cutaway body accessing the highest frets.

Sounding a note

Flexible picks protruding from the thumb and forefinger will give a soft, pliable sound. Most jazz guitarists play with a plectrum, or pick, although some sound the notes by plucking "finger style."

Allowing only a small amount of plectrum to protrude stiffens the pick, and the resulting abrupt, clucking sound is often used as a special effect.

Where the strings are struck makes a big difference to their sound. Strings are tightest close to their anchorage at the bridge. Plucking or strumming here gives a hard, bright metallic sound.

Strumming near the center of the tone hole gives a rhythm guitar sound, warm and buoyant on an acoustic instrument. It can be softened further by moving toward the end of the fingerboard.

Playing chords

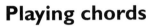

Regular B flat major chord

B flat with an extra 11th note

B flat augmented with a 13th

In blues and earlier jazz, guitar chords were uncomplicated, but bebop's harmonic subtleties led to voicings of greater ambiguity and depth. These were not harder for guitarists to play, although chord changes took place more frequently, as in all bop. To switch easily between melodic "fills" and chords, guitarists often use the thumb rather than the index finger for bass notes.

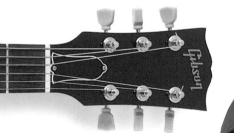

Harmonics — high, glittering overtones — are a delicate guitar special effect. They are sounded by using the left hand normally, but extending the right index finger across the 12th fret, so it rests very lightly on the strings. The curled second finger functions as a plectrum to strike the note.

Special effects

Bending notes is one of the most fundamental of blues guitar techniques, producing a sound of sliding pitch. The finger that stops the string stretches it across the fingerboard as the note is plucked. As the genre has influenced postbop guitarists, the method is still widely used.

The string is pulled to one side

The right hand hits another note

Tapping involves pulling the fretboard finger away from its stopped note to sound it while striking another note with the fingers of the right hand. Before Eddie van Halen and Stanley Jordan pioneered this, plectrum guitarists could only play one melody line.

The index finger is held just above the string

Bass

I T IS EASY to overlook the steady, encouraging murmur of the double bass, until it isn't there — and then an abyss seems to open beneath the music. The bass thickens and colors the low-register texture, but it also frequently lays down the beat. Ragtime tempos made bassists emphasize the strong beats in the bar and, although some 1920s jazz extended the role to a more even tempo, it was bassists of the 1940s who developed a fast, conversational countermelodic style that led to the guitarlike speed common today. Some players never relinquished the weight and depth of the more traditional double bass sound, and a measured, dramatic, tonally rich style resoundingly survived in some hands. In the 1970s, many bassists took up bass guitar, and the best exponents realized that it was an instrument with its own sound and unique demands.

Alec Dankworth

STARS AND STYLES

Ensemble bassists like **Pops Foster** and **John Kirby** supplied harmonic and rhythmic punctuation in the 1920s and 1930s. Basie's **Walter Page** developed the modern even four-beat marking of pulse. Ellington's short-lived bass genius **Jimmy Blanton** reeled off fast countermelodies against ensembles and soloists. Then came **Oscar Pettiford** and **Ray Brown** with a big sound and improvising creativity. In the late 1950s Bill Evans's **Scott LaFaro** intensified the conversational style, making the piano trio a collective improvising group. **Charles Mingus** and disciples **Charlie Haden** and European virtuoso **Eberhard Weber** restored a resonant and deliberate style. Jazz funk brought bass guitar with **Stanley Clarke**, lyrical **Steve Swallow**, and **Jaco Pastorius**.

Bass range The double bass is the lowest-pitched member of the violin family, sounding an octave below its written pitch. The electric bass has the same tuning, an octave below the bottom four strings of a conventional six-string guitar. Some double basses have five strings, the lowest tuned to the third B or C below middle C.

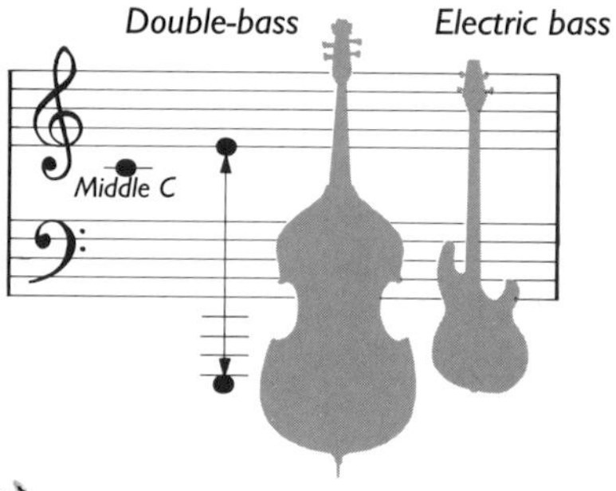

Double-bass   Electric bass

Middle C

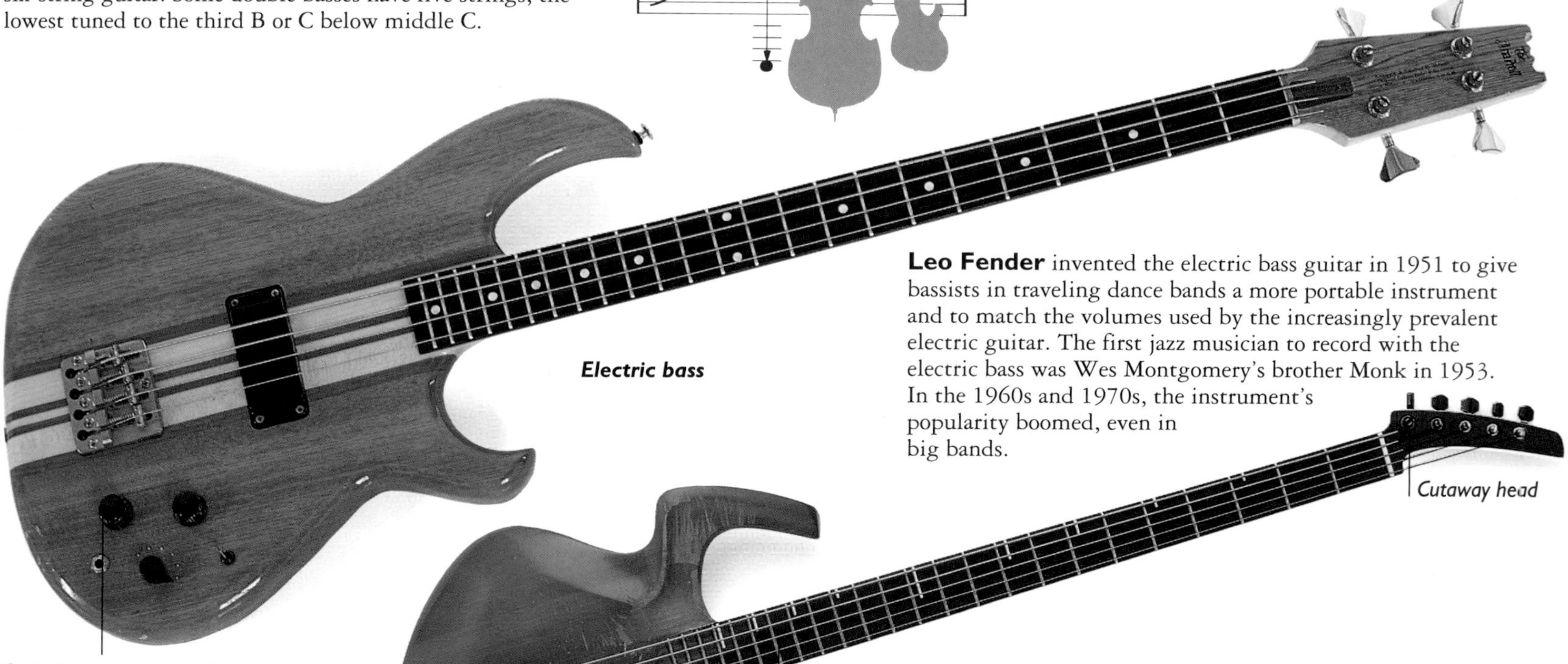

Electric bass

Leo Fender invented the electric bass guitar in 1951 to give bassists in traveling dance bands a more portable instrument and to match the volumes used by the increasingly prevalent electric guitar. The first jazz musician to record with the electric bass was Wes Montgomery's brother Monk in 1953. In the 1960s and 1970s, the instrument's popularity boomed, even in big bands.

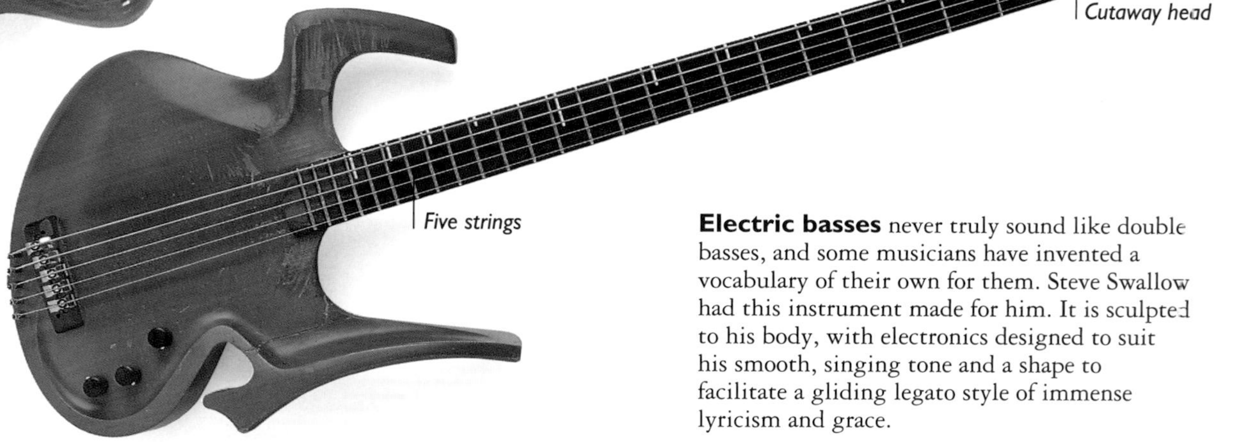

Cutaway head

Controls to alter tone and volume

Five strings

Electric basses never truly sound like double basses, and some musicians have invented a vocabulary of their own for them. Steve Swallow had this instrument made for him. It is sculpted to his body, with electronics designed to suit his smooth, singing tone and a shape to facilitate a gliding legato style of immense lyricism and grace.

Steve Swallow's bass

The double bass

To maximize its deep and reverberating sound, the double bass has a big sound box, heavy strings, and — in its prewar form —gut rather than steel strings and a high bridge, which limited the effective range at the upper register end of the fingerboard. With the faster techniques of bebop, the bridge was lowered to bring the strings closer to the board, and modern bassists now use the whole of the instrument's potential range.

Amplification became more effective in the 1950s when steel strings superseded gut. Originally, microphones were used, but pickups built into the body or clipped on the bridge, as here, are sophisticated enough to magnify the sound without distorting the instrument's natural resonances.

Fingerboard

Pickups amplify the sound

Gut strings

High bridge

F-shaped sound hole

Finger positions

Classical position (right) with the two middle fingers of the left hand together. The hand is rounded as if holding a ball. It is used in positions near the top of the bass where the fingers are stretched. Great pressure must be exerted in order to produce a strong tone.

Open finger position (left), with the two middle fingers apart, is a style adopted from bass guitar and is used in positions nearer the bridge with a finger over each semitone. It makes more notes available in any one position with less shifting of the hand.

In ballad playing (right) the bass line is more widely spaced and the sounding of notes fuller and longer. The right hand is further away from the bridge to soften the sound and the fingers hook the string so that the note can be plucked more vigorously, lengthening its duration.

The high register (left) can only be reached by leaning the left forearm over the upper body of the bass and extending the fingers. In this pose, the index finger cannot be used to "bar" the position, so the thumb is used instead. Sounding notes accurately in this awkward stance requires high skill and great strength in the fingers.

Playing chords

Not all contemporary jazz playing requires a fast countermelodic style. In slower pieces, in theme statements, and to vary solos, bassists will play arpeggios or chords, or sometimes strum the strings like a guitarist. Double and triple-stops are used especially in piano-less groups. This example (right) shows a dominant chord with the root, seventh and tenth notes played simultaneously.

Walking

When Basie's Walter Page extended the occasional use of four even beats to a steady bass pulse beneath the band, it became one of the most familiar sounds associated with jazz. The walking bass line is a test of a player's ability to sustain tempo without losing the cutting edge of the notes. In swing and bop, particularly in open jamming, the bassist may be expected to sustain a fast walking 4/4 for long periods behind soloists. When bop put increasing pressure on bassists' agility, two or three fingers in succession, rather than just the index finger, were used to pluck a fast line.

Electric bass

The thumb slaps against the string

The fingers hit the strings sharply

Slapping technique entered jazz through soul and funk and was popularized by Stanley Clarke. It is a springy, catapulting sound produced by hitting the lower strings with the thumb at the same time as flicking the fingers sharply over the upper strings. The electric bass was first adopted in jazz as simply a loud, portable substitute for the upright instrument, but its exponents in jazz, rock, and soul uncovered unusual techniques for it, such as slapping.

Bowing

A timekeeper's role inevitably made pizzicato, or plucking, technique essential for jazz bassists. But the rich sonorities of the instrument are often explored by techniques with the bow (arco), particularly in suspended time passages or slow, impressionistic overtures. A good bow technique is essential for contemporary bass players.

Harmonics, as on the guitar, are high, delicate overtones produced by holding the fretting finger lightly on the string while plucking it normally with the right hand. Virtuoso players can insert such sounds into a fast bass solo without pause.

Pull offs complement the slapping style, as the smoothness of standard bass technique quickly led the highly adventurous players to search for more bite and vigor. In this method, the finger stopping the string flicks off it the moment the right hand plucks the string, producing an abrupt, drumlike sound.

Sampling

I N GUITARIST Pat Metheny's ballad "Antonia," the mysterious accordionlike sound came from no single instrument but from many performances of the same notes on a soprano saxophone and the high register of a bowed bass blended by electronic sampling. Technology has opened new galaxies of sound to musicians since early synthesizers were made more flexible by computer processes that could memorize and reproduce sounds at a touch. Sampling enabled sounds from acoustic instruments or other sources to be digitized, stored, and remixed. The techniques are used in all new music, but particularly in blending jazz material with rap.

Urban Species with engineer Paul Borg

STARS AND STYLES

Sampling offers more than an orchestra in a box: it opens up nuances not available on synths. **Pat Metheny** explored it on disk, as did **Miles Davis** from the mid-1980s. In jazz dance and hip hop, where deejays are as vital as musicians, jazz horns, bass, and drums sampled from classic grooves mix with vocals. At the fore are **A Tribe Called Quest** and **Gang Starr**.

AKAI S1000 stereo digital sampler. Sounds are recorded onto a computer program.

48 tracks | Computer screen

48-track Solid State Logic mixing console. Each of the 48 tracks has a fader and a series of controls with which to vary the effects. The computer in the center is programmed to operate the different tracks so that the engineer does not need 48 hands.

Cuing up

British hip hop band Urban Species uses samples and live sounds in a recording session, recently working with Flora Purim. Each tune is cued up on the Technics deck and recorded in to the AKAI S1000, which samples the changing waveform several thousand times in a second, storing it as a digital code. When all the ingredients are in, the deejay arranges and mixes them using the computer.

Mixing

Computer screen displays what is happening in the program

Engineer Paul Borg arranges one track

Each track is named

Tracks | Bar numbers

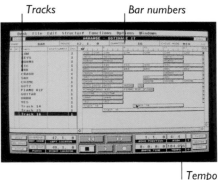

Tempo

The computer screen displays the various tracks sampled for Urban Species's tune "Got 2 Have It." The line along the top shows the bar numbers, the column down the left hand side shows the song's components: horns, piano riff, vocal tracks, etc. The horizontal columns display which samples are playing at any moment and charts when they cut in and out. The engineer manipulates all the elements from the console.

3

JAZZ GIANTS

No single performer created jazz or brought about its periodic changes of direction alone, not even Louis Armstrong. Yet exceptional talents have released new energies in jazz and added new sounds to the palette of jazz materials for others to use. Of the 20 giants of jazz whose stories follow, only five are primarily composers, and all but one are improvising performers, too. Scott Joplin apart, they are pioneers of a different art, the art of spontaneous composition. Although the contributions of these master musicians have unleashed new dreams of how jazz might be played, all the performers were artists of their time, building on history and using the materials around them, but hearing new possibilities in all of it. Many were confronted with abuse, indifference, racism, and deception through their work, and their stories are not always comforting. But the vitality of the music and their creative lives resists the sensationalism that has often clung to them, and it always will.

Scott Joplin

SCOTT JOPLIN'S name does not always fit into jazz books. His music predates jazz and was not improvised but highly formal in design. Joplin saw his identity as that of a black American counterpart to Chopin or Strauss: a composer of music for a new world and new century, blending his own experiences with the European inheritance. But Joplin's troubled life belongs among the stories of the pioneers of this music. The style of which he was the most daring exponent — ragtime — was a vital ingredient in the chemical process from which jazz emerged.

Piano King

Joplin was born in Texas in 1868, the son of a former slave. A piano prodigy with a musical education financed by his mother's work as a domestic servant, he set his sights on a career as a classical concert pianist. After she died in the boy's teens, Joplin traveled throughout the Midwest, studying, performing, even playing at the World's Fair in 1894, and enrolling at the George R. Smith College for Negroes in Sedalia, Missouri. He began writing songs, and news of his talents spread quickly. In 1900 he moved to St. Louis to work with publisher John Stark (one of the most trusted and important relationships of his life) and began to extend his work from songs to full-length pieces including ballets and operas. Short works, however, brought him the greatest acclaim, and the first million-selling song in the history of popular music was Joplin's "Maple Leaf Rag." Classics like this and "The Entertainer" won him the title King of Ragtime.

Negro Eden

Ragtime had already been extensively developed by pianists such as Tom Turpin and James Scott, but Joplin's dreams were bigger. Ragtime's home was the low-life South and Midwest, where it was the background jangle in saloons and brothels. Joplin was obsessed with establishing a more dignified setting for ragtime in the

A piano roll of "Maple Leaf Rag." The sheet music of this Joplin composition sold 75,000 copies in 1899 and made the composer's reputation.

Scott Joplin was not a jazz musician, but his music was a crucial ingredient in the melting pot. The ragtime craze around 1900 obliged most dance bands to feature rags, which brilliant improvisers like Louis Armstrong and Jelly Roll Morton stretched and squeezed into swing.

concert halls and opera houses. Moreover, he wanted to expand the music's scope and emotional weight. A copyright office lost the only copy of his first opera *A Guest of Honor* (it was never subsequently found) and the composer devoted his last years to *Treemonisha*, a flawed, sometimes naive, but massively ambitious three-act grand opera, which his biographer Rudi Blesh described as "the legend of a Negro Eden." *Treemonisha*, a female spiritual leader, is taken by many commentators to be a tribute to Joplin's beloved mother.

The music industry, which had absorbed Joplin's popular rags as fast as he could write them, froze out an opera that seemed to be an expensive and subversive blend of black consciousness-raising and a white middle-class art form. Nobody would touch it. In desperation, Joplin eventually staged the show himself in Harlem in 1915, without scenery, costumes, lighting, or musicians other than the composer himself at the piano. The show was a flop, crushing Joplin's dreams. *Treemonisha* was finally performed again in 1972 on Broadway,

this time to considerable interest, and it was also released on disk in 1976. Nearly sixty years after his death in a mental hospital from syphilis, at the age of 49, Scott Joplin won a Pulitzer Prize for his contributions to American music.

SCOTT JOPLIN
Texas November 24, 1868 –
New York April 1, 1917

Key compositions
"Maple Leaf Rag," "Swipsey Cake-walk,"
"Easy Winners," "Elite Syncopations,"
"The Entertainer," Treemonisha

Key partners
John Stark, Texas Medley Quartet,
second wife Lottie Stokes

Key musical styles
Ragtime, African-American pre-jazz
syncopation of European piano music
with a steady two-beat left hand
against a more florid right, reversing
accents to weak beats.

Jelly Roll Morton

JELLY ROLL MORTON claimed jazz was his invention. It wasn't, but he invented or enhanced enough of its components to make the claim forgivable. In helping ragtime swing and liberating the improviser, he was a towering figure of proto-jazz.

Ferdinand Morton was the son of a black Creole builder and part-time trombonist, F. P. La Menthe. His father's early desertion and his opera-loving mother's downscale marriage left the boy living by his wits, preoccupied with gaining respect — traits that resurfaced in a vanity that alienated many of his contemporaries. During his early years, he tried many ways to make a living: pimp, vaudeville performer, music publisher, gambling house manager, and boxing promoter. But above all, he was a gifted and sophisticated musician.

Reinterpreting Ragtime

Morton's natural environment was the Storyville district of New Orleans. He had learned drums as a child, then harmonica and guitar, but it was as a pianist that he found work in the sporting houses of Storyville. In 1923 he joined the exodus to Chicago and began to record some of the finest examples of early jazz, both as a solo pianist and as the leader of the Red Hot Peppers, one of the most farsighted and pathfinding bands in the music's history. Ragtime was his primary influence but not as played by ragtime piano gurus. Morton improvised, and his interpretation of ragtime did not pursue the ideals of a stately formal black music like Joplin's; it took a more spontaneous, unruly form. He upset ragtime's regular meters and expanded the instrumentation of the orthodox New Orleans band to feature groups of instruments playing harmonically, as in the Red Hot Peppers's "clarinet sections." Conceiving of the jazz ensemble as a palette of contrasting tone colors, Jelly Roll Morton pioneered techniques that would later contribute to orchestral jazz.

Changing times left Morton behind, as 1930s swing developed from the gliding smoothness of upmarket dance music and the raucous charm of New Orleans ensemble sounds. In a famous act of despairing heroism, he defiantly stopped a celebrated swing band in mid-performance of his "King Porter Stomp," getting on stage to show how it should be played. Through the Depression-hit 1930s, Morton did his best with orchestra pit jobs, only returning to the public eye through the tireless efforts of academic Alan Lomax, who extensively recorded Morton's piano playing and shrewd views on jazz for a Library of Congress collection. Morton even recorded again, notably on Sidney Bechet's celebrated Bluebird sessions. He died mocked or ignored by many who had absorbed his ideas but had heard too many grandiloquent claims. He is now considered to be a cornerstone of jazz and a giant of African-American music.

FERDINAND LA MENTHE MORTON "Jelly Roll Morton"
New Orleans October 20, 1890 – Los Angeles July 10, 1941

Key recordings
1923 piano pieces including "King Porter Stomp"; 1926 Red Hot Peppers including "The Pearls," "Sidewalk Blues"; 1938 Library of Congress recordings

Key partners
Omer Simeon, Kid Ory, Baby Dodds

Key musical styles
Ragtime, blues, Hispanic music, minstrel songs and spirituals – all the ingredients that would eventually fuse in jazz.

Song sheet for Morton's "The Naked Dance."

Jelly Roll Morton's Red Hot Peppers, classic exponents of an advanced New Orleans ensemble style in 1926.

Louis Armstrong

FOR ALMOST fifty years, Louis Armstrong dominated first the jazz world, then the wider entertainment business as the best loved and best known of all jazz musicians. He had an unflinching boldness of conception, driving swing, soaring musical imagination, and revolutionary technique, while his music was conceived with all the shape and drama of tantalizing stories. But these virtues were far from obvious to Armstrong himself. His pianist and second wife in the 1920s, Lil Hardin, said that he "didn't believe in himself. I was sort of standing at the bottom of the ladder holding it and watching him climb."

Like many New Orleans musicians, Louis Armstrong came to jazz by hearing its early incarnations on street corners, through open windows, and at funerals and parades. He had no musical education, being the son of a domestic servant and part-time prostitute called Mayann, raised

in poverty by his grandmother when his laborer father Willie took off at his birth. But though the young Louis dressed in rags and often shopped in garbage cans, his genius needed only a spark to ignite it.

The story tells that a teenaged Louis Armstrong was sent to the city's Municipal Boys' Home after firing a revolver in the street to celebrate New Year's Day, 1913. Later investigations suggest that the need to live by his wits meant he was rarely far from the attention of the law. The Home gave him the focus he needed. He had already developed an uncannily accurate ear for improvised harmony by singing on the streets for nickels in a barbershop quartet. Now he could acquire a cornet, some basic instruction, and familiarity with the popular marches, rags, and ballads of the day. When he was released, a musician's life was the only one he wanted.

St. Louis Blues

In the dives and dance halls, honky tonks and brothels of Storyville, musicians worked day and night. A keen, talented youngster had only to walk around the corner to

LOUIS DANIEL ARMSTRONG
"Satchelmouth, Satchmo,
Pops, Dippermouth"
New Orleans ca. 1898 – New York July 6, 1971

Key recordings
*Hot Five and Hot Seven bands 1925–1928,
notably "West End Blues," "Potato Head
Blues," "Cornet Chop Suey," "Weather Bird,"
"Heebie Jeebies"*

Key partners
*Joe "King" Oliver, Lil Hardin Armstrong,
Kid Ory, Earl Hines, Fletcher Henderson,
Jack Teagarden*

Key musical styles
*Grew up with New Orleans ensemble jazz
and created a dominating instrumental solo
style within it. Used rhythmic variations and
composition-based structural balance previously
unthinkable in improvisation.
Popularized an instrumental style of
scat singing without lyrics, echoing in nonsense
syllables the percussive punch of the brass.*

find a chance to play. Armstrong soon met the city's most celebrated musicians, including blues-oriented trumpeter Joe "King" Oliver and trombonist Kid Ory. Oliver befriended the young Armstrong — some accounts suggest that the insecurity of his fatherless childhood made the boy gravitate towards charismatic older men — and the bandleader's patronage opened doors to him all over the city. When Oliver left for Chicago in 1918, Armstrong joined Kid Ory, had a brief first marriage, gained invaluable musical experience working the Mississippi riverboats, and in 1922 took the step that transformed his own career and fueled the development of jazz as a spontaneous art.

At this time, King Oliver was working at a Chicago dance hall called the Lincoln Gardens, and the mixture of disciplined ensemble playing and vocallike instrumental effects in his Creole Band was causing a stir. Oliver sent for Armstrong to join him, and the stir became a storm. The 22-year-old newcomer was louder, more inventive and less bound to the chugging ragtime beat than anyone else on the newly forged jazz scene. Oliver and Armstrong went into the studios in 1923 and, according to jazz

King Oliver's Creole Band at its 1923 recording debut. Armstrong poses with a slide trumpet, bassist Bill Johnson played banjo because the bass made the cutting stylus jump.

The bugle played by a young Louis Armstrong in 1913 at New Orleans Municipal Boys' Home. Teacher Peter Davis made the young Louis the institution's bugler, and unintentionally changed the music world.

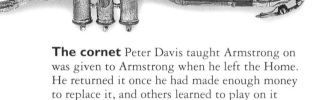

These notches were cut into the mouthpiece of the cornet by Louis Armstrong to suit his particular embouchure.

The cornet Peter Davis taught Armstrong on was given to Armstrong when he left the Home. He returned it once he had made enough money to replace it, and others learned to play on it

By the 1930s, Armstrong was a celebrity. This gold-plated mouthpiece was given to him later in life.

lore, the young man's music was so powerful and penetrating that he had to stand 15 feet behind the others. But Louis Armstrong was not trying to muscle in on his partners' acts. Early New Orleans jazz was an ensemble music, with the players soloing briefly, if at all; Armstrong was evolving a soloistic music out of his own spiritedness and power.

The Golden Years

Believing that her husband's talents could blossom on an even wider stage, Lil Hardin encouraged him to leave King Oliver and join the glamorous, urbane Fletcher Henderson Orchestra in New York. Louis Armstrong's presence transformed Henderson's outfit from a glossy dance-band to an inventive jazz ensemble, crucial to the later evolution of swing music.

In 1925, he became a bandleader in his own right, and through the remainder of the 1920s he made a series of recordings of such quality and variety as to become timeless classics. Not only did these sessions produce jazz of an unprecedented emotional subtlety and strength, with a shifting, rhythmic intensity that constantly tugged and released the listener, but they also

revealed Armstrong as a pioneering vocalist.

Through the 1930s, his career and fame grew. His manager and mentor, Joe Glaser, and the record industry encouraged him to develop as an all-round popular entertainer — which he was far from reluctant to do, since memories of his early deprivations left him with an intense desire to be reminded of the public's affection. In 1931, he separated from Lil Hardin and subsequently re-married twice. He appeared on Broadway, was the first black American to take prominent roles in feature films, fitfully continued to demonstrate his improvising originality, and became one of the world's biggest showbiz celebrities with hits like "Hello Dolly" and "What a Wonderful World." Declining health stopped his horn playing in his last decade, but his death in 1971 made front pages all over the globe.

The best known of all jazz stars, Louis Armstrong appeared in nearly 50 movies and acquired the title Ambassador Satch for his globetrotting tours.

Bix Beiderbecke

WHEN THE 28-year-old trumpeter Bix Beiderbecke returned to his family home in Davenport, Iowa, close to death from alcoholism and pneumonia, he found the records that he had mailed to his parents unopened in a cupboard. To them, Leon Bismarck Beiderbecke was a privileged boy who had gone bad, fallen into dubious company, and rejected their standards of decorum. But though the achievements of his short life were invisible to his family, he had become the first great white performer of jazz, and to many listeners he has never been overtaken.

Beiderbecke developed a startlingly sonorous tone, quite different from the guttural, bluesy sound common to the brass players of his day. He is often considered the first "cool" instrumentalist of jazz — forerunner of a style that was not truly established until the 1950s. His style was not just a sound, but a unique method of storytelling. Beiderbecke absorbed Louis Armstrong's techniques for building a solo of contrasting phrase lengths and varied accents; he unfolded them, however, in a private, intimate atmosphere.

Beiderbecke's mother was a schooled pianist, and the boy was a natural musician, able to teach himself complex ideas by ear. When the jazz boom began in his teens, he was captivated by Nick LaRocca's cornet sound in the Original Dixieland Jazz Band (who made virtually the only jazz disks available from 1917 to 1923).

Already disturbed by their idiosyncratic offspring's apparent unwillingness to fit in, Beiderbecke's parents sent him to the Lake Forest Military Academy near Chicago. He and other jazz lovers spent time in town after lights out discovering the New Orleans Rhythm Kings and, in Bix's case, Prohibition hooch. In 1922 he was expelled and by 1924 he was leading his own band. He heard Louis Armstrong on the Mississippi riverboats that came up from New Orleans and St. Louis, and the appetite of the music business for new dance-bands led to his group, the

---

LEON BISMARCK BEIDERBECKE
"Bix"
*Iowa March 10, 1903 –
New York August 7, 1931*

Key recordings
*"Singing the Blues," "I'm Coming Virginia,"
"At the Jazz Band Ball" 1927;
the Debussyan piano piece "In a Mist"*

Key partners
*Frankie Trumbauer, Jean Goldkette,
Paul Whiteman*

Key musical styles
*Cool variation on New Orleans music.
A wistful sound for an intimate lyrical line.*

If Beiderbecke's short life is material for mythology, his pure, chiming trumpet sound is material for inspiration – musicians everywhere have imitated him.

Bix's cornet, "The Triumph."

Bix Beiderbecke was wearing these cufflinks when he tried to fight pneumonia and appear at a Princeton University concert. It was his final illness.

Wolverines, playing New York's Roseland Ballroom. Although theirs was not the taut, rhythmically bold concept of King Oliver's band with Armstrong, Beiderbecke was clearly a star attraction.

Beiderbecke's most celebrated partnership was with friend Frankie Trumbauer, a technically advanced saxophonist with a tone almost as distinctive as the trumpeter's. Fruitful connections were also made with dance music entrepreneur and bandleader Jean Goldkette (whose outfit often surprised even the leading black ensembles) and with orchestra leader Paul

Whiteman, who did not deserve the title King of Jazz but who led an imaginative, semi-classical, meticulously organized band of great popularity nonetheless.

Beiderbecke was employed by Paul Whiteman till his death, and in a generally nonimprovising orchestra produced some scintillating, tantalizingly brief glimpses of genius. Wracked with respiratory illness and bouts of alcoholic delirium, he died at age 28 in a boardinghouse in New York. He was mentioned only twice in the press in his career but his sound has inspired musicians worldwide.

Sidney Bechet

WHAT ARMSTRONG was to the cornet, then the trumpet, Bechet was to the clarinet, then the saxophone. Like Armstrong, Bechet found a way of playing for which there were no models, then invented the details of it with a fire and panache that made its out-of-nowhere independence hard to credit. All early jazz musicians faced the problem of liberating an improvising style from ragtime's stiff rhythms and relentlessly semaphored placement of strong and weak beats. Bechet grew out of it, then swept it aside with an imperiousness that rings down to the present. Like many aspiring clarinettists in

New Orleans, Sidney Bechet was first taught by a member of the Creole Tio family — Lorenzo Tio — one of the most respected of the pre-jazz clarinet masters. Bechet came from a relatively secure Creole family, but he was an irrepressible wanderer and when barely into his teens was working regularly with local bands. In 1917 he joined the Southern Syncopated Orchestra led by black composer Will Marion Cook, a concert ensemble playing a music between highly orchestrated formal ragtime and light classics. Bechet went to Europe with the band, and Swiss conductor Ernest Ansermet recalled an "extraordinary clarinet virtuoso . . . [an] artist of genius." Bechet was 22.

That European tour was a catalyst for jazz. Bechet discovered the soprano saxophone — through which the headlong charge of his improvisations came into their own — in a music shop in Soho, London. He returned to the States to record and develop a jazz identity to match Louis Armstrong's. Bechet began working with leading jazz artists including Duke Ellington and James P. Johnson, but he was not a natural sideman, preferring to operate in a smaller group, exploring extended improvisation. From 1923, Bechet was with Clarence Williams's Blue Five. Pianist, sometime minstrel and music business entrepreneur, Williams had excellent connections and the band often accompanied blues singers in sessions that the saxophonist invariably

"Did all those old guys swing like that?" asked John Coltrane of Sidney Bechet. Bechet played the soprano saxophone with the force of Louis Armstrong's trumpet, astonishing jazz musicians and classical maestros alike, and he created an indestructible vocabulary for saxophone. He settled eventually in France.

SIDNEY BECHET
*New Orleans May 14, 1897 –
Paris May 14, 1959*

Key recordings
*"Sweetie Dear" 1932; "Blues in the Air,"
"Summertime" 1939; "Strange Fruit" 1941;
"Shag," "Petite Fleur"*

Key partners
*Louis Armstrong, Clarence Williams,
Duke Ellington, Will Marion Cook,
Tommy Ladnier*

Key musical styles
*Steeped in New Orleans and blues. Developed
the saxophone. Unique tone and timing.*

---

enhanced and illuminated. Early in the 1930s, Bechet formed the New Orleans Feetwarmers with trumpeter Tommy Ladnier and, for all the skills of his partners, Bechet was a volcanic solo star. But the Depression almost ended his career. Bechet and Ladnier went into tailoring until an offer from the Blue Note company led to a sensational recording of "Summertime," successful enough to draw him out of semi-retirement. In 1949, Bechet played at the famous Paris jazz festival with Charlie Parker. The French so appreciated Bechet and his work that he stayed on.

Bechet's erratic, atmospheric autobiography was a romantic self-portrait.

Few saxophonists turned regularly to the demanding soprano until the 1950s. Bechet had mastered it by 1925. This is his own.

Duke Ellington

HE DID NOT LEARN his art in a conservatory or with the encouragement of wealthy patrons but as a Harlem bandleader, where the closest species to a patron was the mobster. But Duke Ellington's wonderful music proves him to be one of the finest composers to have emerged from America in the 20th century. Ellington was among the most expressive explorers of a jazz orchestra's palette of sounds, the idiom's unique melodies and rhythms, and the personalities of soloists. He made distinctions of art and pop meaningless. Although he wrote or cowrote thousands of compositions over a prolific half-century, Duke Ellington did not compose in a study with a piano but furiously scribbled his great works in airport lounges and the back seats of cars, endlessly on the road.

Among Ellington pieces are some of the century's most famous songs, but these alone do not explain his genius. Band members like Billy Strayhorn, Johnny Hodges, and Juan Tizol were involved, and it is hard to be certain just how large the leader's contribution was in notes on paper. Ellington was a composer for the 20th century and helped change the way composition works. The vitality and color of his work reflected fast travel, reflexive speed, and relentless deadlines rather than lengthy contemplation. He absorbed himself in improvisation and collaboration, and his relish for throwing a fragment of a tune into rehearsal to see what others made of it gave a mixed input to the massive body of Ellingtonia. Yet nothing would have happened without Ellington, the alchemist.

The pioneer jazz musicians were frequently working class, but many of those who developed orchestral jazz came from the emerging black middle class. Duke Ellington's childhood was founded on Victorian principles, his father an ambitious coachman turned valet whose work for the rich gave him a vision of the good life which he passed on to his son. Ellington's mother, Daisy Kennedy, was the daughter of a police captain and "a real Victorian lady" according to Duke's sister Ruth. Daisy doted on her son, and a sophisticated manner of speech, elegant clothes, and a sense of self-worth led to the lifelong nickname. But the boy did not show his promise early on.

Jungle Nights in Harlem

Duke Ellington married young and had a son (Mercer, with Edna Thompson) in 1918. A good commercial artist, he started a sign-painting business but preferred the atmosphere of the clubs and dance halls. Although a limited pianist, he could keep up with rags and dance tunes and formed a band with friends, eventually dubbed the Washingtonians. When Ellington learned that some dance musicians in New York were getting rich, the Washingtonians moved base, and their fortunes rose on the wave of the Harlem Renaissance of African-American culture. But the band remained undistinguished and rhythmically conservative until the arrival of two "hot jazz" specialists — trumpeter James "Bubber" Miley, a King Oliver admirer, and the impulsive, impassioned saxophonist Sidney Bechet. They transformed the band with trombonist "Tricky Sam" Nanton, a growl-and-mute specialist and another crucial carrier of the urgent New Orleans message. A five-year stint at New York's Cotton Club backing the "jungle" dance theater routines developed Ellington's

During a long residency at the Cotton Club in Harlem, the Duke Ellington band changed from a dance orchestra that incorporated dashes of New Orleans color to a unique and influential jazz band that built miniature tone poems from elements of blues and "hot music."

Ellington was a workaholic. Touring constantly, he wrote fragments of music in planes, trains, airports, or the back of a car driven by his saxophonist/chauffeur Harry Carney.

Those close to Ellington reported that he devoted more than his customary concentration to the suite he wrote for Queen Elizabeth II after a meeting in England in 1959. Only one copy was pressed, for the Queen's personal use, the tapes to be kept secret until after Ellington's death. The suite was a tribute, but not an obsequious one — Ellington was confident of his own royal status in the music world.

The Ellington band was a perennial favorite in Europe after 1933's celebrated debut trip.

conceptual sense and understanding of tone color. The semiclassical composers Will Vodery and Will Marion Cook also helped. During the Cotton Club years, early classics like "The Mooch," "Rockin in Rhythm," and "Mood Indigo" changed jazz. But the Ellington Orchestra often proved it could raise the roof on commercial 1930s swing events, too, and was truly peerless at the atmospheric jazz ballad — for among many fine soloists Duke Ellington employed one of the most sensitive and subtly emotional of saxophonists, Johnny Hodges.

Diminuendo and Crescendo

By the 1940s, a musical high point for the band, Ellington was reinventing jazz with more unexpected outcomes than anyone before him could have imagined, producing such glowing music as "Concerto for Cootie," "Warm Valley," "Harlem Air Shaft," and "Take the A Train." He applied rhythmic devices and key changes that were close to classical music to materi-

al that could only have come from jazz. Moreover, Ellington's rhythm section was strengthened by a revolutionary bassist, the shortlived Jimmy Blanton.

There was a downturn in the early 1950s, not helped by the brief departure of Johnny Hodges, but in 1956 the band staged a tumultuous comeback at the Newport Jazz Festival, when tenorist Paul Gonsalves delivered twenty-seven consecutive choruses of a careening "Diminuendo and Crescendo in Blue." The upswing led Ellington to write and record again, and the long-playing record invited extended pieces. "Such Sweet Thunder," a dedication to Shakespeare, spliced jazz with classical music, several long pieces were inspired by his tireless globetrotting, and in later life he wrote religious music. Ellington stayed on the road into his 70s, received innumerable citations, performed at the White House, and represented the boldest, most openhanded and creative face of American culture to audiences the world over.

EDWARD KENNEDY ELLINGTON "Duke"
Washington D. C. April 29, 1899 – New York May 24, 1974

Key recordings
"Sophisticated Lady," "In a Sentimental Mood," "Take the A Train," "Creole Love Call," "Mood Indigo," "Caravan," "I Got It Bad and That Ain't Good," "Ko-Ko"

Key partners
Sonny Greer, Barney Bigard, "Bubber" Miley, Billy Strayhorn, Johnny Hodges, Harry Carney

Key musical styles
Jazz musicians before Ellington wrote songs and arranged orchestral settings for them. But Ellington revolutionized the music by thinking beyond song forms, using symphonic ideas, but always with the urgency and intonation of jazz and blues. His vision of extended jazz forms was revolutionary, and he composed with his favorite soloists in mind.

Coleman Hawkins

THE TENOR SAXOPHONE is such a potent symbol of a jazz improviser's power that its naive, ungainly sound in 1920s jazz — when the clarinet, trumpet, and trombone had found their voices — is hard to square with its maturity in the hands of Lester Young, Ben Webster, Herschel Evans, Chu Berry, and Don Byas ten years later. The bridge between ugly duckling and the imperiously graceful bird it became was Coleman Hawkins.

Hawkins acquired a tenor on his ninth birthday. He already played piano and cello

Hawkins's pioneering work laid the foundation for a tenor approach for Sonny Rollins, John Coltrane, and young performers today.

and by age 12 was performing at dances. High school and college helped his harmony and composition, and at 16 Hawkins played in a Kansas City theater orchestra. Hired to the Jazz Hounds, touring band of popular vaudeville singer Mamie Smith, he was billed as Saxophone Boy. Hawkins's style in 1922 had none of the presence of Armstrong or Bechet, but he had a good sound, was a remarkable sight reader, and was developing as an improviser.

In 1923 Fletcher Henderson, booking musicians for demonstration sessions for a music publisher, heard and liked Hawkins, although the horn on which the boy sounded so authoritative was sprung by elastic bands. With Henderson's band, Hawkins recorded his first substantial solo on

"Dicty Blues," an assured performance if unremarkable in construction. Henderson's remained a recording band until January 1924 and became one of the most soughtafter black groups in jazz. Hawkins quickly developed — sometimes through reverses. In 1924, he lost to Sidney Bechet in an all-night "cutting contest," pursued into the street by a manic Bechet blasting soprano figures into the night. He dropped the slap-tongue novelty effects (a staple of vaudeville tenor), his sound acquired the clout of Louis Armstrong's trumpet, and his tone was full and rich.

Bean a Re-Bop

Armstrong's methods greatly influenced Hawkins's approach to swing and solo construction (although he felt the trumpeter had usurped his role in the band), but the tenorist started to base his improvisation around a knowledge of chords, rather than melody alone. In this, Hawkins paralleled pianist Art Tatum and anticipated bebop. The rhythmic undertow of the music between New Orleans and swing retained a steady, chugging beat. Via Tatum, Hawkins realized he could fly above it without losing the rhythm. Hawkins began playing fast, double tempo passages and often sowed complex ornamental arpeggios and triplets between the emphatic landmarks of an improvisation without sounding gratuitous or coy. And he transformed tenor ballad playing — startlingly in a 1929 performance of "One Hour" with the Mound City Blues Blowers.

In the mid-1930s, Hawkins, always a loner, went to Europe as soloist. The journey he told Henderson would take a month lasted nearly six years: he played in Britain, Holland, Switzerland, and France, jamming with guitarist Django Reinhardt in Paris. Hawkins's flawless technique and power to move audiences intrigued his colleagues. In Britain, needled by an article by Hawkins in *Melody Maker* claiming that improvising in all keys was just practice, the Ennis Hylton dance band transposed "It's the Talk of the Town" by a semitone without telling Hawkins — but he breezed through the change in a live show, and he never mentioned the incident to his tormenters.

Coleman Hawkins was a born competitor on saxophone. The Jazz at the Philharmonic concerts were jam sessions that often galvanized him, like this British tour also starring Roy Eldridge, Benny Carter, and Nat and Cannonball Adderley.

COLEMAN RANDOLPH
HAWKINS
"Bean"
Missouri November 21, 1904 –
New York May 19, 1969

Key recordings
"Body and Soul" 1939; with Dizzy Gillespie and Thelonious Monk 1944; solo improvisation on "Picasso" 1948; recordings with Ben Webster around 1957

Key partners
Fletcher Henderson, Ben Webster, Thelonious Monk

Key musical styles
Virtually invented the mature sound and style of the tenor sax in jazz. Swing player sympathetic to bebop. Inspired solo sax pieces with "Picasso."

Miles Davis (right) was a long-time admirer of the confidence, weight, and discipline of Hawkins's playing, like many of the younger bebop generation.

Hawkins returned to the States in July 1939 and recorded two superb choruses that made "Body and Soul" a classic. A commercial hit, it was also an improvisational masterpiece, with an unsurpassed poise, balance, shape, and relaxation with double time and upper register. In the mid-1940s, with swing musicians including pianist Teddy Wilson and trumpeter Roy Eldridge, Hawkins produced delicious variations on

"Sweet Lorraine," "Crazy Rhythm," and "The Man I Love." He also collaborated with beboppers, whose music his harmonic awareness enabled him to follow with relative ease. The 1944 band he led with Dizzy Gillespie and Max Roach made the first explicit bebop recordings.

In the late 1940s and 1950s, Hawkins toured with Jazz at the Philharmonic packages, recorded with Miles Davis, Fats Navarro, and Milt Jackson, and cut an unaccompanied improvisation, "Picasso," remarkable even by the high technical standards of bop and a truly avant-garde performance for the period. In the early 1950s Hawkins's prestige slipped. He trailed in the polls behind Lester Young and his imitators. By the mid-1950s, working with younger musicians, busy on J.A.T.P. tours, and inspired by the long-playing record, he blossomed again, although he was drinking heavily and was disillusioned with the music business. He recorded extensively and rose to any challenge (including work with Thelonious Monk, Sonny Rollins, and Max Roach). He appeared in movies and on television, and ran a small club group that included pianist Tommy Flanagan. Hawkins became increasingly neglectful of his health but could summon remarkable performances, even when promoters despaired of getting him on stage.

Billie Holiday

IN 1986, ALMOST 27 years after her death and on what would have been her 71st birthday, Billie Holiday had a star in her honor set into Hollywood's Walk of Fame. Holiday, perhaps the only jazz vocalist unequivocally regarded as a great jazz musician by the standards that would be applied to instrumentalists like Louis Armstrong, Miles Davis, or Sonny Rollins, finally received mainstream acknowledgment for achievements often obscured by scandal and sensationalism during her lifetime. Because the mythology of Billie Holiday's strife-torn life fitted so conveniently with the cliché of the self-abusive jazz genius, her newsworthiness was more often based on stories of childhood prostitution, drug dependency, stretches in jail, scandals, and a narcotics charge on her deathbed. Even in her prime, meetings with the press both at home and abroad would always involve fending off questions on these subjects, and they rarely provided opportunities to talk about the music and musicians she loved.

Billie Holiday's early life is hard to place accurately. Although she collaborated in an autobiography with the author William Dufty, its evidence is unreliable. But even allowing for the vagaries of Holiday's own early memories, there are some consistent threads. Her father, Clarence Holiday, a musician who worked fitfully with the Fletcher Henderson band, left the family early in her childhood. The girl was often looked after by relatives when her mother went to New York to look for work. They were unsympathetic, by her own account, and she recollects this period of her life as a catalog of abuse and neglect, probably embroidered a little, but unquestionably tough.

T'ain't Nobody's Business

In her mid-teens, Holiday and her mother moved to New York, where the girl was drawn into prostitution and served her first prison sentence. She began to look for work in the Harlem clubs as a dancer, but discovered singing one night in desperation for money to forestall her mother's eviction from an apartment. Whether on that night in 1930 she really did reduce an audience to tearful and generous gratitude by singing "Trav'lin All Alone" and "Body and Soul," undoubtedly she quickly acquired a reputation. By 1933 she had been discovered by impresario John Hammond, joined Louis Armstrong's manager Joe Glaser, and was then paired with pianist Teddy Wilson in 1936 to make a series of small-group records for the emerging juke box market. They became classics of popular music. Songs like "Why Was I Born," "Mean to Me," "Easy Living," and "The Man I Love," many performed in uncanny conversation with Lester Young's tenor, are unsurpassed examples of a vocalist transforming a song in her own image. They are also superb vignettes of small-group jazz, her voice and the instruments operating in the same spontaneous manner.

Even as a teenager (left) Billie Holiday's subtlety and timing impressed jazz instrumentalists like Ben Webster. The white gardenias (above) were a later trademark.

Holiday claimed that she listened to jazz instrumentalists to shape her style, although she admired Bessie Smith. Untrained, she could hear how musicians like Louis Armstrong and Lester Young surprised the listener by constantly avoiding the obvious in placing accents, unexpected weighting of openings, and resolutions of phrases. She also appreciated that the lyrics of many Tin Pan Alley songs do not bear too much examination and reworked them in such a way that her personality, sense of irony, and unsentimental pragmatism, coupled with a yearning tenderness and empathy with the instability of human affections, transformed the originals.

John Hammond arranged for Billie Holiday to join Count Basie the following year, although they never officially recorded together and the singer's unpunctuality cut the relationship short. In 1938 Holiday began touring with the prestigious dance orchestra led by clarinetist Artie Shaw, with whom she had a brief affair. This was a tough assignment. Shaw's band was white, so in the South Holiday had to eat by herself in the bus while the others sat in a diner. But it was still a landmark in race relations in the music business. Although these were significant openings, Billie Holiday's associations were primarily with

Holiday's composition "Fine and Mellow" was a perfect blend of her early mixture of playfulness and realism and, for her, a rare blues.

BILLIE HOLIDAY
"Lady Day"
Baltimore April 7, 1915 –
New York July 17, 1959

Key recordings
With Teddy Wilson and Lester Young 1935-39, notably "Mean to Me"; "Strange Fruit" 1939; 1950 Decca sessions including "Don't Explain," "God Bless the Child"

Key partners
Teddy Wilson, Lester Young

Key musical styles
Pioneered an intimate microphone style. Exceptional manipulator of the beat and nuances of songs. Saxophonelike sound without any obvious instrumental mimicry.

the desire for a father figure. A succession of men helped themselves to her fast-expanding income, contributed to her heroin addiction, and one, John Levy, is alleged to have framed her to get a reprieve on a jail sentence, after which the singer nonetheless returned to him. Her attempts to straighten out were public knowledge: she wore long gloves to conceal the needle marks she was convinced her audiences were obsessed with. But the music of this period, though more commercial, is sublime, too, particularly on cuts like "Don't Explain" and "God Bless the Child."

Say It Isn't So

In the mid-1950s Holiday's health and prospects improved, and with the help of impresario Norman Granz she toured, recorded again, and the dubiously accurate autobiography *Lady Sings the Blues* was published. But if she managed to avoid hard drugs, her performances became more erratic, and her depressions grew. Refused permission to adopt a child, she reportedly fed her Chihuahua from a baby's bottle. In May 1959, a few months after the death of musical soulmate Lester Young, Holiday collapsed, dying ten weeks later. Diana Ross played Holiday in the 1970s in the big budget movie *Lady Sings the Blues*, much of it as unrelated to her life as the earlier autobiography had been.

By the mid-1940s Billie Holiday was a major star. She seemed to represent a chemistry of innocence and experience that jazz and non-jazz audiences alike could share.

jazz musicians in give-and-take partnerships which confirmed her instinctive musicianship but were not commercial enough to make her rich. A run at the newly opened, multiracial Cafe Society club in Greenwich Village introduced Holiday to a liberal audience keen to embrace the emotions of a life of mingled sensuality and suffering that seemed to inhabit every musical sound she made, and in 1939 the antiracist poem by Lewis Allen, "Strange Fruit" (a chilling image of south-

ern lynchings), became an unexpected hit for her. More commercial recordings followed in the next decade, often with the addition of a string section.

A solo career both attracted and terrified Billie Holiday. The insecurities of childhood poverty and neglect never faded, nor did

Lester Young

THE TWO TENOR GIANTS in the 1930s could not have been more different. Coleman Hawkins approached the horn with the harmonic conception of a pianist and a huge foghorn sound; Lester Young sketched a series of ethereal impressions, resembling an alto saxophone or even a clarinet. Young's influence was for a while more extensive: in the 1940s saxophonist Brew Moore said that anyone who didn't play like him was playing wrong. Young's way of improvising did much to galvanize modern jazz, and his soft sound inspired the postwar cool school.

Young acknowledged his inspirations to be the white saxophonists Frankie Trumbauer and Jimmy Dorsey, but his loose phrasing was affected by Louis Armstrong. Young used hardly any vibrato, low volume, fewer notes, and did not lock phrases within the cages of bar lines: he let a single note fill one bar, a continuous phrase bridge several, then silence. He would anticipate a chord change by playing the relevant notes early or sustain them

into a new chord. His ear guided him infallibly in his early years: he seemed incapable of ugly or graceless music. Remarkable in any jazz context, playing like this within the furor of big bands was a measure of the charisma of his voice. He suggested that the course of his musical life had been to explore "alto tenor" early on, "tenor tenor" in the middle years and "baritone tenor" near the end. The high, airy period was the most fertile and most imitated: the famous "soundless laughter."

Lester Leaps In

Oldest of three children who performed in their father's vaudeville band, Young took up alto in his teens and, after an acrimonious break with his father, joined bassist Walter Page's Blue Devils. Young settled in Kansas City — town of powerful tenorists and punchy, bluesy ensemble music — working with Bennie Moten, King Oliver and, one night when Coleman Hawkins did not show, the touring Fletcher Henderson band. The ease with which the unknown Young deputized the best-known American tenorist provoked the competitive Hawkins to seek a jam session. Young's effortless originality so provoked Hawkins that the established star went on blowing through the next morning and into the afternoon, trying to see him off. Young's victory led to the nickname New President, shortened to Pres. After this episode, Young replaced the Europe-bound Hawkins in the Henderson band, but his light sound was disliked. Henderson's wife played him Hawkins's records to toughen him up.

In 1936 Young made his first recordings, with Count Basie. The phrasing and timing made these recordings bibles for other musicians. The young Charlie Parker bought every release and wore out the grooves on "Lady Be Good." His version with Jay McShann, if played at half speed to lower the alto to tenor register, sounds virtually identical. Before World War II, Young mixed a series of remarkable Basie performances with small-group sessions and

LESTER WILLIS YOUNG
"President, Pres, Prez"
*Mississippi August 27, 1909 –
New York March 15, 1959*

Key recordings
*"Lady Be Good" from first recordings
in 1936; "Jumpin' at the Woodside,"
"Lester Leaps In" with Count Basie;
"These Foolish Things" 1956*

Key partners
Billie Holiday, Count Basie

Key musical styles
*Made a light, non-macho altolike sound his
own. Much copied by later cool saxophonists.*

partnerships with Billie Holiday — some of the most sublime examples of musical rapport in jazz. There were also echoes of his phrasing and timing in many bebop players, although Young himself disliked harmony improvising.

He became better known, but was drafted in September 1944, and the abrupt shift from bohemian to institutionalized life for an introverted, often naive personality was insufferable. Young was caught with drugs, court-martialed and served desperate months in detention. When he emerged his first recordings seemed as distinctive as ever, but the airy, dancing quality was receding. Young joined the popular Jazz at the Philharmonic tours, and his style became more aggressive and bluesy, but he drank, was hospitalized, and his vocabulary ("eyes" for desire, "bells" for approval) turned from being lyrical insights to signs of mental isolation. Some say his last decade was one of unremitting depression and decline, but contemporaries' accounts and his own recordings suggest otherwise. After an unsuccessful engagement in Paris in early 1959, Young returned to the States a sick man and died that year. His life was the basis of Bertrand Tavernier's film *Round Midnight*, played by saxophonist Dexter Gordon.

The bohemian hipster with pork pie hat and tangential speech called Harry Edison "Sweets," musicians "ladies;" Holiday was "Lady Day."

Lester Young played with the tenor held at an angle to his right — a habit picked up in the cramped Kansas City Reno Club of his youth.

Count Basie

THE INFLUENCE of William "Count" Basie is heard in virtually every big jazz band to this day. The challenge facing early jazz orchestras was to make a big group push forward with the same relaxed urge as soloists like Louis Armstrong and Sidney Bechet. When pianist Bill Basie joined Bennie Moten's Kansas City band with others from bassist Walter Page's Blue Devils, a big band style simpler than Henderson's or Ellington's developed. It relied on short phrases, "riffs," exchanged between the sections, call-and-response, plenty of space for soloists, and lots of blues.

William Basie had learned piano at home in Red Bank, New Jersey. In New York, he heard the leading stride pianists and joined the vaudeville circuit. As a pianist, Basie was influenced first by Fats Waller, and later a little by Earl Hines and Teddy Wilson, and his own minimal style influenced many modern jazz pianists. He smoothed out the syncopated thump of stride and concentrated on a simple solo style, discreetly prompting the band.

In 1927, Basie got a job accompanying silent movies. The following year he joined Walter Page's Blue Devils, and eventually

---

WILLIAM BASIE
"Count"
New Jersey August 21, 1904 –
Florida April 26, 1984

Key recordings
"One o'Clock Jump," "Roseland Shuffle,"
"Taxi War Dance" late 1930s with Lester
Young; The Atomic Mr. Basie 1959

Key partners
Lester Young, Herschel Evans, Jo Jones

Key musical styles
Kansas City sound, an ensemble approach with
less "orchestral" scoring, more riffs, exchanged
motifs, improvisation, and blues.

Basie's band revolutionized jazz brass, was as insistent as a preacher, and had a rhythm section the envy of every 1930s jazz orchestra. At the Famous Door in 1938, Herschel Evans solos, Pres (far right) snaps his fingers.

The Count claimed popular success with his only big hit, 1947's "Open the Door, Richard." It featured less of the genuine Basie magic than almost anything else he put out.

Bennie Moten's band. Moten died in 1935, and Basie formed a nine-piece that included Lester Young and drummer Jo Jones. As the Barons of Rhythm, they attracted attention through live radio broadcasts from the Reno Club. A powerful swing, intensified by Basie's frequent practicing with the rhythm section alone, gave the band an identity, and Basie's stature compared with Duke Ellington's led to the title "The Count."

Door to Success

A national agency booked the band for a run at Chicago's Grand Terrace, initially without much effect. But when it came to New York's Famous Door on 52nd Street, Basie expanded to fifteen players and the band took off. Although ragged, it had an exuberance that stemmed from redefining swing for a bigger group, and it poleaxed witnesses to early live shows.

Basie drew his early repertoire from Fletcher Henderson and the Mills' Blue Rhythm Band — simple riffs shot through with blues in memorized ("head") arrangements. Jones's lighter, cymbal-oriented drumming made the beat looser and more focused on Page's steady bass, and Basie's piano offered a swinging understatement.

Big bands suffered financially during and after World War II, and in 1950 Basie called it a day, running an octet instead. In 1952 he was back with an orchestra, with saxophonists Frank Foster and Eddie "Lockjaw" Davis, trumpeters Thad Jones and Joe Newman, and rugged, eloquent blues singer Joe Williams. Basie put out many recordings from the 1950s, and some of his band's work was issued under the names of vocal stars, notably Frank Sinatra, Tony Bennett, Sammy Davis, Jr., Sarah Vaughan, and Bing Crosby.

The 1960s and 1970s saw a more varied repertoire, although the band was not at its happiest with pop. In the 1980s, illness hampered Basie, but at the keyboard he was still irrepressible.

Charles Mingus

Both Basie's and Ellington's bands liberated the jazz orchestra by letting gifted improvisers fly. Charles Mingus did not become as famous, but his groups could shout with Basie's bravura, and show the breadth, subtlety, surprise, and atmosphere of Ellington. He could not, however, contain an embattled, rebellious, and combative temperament and was more likely to yell at his musician or a disrespectful audience than play a piece polished to a gleam. Yet, as a double bass virtuoso with a tone like a cathedral bell, and as a visionary bandleader, Mingus is an undisputed jazz giant, his loosening of swing band rigidity now absorbed by almost all larger creative jazz ensembles.

Mingus was raised in Los Angeles. He learned double-bass in high school, was taught by bassist Red Callendar, and took some formal composition studies. In the 1940s, he avoided bebop, touring with bands led by Louis Armstrong and Kid Ory and working briefly with Lionel Hampton and Duke Ellington, to whom he admitted a massive debt. But he also rammed home his sweeping grasp of all jazz styles when he accompanied Charlie Parker, Dizzy Gillespie, Max Roach, and Bud Powell at the famous 1953 Massey Hall concert.

Composition dominated. Between 1953 and 1955, he became involved first in the Jazz Composers' Workshop, then in a productive workshop of his own. Like all composers of his stature, Mingus wanted written parts to have the flair of improvisation, which he achieved by extending more freedom to soloists than anyone before, often prefiguring

Rebellious visionary Charles Mingus lived on the high wire of jazz composition, dynamically reworking the entire legacy of African-American music.

CHARLES MINGUS
Arizona April 22, 1922 – Mexico January 5, 1979

Key recordings
Pithecanthropus Erectus 1956,
Blues and Roots 1959,
Black Saint and the Sinner Lady 1963

Key partners
Dannie Richmond, Eric Dolphy

Key musical styles
Majestic bass tone; compositions use improvisation, with frequent tempo changes.

free music. His pieces could be as raucous and colorful as a street parade, as manically soulful as a revivalist service, but darker, more somber, less bound to the song than Basie and less optimistic than Ellington. Mingus gathered musicians of the stature of saxophonists Jackie McLean, Booker Ervin, John Handy, Rahsaan Roland Kirk, and eventually the gifted Eric Dolphy. His music embraced more jazz history and technical range than any composer — evident in pieces as diverse as "Fables of Faubus," "Saturday Night Prayer Meeting," "Better Git It in Your Soul," and "Goodbye Pork Pie Hat."

The Black Saint

Mingus did not trust what he saw as an exploitative entertainment industry — but his independent labels and promotional activities lost money and discouraged him so much that he virtually stopped work in the late 1960s. A Guggenheim fellowship and the publication of his powerful autobiography, *Beneath the Underdog*, brought him back in the early 1970s when he collaborated on movie music and made an album with folk singer Joni Mitchell. After his death in 1979, a huge symphonic piece, *Epitaph*, was found in a jumble of manuscripts. Reconstructed by Gunther Schuller, it expanded perceptions of Mingus's unruly genius. Begun in his teens, the work embraced Jelly Roll Morton's "Wolverine Blues," Vernon Duke's "I Can't Get Started," and notated work from other musical traditions, with hints of Schönberg, Bartók, and Stravinsky.

Charlie Parker

THERE WAS THE ERA of jazz preceding Charlie Parker and the era transformed by him — just as there had been the period before Louis Armstrong arrived and a new landscape after his vision of jazz lit the future of the music. Charlie Parker was the messiah of modern jazz, and when he died, graffiti artists scrawled the words "Bird Lives!" in New York's subways and around Greenwich Village.

Like Armstrong, Parker changed jazz with a unique approach to rhythm and phrasing: a profound conviction that stories in music could be told differently. Like Armstrong, he too played with a passion and fervor that went far beyond technical mastery. Parker, however, was not playing in an idiom that enhanced and extended the potential of popular dance music as Armstrong's work did. He arrived at a point when at least part of his audience was ready to perceive jazz as a serious art form and a symbol of youthful rebellion. Bebop became the soundtrack for bohemian disengagement and the alto saxophone of Charlie Parker a comet in sound devoted to the intense and fleeting moment.

Parker's Mood

Charlie Parker was the son of a Kansas vaudeville performer who left the family home around 1931. Charlie's mother, Addie Parker, devoted to her son, would not let him do odd jobs for pocket money like other kids and gave him everything she could, including his first saxophone. When she secured a job as a night cleaner, Charlie, age 14, went out into Kansas City's clubland, listening to saxophone players like Ben Webster and Lester Young. Young was Parker's hero, an improviser of immense tonal subtlety. Indifferent to his formal education, Charlie Parker devoted all his learning energies to the saxophone, which he taught himself in a personal, eccentric, yet liberating way.

CHARLIE PARKER
"Yardbird, Bird"
*Kansas August 29, 1920 –
New York March 12, 1955*

Key recordings
*Particularly "Now's the Time," "Ko-Ko,"
"Billie's Bounce" 1945; "Ornithology,"
"Yardbird Suite," "A Night in Tunisia"
1946; "Au Privave" 1951*

Key partners
Dizzy Gillespie, Miles Davis, Max Roach

Key musical styles
*Leading founder of bop. Enriched song harmony
to free melodic ideas. Spontaneous
rhythmic and melodic imagination.
Influence only rivaled
by Louis Armstrong.*

Charlie Parker's soaring alto sound was one of the most imitated in jazz. He was regarded as a messiah of post-1940s music, as a virtuoso and conceptual genius, and as a symbol of bohemian dissidence.

Jazz at the time was mostly played in a few key signatures convenient for regular instrumentation. The young Parker was unaware of this, and he learned to play in all of them. One of the characteristics of bebop, which Parker was crucial in developing, was an agility in transposing from one key to another. He practiced constantly, convinced that his methods were right — but it was a confidence that sometimes made him overstep. Sitting in one night at the Reno Club, attempting the kind of key change that players much older than him found difficult, in the midst of a furious "I Got Rhythm," the young Parker became

hopelessly lost. Count Basie's whirlwind drummer Jo Jones completed the humiliation, hurling a cymbal at his feet to gong him off. Parker told his mother, "There's got to be a way." By 1939 he had found it.

When Parker joined Jay McShann, who ran the last of the big-time Kansas City bands at the end of the 1930s, he had made it. He left his hometown at age 19, already married, divorced, and the father of a son. Parker stayed with McShann until 1942, by which time he had made the breakthrough of method. "I kept thinking there's bound to be something else," he said later. "I could hear it but I couldn't play it … I was working over 'Cherokee,' and as I did, I found that by using the higher intervals of a chord as a melody line and backing them with appropriately related [chord] changes, I could play the thing I'd been hearing. I came alive."

Now's the Time

Parker soon met the other New York musicians working toward the same ends: drummer Kenny Clarke, pianist Thelonious Monk, guitarist Charlie Christian, and trumpeter Dizzy Gillespie. The beginnings of bop were explored at Minton's Playhouse and in after-hours and occasional onstage experiments with sympathetic employers like Earl Hines, Coleman Hawkins, and Billy Eckstine. At this point in his life, Charlie Parker's use of narcotics and alcohol — dependencies started in those long Kansas City nights as a teenager —was already a professional liability. But although his punctuality was a problem, his imagination teemed with music.

In 1944, Parker began to record under his own name with a mixture of swing and modern players, and a year later cut the immortal tracks that were to make his reputation. On scraps of paper or during the warm-up to a recording session, Parker wrote tunes that became beacons to jazz musicians everywhere. His improvisations on scalding themes like "Now's the Time," "Billie's Bounce" and "Ko-Ko" were displays of technical virtuosity and energy, switchbacks of phrasing and timing that would constantly subvert expectations, all couched in a tone that could only have descended from the blues. Only Louis Armstrong's playing on his recordings with the Hot Fives and Hot Sevens rivaled Charlie Parker's work in the mid 1940s for sheer fire, originality, and revolutionary influence. *Down Beat* magazine did not appreciate these qualities at the time: it gave "Now's the Time" a no-star rating.

Parker in 1949 with Lennie Tristano, Eddie Safranski, and Billy Bauer during a session at the RCA Victor studio in New York. Tristano's music, although much cooler than Parker's, was strongly influenced by his melodic ideas.

The following year, Parker joined Dizzy Gillespie's band at Billy Berg's West Coast club, stayed on after the group left, and signed to Ross Russell's Dial label. From seven sessions, six albums of phenomenal improvisation resulted, including "A Night in Tunisia," "Ornithology" and "Yardbird Suite." But Parker's physical and mental health were worsening. On the second Dial session, he could barely stand — but he played. His fraught, anguished "Lover Man" is one of the most revealing and emotional of all jazz sessions.

As Parker became better known, impresario Norman Granz involved him in more elaborate but less spontaneous projects, often with strings. Parker was not an unwilling participant, believing that the tribulations of jazz life would ease if he shared the status of conservatory composers like Stravinsky and Varèse. Although some of the Verve recordings with strings show his alto still soaring and a capacity to be romantic as well as brittle and defiant, the earlier small-group sets remain among the most unforgettable 20th-century music.

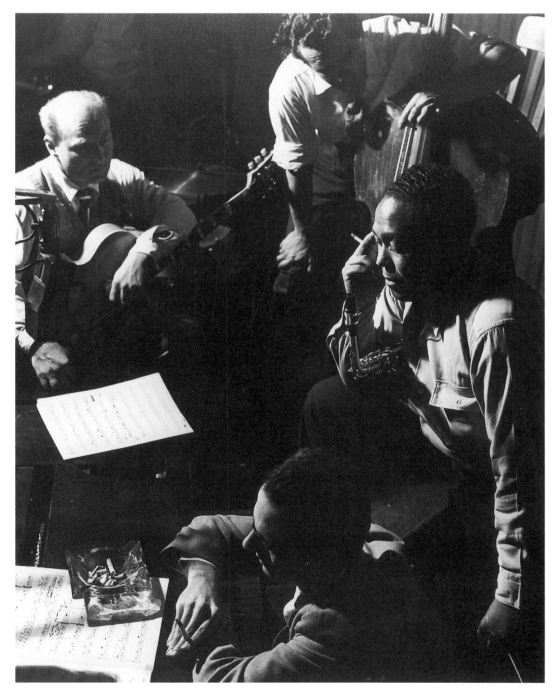

Dizzy Gillespie

WITH CHEEKS INFLATED to bursting and neck muscles like a wrestler's biceps, the image of Dizzy Gillespie at work is a memorable symbol of a music's demands on energy, imagination, and body-and-soul commitment. Throughout the 1940s and until the maturing of Miles Davis, Gillespie was the most imitated trumpeter in jazz, as his partner Charlie Parker was the most imitated saxophonist. With Parker, Charlie Christian, Thelonious Monk, and Kenny Clarke, Gillespie founded the bebop movement, developing a more ambiguous, harmonically complex music out of the materials and methods of swing. Originally an admirer of trumpeter Roy Eldridge, the most dramatic, techni-

cally ambitious brass player bridging New Orleans music and modern jazz, Gillespie developed into an improviser of astonishing accuracy and inventiveness at apparently treacherous tempos, redefining the capabilities of an instrument dependent on embouchure changes rather than keystrokes.

Dizzy Atmosphere

Gillespie was a natural clown and indefatigable showman. While many beboppers cultivated an image of cool reserve to all but a privileged inner circle, Gillespie was prepared to go out and win friends for this music. Originally John Birks Gillespie, he gained his nickname for his antics onstage — hilarious introductions to his material

and musicians and a stream of inspired gibberish as a scat singer. Gillespie also contributed striking compositions, helped engineer the mingling of jazz and Latin music that expanded after the late 1940s, and in his later years virtually defined the role of globetrotting "jazz ambassador." He was to postwar jazz what Louis Armstrong had been to its earlier phases, and he shook hands with enough presidents to tax his memory.

The youngest of nine children, Gillespie was born in South Carolina, son of a bricklayer and amateur bandleader who encouraged an enthusiasm for music and something of a formal education in it. He won a scholarship to Carolina's Laurinburg

A captivating blues player, Gillespie blended vocalized sounds with showers of short note runs and unpredictable shifts of pace, volume, and intensity.

Institute and practiced both trumpet and piano — a pursuit that helped develop the harmonic awareness that was to prove significant as bop, a form of improvisation liberated by harmonic insights, began to blossom. Gillespie imitated Roy Eldridge initially, so successfully that he replaced his departing idol in Teddy Hill's swing band in 1937. There followed a liaison with the commercially successful vocalist and bandleader Cab Calloway, before Calloway finally fired the trumpeter for general disruptiveness and a physical fracas that Calloway would later concede was his fault.

Groovin' High

Gillespie gravitated toward those young swing stars who thought along the same lines as him. Like Charlie Parker and Charlie Christian, he had found the route to fresh phrasing in stacking chords with extra notes and developing techniques for migrating to distant keys in midsolo and finding the way back without a hitch. Parker and Gillespie collaborated in the mid-1940s on the most significant recordings of bebop. Their breathtaking empathy conveyed the adrenaline charge, musicality, and sheer cliff-hanging enthusiasm that bop's pioneers experienced in its early incarnations.

Parker's unpredictability contributed to Gillespie's departure, and Miles Davis, Gillespie's diametric opposite as a player and personality, replaced him. Gillespie meanwhile explored the possibilities for performing bop-oriented music with a big band. He also introduced sidemen such as the short-lived, highly influential Cuban percussionist Chano Pozo to explore Latin-flavored jazz that kept the same urgency and drive to surprise. In *To Be or Not to Bop*, Gillespie wrote: "the people of the calypso, the rhumba, the samba and the rhythms of Haiti all have something in common from the mother of their music. Rhythm. The basic rhythm, because Mama Rhythm is Africa."

Bebop was criticized as antijazz at first, but it soon won a big following.

JOHN BIRKS GILLESPIE
"Dizzy"
South Carolina October 21, 1917 – Englewood, New Jersey January 6, 1993

Key recordings
With Coleman Hawkins in 1944; other all-time great bebop sessions with Charlie Parker 1944-45; "Cubana-Be, Cubana Bop" and "Manteca" with 1947 big band

Key partners
Charlie Parker, Billy Eckstine, Chano Pozo

Key musical styles
Co-founder of the 1940s bebop movement. Fused jazz with Latin music. One of the most widely imitated trumpeters in jazz.

Someone fell on Gillespie's trumpet in 1953, bending the bell. Gillespie liked the result because "I hear the sound quicker." He subsequently had an instrument designed that became a trademark (left).

Dizzy Gillespie not only toured constantly from the 1950s on, but encouraged younger trumpeters: Fats Navarro, Clifford Brown, Lee Morgan, and two younger men he regarded as musical sons, Jon Faddis and Arturo Sandoval. Though a demanding schedule and the popular pressure for a spectacular, pyrotechnical style (seen during his frequent participation in the Norman Granz Jazz at the Philharmonic tours) sometimes seemed to dim his creativity and lessen the clarity of his phrasing, he was capable of scorching performances into his seventh decade.

Jazz Ambassador

A lifelong campaigner for civil rights, for proper treatment of artists regardless of race, and an energetic defender of African-American music's entitlement to the status and investment of a major art form, Gillespie often made apparently frivolous political statements that were underpinned by serious intent. He threatened to run for president in the 1980s, claiming he would rename the White House the Blues House and install Miles Davis as chief of the CIA. He also led the United Nations Band on punishing city-a-night tours in his 70s, reveling in collaborations with younger Latin jazz stars (saxophonist Paquito D'Rivera and trumpeter Arturo Sandoval) as well as long-time partners like saxophonist and composer James Moody.

Gillespie's surreal humor and bohemian dress became models for hipster style. A beret, shades, and goatee were, for awhile, a uniform for "modern jazz."

Miles Davis

No JAZZ MUSICIAN ever played an instrument nearer the most intimate and elusive emotions than Miles Davis. His notes change color like jewels turning at shifting angles to the light, his sound is poignant and personal, and his sense of swing is founded on as instinctive a feel for when not to play as any musician has ever possessed in the often hyperactive music of jazz. When Miles Davis unfolded a story in a solo, he predicted the shape from beginning to end so clearly that his lines effectively disguised the underlying structure and made it all but evaporate. Yet the sense of forward movement was never lost. To have been simply a solo trumpet player of this quality would have been enough. But Miles Davis was also a great innovator and was repeatedly impatient with accepted forms. A true giant of 20th-century music, he profoundly influenced the way jazz is played, not once, but several times during his long career. When he died in September 1991, he was working with Prince and on a rap disk with New York dance-floor producer Easy Mo Bee.

MILES DEWEY DAVIS
*Illinois May 26, 1926 –
California September 28, 1991*

Key recordings
Birth of the Cool *and Blue Note disks
1952-1954;* Workin' *and* Steamin' *1956;*
Kind of Blue *1959;* Miles Ahead *1957;*
Bitches Brew *1970;* You're Under
Arrest, Aura *1985*

Key partners
*Charlie Parker, Gil Evans, John Coltrane,
Herbie Hancock, Tony Williams,
Marcus Miller*

Key musical styles
*Davis made his version of bebop soft and
spacious. Influential exponent of fifties modal
improvising; concertolike orchestral jazz (early
sixties); collective playing mingling hard bop
and modalism (sixties); fusion (late sixties on).*

Son of a St. Louis dentist, Miles Dewey Davis took up the trumpet at 13. He seemed destined for a classical training but became obsessed with the music of Charlie Parker as a teenager. On moving to New York, Davis largely abandoned his studies to follow the saxophonist from club to club, eventually rooming with him and substituting for Dizzy Gillespie in Parker's quintet. At the outset, Davis did not sound like an ideal bop trumpeter. He frequently missed notes, had faulty intonation, and was uncomfortable with fast tempos. But it was not because he had difficulty getting his fingers around bop that he developed a new music out of it. Temperamentally, Davis was a different kind of player, an artist who could hear an as-yet unformed jazz in which improvisation depended on subtleties of tone and timing. These would deepen its emotional appeal and eventually hypnotize the jazz world.

So What
In 1949, at 23, Davis formed a band that sounded like an expanded, tonally enriched version of his trumpet sound — a nine-piece group including French horns and saxophonists Gerry Mulligan and Lee Konitz who were more reserved and low-key than most beboppers. The band's sound depended extensively on the richly layered, ethereal arrangements of a young Canadian, Gil Evans. The band performed rarely, and Davis spent the early 1950s in difficulties with narcotics. When he broke the habit, he made a comeback at the 1955 Newport Jazz Festival. The event gave him the publicity and encouragement to re-engage a working band. His principal partner was a young tenor saxophonist, as fast, dense, and emotionally heated as Davis was withdrawn — John Coltrane. With pianist Red Garland, bassist Paul Chambers, and drummer Philly Joe Jones, the band became one of the most expressive and dynamic in the hard bop movement, enhanced by the marked contrast between Davis's trumpet and the shoulder-charging

Miles Davis
made headlines for turning his back on audiences in the 1950s. In the 1980s, his charisma had not stopped growing. He wanted only that his music should speak for itself and disliked interviews.

vigor of his partners. Davis increasingly used the Harmon mute to make his ballad sound even more brittle and oblique.

This band played with a freedom that made its mid-1950s records classics, but hard bop was still a chordal music, and Davis was growing impatient with it. With records like *Milestones* and *Kind of Blue*, he turned to cycles of scales, or modes, to allow the soloists to stretch. On tracks like "So What" the music began to ripple like waves radiating from stones thrown into water, displacing the linear movement of bop. Davis did not search for his version of freedom only in small groups (the free jazz movement he disliked was taking place simultaneously). Working with arranger Gil Evans, he investigated improvisation against orchestral textures on *Porgy and Bess* and *Sketches of Spain*. Using both the trumpet and the softer-sounding flügelhorn, he was the only soloist, delivering personal soliloquies like a singer.

In the 1960s, Miles Davis moved as close to free jazz as his sense of lyricism and swing would allow, hiring young musicians like 16-year-old drummer Tony Williams, pianist Herbie Hancock, Wayne Shorter from Art Blakey's band on saxes, and Ron Carter on bass. The band still worked modally but abandoned standards to develop a singular empathy that rivaled the mid-1950s band with Coltrane. Moreover, it came close to collective improvisation. The Hancock/Carter/Williams rhythm section's elastic approach to the regular jazz meters altered Davis's style, inviting him to play longer lines, depart from the middle register more often, and at times sound spine-chillingly intense.

But for all the soft poetry of his music, Davis remained a worldly, strong-willed

Davis's trumpet is one of the most imitated and immediately identifiable of all jazz sounds. A self-contained, often demanding man, Davis projected a bruised, mysterious tenderness in his music, allied to a rhythmic sense second to none.

artist. When he realized that more sensitive, spontaneous rock was displacing jazz in the 1960s, and that artists like Jimi Hendrix and Sly Stone were drawing big crowds and making a fortune, Davis tried to recapture the young black audience which was drifting away from jazz. Using his modal quintet, he fused jazz improvisation with rock instrumentation and structures. In the early atmospheric experiments, *In a Silent Way* and *Bitches Brew*, he developed electronic textures — contemporary versions of the tableaux Gil Evans had stretched behind him ten years earlier.

Not all the products of this shift were fruitful. A raft of sensational younger players passed through Davis's fusion bands — Keith Jarrett, Jack DeJohnette, Chick Corea, Dave Holland, John Scofield —

but the music sometimes lacked the light touch and freshness of his earlier recordings and the best new pop to which he was listening closely. Ill health and bouts of uncertainty about his work led to a long layoff in the late 1970s. He returned with a more explicit blend of jazz and pop that linked his eloquent trumpet to pop songs. The magic still worked. The poetry of Miles Davis's sound and conception still bridged cultural and generational divides. His music has had an incalculable effect on almost every idiom currently played.

Thelonious Monk

JAZZ OBSERVERS are often graphic in describing how demanding a Thelonious Monk tune is. John Coltrane, who played in one of the most inventive of Monk groups in the 1950s, said that if you missed a chord change, it was "like falling into an empty elevator shaft." The *New Yorker* critic Whitney Balliett wrote that Monk's use of long pauses made the listener wonder if he had left the recording studio, and that the unexpected twists and suspensions of his melodies were "like missing the bottom step in the dark."

Baptist to Bebop

None of this seemed odd to Monk, who pursued his own course, either bewildered or indifferent to the prevailing view in the 1950s that his music was unusual. Thirty years later, the jangling dissonances in his inimitable tunes no longer obscure the melodic audacity and shapely composition of his pieces, and classical pianists now include them on tributes to the wealth of modern American music.

Monk is generally perceived to be part of the bebop revolution of the 1940s — and not just for his music. His bohemian appearance and an affection for shades and eccentric hats did much to define the image of the postwar hipster. But at root he was a stride player with an adventurous and sophisticated grasp of harmony and an utterly personal sense of time and spacing. Taught piano as a child, he adapted his lessons to accompany his mother's singing in church, and gospel music was a lifelong influence on his playing. Monk worked with a wide range of musicians before he began frequenting the famous Minton's Playhouse where bop was spawned, and in 1943, he joined Coleman Hawkins — a swing musician with a harmonic awareness that could rival that of the beboppers.

False imprisonment on a drug offense and a subsequent ban from the New York clubs kept Monk out of circulation until

Monk's rugged, jolting piano sound is instantly recognizable, his compositions played everywhere today. In the 1950s, his harmonies and timing seemed odd, and work opportunities were unsteady.

the mid-1950s, but not before he had recorded a series of piano improvisations on compositions that were to become jazz classics. Monk's "52nd Street Theme" was recorded by Dizzie Gillespie and Cootie Williams, and "Epistrophy" became Williams's radio theme song. In the 1950s, Miles Davis did much to enhance respect for Monk as a composer with subtle interpretations of his tunes. Monk's own memorable appearance in the movie *Jazz on a Summer's Day* also helped put him back on his rightful throne.

Because Monk's music was so full of dissonances, jagged sounds and idiosyncratic use of space, many jazz soloists found him hard to work with, although the young Coltrane and soprano saxophonist Steve Lacy were ideal partners. As the underlying simplicity and beauty of Monk's ideas became more apparent, tunes like "Well You Needn't" and "Straight No Chaser" became part of the repertoire for many musicians, from swing players to the avant-garde, and the uncharacteristically mellow "Round Midnight" is now one of the most widely played tunes in all jazz. Monk's clangy dissonances and pacing that veered from a long silence to an unexpected gallop made him a refreshingly candid player, indifferent to displays of technique.

Art Blakey

Art Blakey was one of the most thrilling drummers in jazz history, but that was only half the story. Well into his 70th year he continued to campaign for the wider acceptance of jazz and to scout talent among the young. "Tell your square friends about us," Blakey would cajole a club crowd. "I'd hate for a human being to pass through this life and miss out on this music."

Art Blakey emerged in the 1940s when the urbanity of big band swing was being shaken by young bebop stars like Charlie Parker, Dizzy Gillespie, and Thelonious Monk – players whose transformations of Tin Pan Alley song forms were changing jazz forever. The movement's leading drummer, Kenny Clarke, believed that the drums could be a frontline instrument in a band as well as make it swing. Blakey developed a repertoire of explosive snare drum rolls, nudging, hustling accents, and a whirlwind cymbal beat that could create as colorful a sound as an entire ensemble of melody instruments in other bands.

Straight Ahead

In 1954, he formed the first version of the Jazz Messengers with pianist Horace Silver. It became a virtual definition of hard bop, a small band style of longer solos, a strong flavor of blues and gospel, and an excitable, bustling quality that countered the often dispassionate "cool school." Blakey had been a pianist at first, but the presence of a young Errol Garner in the band Blakey led at the age of 15 created difficulties. Blakey would relate how a club owner shifted him from keyboard to drums at gunpoint, and he never looked back. After working with Mary Lou Williams, Billy Eckstine, Thelonious Monk, Miles Davis, and many others, the Messengers became his natural home from the 1950s on, and his gifts as a talent scout

Art Blakey's drumsticks. In use they would be a blur. Blakey pioneered drum techniques used in many musics today.

flowered. Trumpeters Lee Morgan, Clifford Brown, and Freddie Hubbard and saxophonists Johnny Griffin and Wayne Shorter all passed through, with Blakey never shrinking from trusting his younger partners to take care of Messengers arrangements as they saw fit. Through the 1980s, young stars like Wynton and Branford Marsalis, Bobby Watson, and trumpeter Terence Blanchard kept rejuvenating the formula. In his later years, Blakey also became a guru of the "jazz renaissance," a tireless defender of an exuberant and danceable bop-derived jazz that in the 1980s and 1990s was never far from the turntables of young deejays.

Art Blakey was a jazz musician who did not know the meaning of giving less than one hundred percent. Coupled with the youth of most of his partners, it made the Jazz Messengers a consistently compelling outfit. But for all his sound and fury, Blakey was an empathetic listener.

"From the Creator, to the artist, direct to the audience, split-second timing, ain't no other music like that," was Art Blakey's creed. A devoted jazz evangelist, supporting younger fans and players, Art Blakey was a true original.

ART BLAKEY
Abdullah Ibn Buhaina, "Bu"
*Pittsburgh October 11, 1919 –
New York October 16, 1990*

Key recordings
Horace Silver and the Jazz Messengers
1954; Moanin', Blues March *1958;*
A Night in Tunisia *1960;*
Free For All *1964*

Key partners
*Horace Silver, Lee Morgan, Wayne Shorter,
Freddie Hubbard, Wynton Marsalis*

Key musical styles
*Pioneer of hard bop – bebop with a strong
flavor of blues and gospel.
African drumming was a great influence
on Blakey's playing.
His explosive high-hat and snare sounds
cajoled and energized soloists
from the 1950s to the 1990s.*

Sonny Rollins

THEODORE WALTER
ROLLINS
"Sonny," "Newk"
New York September 9, 1930 –

Key recordings
Saxophone Colossus 1956; Way Out
West 1957; The Freedom Suite 1958
The Bridge 1962; Sunny Days,
Starry Nights 1984

Key partners
*Thelonious Monk, Max Roach,
Miles Davis, Don Cherry*

Key musical styles
*Uncompromisingly personal player, uniting
swing sax weight and thematic approach with
bebop's speed. Fondness for Caribbean music.*

I N TODAY'S JAZZ, a player whose style encompasses bop, blues, calypso, and funk isn't a rarity. But Sonny Rollins has been applying the intuition that virtually expels cliché from improvisation to a mixture of popular and quirkily personal materials for forty years. Rollins's parents came from the Virgin Islands, and Caribbean dance music has always appealed to him. He came to the saxophone in the "jump music" era that preceded rock and roll, and this also left a lasting taste. But there is so much more to Sonny Rollins: a single extended saxophone improvisation by him (and some are very extended) can sound like a fast rewind through the history of Western popular music, assembled in such an idiosyncratic manner as to border on the abstract.

Rollins's siblings were all students of classical music, but a saxophone-playing uncle who liked the blues diverted him. He absorbed the styles of the saxophone idols of the 1940s: Coleman Hawkins's dramatic big tone and skill as an embellisher of chords rather than tunes, Lester Young's more whimsical storytelling skills, and Charlie Parker's headlong synthesis of both. Combining these with his affection for Louis Jordan's jump-style sax playing, Rollins emerged with a unique clout, speed, swing, and teeming spontaneous invention. The bop pianist Thelonious Monk also influenced Rollins greatly, making his solos more fragmented and unpredictable in melodic direction, and adding an inclination to beachcomb familiar material and subvert it, often with sardonic humor.

Rollins worked with Miles Davis for a while in the early 1950s and joined Clifford Brown, and Max Roach's great hard-bop group in 1956. By the end of the decade, often with Roach, he had recorded some of his most enduring work, including the classic albums *Saxophone Colossus*, *Way Out West* and *Newk's Time*. *Saxophone Colossus*, besides including one of Rollins's most energetic calypsos in "St. Thomas" and an imperious version of "Mack the Knife" ("Moritat"), featured a long improvisation on a baleful mid-tempo blues, "Blue Seven," full of slurred, bleary notes, spiraling bursts of bebop, and a steadily building intensity that makes it rightly regarded as one of the greatest recorded jazz solos. Rollins does much the same on "Come Gone" from *Way Out West*, a mixture of dogged worrying at recurrent phrases and blistering double time; his characteristic affection for odd materials is borne out by the inclusion of tunes such as "Wagon Wheels" and "I'm an Old Cowhand." The celebrity status that came to Rollins during this period never blunted his natural desire to learn and develop, which he traces back to competition with older brothers and sisters.

Rollins was once as famous for his idiosyncrasies as for his devastating horn playing: Mohawk haircut, shaved head, exotic hats. He would sometimes arrive at clubs already playing his opener in the cab.

Coinciding with the rise of the avant-garde, Rollins took a two-year sabbatical from 1959 to 1961, to investigate complex problems he was setting himself over the relationship of improvisation and structure. He had known the major architect of free jazz, Ornette Coleman, in the 1950s, and on returning from the layoff, began working with two key Coleman sidemen, trumpeter Don Cherry and drummer Billy Higgins. The resulting music was looser and rougher but still infused with the unflagging energy with which he could pile new ideas on top of each other in the course of a single furious solo.

Rollins recorded six albums in the three years after his comeback in 1961. *The Bridge* was one of the best known, named after his penchant for practicing on the catwalk of the Williamsburg Bridge during his withdrawal from performance. But the restless Rollins was still unconvinced that his methods were right, and in 1966 he took a second and longer sabbatical, this time lasting five years.

A New Perspective

In more recent times Sonny Rollins has allowed the musical enthusiasms of his early years to surface more often, and many of his recordings of the past decade have included a good deal more relaxed funk, romantic balladeering and infectious soul music. But Rollins is a peerless unaccompanied improviser. At some point in a live performance, he will enter the spotlight on his own and allow that still mercurial and willful musical intelligence to ransack the immense store of melody in his head and reassemble it in bewitchingly unpredictable ways. At London's Ronnie Scott's Club, they still recall the finale of a Rollins performance in the 1960s. The act of saying goodnight to the audience suddenly triggered a string of memories for Rollins of every Tin Pan Alley song he could remember with "goodnight" in the title. He went on unaccompanied for another hour, barely taking a breath. The drive constantly to remake new music out of old is part of the spirit of jazz, and Sonny Rollins remains a dazzling exponent of it.

One of the few musicians of the first hard bop generation still functioning in an imposing way, Sonny Rollins plays more light fusion than before, but his solo performances remain spontaneous imaginative triumphs.

John Coltrane

WHEN JAZZ MUSICIANS in the 1960s developed styles that broke with accepted notions of what songs and swing were, neither the record industry nor the public was impressed. John Coltrane was an exception. His saxophone would wail and thunder, or be soulful and tender, but in any mood it reached far beyond the inner circle of jazz fans. *A Love Supreme*, Coltrane's most famous recording, sold well enough to turn a generation of rock fans toward a musical leader who did not play guitar.

Coltrane was the ideal symbol for a generation mistrustful of consumerism. Deeply religious, he seemed like a man on a mission, devoted to expressing the music of another dimension through a saxophone. He was shy and obsessively hardworking, yet, for all his unworldliness, engaged with the political ferment of his time. Explicit civil rights messages ("Alabama" was drawn from a Martin Luther King speech) confirmed this and conveyed the opposite message to 1950s cool jazz.

Coltrane's complex journey began with alto horn and clarinet, and saxophone at 15. Like many young black saxophonists, his early experience was in rhythm and blues, with stars of the style, Eddie "Cleanhead" Vinson and Earl Bostic. Coltrane also absorbed bebop, working in the Dizzy Gillespie Orchestra in the late 1940s, then with Johnny Hodges. A model at this time was tenorist Dexter Gordon's attack and big bluesy sound. Charlie Parker, Sonny Rollins, and Sun Ra's tenorist John Gilmore affected his style too.

Workin' and Steamin'

When Miles Davis made his triumphant return to the spotlight in 1955, Coltrane became the typhoonlike counterbalance to his celebrated reticence. But as steadily as Miles Davis was moving away from bebop chords, the saxophonist was digging relentlessly deeper into them. In a famous exchange, Coltrane told his boss that, once immersed in a solo, he didn't know how to

Though Sidney Bechet adopted the soprano saxophone in 1919, it was rarely used until Coltrane popularized it. The penetrating, passionate *My Favorite Things* turned a generation of saxophonists on to it.

stop. "Try taking the saxophone out of your mouth," said Davis. But he knew Coltrane's style was unique, claiming it was like hiring three saxophone players in one.

If Parker was a bird in flight, Coltrane was a river bursting its banks. To make the onrush of sound ever more urgent, he experimented by substituting even more chords than bebop had, at times shifting the harmony virtually every beat. He told Wayne Shorter that his aim was to start in the middle of a sentence and progress to its beginning and end at the same time.

Coltrane was hooked on narcotics and alcohol for much of the 1950s, and when a deepening religious conviction guided him away from them, it became the focus of his life and work. In 1957, he joined Thelonious Monk's quartet, and this short-lived group became a classic band. The saxophonist's harmonic insights made him

one of the few able to improvise over the pianist's angular themes. Coltrane reappeared with Miles Davis for the pioneering *Kind of Blue*, his tone now a full-throated majestic sound like a gospel singer, his ballad style starkly tender. As Coltrane's phrasing became increasingly impacted and layered, critic Ira Gitler dubbed it "sheets of sound," an expression that stuck.

Giant Steps

Around 1960, two records pointed to the future — *Giant Steps* and *Coltrane Jazz*. *Giant Steps* wrung every last gasp of life from bebop chord change playing. "Harmonique" on *Coltrane Jazz* shows the tentative use of overtones to play several notes at once, exploring a previously unconsidered upper range. Miles Davis's modal investigations also released Coltrane from overloading chords with notes. He began to improvise around cycles of scales, the escape offered by modalism (see page 136).

Coltrane settled on the ideal partners for his own group in pianist McCoy Tyner, bassist Jimmy Garrison, and drummer Elvin Jones. Jones had as powerful an impact on drumming as Kenny Clarke and Max Roach had twenty years before. He spread the pulse away from the ride cymbal to a tidal surge of sound, using fully all the kit. Tyner's piano was so percussive that it often carried the beat, allowing Jones to concentrate on texture. Coltrane took up the little-used soprano saxophone, capturing the whooping, exultant upper

Coltrane's records were pored over by aspiring sax players.

range he was trying to reach on the tenor. Following the more radical *Ascension* in 1965 (a wild celebration of group dynamics and timbres), he made an ever more intense, incantatory succession of recordings in his last two years, eventually with a new group including saxophonist Pharoah Sanders and second wife Alice on keyboards.

John Coltrane died of liver failure in 1967. His work was sometimes unresolved and seemed like the pursuit of the inexpressible, but energy and humility were his twin strengths and the source of his charisma. "You can't ram philosophies down anybody's throat," he told Frank Kofsky. "I think the best thing I can do . . . is try to get myself in shape and know myself." That discipline spoke so clearly to the future that musicians not yet born when Coltrane died find him as powerful a mix of teacher and saint as did his own generation.

JOHN COLTRANE
"Trane"
North Carolina September 23, 1926 –
New York July 17, 1967

Key recordings
Blue Train *1957;* Kind of Blue *with Miles Davis,* Giant Steps *1959;* My Favorite Things *1960;* A Love Supreme *1964;* Ascension *1965*

Key partners
Miles Davis, Thelonious Monk, McCoy Tyner, Elvin Jones, Alice Coltrane, Pharoah Sanders

Key musical styles
Learned tenor in r & b bands. Concentrated on deepening scope of bebop harmonies in 1950s. Studied scales and modes exhaustively, developing unprecedented speed and facility to play two lines at once. Greatly extended upper range.

Coltrane's uncompromisingly personal jazz is still idolized and imitated by players everywhere. He revolutionized saxophone technique and intensified the small-group sound.

Ornette Coleman

THE YOUNG swing rebels of the 1930s broke the treadmill of dance music chords and jazz improvisation dependent on Tin Pan Alley. But bop became a treadmill itself. If jazz improvisation meant only juggling the related scales of pop songs, reasoned Texan saxophonist Ornette Coleman, why not forget improvising and just learn solos note for note? Coleman's bold dismissal of previously crucial material was one of the most startling departures in jazz history, and he became the principal and most volatile catalyst of free jazz or the New Thing in the early 1960s.

Coleman began to play professionally in his teens, in the blues bands popular in his native Fort Worth. Though his early playing echoed Charlie Parker's phrasing, Coleman was absorbed in the saxophone's sound. As he practiced he repeated the same note over and over, exploring colorations of tone. Steeped in southern blues, his sax resembled a blues singer's voice, had a strong beat, and echoed bop phraseology, but was dislocated from chords. Coleman made it clear that he was interested in the song, not the structure. Moving to Los Angeles later in the 1950s, he found sympathetic partners in bassist Charlie Haden, trumpeter Don Cherry, and the drummers Billy Higgins and Ed Blackwell. In a Los Angeles garage, they developed a collaborative music in which shifts of line, rhythm, and mood evolved organically, one performer picking up another's ideas. *Something Else* and

Tomorrow Is the Question announced these changes almost overnight and instantly polarized the jazz world. Some nonjazz composers (Gunther Schuller and Leonard Bernstein) and the Modern Jazz Quartet's John Lewis embraced Coleman's adventurousness. Others labeled him an inept musician taking the arts establishment for a ride.

Gradually, sympathetic listeners realized that his improvisations were far from random. Though he might color a fluid ballad with sudden guffaws, or play blues in compressed or extended forms, his music reflected the passions and ambiguities of life as vividly as early blues. Much of his work bridged formal music and jazz, with string quartets, wind quintets, and powerful symphonic works. In 1967, he won the first Guggenheim Fellowship for jazz. In the early 1970s he embraced electronic dance music and funk, bringing to them his "harmolodic" theory of spontaneous ensemble ideas (see page 136) in the electric band Prime Time. This unleashed an imposing group of young, free funk, "no wave" musicians. Above all, many regard him as one of the great geniuses of the blues.

ORNETTE COLEMAN
Fort Worth, Texas March 9, 1930 –

Key recordings
Something Else – The Music of Ornette Coleman *1958;* The Shape of Jazz to Come *1959;* Free Jazz *1960;* Dancing In Your Head *1975;* Song X *1988*

Key partners
Ed Blackwell, Billy Higgins, Don Cherry, Charlie Haden, Denardo Coleman

Key musical styles
Fundamentally a blues player, Coleman adopted collective improvising based on shifting tone centers, intuitively picked up. He developed this into his harmolodic theory.

Ornette Coleman became a guru to the 1960s free jazz movement. Though he was controversial at the outset, his links with the expressiveness of early jazz and blues later became self-evident.

Coleman's live shows grew fewer as he fought for fair pay for jazz.

Keith Jarrett

Pianist Keith Jarrett is one of the biggest box-office attractions in the jazz world. He records constantly, tours extensively, and improvises in the world's most prestigious concert halls under the most testing circumstances, unaccompanied or with only drums and bass. Jarrett refuses to be constrained by musical differences. A virtuoso pianist in any idiom, he has written symphonic works and recorded Bach on church organ and harpsichord. Some speculate that if Liszt had been born in the same time and place, this is how he would play. Jarrett's 1975 disk *The Köln Concert* is the best-selling solo piano record ever.

Jarrett's unique chemistry forces nineteenth-century romanticism, country music, gospel, and blues to react together. An infant prodigy at age three, he gave recitals of classical music and his own compositions at age seven, and after a stormy relationship with formal music education, he rose spectacularly to the front rank of jazz artists through periods with Blakey's Jazz Messengers, the Miles Davis band, and a pioneering jazz-rock fusion group led by cult saxophonist Charles Lloyd.

Keith Jarrett is visually as well as musically charismatic, leaping from the stool while playing, and making ecstatic cries.

Working as a sideman in someone else's band never suited Jarrett. During the stint with Davis, he began to develop his own music with partners including bassist Charlie Haden, drummer Paul Motian, and saxophonist Dewey Redman. The music suggested the mingled influences of Ornette Coleman, Paul Bley, and Bill Evans. Jarrett found Miles Davis's music too restrictive and developed an intense dislike of electric instruments. His natural habitat outside his classical exploits became composed work under his own control, a small group of empathetic partners, or the solo recital. Despite being one of the strongest musical personalities in contemporary jazz and improvised music, Jarrett's appeal for many over the last decade has been his celebration of great Tin Pan Alley standards in the company of creative partners bassist Gary Peacock and drummer Jack DeJohnette. The Standards Trio's name describes both the material played and the reassertion of traditional "standards" of craft and music making reminiscent of the late Bill Evans's trios.

A contemplative man and a combative thinker, Keith Jarrett is dedicated to the

A brief participator in fusion, Jarrett now vehemently opposes electronic music.

notion of musicians deepening and broadening their consciousness of personal potential, regardless of any commercial considerations. He believes that making this discovery "rather than just playing all the notes" marks an irreversible life change for any musician.

KEITH JARRETT
Pennsylvania May 8, 1945 –

Key recordings
Charles Lloyd's Dream Weaver *1966;*
Belonging *1974;* The Köln Concert
1975; Standards *1983*

Key partners
*Charlie Haden, Paul Motian,
Gary Peacock, Jack DeJohnette*

Key musical styles
Embraces many styles of jazz and romantic classical music. His 1970s group albums echoed Ornette Coleman, his 1980s trio the classic Bill Evans band.

4

TECHNIQUES

Marginalized or romanticized for decades, jazz has been surrounded by misconceptions that seem superficially too glamorous to make way for the truth.

One of the most enduring is that jazz performers simply make it all up as they go along, freewheeling without structure or theory. While the improviser's imagination of a Charlie Parker or Miles Davis is not given to everyone, jazz does have its formal principles — and although they are constantly evolving, they have guided the music's performers from the most supremely gifted like John Coltrane, to modest supper club entertainers in thousands of dimly lit rooms around the globe.

In principles of harmony and melody, jazz and Western classical music often come together; in rhythm they are far apart. These pages focus on the formal elements that combine to unleash the incandescent chemistry of improvisation, and also look at the vocabulary of jazz dance, which has accompanied the music since its birth.

Musical roots

JAZZ IS NOT A MUSIC of Africa or the New World alone. A 1920s West African village musician would not have recognized the King Oliver Creole Band as a branch of the same tree. Western listeners to African drum choirs, overlaying rhythms to deliver a message as rich in meaning and emotion as European classical music, first heard a wall of noise. The fusion of two ancient cultures in a new land gave the 20th century a true "rhythm of the world."

North America

African ritual, celebration, work song, and multirhythmic sounds met the European music of the army, church, and recital room in North America in the 18th and 19th centuries. Expressive hybrids evolved.

The blues, the song form central to jazz, then rock and roll, developed in the late 19th century from a mix of African field hollers and Christian hymn harmonies.

Psalm-singing, as practiced in New England churches from the 1600s, revealed antiphony, the congregation responding to a preacher.

Ragtime was a European style of piano music with a distinctly African rhythmic undertow.

In New Orleans, Dahomean *voudun* rituals were smuggled into Catholicism. French army brass traditions had been absorbed by the city's freed slave population, and around 1900 the gleeful thump of a street band was the perfect basis for a new form of music. The first wave of jazz broke when the marching bands began to swing and to play the blues.

Central and South America

Of the 12 million Africans brought to the Americas as slaves, two-thirds went to Central or South America and the Caribbean. The musical traditions they brought with them were as distinctive as the tribes that were forced to sing, dance, and drum for their captors on those floating prisons.

In Catholic-run colonies, dancing and drums were not outlawed as morally suspect and politically disruptive as they were in the Protestant North, so the rhythmic subtlety of the African rituals was better preserved. The celebratory, ritualistic elements of Catholicism, with its frequent festivals, provided opportunities to nourish them. The dominant beat in Latin America works in groups of paired pulses, with varied accents quite different from conventional jazz swing's jumpy triplets. It found a way into jazz almost at the outset, with versions from Cuba and Brazil becoming most common.

In Cuba the predominant African music came from the Yoruba people and was maintained in secret societies and the religious cults of *Shango* and *santeria*. African drums mingled with Spanish song melodies, and dances developed like the rhumba, conga, and cha-cha. The tango (from an African word) developed from the habanera (Havana). Cuban rhythms fed into jazz at its birth, with real prominence from the 30s.

Jamaica, a British colony, has a musical life in Rastafarian drumming, dub, ska, reggae, and even ragga that is still traceable to the Ashantis who began to work its fields more than 200 years ago.

In Trinidad, strong West African traditions like ridicule songs merged with Spanish and French influences to create calypso. Steel bands evolved after the British banned drums. Both are the essence of the "mas" Carnival processions.

In Haiti, *voudun* (voodoo) traditions have strong remains of pure African ritual — despite crossovers like the meringue based on French folk song — because the blacks threw off French rule in 1804, and were less influenced by Europe.

Brazilian plantations were worked by Sudanese, Bantu, and Muslim Guinea-Sudanese people in whom Portuguese slave traders specialized. Colonies of runaway slaves kept the cultures strong. Musicians there today play a wider variety of African, European, and indigenous percussion than anywhere in the Americas. The samba (from an African beat) was played in Brazilian street festivals by schools of drummers before it was ever a hit in the world's ballrooms.

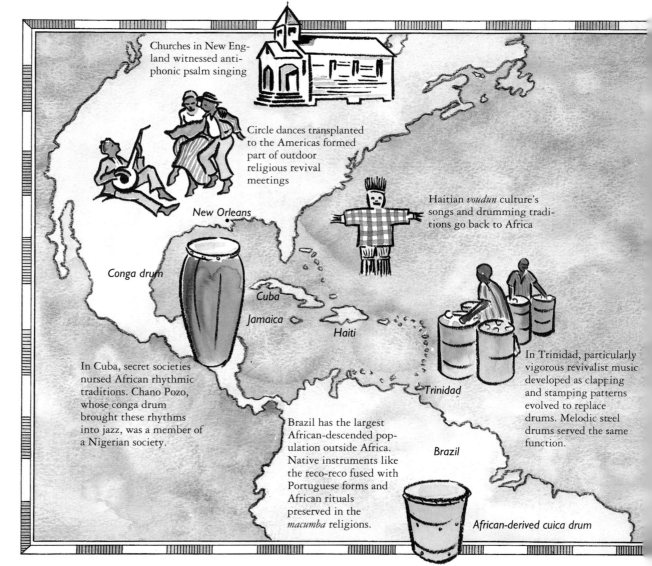

Churches in New England witnessed antiphonic psalm singing

Circle dances transplanted to the Americas formed part of outdoor religious revival meetings

New Orleans

Haitian *voudun* culture's songs and drumming traditions go back to Africa

Conga drum

Cuba

Jamaica

Haiti

In Cuba, secret societies nursed African rhythmic traditions. Chano Pozo, whose conga drum brought these rhythms into jazz, was a member of a Nigerian society.

In Trinidad, particularly vigorous revivalist music developed as clapping and stamping patterns evolved to replace drums. Melodic steel drums served the same function.

Trinidad

Brazil has the largest African-descended population outside Africa. Native instruments like the reco-reco fused with Portuguese forms and African rituals preserved in the *macumba* religions.

Brazil

African-derived cuica drum

Europe

The traditional songs of French, Spanish, English, Scottish, Irish, Italian, German, and Slavonic music all went into the melting pot of the 19th-century seaport New Orleans with its unique location. Jigs, hornpipes, and square dances from northern Europe were incorporated into African dances by the slaves in the hope of making the entertainment of their captors more palatable. In the sea chanteys sung by black roustabouts in the Southern cotton ports, African work songs blended with material sometimes even adapted from the English music hall.

The English church custom prevalent in the 17th century of "lining out" — in which illiterate congregations were obliged to repeat phrases from the preacher — mixed readily with African call-and-response practice.

French quadrilles were the base of many rags. The French education of many of New Orleans' mixed-race Creoles contributed much to the instrumental virtuosity of the district, heard in musicians like Jelly Roll Morton and Sidney Bechet.

The flamenco tradition of Spain, reflected in Latin American music that has constantly recrossed the path of jazz, is rhythmically complex and improvisational. It derives from the Moorish connection with Africa.

The brass band common in every French village since the time of Napoleon had a profound influence on early jazz, which took its lineup and instrumentation.

European military band

Spanish flamenco

West Africa

As the Muslim culture penetrated Africa, Middle Eastern musical traditions fused with indigenous forms

The complex polyrhythms of drum choirs define African rhythm

The pentatonic scale, common in Africa, consists of five notes, as opposed to the European seven-note diatonic scale

Africa's music was the machinery of a community's rituals rather than the oil on its wheels. This carved staff was part of Yoruba funeral rites.

African malleable tonality and indeterminate pitch produced abrupt, exclamatory accents. A conventionally pitched note would range into dramatic, upward-skidding whoops — falsetto sounds that have echoed all the way from distant greetings across the African bush to the cotton fields, railroad boxcars, and urban streets of the United States, and eventually to both black and white rock and roll artists of the 1950s and singers of free jazz rediscovering their musical roots in the 1960s and 1970s.

Call-and-response (antiphony) is another characteristic musical pattern found all over West Africa, particularly in work-related song. Several participants, even one person and an instrument, announce, then echo and embellish a significant phrase. It resurfaced in America's revivalist church, and swing bands.

The Middle East and Asia

The worlds of the Middle East and Asia have affected jazz more in philosophical terms than musical, although the Muslim influence of Middle Eastern music on Africa must be considered. Particularly from the 40s, African-American musicians embraced Islam, and in the 60s Indian spiritual principles affected jazz and rock performers. Jazz musicians have often used instruments from these cultures to vary texture and tone. Since both Arabic and Indian forms of music are founded on modes, there has been a continuing dialogue with jazz as modal principles have increasingly come to influence jazz improvisation.

Africa

Slave traders thought that the wealth they discovered in West Africa was powerful enough to cut cotton, but powerless to take a percentage of its receipts. Inadvertently, they also shipped a fortune of another kind — the wealth of musical traditions and ideas in the hearts and minds of the newcomers.

Overlapping rhythms in West African ritual dance — the beats of several percussion instruments, claps, shouts, and stamps — become so convoluted as to be indecipherable to an untrained ear. Writer Marshall Stearns observed that a simultaneous combination of 3/4, 6/8 and 4/4 time — a mix of tempos far more complex than anything in the Western classical tradition — was not uncommon for a drum choir.

The melody line is different, too. When the African five-note (pentatonic) scale met a seven-note European (diatonic) scale in the Americas, odd pitch intervals arose where the extra notes in the European system occurred. The result was a way of hitting notes that was quite different from the way musicians traditionally approached the "purer" — or more inflexible — tempered European scale.

Religious music, particularly that connected with ancestor worship, is a tradition common to many African peoples that was transmitted to the New World, as were ring-shout dances, where people become possessed through dance and rhythm.

Melody

Melody is much older than harmony, although in European classical music they are often thought of as inseparable. Jazz melody first grew from that European connection, as the "top line" of the harmonies of marches, hymns, polkas and waltzes, and their pop song descendents. But melodies used in jazz were often tinged with the bent, sliding sounds of African music. As the rhythmic ambiguities of swing evolved, revolutionary improvised jazz phrasing like Armstrong's changed ideas about accent and emphasis, and the effect rubbed off on the way jazz melody was conceived. The earthiest, bluesiest tunes of early jazz came back in the free era, although often in apparently random sequences, and melodies based on rhythmic patterns and riffs returned with funk. Modal music, scale-based melody, allowed African-American music to draw on melodic ideas from the great musical cultures of the Middle East and

Miles Davis constantly helped redefine jazz melody – notably on modal principles in the 1950s.

The musical scale

When locating pitch, blues and early jazz musicians – many of whom never wrote their material down – turned to the shorthand of European classical music as the most practical language. The ascents and descents of pitch were thus recorded as steps on a ladder or "staff," expressed horizontally to indicate their duration in time, as well as vertically to indicate pitch.

𝄞 **The treble clef,** an embroidered G centered on the G line, represents the middle to upper range on the staff – musical notation is divided between low- and high-pitched instruments on two separate staves.

𝄢 **The bass clef,** symbolized by a stylized F, represents the notes below middle C. It is used to notate deeper instruments such as the trombone and double bass, or lower piano parts.

Extra "ledger lines" above or below the staves are added to represent exceptionally low or high notes outside the outer limits of the treble and bass clefs.

Middle C – the piano keyboard's central note – is a focal point in notation

Treble clef

Staff

Bass clef

G A B C D E F G A B C D E F G A B C D E F

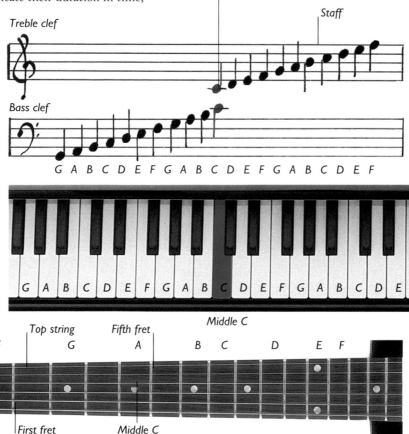

Accidentals Singing the "major scale" – do-re-mi-fa-sol-la-ti-do – covers the simple intervals of music. But the gaps between notes can be narrower – half the value in European music, narrower still in other cultures. "Accidental" signs indicate these. A half step up is

|Sharp |Flat |Natural

represented by the sharp sign #, a half step down by the flat sign ♭. To cancel these half steps, a composer uses a natural sign ♮.

On the piano keyboard notes are arranged in a linear format. The sequential way in which scales ascend or descend, and chords (harmonious "vertical" combinations of notes) are constructed, means that many jazz musicians find it easier to compose or arrange on the piano keyboard, even if it is not their usual instrument.

Middle C

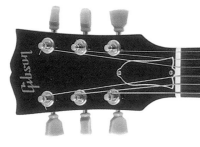

Top string   *Fifth fret*

F   G   A   B   C   D   E   F

First fret   *Middle C*

The guitar fretboard is a sequence of "positions" – E on the top and bottom open strings, A at the fifth fret, and so on. A scale is played by moving up the string to the bridge, or playing equivalent notes on adjoining strings across the neck.

Scales in action

The major scale is the simplest, most widely used scale in European music, and has clear and emphatic characteristics. It involves a sequence of eight notes, passing from a key note (here C) up to the same note an octave (eight notes) away. Many hymns, children's songs, anthems, and military themes are derived from these sequences, as is much conventional jazz.

C major scale

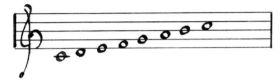

Minor scales are often subjectively described as sounding sadder or more contemplative. The steps between the notes are reduced in some places, and the effect is as if the purposeful march of the major scale is made more hesitant or tentative by the shorter "steps." Many pop and jazz ballads are composed in minor scales.

C minor scale

The blue note scale gives jazz much of its character. In it, the third and seventh notes of a conventional scale are played or sung slightly flat or between pitches. Its origins may lie in the attempts of voices untrained in European music to sing hymns, but African spoken languages also depend more on subtle pitch variation for meaning.

Blue note scale

Modal scales from older musical systems, non-European cultures, and the medieval church use sequences of scales as a base for melody. There are seven sequences of notes, each starting at a different note of a major scale and ascending to the same note an octave above. Because the tones and half tones appear in different places in each mode, depending on the first note, every one has its own character and classical Greek name.

Dorian scale

"Sweet Georgia Brown," a classic, 32-bar early pop song, uses almost all the notes in the major scale, some only slightly reordered. The main characteristic of the scale – its "major third" note (E) – occurs in each bar, and imparts the tune's jaunty, positive feel.

The third note in the major scale – E – known as the major third appears in each bar

The tune is rooted in the tonic, or first note of the scale – C

"Round Midnight," the Thelonious Monk classic, passes through several key changes that add to its ambiguous quality – but the "minor third" note (E flat) establishes its ruminative mood.

The phrase ends on the third note of the minor scale, E flat

Such indeterminate pitches elude classical notation, because the degree of inflection is governed only by the performer's technique and responses to the music. Their occurrence in African-American music as evolved in the United States is unique, and the use of blue notes gives jazz much of its character. In traditional blues, the third, seventh, and occasionally the fifth of the scale gets this treatment, but in modern jazz, as exemplified by the work of Ornette Coleman in particular, this flexibility of pitching may be applied to any note.

"So What," recorded by Miles Davis on *Kind of Blue*, is based on the Dorian scale, the C major notes beginning a tone further up on D. This mode evokes a floating, suspended feeling. *Kind of Blue* established the popular use of modal scales in jazz, for a displaced, ethereal feel.

All the notes are from the Dorian scale: the white notes on the piano keyboard running from D to D

The key phrase of the melody begins and ends on the first note of the scale, D

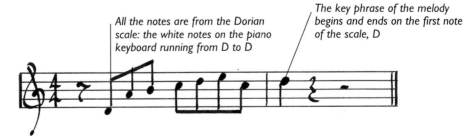

Rhythm

RHYTHM IS THE PATTERN of music in time. The pattern of heartbeats and the patterns of beats in music are both the materials of rhythm, and while a rhythmic music can exist on its own (like drum music, or like some hip hop and rap), a melodic music cannot exist without rhythm. Because its early history was intimately connected with dance, and because of earlier antecedents in African music, rhythm has assumed a significance higher than that of melody in the development of jazz. Yet "swing," the elusive and unique rhythmic quality of jazz, existed neither in traditional African music nor in Europe but grew in the New World. Swing is the creative tension between clock time and feeling time, of objective and subjective time, that gives jazz its distinctive sound.

With drummer Elvin Jones jazz rhythm evolved from a steady march time to complex polyrhythms recalling an African inheritance.

Note values

The vertical positioning of a note shows its pitch, and small variations in the symbol show how long or short it is. But just as fractions of clock time mean nothing unless the length of a day is also known, subdivisions of musical time are related to groupings of beats occurring between the bar lines of a particular piece. On the right are the variations in notes and their equivalent silences (rests), from the whole note — lasting a bar — down.

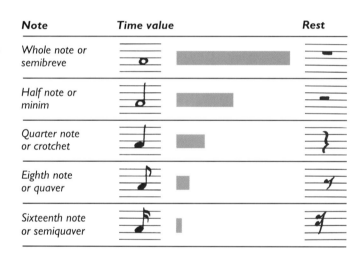

Note	Time value		Rest
Whole note or semibreve			
Half note or minim			
Quarter note or crotchet			
Eighth note or quaver			
Sixteenth note or semiquaver			

A dot placed after a note extends its duration by half of the original value, and a double dot adds half the value of the first dot. Using the same formula, dots can be applied to rests. Dots that appear above or below a note indicate staccato (short, detached) playing.

Note	Time value

Grouping notes

At the start of a piece of music, a fractionlike figure describes the basic rhythmic feel. The upper number shows how many beats there are in the bar. The lower number expresses the duration, or value, of each beat: a 4, for example, corresponds to the quarter note.

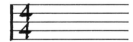

Duple time is the grouping of beats in twos and fours in a bar. Four-four time or common time, written 4/4 (four quarter notes in a bar) or **c**, is familiar in jazz. 2/4 is a steady march; two half notes in a bar, written 2/2 or **¢**, is a samba time.

Triple time describes patterns of notes broken down into threes. The 1-2-3/1-2-3 feel of a waltz is the most common version, written 3/4. A triplet is a group of three notes with 3 written above, played in the same time as two notes.

Ride cymbal · *Snare drum* · *Bass drum* · *High hat cymbal*

Drum notation

Drummers, too, use notated music but it is a form of notation that expresses only rhythm, accent (strong and weak sounds), and the part of the drumkit the sound is played on. A crossed note is commonly used to indicate cymbal beats, which may be on the high hat or the ride cymbal. Arrows above or below the note, called accents, show where the rhythmic emphasis is to fall.

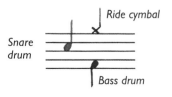

Ride cymbal · *Snare drum* · *Bass drum*

A chronology of jazz drumming

Early New Orleans jazz drumming used military instruments and techniques — two-beat march tempos on bass and snare drums, the cymbal rarely appearing except in resolutions and conclusions. As New Orleans ensemble music developed, drumming became more varied, triplet figures became more common, and percussion ideas adapted from the phrasing of the soloists gave bands a more integrated feel.

Swing arrived too subtly to assign it a particular exponent or debut date. It is also difficult to attribute its effect to the simple accentuation of offbeats rather than strong beats — rather, the whole "feel" changed. Although almost impossible to define or notate accurately, the rhythm is looser, more fluent, sensuous and relaxed, the overlapping of an African and European sense of time.

With bebop, the emphasis on beats two and four — the main carrier of a symmetrical staccato "backbeat" — fades, freeing the accenting of the beat to roam wider. The main rhythmic line moves to the cymbal, and the double bass (not notated) takes over the "even-four" marking of the pulse as the beats on different parts of the drumkit coincide more irregularly.

In fusion, the triplet feel is displaced by the old duple rhythm, but in a multiple form based on funk style straight eighth-note patterns. Early jazz rock drumming emphasized the backbeats — two and four — against a flow of eighths (pairs of strokes on a single beat). Newer versions are more fluid: some drummers even work to their own displaced parallel bar lines.

Latin music has been a constant influence on jazz. As in jazz rock, the basic subdivision of the beat is a pair, not a jazzy triplet, but the accented beats have an irregular pattern. Cuban music constantly found its way into jazz until the 1950s, as did Brazilian dance rhythms from the samba and bossa nova in the next decade. Brazilian percussionists introduced new subtlety to the complex chemistry of bop and rock.

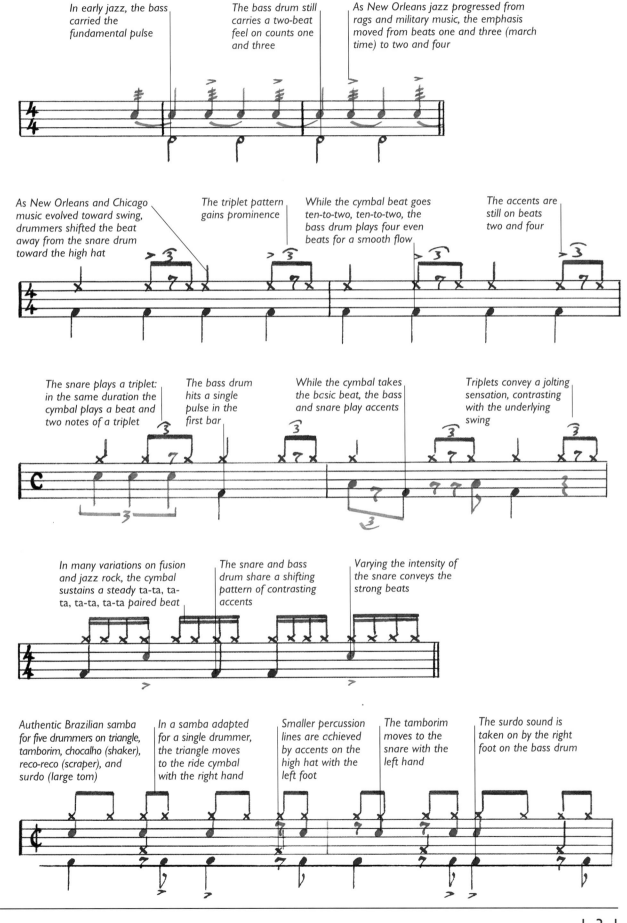

In early jazz, the bass carried the fundamental pulse

The bass drum still carries a two-beat feel on counts one and three

As New Orleans jazz progressed from rags and military music, the emphasis moved from beats one and three (march time) to two and four

As New Orleans and Chicago music evolved toward swing, drummers shifted the beat away from the snare drum toward the high hat

The triplet pattern gains prominence

While the cymbal beat goes ten-to-two, ten-to-two, the bass drum plays four even beats for a smooth flow

The accents are still on beats two and four

The snare plays a triplet: in the same duration the cymbal plays a beat and two notes of a triplet

The bass drum hits a single pulse in the first bar

While the cymbal takes the basic beat, the bass and snare play accents

Triplets convey a jolting sensation, contrasting with the underlying swing

In many variations on fusion and jazz rock, the cymbal sustains a steady ta-ta, ta-ta, ta-ta paired beat

The snare and bass drum share a shifting pattern of contrasting accents

Varying the intensity of the snare conveys the strong beats

Authentic Brazilian samba for five drummers on triangle, tamborim, chocalho (shaker), reco-reco (scraper), and surdo (large tom)

In a samba adapted for a single drummer, the triangle moves to the ride cymbal with the right hand

Smaller percussion lines are achieved by accents on the high hat with the left foot

The tamborim moves to the snare with the left hand

The surdo sound is taken on by the right foot on the bass drum

Harmony

Listeners to any pop song containing harmony — two or more notes sounded at the same time — know when the end is coming and when it is being postponed, whether they understand music or not. Composers describe the "pull" of harmony as music's gravitational force. Yet it is a relatively recent development. Musicians have always combined different sounds, but this was fraught with problems until they agreed on a system for tuning instruments. When Europeans did so in the 1700s, it released a rich, new music of sonorous note clusters and startling key changes that sounded as if they made sense together. Harmony became European music's expressive force, as rhythm was Africa's. Its role grew in jazz, which needed a framework for improvisation. Jazz is an even newer form that has drawn ideas from two old civilizations, a source of vitality, allowing subtle rhythms evolved out of Africa to enrich European harmony.

Louis Armstrong picked up harmony in a New Orleans sidewalk singing group. His improvised horn lines harmonized with others' tunes.

Creating chords

Harmony simply means playing several notes at the same time. One combination of notes (or "chord") may seem close to the "home" note of the key the music is in, others will sound more distant. Music's evocation of order, movement, urgency, contemplation, exuberance, sadness, and an infinity of other emotional impressions, is rooted not only in the qualities of sounds, but also in the nuances of tension and relaxation that build up as the sounds move harmonically toward or away from the key note, and in the way the notes of one chord echo or develop others in a sequence. Chords deepen the implications created by the movement of lines of single sounds alone. In much jazz, they also underpin increasingly complex tensions and releases between an improviser's impromptu melody line and the harmony it travels on.

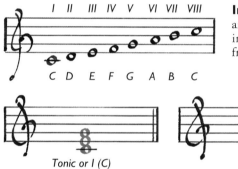

Intervals, or gaps between notes, are shown by Roman numerals, indicating how far each note is from the scale's root.

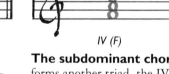

Tonic or I (C)

Triads, three-note chords, are the basis of Western harmony. The tonic triad (chord I) is formed by sounding the first, third, and fifth notes in a scale. In the scale of C major, the triad runs C-E-G, as above.

IV (F)

The subdominant chord forms another triad, the IVth, starting from the fourth note in the C scale, F. Keeping the intervals between the notes the same as for the tonic triad, the chord becomes F-A-C.

V (G)

The dominant chord, the final triad of this sequence, is the Vth, beginning on the fifth note of the scale, G. Keeping the three notes the same intervals apart gives the triad G-B-D.

Extending chords

Before bebop, jazz harmonies were very simple. Even in the 1940s, although departures from Tin Pan Alley sequences led bebop musicians to be described as using "weird chords," the combinations were mostly common to European music. Swing musicians often added a sixth note to the major triad and even placed ninths and elevenths above the root note. Bop players stacked on more still. Charlie Parker described as a personal breakthrough the use of extra top notes of chords as a basis for new improvisation. Bop players also inserted "passing chords," linking one step of the original harmony to another with voicings related to both to create deeper levels of tension and resolution and further expand the palette of related scales for the improviser.

Augmented harmonies in the major scale

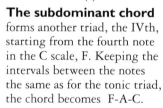

In major scales, stacking notes on top of the regular 1, 3, and 5 in the scale produces extended harmonies. Although many assume bop musicians added the 13th to jazz, big band arrangers and composers like Don Redman and Duke Ellington were using it in the late 1920s for unusual effects. They also increased the rate of harmonic change in jazz.

Minor harmonies

minor 3rd

Minor scales are sequences of notes in which the intervals are reduced in some areas to suggest a more muted and tentative sense of movement. Stacking the notes of minor scales vertically produces minor chords, built on in the same way as major chords. Improvisers use the flattened notes of these scales to establish new tension and release.

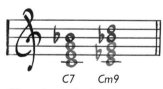

C7   Cm9

Chord symbols are a shorthand way of indicating chords. Formal jazz teaching accelerated with bop and its links to European music, but chord notation — particularly for extended combinations — can be used in practice only by those versed in Western music theory. C7, for example, indicates a C major chord with an added 7th note; "m" represents a minor chord

Chords in action

The 12-bar blues is the most fundamental chord sequence in jazz. The simplest versions of its harmony use the three basic triads: I, IV, and V. The structure is based on three segments, corresponding to early vocal blues pattern of an initial statement confirming the song's "home" position (for instance, the opening line "Born Under A Bad Sign") followed by four bars of shifted harmony focused instead on the IVth ("Been Down Since I Could Crawl"). The last four begin with a still more emphatic shift of gear to the Vth chord (G for a blues in C), sliding back through the IVth (F) to return to the root ("If It Wasn't for Bad Luck/I Wouldn't Have No Luck/At All"). The chord voicings are plain, their direction clear.

Extended chords can support the same melody as the conventional blues, or exciting new ones, by adding a greater variety of notes. The explicit relationship of the tune to the original key and the "message" of a chord's origin and destination dissolve, making the music's direction less apparent. The basic C-chord triad, for instance, may have extra notes added to it, seven, nine, even thirteen away from the root – with the result that the homely emphasis of the original is diffused, perhaps given a floating or brooding feel. "Passing chords" may also be introduced between the originals, so that although the expected "steps" still occur, there are additional linking harmonies between them, delaying the progression and inserting new bases for melodic improvisation.

Modal harmony arose in reaction to the dense developments of chord-based harmony, which culminated in John Coltrane's *Giant Steps*, running at around 100 chord changes per minute and moving in and out of several keys. In a search for a simpler, more atmospheric framework, modal jazz was based on a single scale or sequence of scales. It is closer to Indian music in that it works on horizontal patterns rather than vertical ones like chords. Chords still accompany the melody lines, but they will not necessarily be derivatives of triads and the "harmonic rhythm" of the flow of chords is gone, leaving it all up to the melody. The composer George Russell, one of jazz music's great theoreticians but a great bandleader too, gave immense impetus to the process in the 50s with his treatise *The Lydian Chromatic Concept of Tonal Organization*. John Coltrane exhaustively studied modal structure both from early European and from Eastern music. And Miles Davis performed some of the most famous of all modal jazz improvisations, notably this example from the landmark 1960 album *Kind of Blue*.

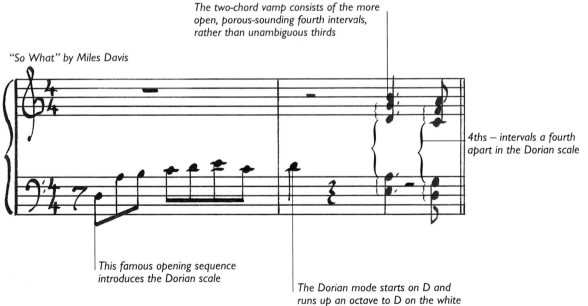

The two-chord vamp consists of the more open, porous-sounding fourth intervals, rather than unambiguous thirds

"So What" by Miles Davis

4ths – intervals a fourth apart in the Dorian scale

This famous opening sequence introduces the Dorian scale

The Dorian mode starts on D and runs up an octave to D on the white notes of the piano keyboard

Improvisation

IMPROVISATION IS OFTEN TREATED as a quirky, even inferior, way of making music in Western cultures — yet it is the most widely practiced method on earth. The standards of Western classical music, with its emphasis on the composer, the tempered scale, and the notated score, have sidelined improvising. Yet Indian classical music, Spanish flamenco, and many forms of African, Middle Eastern, and Celtic music are built around it. Improvisation is, of course, at the heart of jazz. But if the essence of a vital improvising tradition is that the players should be free, its coherence and meaning depend on some shared beliefs. In a good deal of jazz, musicians have favored song structures as frameworks — because of their cyclical form, improvisers always know where they are. Even in the freest, least premeditated jazz, a rhythmic pulse and a tonal center are often a constant guide. Improvisation breaks and redefines musical rules, changing notions of virtuosity.

Two great saxophone improvisers — Charlie Parker (right) and Lester Young (far left). Both improvised on chords, but their concepts of rhythm distinguished swing from bop.

Traditional jazz improvising

Casual listening to early New Orleans ensembles might suggest that although the music is raw, vivid, and robust, it isn't improvised. Nobody seems to solo very often, and the original theme is never far away. But the sound is deceptive. The first New Orleans jazz bands functioned like many marching bands. Everybody played at the same time, interweaving the lines that build the theme in a style generally described as polyphonic,

"many-voiced." But the lines are constantly embellished and reworked, a way of playing described as "free counterpoint." In the traditional New Orleans frontline, the principal interplay is between the cutting power of the lead trumpet or cornet, the sonorous, slithering lines of the trombone, and the mercurial darting of the clarinet. As jazz evolved, the instrumentation changed, but this group sound persisted into the 1930s.

Traditional improvising gains its unique flavour through the personal quirks of particular players' tone and timing. Trumpeter Tommy Ladnier (below), for example, was an old foil of Sidney Bechet's and could be stung into feverish solos by his partner's relentless energy.

As in regular New Orleans clarinet practice, Bechet embellishes the tune while following a line that embraces the work of the other horns

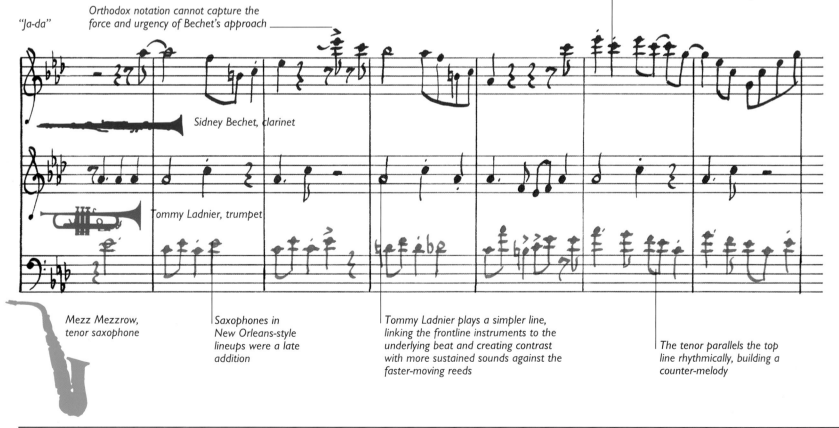

"Ja-da"

Orthodox notation cannot capture the force and urgency of Bechet's approach

Sidney Bechet, clarinet

Tommy Ladnier, trumpet

Mezz Mezzrow, tenor saxophone

Saxophones in New Orleans-style lineups were a late addition

Tommy Ladnier plays a simpler line, linking the frontline instruments to the underlying beat and creating contrast with more sustained sounds against the faster-moving reeds

The tenor parallels the top line rhythmically, building a counter-melody

Chord-based improvising

In classic chord-based solos, the melody is based around the chord sequence of the tune. Soloists are guided toward which notes to play by the harmonic structure, rather than by adhering closely to the original theme. All the examples here use a similar chord sequence.

One of Louis Armstrong's finest solos, roughly based on "I'm a Ding Dong Daddy from Dumas," dates from the start of his work with studio bands featuring the Luis Russell Orchestra. As his confidence grew, Armstrong increasingly played at odds with the background rhythm, and simplified his lines to tightly edited phrases.

Short, out-of-meter runs contrast with longer tones and rests

The three chord changes intensify this cluster of notes in the mid-register

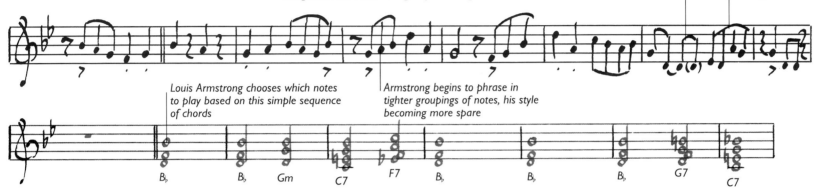

Louis Armstrong chooses which notes to play based on this simple sequence of chords

Armstrong begins to phrase in tighter groupings of notes, his style becoming more spare

Coleman Hawkins dragged the tenor saxophone out of the obscurity of vaudeville shows, quickly influenced by Armstrong's approach and phrasing, and by pianist Art Tatum's improvising on harmony rather than themes, to produce a uniquely rich style.

Even a non-musician's glance at the patterns in this solo, inspired by "How Come You Do Me Like You Do," reveals Hawkins's creative use of the low register, quick flurries of notes, slurs and telling periods of silence.

The higher register opening is contrasted with deeper phrases

Creating an effect of tense expectation, Hawkins leaves a tantalizing pause

Vibrato effect intensifies entrance

A busier passage, pulls at the beat

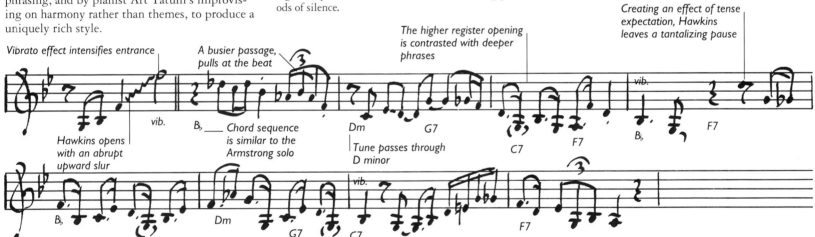

Hawkins opens with an abrupt upward slur

Chord sequence is similar to the Armstrong solo

Tune passes through D minor

With the coming of bebop, musicians improvised far more extensively on the harmonic possibilities of the underlying chords than they ever had in the 1930s – partly to extend improvisation, partly to avoid paying copyright dues on published songs.

In a typical Charlie Parker solo such as this, loosely based on "What a Wonderful World," the genius of bop departs from swing by reducing vibrato, playing faster, moving outside the harmony to intensify the drama of rejoining it, and disrupting the underlying beat.

Runs include fast demisemiquaver triplets

Parker carried dozens of prepared ideas for phrases in his head, but spontaneously reworked them constantly according to the harmony and pulse

Parker's alto enters after the ensemble intro

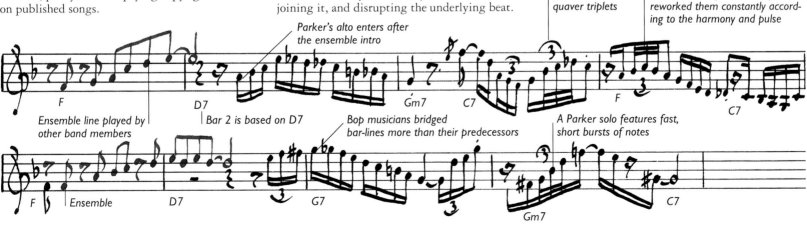

Ensemble line played by other band members

Bar 2 is based on D7

Bop musicians bridged bar-lines more than their predecessors

A Parker solo features fast, short bursts of notes

Modal improvising

The logical development of bop improvising over chords made chord changes so fast that the related note patterns shifted at bewildering speed. Composer George Russell devoted himself to a "war on chords," returning to sequences of pitches, modes, that governed church and folk music before European harmony took over. As modalism gained ground in the 1950s, musicians began to use materials related to Indian music, in which ragas, sequences of notes played over continuous drones, determine the sound palette a player uses to improvise. Accompanists would oscillate between a pair of chords related to the notes of the mode, like the drone.

John Coltrane's "A Love Supreme" was one of the most influential and popular of 1960s jazz recordings, its devotional intensity and spacious feel appealing to listeners outside jazz. Its structure is modal.

The relaxation of the underlying harmony allows Coltrane to repeat and transpose the motif more freely

"A Love Supreme, Part 1"

The first part of the suite is based on this recurring motif

Using more notes increases the intensity of the theme in the absence of harmonic change

Free improvising

Even in spontaneous playing based on forms from Western music, jazz makes the inherited rules irrelevant — it even allows mistakes made in the heat of the moment to change the run of a line and become entirely appropriate. Free improvisation (influential from the late 1950s) may appear to depend on reflexive performances in which the only form is the musicians' responses to each other. But as a group expands, the need for loose ground rules increases if the result is not to stretch expressionism into incoherence. Free bands often determine who will play when, adhere to a tonal center, like a loose conception of key, or let a stable beat determine a solo's rhythmic shape. Ornette Coleman's "harmolodics" music is dictated by the movement of the melody, which sets the harmony.

Saxophonist Albert Ayler was one of free improvisation's most eloquent performers. His tone on saxophone, drenched with gospel intonation and the blues, reached back into the earliest history of jazz. He believed that overattention to complex form restricted the emotional range of spontaneous playing.

Ayler's wailing tone in the upper register of the saxophone was one of his most telling devices, its sound beyond notation

"Ghosts" (Copenhagen version)

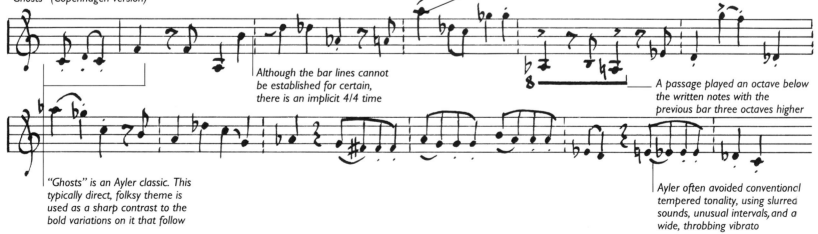

Although the bar lines cannot be established for certain, there is an implicit 4/4 time

A passage played an octave below the written notes with the previous bar three octaves higher

"Ghosts" is an Ayler classic. This typically direct, folksy theme is used as a sharp contrast to the bold variations on it that follow

Ayler often avoided conventional tempered tonality, using slurred sounds, unusual intervals, and a wide, throbbing vibrato

Composing & arranging

JAZZ IS ALWAYS COMPOSED, but often on the wing – and if the spontaneous composition is not recorded, it may never be heard again. The relationship between improvisation and premeditated compositions is a thorny one. In the 1920s, Paul Whiteman was called King of Jazz for jazz-flavored pieces that downplayed improvisation, borrowed from classical music, and cleaned up New Orleans musicians' expressive quirks. In the 1980s, the most hardline free improvisers saw composition as incompatible with the spirit of jazz. Between the extremes lies a rich body of music that balances improvisation and composition in ways that enhance both. Jazz musicians have always put their inimitable stamp on others' work – from early rags and marches, through pop songs, to European art music – and some unique composers, like Thelonious Monk, have used jazz materials only.

Much written jazz is based on conventional notation, with idiosyncratic variations for special sounds. Contemporary versions, like Anthony Braxton's 1983 "Composition No. 107," use new graphic symbols.

At the turn of the century, when jazz did not even have a name, one of its founding figures took it for granted that composition and improvisation could coexist. Jelly Roll Morton had a musical education, but playing piano to an unpredictable clientele in bars, honky tonks, and brothels made improvising skills not just useful, but inevitable. Morton took the intuitive, inflammable materials of New Orleans – solo improvisation, ensemble polyphony, expressive tonality, impulsive breaks – and organized them to create early masterpieces.

For all his reputation as a dilettante, Morton was a sophisticated and erudite musician, and one of the first to draw inspiration both from the sensuality and directness of jazz and blues, and the formal principles of the European classics. He proved that the earthiness and spontaneity of jazz need not necessarily be tamed or blunted by careful preparation, so long as it was preparation of incentives for improvisers, rather than the personal ruminations of an all-powerful composer.

The hot, fervent music coming north from New Orleans in the early years of the 20th century inevitably affected those working elsewhere in the music business, particularly the dance bands. At first inclined to dismiss "hot" music as primitive and unrefined, the big-time commercial arrangers and bandleaders soon started hiring improvisers to add spice to their sound. The impact of such phenomenal instrumentalists as Louis Armstrong and Sidney Bechet was far-reaching. Dance-band leaders Duke Ellington and Fletcher Henderson first ruffled the sleek feathers of their ensembles with the roaring expositions of mavericks like Bechet, Armstrong, trumpeter Bubber Miley, and trombonist Tricky Sam Nanton, and then began to use the phrasing and rhythmic approaches of these performers as a basis for an entirely new approach to orchestral writing.

"Head arrangements"
Count Basie pursued this course rhythmically above all, developing arrangements that elevated the repeated collective horn riff to the status of an alternative rhythm section, an impetus that made the soloists fly. These shorthand forms of organization were not simply the leader's inspiration, but frequently a collaborative effort by the musicians in rehearsal (or even in live performance), and the resulting section-playing was sometimes not even written down but memorized, in what became known as the "head arrangement," usually abbreviated to "the head." Duke Ellington took a more impressionistic and painterly path, exploring the beautiful – and uniquely African-American – timbres of jazz instruments to create structures that were far more ambitious than simple elaborations on songs.

In the postwar era, Gil Evans developed Ellington's method by subtle, subdued use of the riff, unjazzy instrumentation, and avoidance of dynamic extremes. As an arranger with the ambitious Claude Thornhill dance band, Evans was used to augmenting the lineup with such exotica as French horns, and the distinctive textures and subtle chordal movements of the Thornhill ensemble were dubbed "clouds of sound." Evans used these ideas to devastating effect – in collaboration with Gerry Mulligan and John Lewis – on the famous Miles Davis "Birth of the Cool" sessions, and inspired a softer, more ambiguous manner of writing for larger jazz ensembles that had a considerable impact on composition in the 1950s and still influences the music today.

Composition and arrangement took some extreme forms. The "progressive jazz" of Stan Kenton's orchestras attempted to bring modern classical music and jazz together. European and African-American music were often merged at the other end of the scale in pianist/composer John Lewis's work with the chamberlike Modern Jazz Quartet. But it is Gil Evans and Charlie Mingus who are the major influences on bigger jazz ensembles today. So is veteran composer George Russell, one-time collaborator with Charlie Parker and Dizzy Gillespie, now likely to open a show with a 15th-century madrigal, turn it into an erupting volcano of rhythmic density and interweaving horns, and use dissonance, interval leaps, rock percussion, and bravura trumpets spanning 50 years of the big band tradition.

Arrangers in action

Count Basie's direct methods of composing and arranging, though not as complex as Ellington's with its extension of jazz forms beyond the confines of the song and the enrichment of its harmonies, were nevertheless the essence of the swing style. Like Ellington, Basie also used the musical personalities of his sidemen as tone colors, though in freer contexts. The music that came out of Kansas City in the 1930s was bluesy, danceable, and placed the rhythm section at the center. The brass and reeds often played simple "head" (unwritten) arrangements as punchy as percussion effects, plus patterns of chords repeated behind the soloists as riffs.

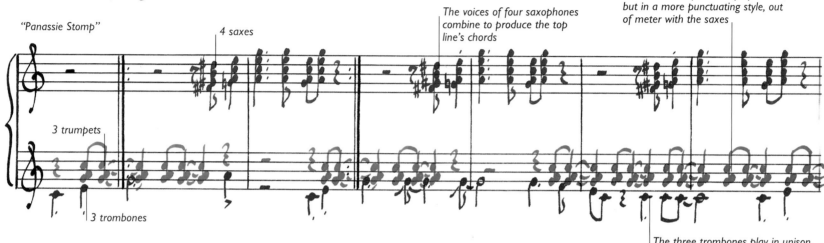

"Panassie Stomp"

4 saxes

3 trumpets

3 trombones

The voices of four saxophones combine to produce the top line's chords

The three trumpets also play chords, but in a more punctuating style, out of meter with the saxes

The three trombones play in unison, adopting a simple rifflike line

Gil Evans was a jazz composer who could make the simplest and most fragmentary of jazz materials glow with a new life. His approach was rooted in both Duke Ellington and an idiosyncratic absorption of the European classics. As a result, Evans was a jazz writer to the tips of his toes, but he used types of instrumentation unusual in jazz, and created the lightest and most ethereal of textures with them. "Blues for Pablo," a showcase for Miles Davis, is one of his most famous pieces, using flutes, French horns, bass clarinets, and tuba as well as regular jazz instruments. Davis plays the deeper and more resonant flügelhorn on this piece, which adds to its sense of obliqueness when coupled with the sustained minor chord of this sequence, given depth and texture by a mix of instrumental voices rarely used in jazz before this point.

"Blues for Pablo"

Flügelhorn (Miles Davis)

2 flutes,
Alto saxophone,
2 French horns

Bass clarinet
Tuba

The first four bars feature Miles Davis playing the theme over a long, brooding minor chord

2 flutes, 5 trumpets,
4 trombones,
2 French horns

Minor chord

Duke Ellington's influence

towers over jazz composition. In a relentless working schedule he is believed to have written some 2,000 pieces of music, some fragmentary, some full-scale orchestral works. His music is still played and reinterpreted constantly, and his song-form pieces such as "Don't Get Around Much Anymore" and "Sophisticated Lady" are classics. Ellington's vision gave even routine and orthodox jazz materials new life. He could invest a single chord with startling richness simply by the choice of unconventional instruments to voice it. He refused to be hamstrung by the simple materials of popular song and blues which provided the vehicle for much early jazz improvisation, extending these forms by added measures and unorthodox departures of key. Ellington was also a remarkably fertile melodist, which is borne out by the frequency with which all interpreters — and not simply jazz musicians either — return to his work for inspiration. And perhaps most remarkably of all, he played his band as if it were an instrument, using the unique and personal sounds of his musicians as the textural materials in his compositions.

The greatest jazz composer and **arranger,** Duke Ellington, used his players' own sounds as his materials, and experimented endlessly with orchestral textures, extended forms, and changing frameworks against which to set improvisation.

The orchestra then echoes the theme

The segment ends with a bluesy phrase from the alto, horn, and trombone

This time the theme is reharmonized with a new bass clarinet and tuba line deep down

The recording

THE FIRST "JAZZ AGE" began when the first jazz records were made. Because the raucous, uninhibited sound of the Original Dixieland Jazz Band was available on a Victor recording to anybody with access to a phonograph, the band and the new idiom it introduced became cults within months. But recording technology also caught the unique qualities of jazz on the wing. Because the rhythmic fluidity of the music was hard to notate, as were the unusual inflections in notes, the vibrancy of a jazz performance could not be recaptured from a written transcription. Records became the staple documentation of jazz and, because no two performances of the same piece are ever exactly alike, they also became the key to the elusive idiosyncrasies of improvisation.

When the Original Dixieland Jazz Band opened in New York, recording had already been under way for over three decades, but not for jazz. The technology was limited, and the fact that music could be captured and replayed at will was a new development to which the public was still acclimatizing itself in 1917.

Musicians played into an enormous horn that worked like a loudspeaker in reverse. Its vibrations shook a cutting stylus attached to the horn's tapered end, which drew a groove in a wax cylinder or disk, the undulations in the groove following the variations of frequency. After three stages of molds from the wax, a metal negative was made which acted as a disk stamper.

It all happened too late, and jazz was too much of an underground phenomenon, for the sounds of the honky tonks, the original bluesmen, the first boogie pianists, and the marching bands to be preserved on wax

Edison originally saw the phonograph as a business tool, but it took off as a medium for entertainment at the turn of the century, both in the United States and in Europe.

(Although rumors persisted of the existence of a long-lost Buddy Bolden cylinder from 1894). Ragtime pianists and the early stride players were recorded, but on piano rolls — punched reels of paper used to activate automatic player pianos.

Even after the Original Dixieland Jazz Band's million-selling debut, the record business executives still saw jazz and blues as music that appealed only to a black-dominated market — in other words, a segment of society too poor to buy phonographs. But when the early blues recordings by Mamie Smith and later, Bessie Smith, sold in unexpected quantities, the "race records" industry (disks specifically for sale to non-Caucasians) began and boomed

An Okeh session in the 1920s. The musicians play into the horn, which records the vibrations as grooves on wax via a cutting stylus. This temperamental technology all but obscured piano, bass, and drums.

In the original phonograph patented by Thomas Edison in 1877, the recording medium was a cylinder, not a disk. Recording time would typically have been three minutes or so.

until the economic slump of 1929. The Gennett, Paramount, and Okeh labels were among the pioneers in the field, although the technical difficulties meant that anything from cold weather to rail traffic outside the studio could ruin recording sessions, and the sounds of drummers and pianists were virtually inaudible on the disks.

Electric recording, using a microphone to turn sound waves into electrical impulses activating a motorized cutter, transformed fidelity in the mid-1920s, allowing bands to sound more natural, and it made field recordings made on mobile equipment more reliable, too. But with the Depression of the early 1930s, the recording industry capsized, and the race labels never recovered. A series of mergers between smaller companies and strenuous efforts to capitalize on the runaway success of network radio stabilized the industry. (Initially perceived as a threat to the record business, radio later became a voracious consumer of its products.) The popularity of swing did the rest.

Mo' Wax

If radio, movie, and recording interests were increasingly coming together, improvements in technology were also encouraging both independent labels and enthusiastic

The 1950s saw the rise of the 33 rpm long-playing record. Jam session atmosphere, and the ambitions of composers like Ellington, could be accurately represented.

amateurs. The famous Dean Benedetti live recordings of the early career of Charlie Parker were produced on a portable disk-cutting machine, and wire recorders, a precursor to tape, were also often used from the bebop years onward. Ironically, this amateur material turned out to be vital documentation of early bebop because the American Federation of Musicians, fearing the effect of radio on live performance opportunities, instituted a recording ban — in pursuit of a percentage on radio transmissions — that lasted from 1942 to 1944.

Large-size transcription disks and longer-running "V – disks" were also made from broadcast material for troop entertainment in the years of the ban, although most of them represent what the authorities assumed would be popular — swing. After the war, the independent recording companies resurfaced to document both the incandescent bebop and the newly revived Dixieland — labels like Commodore, Dial, Clef, Savoy and Blue Note. Because they were run by jazz enthusiasts alive to the needs of musicians, the output of these companies often saw unusual configurations of players, challenging repertoires, and recordings of great sensitivity.

Fats Waller at a Victor records session in 1942 with his Rhythm and the Deep River Boys. Founded in 1901 as the Victor Talking Machine Co. and becoming RCA Victor in the 1940s, it issued the first 45 rpm single in 1949.

New labels sprang up in the 1950s, like Prestige, Riverside, and Pacific, as plastics technology let grooves become narrower and more tightly packed. The long-playing microgroove disk was born, and the complex, open-ended qualities of improvisation were at last properly documented and more ambitious, extended music written.

Editing technology in those days was used less in jazz than other styles of music. After studios began to use multitrack recorders in the early 1960s, the producer and recording studio featured more prominently in the creative process of the session, and making a disk came to be regarded as a separate artistic discipline. The arrival of the compact disc in the 1980s with its laser technology and the development of sophisticated, noise-reducing equipment resulted in massive reissue programs. Now even the earliest jazz can be heard with the shortcomings of the original studios and engineers greatly reduced.

Dance roots

JAZZ AND DANCE grew up together, from the ragtime bounce of early New Orleans jazz, through the blues pianists accompanying the "slow drag" in the Storyville brothels, to swing bands for lindy-hoppers, bebop bands and soul jazz bands for jivers, and jazz funk bands for boogie. The union continues today with the hip hop-influenced jazz of the 1990s. In Africa, dance was the essence of communal and religious life. European style was quite different in technique and meaning. The dynamism of black dance transformed first the social habits of Americans and eventually those of the young-in-spirit all round the world.

Cholly Atkins and Honi Coles — their famous "class act" began in Cab Calloway's band, and they were the epitome of elegant jazz dance.

Before the slave ships came, nothing broke the ancient African continuum that religion was central to life, and dancing central to worship. The movements and their meanings varied from tribe to tribe, but dancing represented the expression of powerful feelings and communication with the spirits of ancestors. Its many rituals have survived into the modern world in Haitian voodoo, *Shango* cults in Cuba, and the Bantu-derived Afro-Brazilian religions, such as *candomblé*. The slave trade broke up families, destroyed lives, and trampled on centuries of African history, but it could not destroy the tribal dances. Because the significance of these dances had for centuries been emotional and spiritual, and because they had become a way to protect a communal memory of African civilization in the Americas, their spark proved inextinguishable.

Dance Wicked

African and European dances mingled as inevitably as did African and European music. From Africa came the shimmying of shoulders and pelvis and sliding, weaving footwork; from Europe came erect, high-stepping folk styles such as English clog dancing and Irish jigs. Dances that evolved from minstrelsy — for all the caricature and racism of the genre — eventually became powerful expressions of African-American sensibility that were to change the way the whole world danced. The cake-walk — the cake being the prize for the best performer — was an elaborately posed, backward-leaning strut, possibly a sardonic reference to the minuet. The Virginia essence was a gliding dance based on shuffling foot movements, from which the famous soft-shoe shuffle seen in 20th-century vaudeville and Broadway shows evolved. Most of the minstrel stars were white entertainers in "blackface" makeup, but the black performer William Henry "Master Juba" Lane topped bills even before the Civil War ("juba" referred to an African mating dance with hand move-

ments suggestive of the Charleston yet to come). The sound of his footwork, a pre-tap mixture of European jigs and reels and African percussive accents, was often compared to drums. Charles Dickens saw Lane's act and was enraptured.

The churches discouraged African-based dance in the southern states after the Civil War, seeing in it incitements to immorality. But when the dancing couldn't be stopped, segregated "jook houses" — derived from *dzugu*, an African word meaning "wicked" — in the black ghetto neighborhoods of southern towns became hothouses for new moves. The famous black bottom began in a Nashville jook.

Minstrelsy turned into the less racist and more eclectic vaudeville, and the dancers of the cakewalk found themselves alongside Irish dancers, Russian dancers, comic dancers, and circus acrobats. Black dance, influenced by the new ragtime craze, began to be incorporated into popular shows in the rapidly expanding district of Harlem and on Chicago's South Side after the migrations of World War I. Spectacular ballrooms opened, like the Savoy, which occupied an entire block between 140th and 141st Streets.

Social dancing boomed early in the 20th century. Formal European ideas were displaced by expressive black dance.

Whites were still dancing in the straight-backed, swirling ballroom style of Vernon and Irene Castle, who advised their pupils that African-American dance styles were ugly. But dances like the black bottom, the Charleston, ballin' the jack (railroad terminology used as an image for fast living), the shimmy and the mooch came up from the South, and new dances mutated from them in the ballrooms — the lindy hop, the shag and the Suzi-Q. The lindy hop had emerged out of the African shimmy, shuffle and free-form movements to become a smooth, fast, energetic dance with improvised breaks whose fluid movements encouraged the progress of an even, four-four swing beat in jazz. A jerkier, more upright, footwork-oriented version of this dance mutated later into the jitterbug, which was predominantly danced by white youth to bands like Benny Goodman's.

White curiosity about black dance, encouraged by the Harlem Renaissance of interest in African-American culture in the 1920s, spread the message. The black musicals *Shuffle Along* and the 1923 *Runnin' Wild* featured spectacular dance routines, the latter launching the Charleston along with James P. Johnson's hit song of the same name. The accompaniment to the new dances was jazz, with its percussive rhythms and swing. Europe embraced the new dance crazes, too, Josephine Baker enrapturing audiences when she took the Charleston and the black bottom to Paris. And with the 1928 American show *Black-birds*, Bojangles appeared.

Steppin' Out

The poet Langston Hughes described the sound of Bill "Bojangles" Robinson's feet as "human percussion . . . little running trills of rippling softness, or terrific syncopated rolls of mounting sound." Bojangles danced on his toes, improvised, and would engagingly watch his own feet while he moved, as if sharing with the audience his astonishment at their independence. In the

same show, the rubber-limbed Earl "Snakehips" Tucker performed the dance that gave rise to his nickname, and throwbacks to his routine were to appear a quarter century later in the stage act of Elvis Presley.

Between the 1930s and the early 1950s, dancers of astonishing skill emerged out of vaudeville and Broadway, notably the Whitman sisters, the sophisticated Williams and Walker, and Buck and Bubbles, and the dazzling tap dance "class act" of Bubbles protegé Charles "Honi" Coles and Charles "Cholly"

Atkins. The term *class act* meant elegance in vaudeville parlance. The spectacular Berry Brothers — who would end their act in a dramatic climax by vaulting 12 feet over the band and landing in the splits — and the Nicholas Brothers were, on the other hand, "flash acts," a label coined to describe the acrobatic minglings of vaudeville and circus performance. The Nicholas Brothers, who grew famous at Harlem's Cotton Club, remained in the business into the 1960s, but by that time the dance world had already been transformed.

Lindy-hopping at the Savoy. The lindy hop was the smoothest, fastest, most acrobatic dancing ever seen in the ballrooms. It developed alongside changes in jazz rhythm.

Jazz dance today

JAZZ AND DANCE were inseparable until the swing era ended. But jazz grew cooler in the 1950s, and a mixture of black rhythm and blues and white country music became so hot that, as rock and roll, it transformed dancing, dress, speech, and the self-image of youth everywhere. Dancing grew more casual, relaxed, and less competitively technical. Latin American dance staked a strong parallel claim, too, following the Cuban and then Brazilian influxes of the 1940s through to the 1970s. But as youth's search for respect has grown more urgent in tougher times, demonstrative and spectacular dancing has returned, and some young dancers have gone back to the "flash acts" of the swing years. Classical dancers, too, have found a rich, new source of inspiration in jazz dance.

Members of the British company Jazz Exchange

By the 1950s, many of the old tap and flash dance partnerships of the prewar years were breaking down or breaking up. Self-taught dancers, performing a punishing routine of competitive workouts to stay ahead of rivals, often launching into cliff-hangingly ambitious maneuvers without warm-ups, were frequently out of the business with injuries before they reached their 30s. And those dancers that survived, even if they could expand their opportunities through the movies, were seeing their hard-won skills superseded by new dance forms as the 1950s dawned.

First came the startling popularity of Cuban music in the 1940s, with Dizzy Gillespie's introduction of Chano Pozo's polyrhythmic ideas into his band and the arrival of many Cuban outfits blending a new pulse with jazz. New American dance crazes accompanied the Latin crossover music, like the mid-1950s mambo, mixing the rhumba and jitterbug, and the later boogaloo, which fused the mambo and rock and roll. With rock and roll emerged a more relaxed and uncompetitive dancing as part of an artless, deprofessionalized return to the fundamental materials of blues and boogie. "Class acts" seemed too glib and elitist, just as big bands suddenly appeared too mechanical, overblown, and preoccupied with technical displays.

Jiving, a simplified form of the swing-out couple movements of the lindy hop, was the staple dance of early rock. But free styles of dancing returned in the 60s, although they weren't as self-consciously or elaborately skillful as the moves the Savoy's regulars had painstakingly developed. Beginning with the twist, a rapid turnover of early disco dances followed, like the mashed potato (which derived from the Charleston), the frug, the hully-gully, and many more. With an intensifying of the Hispanic influence in America and a renewed interest in traditional African dance as part of the search for black identity during the civil rights era, styles were further enriched. Hot Latin salsa, both the music and the dance, hit the streets of New York in the 1970s, played by Cuban and Puerto Rican musicians. Other Latin rhythms and dances included the meringue, and Brazil's samba, and the later lambada.

Makes You Wanna Hustle

In the decades following the 1970s, when youth unemployment began to grow in the West, the disco — the loud, anonymous strobe-lit, basement dance hall of the 1960s and 1970s — changed. Once again, club dance became a demonstration of status and a search for expression and respect, rather than simply a form of relaxation.

In the States, versions of break dancing — a throwback to the "flash act" with its spins, flips, and acrobatic movements — dominated a movement towards newly eclectic musical sources in the clubs. On the streets of Harlem and the South Bronx, too, hip hop culture appeared, with its upfront ethos of rapping, graffiti artistry, and exclamatory, percussive dance, and a new generation of deejays made original music from existing disks through the use of agile and imaginative turntable techniques like mixing and "scratching" (spinning a break on a track forward and back for a percussive effect).

In Britain, young dancers developed dance steps to bebop and fusion music that closely resembled the tap, shuffle, and acrobatic routines of the 1930s. During the 1980s, the jazz dance movement became so popular that dancers traveled widely to visit new clubs, where they could compete with rivals whose reputations preceded them and would frequently astonish veteran bop musicians with their virtuosity.

Black Classicism

Until the 1960s, it was rare to see black classical ballet, and until the assault on segregation, it was tacitly assumed that ballet companies did not admit black dancers. Pressure for self-determination led to the founding of black ensembles such as Alvin Ailey's. Influential, popular styles developed, mingling the grace of orthodox ballet and contemporary techniques with the music and movement of jazz.

This choreography is danced to the Dirty Dozen's tune "My Feet Can't Fail Me Now"

Choreographed leap

Show dance

Show dance and ballet movements to jazz and funk grooves mingle in the work of some young dance groups. "Air steps," tap, stylized gestures, and balletic choreography build complex routines that are both contemporary and reflect the history of vaudeville and Broadway. The eyes are on the audience, coaxing a reaction. There is relatively little improvising, but the accents and rhythms draw on jazz. The right clothes matter for the right dance, but traditional gender roles are no more insistent now than they were in the era of the Whitman Sisters of the 1920s in their men's suits and hats. The tradition comes from vaudeville, where "self-expression" has always taken second place to figuring out a routine that will stun an audience.

Fluid, statuesque poses (unlike those used in club dance) derive from a background in classical and contemporary dance

Black classical dance

Ballet dancers who have moved toward the special freedoms and fluencies of jazz have created forms of dance that retain the statuesque, frozen movement visual poetry of classical dance but in which the meters are different. This routine, danced to a music midway between the elegiac romanticism of Jan Garbarek and soft funk, is as graceful as any orthodox ballet, full of pliant, swirling movements and briefly held poses in which the dancer's body and clothes appear to be painting glowing shapes in space. Yet the rhythms of the body's movement blend the sharp, impulsive turns of jazz accents, the robotic gestures and right angles of 1980s techno-funk disco styles, and the flowing shapes of ballet.

The dress and the shapes made by the lower limbs are all part of the moving picture

Dancer Sheron Wray seeks to expand the jazz dance vocabulary

Club dance

DYNAMIC DANCES like the black bottom emerged from the ghetto "jook" of the early years of the century. While dance has often been a social code to ease access to a dominant class, it has also been an expression of independence, defiance, exultation, and solidarity. As in the "jooks" of the 19th century, so on the streets and club dance floors of the late 20th century. No matter what their status or background, the young have found release and respect from creative and ever-changing variations on the dance styles of the past. Many of the variations of the past decade have evolved to a background of rediscovered jazz.

In the club-dance world, older definitions of "jazz," "fusion," and "swing" have taken on new meanings. But they all have their own codes of dress and steps, being constantly reworked by young disciples for whom dance is a religion

Mambo, derived from the Latin tradition, features fixed, gestural poses made using the whole body, moody shapes, and bohemian dress, such as the black turtleneck and beret or Lester Young-inspired pork pie hat.

Slow, freeze-frame movements

The "jazz" style developed in the 1980s. Baggy jeans, boots, an earring, and fast, punchy movements coupled with a frequently competitive approach on the dance floor characterized its early forms.

The pose is bold, firm, assertive, and aggressively mobile

High jumps are part of this style. Dancers, sparring, shout at each other to jump higher

Fusion is gestural, establishing a gregarious rapport with the club audience

Moves derive from earlier funk and boogie

Fast, jerky movements are executed near the floor

Fusion dancer, Legs

In fusion, the dancer uses gimmicks to get a laugh and spar with others. Dancers call the style's characteristic moves "bulky"— stamping feet and a rougher, street-oriented mode like stylized walking. The style also features astonishingly fast footwork and displays of virtuosity like knee-landing "drops."

Swing is graceful and is often performed to bebop tracks. The footwork is deft and quick, but the predominant features are large, sweeping moves, "flash dance" high kicks, and the elegant swing uniform of baggy jacket, tie, and trousers, Oxford shoes, and sometimes a tuxedo.

Poses such as this (and like all those shown on these pages) derive from the street, not the dance school, although some dancers take classes to lessen the chance of injury

Irven, from the British jazz dance group Brothers in Jazz

The moves are fast, aggressive, and showy

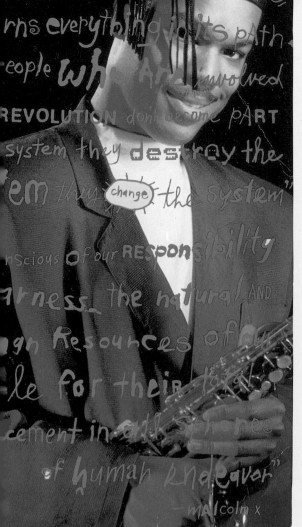

A GALLERY OF CLASSIC RECORDINGS

Jazz is almost the same age as the record industry. When the first disks were made in 1917, jazz was little known outside a handful of locations in the United States, notably New Orleans. A few years later, thanks to the phonograph, the whole world knew about it.

Recorded jazz is not simply a source of fascination for fans, it is an essential body of reference for players. Because much of what makes jazz unique is difficult or impossible to score conventionally, hearing the performers themselves is crucial to learning.

What follows is a selective discography of creative and influential jazz. Many of the early examples are now unavailable rarities, but most of the music on these sessions has been reissued in new formats. Specialized jazz stores will know what you are looking for.

Blues & roots

For 300 years, West African and European music has intermingled in the Americas. In the early 20th century the relationship gave birth to jazz. By the time its first recordings were made, the roots of this fiery new music were already changing. The field hollers, work songs, blues, and boogie woogie, rarely written down but passed informally and embroidered in every transaction, were finally recorded by those musicians who had inherited the tradition and cherished it. But the music was so vital, its impact on successive generations so powerful, that recordings made as late as the 1960s retain the immediacy and flavor of music that might have been first conceived a century before.

Various Artists
BOOGIE WOOGIE RARITIES

Date recorded 1927 – 1932
Label Milestone
Musicians Meade Lux Lewis, Wesley Wallace, Blind Leroy Garnett, Cripple Clarence Lofton, Will Ezell, Charlie Spand, Jabo Williams, Cow Cow Davenport, Henry Brown, Charles Avery *piano, vocal*, B. T. Wingfield *cornet*, Blind Blake *guitar, vocal*, George Hannah, Louis Johnson *vocal*
Tracks Honky Tonk Train Blues ❑ Molasses Sopper Blues ❑ Number 29 ❑ Chain 'Em Down ❑ On the Wall ❑ Playing the Dozens ❑ Just Can't Stay Here ❑ Hastings Street ❑ Levee Camp Man ❑ Jab Blues ❑ Chimes Blues ❑ New Cow Cow Blues ❑ Deep Morgan ❑ Dearborn Street Breakdown
Appraisal Compilation of various boogie classics. Meade Lux Lewis's "Honky Tonk Train Blues" spawned countless train-rhythm imitations by boogie pianists, but Wesley Wallace's cross-rhythmic "Number 29" is not far behind.

Various Artists
CHICAGO/THE BLUES/TODAY! VOL. 1

Date recorded 1966
Label Fontana
Musicians The Junior Wells Chicago Blues Band: Junior Wells *harmonica, vocal*, Buddy Guy *guitar*, Jack Myers *bass*, Fred Below *drums*; J. B. Hutto and his Hawks: J. B. Hutto *guitar, vocal*, Herman Hassell *bass*, Frank Kirkland *drums*; Otis Spann's South Side Piano: Otis Spann *piano, vocal*, S. P. Leary *drums*
Tracks A Tribute to Sonny Boy Williamson ❑ It Hurts Me Too ❑ Messin' With the Kid ❑ Vietcong Blues ❑ All Night Long ❑ Going Ahead ❑ Please Help ❑ Too Much Alcohol ❑ Married Woman Blues ❑ That's the Truth ❑ Marine ❑ Burning Fire ❑ S. P. Blues ❑ Sometime I Wonder ❑ Spann's Stomp
Appraisal Much later examples of Chicago blues continue the forthright, clamorous delivery of younger days. Wells's slow harmonica stands out, as does the uncompromising J. B. Hutto trio on "Too Much Alcohol."

Leadbelly
LEADBELLY'S LAST SESSIONS

Date recorded 1953
Label Folkways
Musicians Leadbelly *guitar, vocal*
Tracks I Was Standing in the Bottom ❑ Yes, I'm Goin' Down in Louisiana (2 takes) ❑ I Ain't Goin' Down to the Well No More (2 takes) ❑ Dick Ligger's Holler ❑ Miss Liza Jane ❑ Dog-Latin Song ❑ Leaving Blues ❑ Go Down Ol' Hannah ❑ Blue Tail Fly ❑ Nobody in This World Is Better Than Us ❑ We're in the Same Boat, Brother (2 takes) ❑ Look-y, Look-y Yonder ❑ Jolly O the Ranson ❑ Ship of Zion ❑ Bring Me a Little Water ❑ Mistreatin' Mama ❑ Black Betty ❑ I Don't Know You, What I Done ❑ Rock Island Line (2 takes) ❑ Old Man Will Your Dog Catch a Rabbit ❑ Shorty George ❑ Stewball ❑ Bottle Up and Go ❑ You Know I Got to Do It ❑ Ain't It a Shame to Go Fishin' on a Sunday ❑ I Ain't Going to Drink No More ❑ My Lindy Lou ❑ I'm Thinking of a Friend ❑ He Never Said a Mumblin' Word ❑ I Don't Want No More Army Life ❑ "In the World" ❑ I Want to Go Home ❑ Springtime in the Rockies ❑ Chinatown ❑ Backwater Blues ❑ Sweet Mary ❑ Irene ❑ Easy, Mr. Tom ❑ In the Evening When the Sun Go Down ❑ I'm Alone Because I Love You ❑ House of the Rising Sun ❑ Mary Don't You Weep and Don't You Moan ❑ Talk About Fannin' Street ❑ Sugar'd Beer ❑ Didn't Ol' John Cross the Water ❑ Nobody Knows You When You're Down and Out ❑ Bully of the Town ❑ Sweet Jenny Lee ❑ Yellow Gal ❑ He Was the Man ❑ Leaving Blues
Appraisal A one-man archive of black folk music and blues, Huddie "Leadbelly" Leadbetter made these informal recordings close to the end of his life but covered a massive sweep of African-American musical history in the process. He is said to have kept some 500 songs in his head, and many have been passed down from the repertoire of itinerant musicians even preceding the blues. Leadbelly's 12-string guitar accompaniments had a chilling power, his voice was rich, grainy, and expressive, and he had no inclination to modernize or streamline his music to suit the blues market of the day. This famous collection includes work songs, prison songs, blues, spirituals, and ballads.

Ma Rainey/Various Artists
THE CLASSIC BLUES SINGERS

Date recorded 1920 – 1939
Label CBS
Musicians Ma Rainey, Mamie Smith, Clara Smith, Martha Copeland, Eliza Brown, Sippie Wallace, Edith Wilson, Lillian Glinn, Bessie Smith, Mary Dixon, Liza Brown, Ann Johnson, Sara Martin, Victoria Spivey, Ida Cox *vocal*, Kid Henderson, Johnny Dunn, Shirley Clay, Joe Smith, Ed Allen, Louis Metcalfe *cornet*, Hot Lips Page *trumpet*, Dope Andrews, Al Wynn, Herb Fleming, Charlie Green, J. C. Higginbotham *trombone*, Lucien Brown *alto sax*, Arville Harris *tenor sax*, Garvin Bushell *clarinet, alto sax*, Ernest Elliot, Artie Starks, Ed Hall *clarinet*, Lil Henderson, Willie "The Lion" Smith, Porter Grainger, Wesley Wilson, J. C. Johnson, Dan Wilson, Leroy Tibbs, John Erby, Fletcher Henderson, Clarence Williams *piano*, George Williams, Buddy Christian, John Mitchell *banjo*, Jim Jackson, Lonnie Johnson, Sylvester Weaver, Charlie Christian *guitar*, Art Bernstein, Cyrus St. Clair *bass*, Leroy Parker *violin*, Happy Bolton, Lionel Hampton *drums*
Tracks Rough and Tumble Blues ▢ Crazy Blues ▢ Jelly, Jelly, Look What You Done Done ▢ Nobody Rocks Me Like My Baby Do ▢ Peddlin' Man ▢ Ma Rainey's Black Bottom ▢ I'm a Mighty Tight Woman ▢ Rules and Regulations (Signed Razor Jim) ▢ Cravin' a Man Blues ▢ Hot Springs Blues ▢ I've Got What It Takes (But It Breaks My Heart to Give It Away) ▢ Fire and Thunder Blues ▢ Let's Get It Straight ▢ Black Hearse Blues ▢ T. B. Blues ▢ Hard Times Blues
Appraisal Dubbed the Mother of the Blues, Gertrude "Ma" Rainey guided Bessie Smith, and although she was closer to both the rural tradition and to minstrelsy and vaudeville, her voice was so majestic and her sound so rich in nuances that she could transform the hollowest songs. Although she recorded extensively in the mid-1920s, the sessions mostly captured her power but not her individuality, so "Ma Rainey's Black Bottom" on this collection is a rare demonstration of her entertainer's skills with a vaudeville song. The warm mellow sound of Sippie Wallace (on "I'm a Mighty Tight Woman"), the harder, more abrasive singing of Victoria Spivey ("T. B. Blues," with Red Allen and J. C. Higginbotham) and, of course, the blazing power of Bessie Smith are among the highlights of this collection.

Various Artists
NOTHIN' BUT THE BLUES

Date recorded 1922 – 1938
Label Fontana
Musicians include Snitcher Roberts, Bessie Smith, Clara Smith, Helen Humes, Bessie Jackson, Ruby Smith *vocal*, "Barbecue Bob" (Robert Hicks) *guitar*, Jack Kelly and his South Memphis Jug Band, Johnny Dunn's Original Jazz Hounds, Dixie Stompers, Troy Floyd and his Shadowland Orchestra, Clarence Williams Washboard Band, Trombone Red and his Blue Six, Sonny Greer and his Memphis Men, J. C. Higginbotham and his Six Hicks
Tracks Heart Is Right Blues ▢ Motherless Child Blues ▢ Dyin' by the Hour ▢ Empty House Blues ▢ Cross-Eyed Blues ▢ Highway No. 61 Blues ▢ T. N. & O. Blues ▢ Back Water Blues ▢ Four o'Clock Blues ▢ Jackass Blues ▢ Dreamland Blues No. 1 ▢ Log Cabin Blues ▢ Red River Blues ▢ B Flat Blues ▢ Beggar's Blues ▢ Higginbotham Blues
Appraisal This compilation embraces a variety of idioms, from the sinewy, oddly accented Georgia blues style of Robert Hicks ("Barbecue Bob"), to the earthy southern dance hall simplicity of Jack Kelly's jug band, Bessie Smith's magnificent evocation of the Mississippi floods ("Back Water Blues"), and the swing-influenced blues of J. C. Higginbotham and Ellington's drummer Sonny Greer.

Various Artists
WASHBOARD RHYTHM

Date recorded 1926 – 1932
Label Ace of Hearts
Musicians Jimmy Bertrand's Washboard Wizards: Jimmy Bertrand *washboard*, Louis Armstrong *cornet*, Johnny Dodds *clarinet*, Jimmy Blythe *piano*; Clarence Williams's Washboard Band: Clarence Williams *piano*, Ed Allen *cornet*, Buster Bailey *clarinet, alto sax*, Ben Whittet *clarinet, tenor sax*, Floyd Casey *washboard*; Beale Street Washboard Band: Herb Morand *cornet*, Johnny Dodds *clarinet*, Frank Melrose *piano*, Baby Dodds *washboard*; Alabama Washboard Stompers; Chicago Stompers: Alfred Bell *kazoo*, Jimmy Blythe *piano*, Jasper Taylor *washboard*
Tracks Little Bits ▢ Idle Hour Special ▢ 47th Street Stomp ▢ Cushion Foot Stomp ▢ P. D. Q. Blues ▢ I'm Goin' Huntin' ▢ Forty and Tight ▢ Piggly Wiggly ▢ Pigmeat Stomp ▢ Wild Man Stomp ▢ Stomp Your Stuff ▢ Pepper Steak
Appraisal Most country-born American folk music drew extensively on jazz, blues, and vaudeville-rooted material but performed it on makeshift instruments such as washboards, jugs, and "washtub" basses in an indefatigable style.

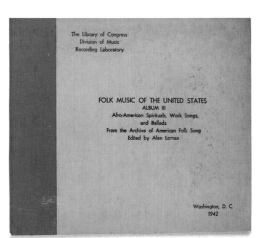

Various Artists
FOLK MUSIC OF THE UNITED STATES

Date recorded 1934 – 1939
Label Library of Congress
Musicians Rural singers, and groups at penitentiaries
Tracks include various African-American spirituals, shouts, and work songs
Appraisal In the 1930s and 1940s, the Library of Congress in Washington, D.C., authorized musicologists to record the widest possible range of American folk songs. These recordings made by Alan, John, and Ruby Lomax are indispensable to the study of early African-American music, featuring fascinating spirituals, work songs, ballads, and blues.

Ragtime & stride

MUCH OF JAZZ MUSIC'S CAPACITY to move listeners came from blues. Much of its capacity to entertain, to laugh and dance, came from ragtime. "Ragged time" was more European than other elements of jazz and, in its original form, was not an improviser's music, but its sparky cross rhythms and bright, pearly compositions surfaced in many early jazz ensembles. The New Orleans jazz of King Oliver and Louis Armstrong dominated early recordings, but the chugging, more formal amiability of the raglike music preceding it, was captured on disk years later by revivalist veterans. Ragtime piano patchily survived piano rolls and turned into jazz in the stride styles of Harlem virtuosos James P. Johnson, Fats Waller and Art Tatum, who stretched the oom-pah rhythms and freed the right hand's variations from being just the syncopated flipside of the beat. Ragtime's legacy also survived in the work of Jelly Roll Morton, whose experiments with rag rhythms were foundation stones of jazz.

Jelly Roll Morton
THE SAGA OF MR. JELLY LORD

Date recorded 1938
Label Circle
Musicians Jelly Roll Morton *piano, vocal*
Tracks Mr. Jelly Lord ❑ Boyhood Memories ❑ Original Jelly Roll Blues ❑ Alabama Bound ❑ King Porter Stomp ❑ You Can Have It ❑ Tiger Rag ❑ Panama
Appraisal Morton's work embraces many elements in early jazz. Its loosening of stiff ragtime rhythms had an incalculable effect, and his methods are highlighted on this late disk which also includes reminiscences.

Bunk Johnson and his Band
THE LAST TESTAMENT

Date recorded December 1947
Label Philips
Musicians Bunk Johnson *trumpet*, Ed Cuffee *trombone*, Garvin Bushell *clarinet*, Don Kirkpatrick *piano*, Danny Barker *guitar*, Wellman Braud *bass*, Alphonso Steele *drums*
Tracks The Entertainer ❑ Someday ❑ Chloe ❑ The Minstrel Man ❑ Till We Meet Again ❑ You're Driving Me Crazy ❑ Kinklets ❑ Maria Eleria ❑ Some of These Days ❑ Hilarity Rag ❑ Out of Nowhere ❑ That Teasin' Rag
Appraisal Johnson was the only musician of Buddy Bolden's generation to record extensively, as late as the New Orleans revival era of the 1940s. These variations on rags and popular songs are simple, thematically logical, and disciplined — fascinating insights into how prerecording era jazz might have sounded.

Fats Waller
FRACTIOUS FINGERING

Date recorded 1929 – 1936
Label RCA Victor
Musicians Fats Waller *piano, vocal*, Herman Autrey *trumpet*, Gene Sedric *clarinet, tenor sax*, Al Casey *guitar*, Charles Turner *bass*, Slick Jones, Yank Porter *drums*
Tracks The Curse of an Aching Heart ❑ S'posin' ❑ 'Taint Good ❑ Gladyse ❑ Nero ❑ I'm Sorry I Made You Cry ❑ My Feelin's Are Hurt ❑ Floatin' Down to Cotton Town ❑ Fractious Fingering ❑ La-De-De La-De-Da ❑ Sweet Savannah Sue ❑ Bye Bye, Baby ❑ I'm at the Mercy of Love ❑ Please Keep Me in Your Dreams ❑ Who's Afraid of Love? ❑ Swingin' Them Jingle Bells
Appraisal Fats Waller was a brilliant musician, although his showbiz career often obscured it. This happens on this disk, too, but there are some stride-derived gems.

Various Artists
CLASSIC JAZZ PIANO STYLES

Date recorded 1929 – 1941
Label RCA Victor
Musicians Fats Waller, Albert Ammons, Pete Johnson, Earl Hines, Jelly Roll Morton, Jimmy Yancey *piano*
Tracks Freakish ❑ Fat Frances ❑ Pep ❑ Handful of Keys ❑ E-Flat Blues ❑ Tea for Two ❑ Russian Fantasy ❑ Rosetta ❑ Body and Soul ❑ On the Sunny Side of the Street ❑ My Melancholy Baby ❑ Yancey Stomp ❑ State Street Special ❑ Boogie Woogie Man ❑ Cuttin' the Boogie
Appraisal Ragtime's descendants: Jelly Roll's fine piano solos from 1929, four Fats Waller solo stride classics, mutating into the sporadic stride bass of Earl Hines's "trumpet style" piano sound, and echoes of the pounding momentum of boogie woogie.

Various Artists
PIANOLA JAZZ

Date recorded circa 1895 – 1925
Label Saydisc
Musicians featuring Pete Wendling, Billy Mayerl, Victor Ardey *piano*
Tracks Skip Along ❑ Maple Leaf ❑ Blame It on the Blues ❑ For Me and My Gal ❑ Aunt Hagar's Blues ❑ I'll Dance till de Sun Breaks Through ❑ Rose of Washington Square ❑ Georgia Camp Meeting ❑ Stumbling ❑ French Trot ❑ Alabama Dream ❑ Creole Bells ❑ Old Fashioned Girl
Appraisal Paper perforations activate automatic player-pianos in this music, often based on rags.

Scott Joplin
SCOTT JOPLIN – 1916

Date recorded January – February 1916
Label Biograph
Musicians Scott Joplin *piano*
Tracks Maple Leaf Rag (2 takes) ❑ Something Doing ❑ Weeping Willow Rag ❑ Ole Miss Rag ❑ Magnetic Rag ❑ Ragtime Oriole ❑ Quality Rag ❑ Agitation Rag ❑ Tickled to Death ❑ Grace and Beauty ❑ 12th Street Rag ❑ Anoma ❑ Cannon Ball
Appraisal Joplin's rags were massive hits, but he did not record himself until his health was failing. These historic rarities include some classics, although his declining energies are obvious.

James P. Johnson
SNOWY MORNING BLUES

Date recorded 1930 – 1944
Label Decca/MCA
Musicians James P. Johnson *piano*, Eddie Dougherty *drums*
Tracks What Is This Thing Called Love? ❑ Crying for the Carolines ❑ You've Got to be Modernistic ❑ Jingles ❑ I've Got a Feeling I'm Falling ❑ Honeysuckle Rose ❑ Keepin' Out of Mischief Now ❑ My Fate Is in Your Hands ❑ Blue Turning Gray Over You ❑ Squeeze Me ❑ I'm Gonna Sit Right Down and Write Myself a Letter ❑ Ain't Misbehavin' ❑ Snowy Morning Blues ❑ Carolina Shout ❑ Keep Off the Grass ❑ Old Fashioned Love ❑ If I Could Be with You (One Hour Tonight) ❑ A Porter's Love Song ❑ Over the Bars ❑ Riffs
Appraisal Johnson's left-hand beat suggests a more relaxed ragtime, and his right flows freely rather than following the syncopation, with ideas suggestive of blues and the black churches. The title track is an atmospheric original.

Art Tatum
SOLO MASTERPIECES

Date recorded 1953 – 1954
Label Pablo
Musicians Art Tatum *piano*
Tracks include Blues in My Heart ❑ Aunt Hagar's Blues ❑ Jitterbug Waltz ❑ Stardust ❑ Ain't Misbehavin' ❑ Tea for Two ❑ Tenderly ❑ Yesterdays ❑ Willow Weep for Me ❑ Embraceable You ❑ This Can't Be Love ❑ Makin' Whoopee ❑ Taboo ❑ I Don't Stand a Ghost of a Chance with You ❑ Louise ❑ I'll See You in My Dreams ❑ Heat Wave ❑ September Song
Appraisal A pianistic and improvising genius, Tatum awesomely demonstrated how much music he could apparently pack into short tracks on this massive multidisk project. He reveals his transformations of stride into swing, a constant rhythmic variation, and imaginative use of substitute harmonies.

13 LP set 2625 703

New Orleans style

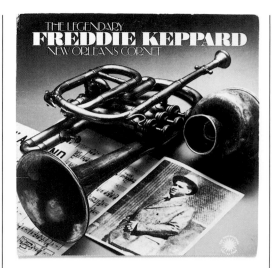

B<small>Y 1910 GRAMOPHONES</small> were growing in popularity as fast as the dance band, a foretaste of jazz to come. The Original Dixieland Jazz Band made the first outright jazz recordings in 1919, signing up with the legendary Victor company. Key black twenties performers appeared for Gennett — an Indiana label recording Jelly Roll Morton and King Oliver — and Okeh, the most successful "race record" label. Okeh captured the best musicians who had moved north — such as King Oliver and Louis Armstrong — and those who had not, like Bennie Moten in Kansas. Bands played into large recording horns, which vibrated a stylus and scratched a low-fidelity imprint onto wax. Reproduction improved after 1925, when electric recording enabled sound to be turned into electrical impulses activating the cutting head.

Freddie Keppard/Doc Cooke
THE LEGENDARY FREDDIE KEPPARD

Date recorded 1924 – 1927
Label Smithsonian
Musicians Freddie Keppard *cornet*, Doc Cooke *director*, Fred Garland, Eddie Vincent, Eddie Ellis *trombone*, Elwood Graham *cornet*, Jerome Pasquall *tenor sax*, Clifford King *clarinet, alto sax*, Jimmie Noone *clarinet, alto sax, vocal*, Joe Poston *clarinet, alto sax, tenor sax, vocal*, Johnny Dodds *clarinet*, Jimmy Bell *violin*, Tony Spaulding, Kenneth Anderson, Arthur Campbell, Tiny Parham *piano*, Stan Wilson, Johnny St. Cyr, Robert Shelly *banjo*, Bill Newton, Rudolph "Sudie" Reynauld *brass bass*, Bert Greene, Andrew Hilaire *drums*, Jasper Taylor *washboard*, Papa Charlie Jackson *vocal*
Tracks Scissor Grinder Joe ❑ So This Is Venice ❑ Moanful Man ❑ The Memphis Maybe Man ❑ The One I Love Belongs to Somebody Else ❑ Messin' Around ❑ High Fever (2 takes) ❑ Here Comes the Hot Tamale Man (2 takes) ❑ Stock Yards Strut ❑ Salty Dog (2 takes) ❑ Stomp Time Blues ❑ It Must Be the Blues
Appraisal Buddy Bolden remained the most darkly angelic of legends because the stories of his exploits were not compromised by surviving recordings. Freddie Keppard was the New Orleans cornet star who followed Bolden and was reluctantly recorded (he was scared rivals would rip off his ideas), although by this time his early reputation was muffled by big ensembles and crowded, self-conscious arrangements. "Salty Dog" and "Stock Yards Strut" by Keppard's Jazz Cardinals with blues singer Papa Charlie Jackson are the standouts, a raucous, elemental black music in which Keppard's strident cornet constantly declaims a street music predating jazz. Sound quality is poor, although some reissues have improved it.

The Original Dixieland Jazz Band
THE ORIGINAL DIXIELAND JAZZ BAND

Date recorded 1917 – 1936
Label RCA Victor
Musicians Nick LaRocca *cornet, trumpet*, Eddie Edwards *trombone*, Benny Krueger *alto sax*, Larry Shields *clarinet*, Henry Ragas, J. Russel Robinson *piano*, Tony Sbarbaro *drums*
Tracks Livery Stable Blues ❑ Dixie Jazz Band One-Step ❑ Tiger Rag ❑ Sensation Rag ❑ Clarinet Marmalade Blues ❑ Lazy Daddy ❑ Home Again Blues ❑ Margie ❑ Palesteena ❑ Broadway Rose ❑ Barnyard Blues ❑ Original Dixieland One Step ❑ Tiger Rag ❑ Skeleton Jangle ❑ Clarinet Marmalade ❑ Bluin' the Blues
Appraisal The Original Dixieland Jazz Band's music, learned in the Storyville ghetto, displayed stiff raglike rhythms, vaudeville antics, and limited material, but it had fresh excitement and three clamorously urgent voices in Shields, Sbarbaro, and LaRocca, the last an influence on Bix Beiderbecke.

King Oliver's Jazz Band
THE COMPLETE 1923 OKEHS

Date recorded June – October 1923
Label EMI
Musicians Joe Oliver, Louis Armstrong *cornet*, Honoré Dutrey *trombone*, Charlie Jackson *bass sax*, Johnny Dodds *clarinet*, Lillian Hardin *piano*, Arthur "Bud" Scott *banjo, vocal*, Johnny St. Cyr *banjo*, Warren "Baby" Dodds *drums, slidewhistle*
Tracks Snake Rag ❑ Sweet Lovin' Man ❑ High Society Rag ❑ Sobbin' Blues ❑ Where Did You Stay Last Night ❑ Dipper Mouth Blues ❑ Jazzin' Babies' Blues ❑ Buddy's Habits ❑ Tears ❑ Ain't Gonna Tell Nobody ❑ Room Rent Blues ❑ Riverside Blues ❑ Sweet Baby Doll ❑ Workin' Man Blues ❑ Mabel's Dream
Appraisal These were the poised and dignified first recordings of King Oliver's ensemble featuring the young Louis Armstrong. "Dipper Mouth Blues" and "Snake Rag" are among the high spots on this British compilation, highlighting both the expressive discipline of the band's ensemble sound and Armstrong's imposing individuality.

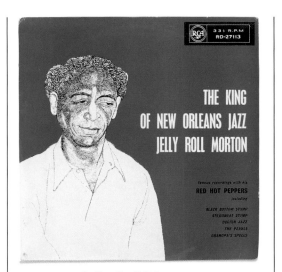

Jelly Roll Morton
THE KING OF NEW ORLEANS JAZZ

Date recorded 1926 – 1928
Label RCA
Musicians Jelly Roll Morton and his Red Hot Peppers featuring Jelly Roll Morton *piano*, Ward Pinkett *trumpet*, George Mitchell *trumpet, cornet*, Lee Collins *cornet*, Kid Ory, George Bryant, Geechy Fields *trombone*, Quinn Wilson, Bill Benford *tuba*, "Stomp" Evans *alto sax*, Omer Simeon, Darnell Howard, Barney Bigard, Johnny Dodds *clarinet*, Johnny St. Cyr, Lee Blair *banjo*, John Lindsay *bass*, Andrew Hilaire, Baby Dodds, Tommy Benford *drums*
Tracks Black Bottom Stomp ❏ The Chant ❏ Smoke House Blues ❏ Steamboat Stomp ❏ Sidewalk Blues ❏ Dead Man Blues ❏ Cannon Ball Blues ❏ Grandpa's Spells ❏ Doctor Jazz ❏ Original Jelly Roll Blues ❏ Jungle Blues ❏ The Pearls ❏ Beale Street Blues ❏ Kansas City Stomp ❏ Shoe Shiner's Drag ❏ Georgia Swing
Appraisal Jelly Roll Morton was the first great jazz composer, reinventing the regular New Orleans instrumentation in audacious ways, and organizing groups of instruments to predate big band "sections." Morton's Red Hot Peppers was one of the most original of all jazz bands. on such classics as "The Chant," "Grandpa's Spells," and "Doctor Jazz," and with the expanded clarinet sections on "Steamboat Stomp" and "Sidewalk Blues," Morton constantly varies tone color, structure, and dynamics.

The Clarence Williams Blue Five
WITH LOUIS ARMSTRONG AND SIDNEY BECHET

Date recorded 1923 – 1925
Label CBS
Musicians Clarence Williams *piano*, Louis Armstrong, Thomas Morris *cornet*, Sidney Bechet *soprano sax, clarinet, sarrusophone*, Charlie Irvis, Charlie Green *trombone*, Buster Bailey *soprano sax, clarinet*, Narcisse "Buddy" Christian *banjo*
Tracks Kansas City Man Blues ❏ Wild Cat Blues ❏ New Orleans Hop Scop Blues ❏ O Daddy Blues ❏ Pickin' on Your Baby ❏ You've Got the Right Key but the Wrong Keyhole ❏ Texas Moaner Blues ❏ Cake Walking Babies from Home ❏ Everybody Loves My Baby ❏ Of All the Wrongs You've Done to Me ❏ Mandy Make Up Your Mind ❏ I'm a Little Blackbird ❏ Papa de Dada ❏ Just Wait Till You See ❏ Livin' High ❏ Coal Cart Blues
Appraisal Clarence Williams was an artists-and-repertoire man for Okeh Records, an average pianist but an ambitious leader. Williams brought about Sidney Bechet's first recordings, and although the sound quality is indifferent, the partnership of the two most uninhibited and imaginative soloists of early jazz in Armstrong and Bechet on "Cake Walking Babies from Home" and "Mandy Make Up Your Mind" soars over all obstacles.

New Orleans Rhythm Kings
VOLUME TWO

Date recorded 1923 – 1925
Label Village
Musicians George Brunies, Santo Pecora *trombone*, Paul Mares *cornet*, Glenn Scoville *alto & tenor sax*, Don Murray, Charlie Cordella *tenor sax, clarinet*, Jack Pettis *C-melody sax*, Leon Roppolo *clarinet*, Jelly Roll Morton, Kyle Pierce, Glyn Lea "Red" Long *piano*, Bob Gillette, Bill Eastwood *banjo*, Chink Martin *brass bass*, Ben Pollack, Leo Adde *drums*
Tracks Sobbin' Blues ❏ Marguerite ❏ Angry (2 takes) ❏ Clarinet Marmalade (2 takes) ❏ Mr. Jelly Lord (2 takes) ❏ London Blues ❏ Milenberg Joys (2 takes) ❏ Mad (Cause You Treat Me This Way) ❏ Baby ❏ I Never Knew What a Gal Could Do ❏ She's Crying for Me Blues ❏ Golden Leaf Strut ❏ She's Cryin' for Me (2 takes) ❏ Everybody Loves Somebody Blues (But Nobody Loves Me) (2 takes)
Appraisal The Original Dixieland Jazz Band may have been the first, but the New Orleans Rhythm Kings was *the* white band of the first wave of jazz. N.O.R.K. gave the smoother, less frantic phrasing of the King Oliver band precedence over the jumpy style of the O.D.J.B., and possessed musicians of stature and influence such as Leon Roppolo with the subtle dynamics and tonal variety of his clarinet, and George Brunies with his broad, relaxed trombone. Jelly Roll Morton joins these later sessions, galvanizing considerable ensemble energy and previewing a Morton classic in "Mr. Jelly Lord."

Louis Armstrong
LOUIS ARMSTRONG AND EARL HINES

Date recorded June - December 1928
Label Philips
Musicians Louis Armstrong *cornet, vocal*, Earl Hines *piano, celeste, vocal*, Fred Robinson *trombone*, Don Redman *alto sax, arranger*, Jimmy Strong *clarinet, tenor sax*, Mancy Cara *banjo, vocal*, Arthur James "Zutty" Singleton *drums*
Tracks Basin Street Blues ❏ Weather Bird ❏ No, Papa, No ❏ Muggles ❏ St. James Infirmary ❏ Tight Like This ❏ West End Blues ❏ Skip the Gutter ❏ Two Deuces ❏ Sugar Foot Stomp ❏ Squeeze Me ❏ Don't Jive Me
Appraisal Louis Armstrong cut the most memorable and revolutionary music of the New Orleans-influenced first phase of jazz when he made these and other recordings with sensational studio bands between 1925 and 1929. All the breakthroughs the trumpeter was making are demonstrated — dislocating the solo line from an obvious adherence to the basic beat, loosening the clunky rag-influenced rhythms, and allowing individual voices to soar out of the collective structure. This recording includes the classics "Weather Bird," "Basin Street Blues," and "Muggles."

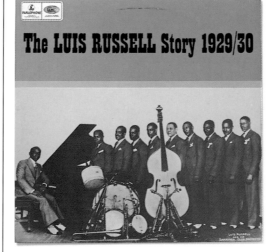

Bennie Moten
THE COMPLETE BENNIE MOTEN

Date recorded 1926 – 1928
Label RCA
Musicians Bennie Moten's Kansas City Orchestra: Bennie Moten *piano, leader*, Paul Webster *trumpet*, Thamon Hayes *trombone, vocal*, Booker Washington *cornet*, Vernon Page *tuba*, Laforest Dent *alto & baritone sax, vocal*, Woody Walder *clarinet, tenor sax*, Harlan Leonard *clarinet, alto sax*, Jack Washington *clarinet, alto & baritone sax*, Lammar Wright, Ed Lewis, Sam Tall, Leroy Berry *banjo*, Willie McWashington *drums*, James Taylor *vocal*
Tracks Thick Lip Stomp (2 takes) ❑ Harmony Blues (2 takes) ❑ Kansas City Shuffle ❑ Yazoo Blues ❑ White Lightnin' Blues ❑ Muscle Shoals Blues ❑ Midnight Blues ❑ Missouri Wobble ❑ Sugar ❑ Dear Heart ❑ The New Tulsa Blues ❑ Baby Dear ❑ Twelfth Street Rag ❑ Pass Out Lightly ❑ Ding Dong Blues (2 takes) ❑ Moten Stomp ❑ Justrite ❑ Slow Motion ❑ Tough Breaks ❑ It's Hard to Laugh or Smile ❑ Sad Man Blues ❑ Kansas City Breakdown ❑ Trouble in Mind ❑ Hot Waters Blues ❑ Get Low Down Blues
Appraisal Moten's orchestra was proof that a more soloistic, blues-based jazz style had formed outside New Orleans. The Kansas City Orchestra was one of the most powerful bands in the Southwest working in the 1920s. The band's early work demonstrated here, prior to the arrival of William "Count" Basie on piano in 1929, is erratic and lacks the solo strength it acquired in the early 1930s. However, it frequently demonstrates uninhibited simplicity over an insistent, thumping rhythm, and "New Tulsa Blues" and "Kansas City Breakdown" are among its early successes.

Luis Russell
THE LUIS RUSSELL STORY

Date recorded 1929 – 1930
Label Parlophone
Musicians Luis Russell *piano*, Louis Metcalf, Henry "Red" Allen, Bill Coleman, Otis Johnson *trumpet*, J. C. Higginbotham *trombone, vocal*, Teddy Hill, Greely Walton *tenor sax*, Albert Nicholas *clarinet, alto sax*, Charlie Holmes *clarinet, alto & soprano sax*, Will Johnson *banjo, guitar*, William "Bass" Moore *brass bass*, George "Pops" Foster *string bass*, Paul Barbarin *drums*, Walter "Fats" Pichon *vocal*
Tracks Savoy Shout ❑ Call of the Freaks ❑ It's Tight Like That ❑ The New Call of the Freaks ❑ Feeling the Spirit ❑ Jersey Lightning ❑ Doctor Blues ❑ Saratoga Shout ❑ Song of Swanee ❑ Louisiana Swing (2 takes) ❑ Poor Li'l Me ❑ On Revival Day ❑ Muggin' Lightly ❑ Panama ❑ High Tension
Appraisal One of the great bands of the 1920s. Its arrangements are modestly but ingeniously geared to highlighting its exceptional soloists: Henry "Red" Allen — a thrilling player second only to Louis Armstrong among trumpet improvisers of the day — Albert Nicholas, J. C. Higginbotham, Charlie Holmes, and the pioneering bassist "Pops" Foster.

Fletcher Henderson
FIRST IMPRESSIONS

Date recorded 1924 – 1931
Label MCA
Musicians Fletcher Henderson *piano*, Louis Armstrong, Russell Smith, Joe Smith, Tommy Ladnier, Bobby Stark, Howard Scott, Elmer Chambers, Rex Stewart *trumpet*, Charlie Green, Jimmy Harrison, Benny Morton, Claude Jones *trombone*, Edgar Sampson *alto sax, violin*, Buster Bailey *clarinet, alto & soprano sax*, Don Pasquall *clarinet, alto & baritone sax*, Don Redman, Russell Procope, Harvey Boone *clarinet, alto sax*, Coleman Hawkins *clarinet, tenor sax*, Charlie Dixon *banjo*, June Coles, Bob Escudero, John Kirby *tuba*, Kaiser Marshall, Walter Johnson *drums*
Tracks Copenhagen ❑ Shanghai Shuffle ❑ Clarinet Marmalade ❑ Hot Mustard ❑ Stockholm Stomp ❑ Have It Ready ❑ Fidgety Feet ❑ Sensation ❑ Hop Off ❑ I'm Crazy 'bout My Baby ❑ Sugar Foot Stomp ❑ Just Blues ❑ Singing the Blues ❑ Low Down on the Bayou
Appraisal This ensemble was a key participant in the invention of big band swing. On "Copenhagen" and "Shanghai Shuffle," the young Louis Armstrong's rhythmic boldness transforms the band from an urbane dance outfit to a swinging jazz ensemble, and an apprentice Coleman Hawkins is in there, too.

Sidney Bechet
THE BLUEBIRD SESSIONS

Date recorded classic sessions from 1932 – 1943
Label Bluebird
Musicians featuring Sidney Bechet *soprano sax, clarinet*, Tommy Ladnier *trumpet*, Victor "Vic" Dickenson *trombone*, Rex Stewart *cornet*, Albert Nicholas *clarinet*, Milton "Mezz" Mezzrow *clarinet, tenor sax*, Jelly Roll Morton *piano, vocal*, Earl Hines, Willie "The Lion" Smith *piano*, Kenny Clarke, Sidney Catlett *drums*
Tracks including Maple Leaf Rag ❑ Shag ❑ Oh, Didn't He Ramble? ❑ Winin' Boy Blues ❑ Blues in Thirds ❑ The Sheik of Araby ❑ Blues of Bechet ❑ Strange Fruit ❑ You're the Limit ❑ Blues in the Air
Appraisal Bechet's Bluebirds were made when New Orleans music was passé, but Bechet's sax is at its most impassioned. "Maple Leaf Rag" and "Shag" are dazzling eruptions of improvisation by a giant of jazz.

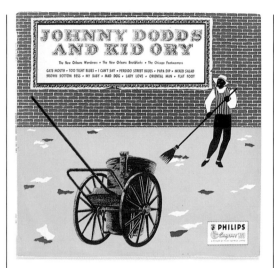

Johnny Dodds/Kid Ory
JOHNNY DODDS AND KID ORY

Date recorded 1926 – 1928
Label Philips
Musicians Johnny Dodds *clarinet*, Kid Ory *trombone*;
The New Orleans Wanderers and Bootblacks
featuring Joe Walker *alto sax*, George Mitchell *cornet*,
Lil Armstrong *piano*, Johnny St. Cyr *banjo*; **The
Chicago Footwarmers** featuring Honoré Dutrey *trombone*, Natty Dominique *cornet*, Jimmy Blythe *piano*, Bill
Johnson *bass*, Baby Dodds *washboard*
Tracks Gate Mouth ❑ Too Tight Blues ❑ I Can't Say
❑ Perdido Street Blues ❑ Papa Dip ❑ Mixed Salad ❑
Brown Bottom Bess ❑ My Baby ❑ Mad Dog ❑ Lady
Love ❑ Oriental Man ❑ Flat Foot
Appraisal Dodds was a great blues clarinetist and
Ory one of the most colorful ensemble trombonists.
Mitchell and Dominique echo the street traditions
of early jazz in these famous sessions.

Jelly Roll Morton
MR. JELLY LORD

Date recorded 1926 – 1930
Label RCA Victor
Musicians Jelly Roll Morton *piano*, Barclay S. Draper,
"Red" Rossiter, Walter Briscoe, Ward Pinkett, Edwin
Swayzee, Eddie Anderson, Bubber
Miley, George Mitchell *trumpet*,
Charles Irvis, Julius "Geechy" Fields,
Bill Cato, Wilbur de Paris, Kid Ory
trombone, Paul Barnes *soprano & alto*

Jelly Roll Morton's roots were
in New Orleans, but he traveled
all over the States in the early
years of the century, absorbing
minstrel and Hispanic music,
country blues, work songs, and
hymns. They were melted down
and reforged in the most fertile
compositional imagination of the
first decades of jazz, by an artist
in whom an organizational
intelligence and an appetite for
improvising were in creative
balance.

sax, Joe Thomas *alto sax*, Joe Garland *tenor sax*, George
Baquet, Johnny Dodds, Russell Procope *clarinet*, Omer
Simeon *clarinet & bass clarinet*, Albert Nicholas *clarinet*,
alto sax, Walter Thomas *clarinet, alto & baritone sax*, Billy
Taylor, Bill Benford *tuba*, Barney Alexander *banjo*, Lee
Blair *banjo, guitar*, Bernard Addison, Johnny St. Cyr
guitar, Ernest "Bass" Hill, Harry Prather *sousaphone*,
"Bass" Moore, John Lindsay *bass*, William Laws, Warren
"Baby" Dodds, Cozy Cole, Manzie Johnson, Tommy
Benford, Andrew Hilaire *drums*, Clarence Black, Wright
Smith *violin*, Billie Young *vocal*; **Wilton Crawley and
his Orchestra** featuring Freddy Jenkins, Arthur
Whetsol *trumpet*, Joe Nanton *trombone*, Johnny Hodges
alto sax, Wilton Crawley *clarinet*, Wellman Braud *bass*,
Paul Barbarin *drums*
Tracks Burnin' the Iceberg ❑ Mr. Jelly Lord ❑ Down
My Way ❑ When They Get Lovin' They's Gone ❑ You
Oughta See My Gal ❑ New Orleans Bump ❑ Load of
Coal ❑ Red Hot Pepper Stomp ❑ Wolverine Blues
(2 takes) ❑ Courthouse Bump ❑ Keep Your Business to
Yourself ❑ Deep Creek Blues ❑ Fussy Mabel ❑ Someday
Sweetheart Blues ❑ Crazy Chords
Appraisal By the late twenties, Morton was writing for
bigger bands. In their themes within themes, textural
variety, and interplay, these tracks point to both a passing music — rhythmically they still echo New Orleans
— and an ensemble sound to come.

Chicago & New York

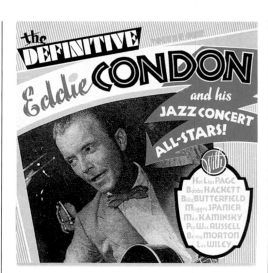

ALTHOUGH MOST "NEW ORLEANS JAZZ" was recorded in Chicago after the black migration north, the city developed its own brand of jazz and blues that survived the antimob crackdown on clubs at the end of the 1920s. Young white musicians heard the black South Side bands and modified the sound into a fast, solo-oriented music later dubbed "Chicago Jazz." New York, on the other hand, first found a jazz identity in the smoother, symphonic dance band style of Paul Whiteman, although it soon became identified with that alchemy of dance band and New Orleans music that set the swing era rolling. Jazz was changing too fast, and its message traveling too quickly for a single city to be identified with a sound, the way New Orleans had been. Although Chicago became famous for its lively small-band music, it also nurtured relationships between jazz musicians and rural blues artists in the Mississippi Delta that prefigured 1940s jump music, rock and roll, the revival of rhythm and blues, and the most expressive ingredients of free jazz.

Eddie Condon
THE DEFINITIVE VOL. 1
Date recorded 1944
Label Stash
Musicians featuring Eddie Condon *guitar*, Billy Butterfield, Muggsy Spanier, Max Kaminsky, Hot Lips Page *trumpet*, Benny Morton *trombone*, Pee Wee Russell *clarinet*.
Tracks include Ballin' the Jack ❑ Sweet Georgia Brown ❑ At the Jazz Band Ball ❑ Royal Garden Blues ❑ Muskrat Ramble ❑ The Man I Love ❑ S'Wonderful ❑ Old Folks
Appraisal Condon was a dynamic rhythm player. These sessions capture the essence of the Chicago style.

Harlem Hamfats
THE HARLEM HAMFATS

Date recorded 1936 – 1937
Label Ace of Hearts
Musicians Herb Morand *trumpet*, Odell Rand *clarinet*, Horace Malcolm *piano*, Joe McCoy *guitar, vocal*, Charlie McCoy *mandolin*, John Lindsay *string bass*, Fred Flynn, Pearlis Williams *drums*
Tracks Tempo di Bucket ❑ The Garbage Man ❑ Southern Blues ❑ My Daddy Was a Lovin' Man ❑ What You Gonna Do? ❑ Growling Dog ❑ Oh! Red ❑ We Gonna Pitch a Boogie Woogie ❑ Black Gal, You Better Use Your Head ❑ Root Hog or Die ❑ Hallelujah Joe Ain't Preachin' No More ❑ Jam Jamboree ❑ Let's Get Drunk and Truck ❑ Hamfat Swing
Appraisal The Chicago-based Hamfats embraced unpolished New Orleans jazz and early rhythm and blues. Louis Jordan's later music developed their line.

Eddie Lang/Joe Venuti
STRINGING THE BLUES

Date recorded 1926 – 1929
Label CBS
Musicians featuring Eddie Lang *guitar*, Joe Venuti *violin*, King Oliver *cornet*, Don Murray *baritone sax, clarinet*, Adrian Rollini *bass sax, goofus*, Clarence Williams *piano*, Lonnie Johnson *guitar, vocal*
Tracks Goin' Places ❑ Doin' Things ❑ Perfect ❑ Cheese and Crackers ❑ Stringing the Blues ❑ I'm Somebody's Somebody Now ❑ Two Tone Stomp ❑ Beatin' the Dog ❑ The Wild Dog ❑ Dinah ❑ In the Bottle Blues ❑ Wild Cat ❑ Guitar Blues ❑ Bull Frog Moan ❑ Jet Black Blues ❑ Penn Beach Blues
Appraisal Scintillating New York guitar-violin duo that inspired Django Reinhardt and Stephane Grappelli. Venuti's rough, hard-driving style was the invigorating antithesis of classical grace.

Earl Hines and his Orchestra
SWINGING IN CHICAGO

Date recorded 1934 – 1935
Label Coral
Musicians featuring Earl Hines *piano*, Trummy Young *trombone*, Darnell Howard *alto sax, clarinet, violin*, Omer Simeon *alto sax, clarinet*, Cecil Irwin, Jimmy Mundy *tenor sax*, Wallace Bishop *drums*, Walter Fuller, Palmer Brothers Trio *vocal*
Tracks That's A-Plenty ❑ Fat Babes ❑ Maple Leaf Rag ❑ Sweet Georgia Brown ❑ Rosetta ❑ Copenhagen ❑ Angry ❑ Wolverine Blues ❑ Rock and Rye ❑ Cavernism ❑ Rhythm Lullaby ❑ Japanese Sandman ❑ Bubbling Over ❑ Blue
Appraisal Hines led a band at Chicago's Grand Terrace for ten years. Its peak came in the mid-1930s, as this disk witnesses, when his brilliant piano figures glittered against increasingly colorful arrangements.

Bix Beiderbecke
THE BIX BEIDERBECKE LEGEND
Date recorded 1924 – 1928
Label RCA Victor
Musicians Bix Beiderbecke *cornet*; Jean Goldkette and his Orchestra: Fred "Fuzzy" Farrar, Tex Brusstar, Ray Lodwig *trumpet*, Bill Rank, Tommy Dorsey, Speigan Wilcox, Lloyd Turner *trombone*, Irish Henry *tuba*, Don Murray, Doc Ryker, George Williams, Frankie Trumbauer, Danny Polo *sax*, Paul Mertz, Itzy Riskin *piano*, Howdy Quicksell *banjo*, Eddie Lang *guitar*, Ray Muerer *guitar, vocal*, Joe Venuti *violin*, Steve Brown *bass*, Charlie Horvath, Chauncey Morehouse *drums*, Al Lynch, the Keller Sisters, Lewis James *vocal*; Paul Whiteman and his Orchestra
Tracks I Didn't Know ❑ Sunday ❑ My Pretty Girl (2 takes) ❑ Slow River ❑ Clementine ❑ Changes ❑ Mary ❑ Lonely Melody ❑ San ❑ Back in Your Own Backyard ❑ There Ain't No Sweet Man That's Worth the Salt of My Tears ❑ Dardanella ❑ Love Nest ❑ From Monday On ❑ Mississippi Mud
Appraisal After his debut with his own band, the Wolverines, Beiderbecke — whose sound Hoagy Carmichael compared to the chiming of a bell — worked with bands bridging popular dance music and jazz, and his solos were brief. He nevertheless produces gleaming classics here, and Frankie Trumbauer lends some ethereal saxophone support.

Bix Beiderbecke
THE BIX BEIDERBECKE STORY
Date recorded 1927 – 1929
Label Philips
Musicians Bix Beiderbecke *cornet, piano*, Harry Goldfield *trumpet*, Bill Rank *trombone*, Doc Ryker *alto sax*, Harold Strickfadden *alto & baritone sax*, Adrian Rollini, Min Leibrook *bass sax*, Frankie Trumbauer *C-melody sax*, Don Murray, Izzy Friedman *clarinet*, Frank Signorelli, Lennie Hayton, Itzy Riskin *piano*, Eddie Lang *guitar*, Howdy Quicksell *banjo*, Matty Malneck *violin*, Chauncey Morehouse, Harry Gate, Georg Marsh *drums*, Scrappy Lambert, Bing Crosby *vocal*; Paul Whiteman Orchestra
Tracks Sorry ❑ Ol' Man River ❑ Somebody Stole My Gal ❑ Since My Best Gal Turned Me Down ❑ Way Down Yonder in New Orleans ❑ I'm Comin' Virginia ❑ In a Mist ❑ Ostrich Walk ❑ Riverboat Shuffle ❑ Borneo ❑ China Boy ❑ Oh, Miss Hannah
Appraisal Bix Beiderbecke's most copied solo is "Singin' the Blues," but "I'm Comin' Virginia" is a corresponding delight for its inspired avoidance of what seemed to most of his contemporaries to be obligatory landmark notes signposting the structure. Bix's sound consequently seems to drift away from a music otherwise locked into the fashions of the time.

Henry Allen Jr. and his New York Orchestra
TREASURY OF JAZZ SERIES
Date recorded 1929 – 1930
Label RCA Victor
Musicians Henry Allen, Jr. *trumpet, vocal*, Otis Johnson *trumpet*, J. C. Higginbotham, James Archey *trombone*, Charlie Holmes *alto sax*, Teddy Hill, Greely Walton *tenor sax*, William Blue *clarinet, alto sax*, Albert Nicholas *clarinet*, Ernest Hill *bassoon*, Luis Russell *piano*, Will Johnson *guitar, vocal*, George "Pops" Foster, Ernest Hill *bass*, Paul Barbarin *drums*, Victoria Spivey, The Wanderers *vocal*
Tracks Swing Out ❑ Feeling Drowsy ❑ How Do They Do It That Way? ❑ It Should Be You ❑ Biff'ly Blues ❑ Make a Country Bird Fly Wild ❑ You Might Get Better, But You'll Never Get Well ❑ Dancing Dave ❑ Singing Pretty Songs ❑ Roamin' ❑ I Fell in Love with You ❑ Patrol Wagon Blues
Appraisal With Louis Armstrong and Roy Eldridge, Red Allen dominated the trumpet playing of the transitional period from New Orleans music to swing. His palette of sound effects offered lessons even to the avant-garde musicians of the 1960s. This strong, raucous mix of New Orleans ensemble playing and the blues catches the early daring of his improvisations.

Various Artists
CHICAGO JAZZ
Date recorded 1939 – 1940
Label Coral
Musicians Eddie Condon and his Chicagoans: Eddie Condon *guitar*, Max Kaminsky *cornet*, Brad Gowans *trombone*, Pee Wee Russell *clarinet*, Bud Freeman *tenor sax*, Joe Sullivan *piano*, Clyde Newcomb *bass*, Dave Tough *drums*; Jimmy McPartland and his Orchestra: Jimmy McPartland *cornet*, Bud Jacobson *clarinet*, Boyce Brown *alto sax*, Floyd Bean *piano*, Dick McPartland *guitar*, Jim Lannigan *bass*, Hank Isaacs *drums*; George Wettling's Chicago Rhythm Kings: George Wettling *drums*, Charlie Teagarden *trumpet*, Floyd O'Brien *trombone*, Danny Polo *clarinet*, Joe Marsala *tenor sax*, Jess Stacy *piano*, Jack Bland *guitar*, Artie Shaparo *bass*
Tracks Nobody's Sweetheart ❑ Friar's Point Shuffle ❑ There'll Be Some Changes Made ❑ Someday, Sweetheart ❑ China Boy ❑ Jazz Me Blues ❑ Sugar ❑ The World Is Waiting for the Sunrise ❑ Bugle Call Rag ❑ I Wish I Could Shimmy Like My Sister Kate ❑ The Darktown Strutters' Ball ❑ I've Found a New Baby
Appraisal Flamboyance and a delight in playing are the abiding characteristics of the hard-swinging Chicago school, well represented on this later session organized by drummer George Wettling. Jimmy McPartland demonstrates some respectful tonal resemblances to Beiderbecke here, and Wettling's rugged, booming drumming drives a crisp band.

Early singers

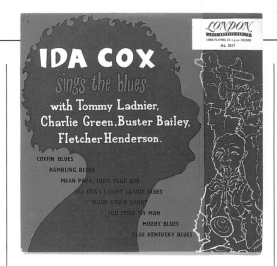

IN EARLY JAZZ, the idiom's pungent tonalities, switchback rhythms, and conversational ensemble sounds lay in the voices of instruments. Singers performed the more ritualized blues or vaudeville's novelty songs, caricature, and double entendres. By the 1920s these strands intertwined; by the 1930s they were inseparable. As the new race records market expanded in the 1920s, blues became commercial, and its most expressive singers made successful disks with session bands of leading jazz stars. Meanwhile, African-American music influenced white popular song more and more, and the connection between Tin Pan Alley and jazz deepened. By the 1930s every swing band had a singer, and the jukebox market created demand for vocals with jazz accompaniment — the launchpad for Billie Holiday. With Holiday, a singing style grew from the rhythmic originality and subtle shadings of horn solos and found its perfect early realization.

Ida Cox
SINGS THE BLUES

Date recorded 1924 – 1928
Label London
Musicians featuring Ida Cox *vocal*, Tommy Ladnier *cornet*, Jessie Crump *organ*, Charlie Green *trombone*, Buster Bailey *clarinet*, Fletcher Henderson *piano*, Charlie Dixon *banjo*
Tracks Coffin Blues ❑ Rambling Blues ❑ Mean Papa, Turn Your Key ❑ Ida Cox's Lawdy Lawdy Blues ❑ Worn Down Daddy ❑ You Stole My Man ❑ Misery Blues ❑ Blue Kentucky Blues
Appraisal Big-time, classic blues artist of the 1920s, linking the folk traditions ("Coffin Blues") to vaudeville ("Mean Papa, Turn Your Key").

Bessie Smith
THE BESSIE SMITH STORY VOL. 3

Date recorded 1925 – 1927
Label CBS
Musicians Joe Smith *trumpet*, Jimmy Harrison, Charlie Green *trombone*, Coleman Hawkins *tenor sax*, *clarinet*, Buster Bailey *clarinet*, Fletcher Henderson *piano*, Charlie Dixon *banjo*, Kaiser Marshall *drums*
Tracks Alexander's Ragtime Band ❑ Baby Doll ❑ The Yellow Dog Blues ❑ One and Two Blues ❑ Money Blues ❑ After You've Gone ❑ Cake Walking Babies (from Home) ❑ Young Woman's Blues ❑ At the Christmas Ball ❑ There'll Be a Hot Time in the Old Town Tonight ❑ Lost Your Head Blues ❑ Muddy Water
Appraisal How New Orleans jazz, popular song, and blues intensity most profoundly merged, with the greatest ever blues singer and a fine Fletcher Henderson small group.

Billy Eckstine and his Orchestra
BILLY ECKSTINE

Date recorded 1944 – 1946
Label Ember
Musicians featuring Billy Eckstine *vocal*, Dizzy Gillespie *trumpet*, Trummie Young *trombone*, Dexter Gordon, Gene Ammons, Wardell Grey *tenor sax*, Leo Parker *baritone sax*, Clyde Hart *piano*, Tommy Potter, Oscar Pettiford *bass*, Rossiere "Shadow" Wilson, Art Blakey *drums*, Sarah Vaughan *vocal*
Tracks Blowing the Blues Away ❑ If That's the Way You Feel ❑ I Want to Talk about You ❑ The Real Thing Happened to Me ❑ I'll Wait and Pray ❑ I Got a Date with Rhythm ❑ Good Jelly Blues ❑ Opus X ❑ I Stay in the Mood for You ❑ I'm the Caring Kind
Appraisal Eckstine, with lustrous voice and pulsating vibrato, was the first black pop idol. His magnificent baritone was enhanced by emerging bop stars he hired, here Dizzy Gillespie, Sarah Vaughan, and Art Blakey.

Billie Holiday
THE GOLDEN YEARS VOL. 2

Date recorded 1937 – 1938
Label CBS
Musicians featuring Billie Holiday *vocal*, Buck Clayton, Harry James *trumpet*, Benny Morton, Dickie Wells *trombone*, Benny Carter *alto sax*, Lester Young, Herschel Evans *tenor sax*, Buster Bailey *clarinet*, Teddy Wilson, Claude Thornhill *piano*, Freddie Green *guitar*, Walter Page *bass*, Cozy Cole, Jo Jones *drums*
Tracks include Mean to Me ❑ I'll Get By ❑ Sun Showers ❑ He's Funny That Way ❑ My Man ❑ Nice Work if You Can Get It ❑ Can't Help Lovin' Dat Man
Appraisal Some of Holiday's most unforgettable sessions, with pianist Teddy Wilson, and featuring Lester Young in a selection of the most intimate musical conversations in jazz. Delaying the beat, rising above indifferent lyrics, improvising barely perceptible nuances, she brought about a new era of jazz singing.

Ella Fitzgerald
ELLA FITZGERALD VOL. 1

Date recorded 1935 – 1941
Label Classics
Musicians featuring Ella Fitzgerald, the Mills Brothers *vocal*, Chick Webb, Bill Beason *drums*, Taft Jordan *trumpet*, Benny Goodman *clarinet*, Louis Jordan, Ted McRae, Eddie Barefield *sax*, Teddy Wilson *piano*
Tracks 138 tracks include My Melancholy Baby ❑ Goodnight My Love ❑ Dedicated to You ❑ Mr. Paganini ❑ Darktown Strutter's Ball ❑ Organ Grinder's Swing ❑ I Want to Be Happy ❑ Gotta Pebble in My Shoe ❑ Undecided ❑ A-Tisket A-Tasket ❑ Please Tell Me the Truth ❑ Lindy Hoppers' Delight ❑ Take It from the Top ❑ Taking a Chance on Love ❑ I Got It Bad ❑ The Lonesomest Gal in Town ❑ Three Little Words
Appraisal Ella Fitzgerald became a jazz star — and a bandleader — almost overnight. Her fresh, relaxed performances from the early years are caught here, chronologically starting at the age of 16 until the moment when she launched into a career in her own right at the age of 23. Her output during these years was varied — a mixture of inventive jazz outings and more dated-sounding novelty songs.

Billie Holiday
BILLE HOLIDAY ON COMMODORE

Date recorded 1939, 1944
Label Commodore
Musicians Billie Holiday *vocal*, Frankie Newton, Doc Cheatham *trumpet*, Vic Dickenson *trombone*, Tab Smith, Lem Davis *alto sax*, Stan Payne, Kenneth Hollon *tenor sax*, Sonny White, Eddie Heywood *piano*, Teddy Walters, Jimmy McLin *guitar*, John Williams, John Simmons *bass*, Eddie Dougherty, Big Sid Catlett *drums*
Tracks Yesterdays ❑ Fine and Mellow ❑ I Gotta Right to Sing the Blues ❑ How Am I to Know ❑ My Old Flame ❑ I'll Get By ❑ I Cover the Waterfront ❑ I'll Be Seeing You ❑ I'm Yours ❑ Embraceable You ❑ As Time Goes By ❑ She's (He's) Funny That Way ❑ Lover Come Back to Me ❑ Billie's Blues ❑ On the Sunny Side of the Street
Appraisal "My Old Flame," "Embraceable You," and "Lover Come Back to Me" are among her most sublime performances, before a more mainstream era to come.

Ethel Waters
JAZZIN' BABIES' BLUES VOL. 2

Date recorded 1921 – 1927
Label Biograph
Musicians Ethel Waters *vocal*, Joe Smith *cornet*, Fletcher Henderson, Pearl Wright *piano*; **Albury's Blue and Jazz Seven** featuring Wesley Johnson *trumpet*, Jim Reevy *trombone*, Clarence Harris *alto sax*, Wilson Kyer *piano*, Ralph Escudero *tuba*, Kaiser Marshall *drums*; **Waters's Jazz Masters** featuring Garvin Bushell *clarinet, alto sax*, Chink Johnson *tuba*; **The Jazz Masters** featuring Henry Brashear *trombone*, June Clark, Howard Scott *cornet*, Clarence Robinson *clarinet*, Chink Johnson *tuba*, Johnny Mitchell *banjo*; **Lovie Austin's Blues Serenaders** featuring Lovie Austin *piano*, Tommy Ladnier *cornet*
Tracks The New York Glide ❑ At the New Jump Steady Ball ❑ Dying with the Blues ❑ Kiss Your Pretty Baby Nice ❑ Jazzin' Babies' Blues ❑ Kind Lovin' Blues ❑ Brown Baby ❑ Ain't Goin' Marry ❑ You'll Need Me When I'm Long Gone ❑ I Want Somebody All My Own ❑ Black Spatch Blues ❑ One Sweet Letter from You
Appraisal Although she is not always credited for it, the influence of Ethel Waters on 20th-century popular singing has been immense. She disliked traditional blues singing as inelegant (although she had much of its sonority), and her breakthrough was to bridge white music hall polish and black music's sensuality and rebelliousness, opening up Tin Pan Alley to black artists. Lighter in sound than the blues singers, less wayward than jazz, but a perfectionist in phrasing, Waters is even a shadowy influence on Billie Holiday.

Swing

EARLY SUCCESS with jazz and blues evaporated under the influence of radio and the Depression, and by 1933 American record sales had crashed. But music was changing nonetheless. Duke Ellington had become more popular than Paul Whiteman; Fletcher Henderson and Don Redman had set brass and reeds in jubilant conversation in an invigorating new ensemble music. Jazz orchestras were struggling for work but were generating ideas whose time had almost come. When John Hammond sold some recordings by clarinetist Benny Goodman to English Columbia, a branch of the industry not in such poor shape, the swing era was on the slipway. The disks won Goodman a deal at home, and new radio deejays did the rest.

McKinney's Cotton Pickers
McKINNEY'S COTTON PICKERS

Date recorded 1930 – 1931
Label RCA Victor
Musicians McKenney's Cotton Pickers: Rex Stewart, Buddy Lee, Langston Curl, Clarence Ross *trumpet*, Ed Cuffee, Quentin Jackson *trombone, vocal*, Don Redman *clarinet, alto & soprano sax, cello, vocal, arranger*, Benny Carter *clarinet, alto sax, arranger*, Prince Robinson *clarinet, tenor sax*, Todd Rhodes *piano, cello*, Dave Wilborn *banjo, vocal*, Ralph Escudero *tuba*, Cuba Austin *drums*, George Bias, Lois Deppe, Donald King *vocal*; **McKinney's Cotton Pickers**: also featuring Joe Smith, Adolphus "Doc" Cheatham *trumpet*, Billy Taylor *bass & tuba*; **The Carolina Dandies**: John Nesbitt, Tom Howell *trumpet*, Lee Howell *trombone*, Benny Carter, Don Redman, Sunny Clapp *clarinet, alto sax*, George Marks *piano, vocal*, Roy Smeck *guitar*, Francis Palmer *tuba*, Joe Hudson *drums*
Tracks Hello! ❑ After All, You're All I'm After ❑ I Miss a Little Miss ❑ To Whom It May Concern ❑ You're Driving Me Crazy ❑ Come a Little Closer ❑ It's a Lonesome Old Town (2 takes) ❑ She's My Secret Passion (2 takes) ❑ Come Easy, Go Easy Love ❑ When I Can't Be with You ❑ Do You Believe in Love at Sight? (2 takes) ❑ Wrap Your Troubles in Dreams (2 takes)
Appraisal A fascinating and popular black band on the cusp of the twenties and thirties, formed out of disaffected Fletcher Henderson employees by Jean Goldkette while searching for entertainers for the Graystone Ballroom. It uses a prejazz blown bass and a banjo instead of a piano, but the arrangements (by Fletcher Henderson's Don Redman, altoist Benny Carter, and John Nesbitt) begin to suggest the glide of the swing bands, and the tightness of the ensemble playing gives the music immense verve.

Fats Waller
'34/'35

Date recorded 1927 – 1935
Label RCA Victor
Musicians Fats Waller *piano, vocal*, Herman Autrey, Bill Coleman *trumpet*, Floyd O'Brien *trombone*, Gene Sedric *tenor sax, clarinet*, Rudy Powell, Milton "Mezz" Mezzrow *clarinet*, Al Casey, James Smith *guitar*, Bill Taylor, Charles Turner *bass*, Harry Dial, Arnold Bolden *drums*
Tracks Don't Let It Bother You ❑ If It Isn't Love ❑ Serenade for a Wealthy Widow ❑ Blue Black Bottom ❑ Mandy ❑ You've Been Taking Lessons in Love ❑ Numb Fumblin' ❑ Dust Off That Old Pianna ❑ Somebody Stole My Gal ❑ Breakin' the Ice ❑ I Ain't Got Nobody ❑ Goin' About ❑ Dinah ❑ Whose Honey Are You? ❑ Blue Because of You ❑ 12th Street Rag
Appraisal Fats Waller's dazzling stride piano is best caught alone, but it also drove the Rhythm band, a commercial, high-spirited swing group set up to showcase the star.

Artie Shaw
THE EARLY ARTIE SHAW

Date recorded August – October 1937
Label Ajaz
Musicians Artie Shaw *clarinet*, John Best, Tom DiCarlo, Malcolm Crain *trumpet*, George Arus, Harry Rodgers *trombone*, Les Robinson, Hank Freeman *alto sax*, Tony Pastor, Jules Rubin *tenor sax*, Les Burness *piano*, Al Avola *guitar*, Ben Ginsberg *bass*, Cliff Leeman *drums*, Leo Watson, Peg LaCentra, Bea Wain, Dolores O'Neil *vocal*
Tracks Am I in Love? ❑ Fee Fi Fo Fum ❑ Please Pardon Us We're in Love ❑ The Chant ❑ The Blues (2 takes) ❑ It's a Long, Long Way to Tipperary ❑ If It's the Last Thing I Do ❑ Nightmare ❑ Shoot the Likker to Me, John Boy ❑ Free Wheeling ❑ I've a Strange New Rhythm in My Heart ❑ Let 'er Go ❑ A Strange Lonliness
Appraisal Shaw was Benny Goodman's closest thirties rival, with a more reserved attack, but as faultless a technique. This band was no fireworks display but had swinging elegance, and the leader's solos here are gems.

Coleman Hawkins All Stars
COLEMAN HAWKINS ALL STARS

Date recorded 1935 – 1946
Label HMV
Musicians Coleman Hawkins *tenor sax*, Stephane Grappelly *piano*, Django Reinhardt *guitar*, Eugene d'Hellemes *bass*; **Coleman Hawkins All Star Jam Band** also featuring Benny Carter *alto sax*, *trumpet*, Andre Ekyan *alto sax*, Alix Combelle *tenor sax*, *clarinet*, Tommy Benford *drums*; **Coleman Hawkins Orchestra** also featuring Joe Guy *trumpet*, Earl Hardy *trombone*, Jackie Fields, Eustis Moore *alto sax*, Tommy Lindsay, Gene Rodgers *piano*, William Oscar Smith *bass*, Arthur Herbert *drums*; **Coleman Hawkins All Star Octet** also featuring J. C. Higginbotham *trombone*, Danny Polo *clarinet*, Lawrence Lucie *guitar*, Johnny Williams *bass*, Walter Johnson *drums*; **Coleman Hawkins 52nd Street All Stars** also featuring Charlie Shavers *trumpet*, Pete Brown *alto sax*, Allen Eager *tenor sax*, Jimmy Jones *piano*, Mary Osborne *guitar*, Al McKibbon *bass*, Shelly Manne *drums*
Tracks Crazy Rhythm ❑ Stardust ❑ Sheik of Araby ❑ Out of Nowhere ❑ Honeysuckle Rose ❑ Bouncing with Bean ❑ Body and Soul ❑ Sweet Georgia Brown ❑ When Day Is Done ❑ Spotlite
Appraisal In the course of a long and spectacular career, saxophonist Coleman Hawkins helped the Fletcher Henderson band become one of the best early swing ensembles, developed a flowing, even, inexorable rhythmic momentum as a soloist that mirrored the thirties big band beat, and performed in an immense variety of bands, delivering different versions of the idiom. This British compilation takes in the historic encounters with Belgian guitarist Django Reinhardt and with Benny Carter and some excellent Europeans in the lively Jam Band (both on Hawkins's five-year European tour from 1934 to 1939). It includes one of the greatest solo improvisations in all jazz – the 1939 "Body and Soul." Hardly pausing, without ever veering from a quiet, insistent swing, and briefly stating the theme of the tune only once, Hawkins delivers a masterpiece of harmonic inventiveness.

Duke Ellington and his Orchestra
AT HIS VERY BEST

Date recorded 1927 – 1946
Label RCA
Musicians Duke Ellington *piano*, Wallace Jones, Cootie Williams, Rex Stewart, Shelton Hemphill, Ray Nance, Harold Baker, Taft Jordan, Cat Anderson, Francis Williams, Louis Metcalf, Bubber Miley *trumpet*, Lawrence Brown, Juan Tizol, Joe Nanton, Claude Jones, Wilbur De Paris *trombone*, Otto Hardwicke, Johnny Hodges, Russell Procope *alto sax*, Ben Webster, Al Sears *tenor sax*, Harry Carney *baritone sax*, Barney Bigard, Jimmy Hamilton *clarinet*, Rudy Jackson *clarinet*, *tenor sax*, Fred Guy *guitar*, *banjo*, Jimmy Blanton, Oscar Pettiford, Alvin Raglin, Wellman Braud *bass*, Sonny Greer *drums*, Adelaide Hall, Kay Davis *vocal*
Tracks Jack the Bear ❑ Concerto for Cootie ❑ Harlem Air Shaft ❑ Across the Track Blues ❑ Chloe ❑ Royal Garden Blues ❑ Warm Valley ❑ Ko-Ko ❑ Black, Brown, and Beige ❑ Creole Love Call ❑ Transblucency
Appraisal More personal, impressionistic, and less inclined to a pop repertoire, Duke Ellington's band never became as popular as Benny Goodman's or Artie Shaw's, but it knew all about swing. In 1939, Ellington hired the great saxophonist Ben Webster and young bass prodigy Jimmy Blanton. Some of Ellington's finest pieces followed, notably "Jack the Bear," the devastating feature for Blanton; "Ko-Ko," a remarkable minor blues with harmonies anticipating modal jazz; and "Transblucency" for singer Kay Davis.

Duke Ellington and his Orchestra
SATURDAY NIGHT FUNCTION

Date recorded 1927 – 1929
Label HMV
Musicians including Duke Ellington *piano*, *arranger*, Bubber Miley, Arthur Whetsol *trumpet*, Johnny Hodges *sax*, Barney Bigard *clarinet*
Tracks Creole Love Call ❑ Got Everything but You ❑ Black and Tan Fantasy ❑ East Saint Louis Toodle-Oo ❑ Black Beauty ❑ Jubilee Stomp ❑ The Mooche ❑ Flaming Youth ❑ Saturday Night Function ❑ High Life
Appraisal Although Ellington wrote many extended compositions in a prolific career, he frequently demonstrated that he needed no more than miniature forms to be as eloquent as any composer in 20th century music. These earlier pieces, inspired by the Cotton Club period, show how the first great Ellington band had a rhythmic momentum that derived as much from the narrative drive of its structures as from the rhythm section. It also includes "Black and Tan Fantasy," which opens as a blues and ends as Chopin's "Funeral March." Far from a mature piece, it is still proof enough that here was an artist seeking to use the jazz orchestra in ways that had not been attempted before.

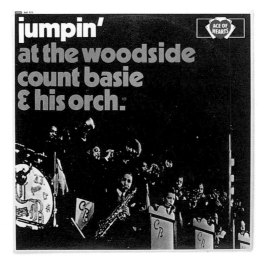

Count Basie and his Orchestra
JUMPIN' AT THE WOODSIDE

Date recorded 1937 – 1939
Label Ace of Hearts
Musicians Count Basie *piano*, Harry Edison, Shad Collins *trumpet*, Eddie Durham, George Hunt, Dan Minor, Benny Morton, Dickie Wells *trombone*, Earl Warren, Herschel Evans, Lester Young, Jack Washington *sax*, Freddie Green, Eddie Durham *guitar*, Walter Page *bass*, Jo Jones *drums*
Tracks Jumpin' at the Woodside ❑ Every Tub ❑ Out the Window ❑ Shorty George ❑ Time Out ❑ Doggin' Around ❑ Texas Shuffle ❑ Blue and Sentimental ❑ Cherokee ❑ Topsy ❑ John's Idea
Appraisal For sheer swing and energy, Basie's prewar band swept the board. The rhythm section perfected the pulse; soloists Young, Evans, and Edison did the rest, with classic Young solos on the title and "Every Tub."

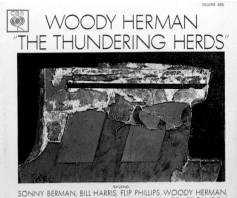

Woody Herman
THE THUNDERING HERDS
Date recorded February – November 1945
Label CBS
Musicians Woody Herman *clarinet, alto sax, vocal*,
Sonny Berman, Pete Candoli, Chuck Frankhauser, Carl
Warwick, Ray Wetzel, Irv Lewis, Conte Candoli,
Shorty Rogers, Ray Linn *trumpet*, Neal Hefti *trumpet,
arranger*, Bill Harris, Ed Kiefer, Ralph Pfeffner
trombone, Sam Marowitz, John LaPorta *alto sax*, Flip
Phillips, Pete Mondello, Mickey Folks *tenor sax*, Skippy
DeSair *baritone sax*, Ralph Burns *piano, arranger*, Tony
Aless *piano*, Billy Bauer *guitar*, Chubby Jackson *bass*,
Dave Tough, Don Lamond *drums*, Red Norvo, Margie
Hyams *vibes*, Frances Wayne *vocal*
Tracks Apple Honey ❑ Laura ❑ Caldonia ❑ Happiness
Is a Thing Called Joe ❑ Goosey Gander ❑ I Wonder ❑
A Kiss Goodnight ❑ Northwest Passage ❑ The Good
Earth ❑ I've Got the World on a String ❑ Bijou ❑ Gee,
It's Good to Hold You ❑ Put that Ring on My Finger
❑ Blowin' Up a Storm ❑ Your Father's Moustache ❑
Wild Root
Appraisal Herman's band was one of the forties'
most popular. Starting closer to Dixieland and vaude-
ville than many outfits — "Woodchoppers' Ball" was
its 1939 million-seller — it developed fast through
Ralph Burns's arrangements, great drummer Dave
Tough, and soloists like Bill Harris and Flip Phillips.
The trumpets' unison playing on "Caldonia," and Bill
Harris's solo on "Bijou" are late swing classics.

Chick Webb
MIDNITE IN HARLEM
Date recorded 1934 – 1939
Label Ace of Hearts
Musicians Chick Webb *drums*, Mario Bauza, Bobby
Stark, Taft Jordan, Dick Vance *trumpet*, Nat Story,
Sandy Williams, George Matthews, Claude Jones *trom-
bone*, Garvin Bushell, Hilton Jefferson, Teddy McRae,
Wayman Carver, Pete Clark, Edgar Sampson,
Chauncey Haughton, Louis Jordan *sax*, Tommy
Fulford, Joe Steele *piano*, Bobby Johnson *guitar*, John
Trueheart *guitar, banjo*, Beverly Peer, John Kirby,
Bill Thomas *bass*
Tracks Liza ❑ Blue Lou ❑ Azure ❑ Clap Hands!
Here Comes Charlie ❑ Go Harlem ❑ What a Shuffle
❑ In the Groove at the Grove ❑ Strictly Jive ❑
Squeeze Me ❑ Don't Be that Way ❑ Blue Minor ❑
Midnite in Harlem
Appraisal Drummer Webb's great band was one
of the most popular ever to play at Harlem's famous
Savoy Ballroom, and on tracks like "Go Harlem" and
"Clap Hands!" you can hear why. Although Gene
Krupa was the most popular drummer of the 1930s,
Webb's furious intensity was technically unrivaled at
the time, and the band's attack always suggests they're
playing for their lives. Ella Fitzgerald was yet to be
discovered by Webb at this time.

Lester Young/Count Basie
LESTER YOUNG MEMORIAL
ALBUM
Date recorded 1936 – 1940
Label Fontana
Musicians Lester Young *tenor sax*, Count Basie
piano; **The Count Basie Orchestra** featuring Ed
Lewis, Harry Edison, Shad Collins, Buck Clayton,
Al Killian, Carl Smith *trumpet*, Dickie Wells, Dan
Minor, Benny Morton, Vic Dickenson *trombone*, Earl
Warren, Jack Washington, Buddy Tate *sax*, Tab Smith
alto sax, Freddy Green *guitar*, Walter Page *bass*, Jo
Jones *drums*
Tracks Pound Cake ❑ Rock-a-Bye Basie ❑ Riff
Interlude ❑ Shoe Shine Boy ❑ Clap Hands, Here Comes
Charlie ❑ Taxi War Dance ❑ Ham 'n' Eggs ❑ Lester
Leaps In ❑ Dickie's Dream ❑ Blow Top ❑ Broadway ❑
Boogie Woogie
Appraisal Of all the star soloists of swing, Lester
Young seemed the one most casually inventing his
own rules. He proved it wasn't necessary to shout to
swing, he developed false fingering techniques now
commonplace in sax playing, and his use of space was a
constant surprise. Classic Young solos here are "Taxi
War Dance" and "Lester Leaps In."

Django Reinhardt
DJANGO AND HIS AMERICAN FRIENDS
Date recorded 1937 – 1939
Label EMI
Musicians Django Reinhardt *guitar*, Eddie South *violin*,
Wilson Myers *bass*; **Bill Coleman and his Orchestra:**
Bill Coleman *trumpet*, Frank "Big Boy" Goodie *clarinet,
tenor sax*, Christian Wagner *clarinet, alto sax*, Emil Stern
piano, Lucien Simoens, Paul Cordonnier *bass*, Jerry Mengo
drums; **Benny Carter and his Orchestra:** Benny Carter
trumpet, alto sax, Fletcher Allen *alto sax*, Alix Combelle
tenor sax, Bertie King *tenor sax, clarinet*, York de Souza
piano, Len Harrison *bass*, Robert Montmarché *drums*; **Rex
Stewart and his Feetwarmers:** Rex Stewart *cornet*,
Barney Bigard *clarinet, drums*, Billy Taylor *bass*
Tracks Eddie's Blues ❑ Sweet Georgia Brown ❑ I Ain't
Got Nobody ❑ Baby Won't You Please Come Home ❑
Big Boy Blues ❑ Bill Coleman Blues ❑ Somebody Loves
Me ❑ I Can't Believe that You're in Love with Me ❑ I'm
Coming, Virginia ❑ Farewell Blues ❑ Blue Light Blues ❑
Montmartre ❑ Low Cotton ❑ Finesse ❑ I Know that You
Know ❑ Solid Old Man
Appraisal In the prewar years, Belgian gypsy guitarist
Django Reinhardt was acknowledged as the most
significant European jazz musician by a considerable
margin. He was a performer of explosive speed but tender
elegance on ballads. The word about Django went back to
the States via a series of performances he recorded with
touring American musicians before the war, and although
the bands chug occasionally on this album, most of the
soloing sizzles.

Lionel Hampton
ALL AMERICAN AWARD CONCERT

Date recorded April 15, 1945
Label Brunswick
Musicians Lionel Hampton *vibes, piano, drums,* Dizzy Gillespie, Al Killian, Joe Morris, Wendell Culley, Lammar Wright, Jr., Dave Page *trumpet,* John Morris, Andrew Penn, Abdul Hamid, Al Hayse *trombone,* Herbie Fields, Gus Evans *alto sax,* Arnett Cobb, Jay Peters *tenor sax,* Charlie Fowlkes *baritone sax,* Milt Buckner *piano,* William Mackel *guitar,* Charlie Harris, Teddy Sinclair *bass,* Fred Radcliffe *drums,* Dinah Washington *vocal*
Tracks Hamp's Blues ❑ I Know that You Know ❑ Loose Wig ❑ Hamp's Boogie Woogie ❑ Oh, Lady Be Good ❑ Evil Gal Blues ❑ Red Cross ❑ Flying Home
Appraisal Hampton's bands seemed to start flat out, then accelerate, as this 1945 live performance shows.

Benny Goodman
CARNEGIE HALL JAZZ CONCERT

Date recorded January 16, 1938
Label Philips
Musicians Benny Goodman *clarinet,* Harry James, Ziggy Elman, Gordon Griffin, Cootie Williams, Buck Clayton *trumpet,* Vernon Brown, Red Ballard *trombone,* Bobby Hackett *cornet,* Hymie Schertzer *alto sax,* Johnny Hodges *alto & soprano sax,* George Koenig, Babe Russin, Arthur Rollini, Lester Young *tenor sax,* Harry Carney *baritone sax,* Count Basie, Teddy Wilson, Jess Stacy *piano,* Allan Reuss, Freddy Green *guitar,* Walter Page *bass,* Gene Krupa *drums,* Lionel Hampton *vibes,* Harry Goodman, Martha Tilton *vocal*
Tracks Don't Be That Way ❑ One o'Clock Jump ❑ Dixieland One Step ❑ I'm Coming Virginia ❑ When My Baby Smiles at Me ❑ Shine ❑ Blue Reverie ❑ Life Goes to a Party ❑ Stompin' at the Savoy ❑ Dizzy Spells ❑ Sing Sing Sing ❑ Big John's Special
Appraisal Goodman's crowning achievement, and a landmark of jazz history. Having triggered a cult, the bandleader eventually had it endorsed by the arts establishment and put jazz in Carnegie Hall. This was also one of Goodman's finest performances, warmer and deeper than formerly, thrilling on "Sing Sing Sing," and featuring walk-on parts for some star guests such as Count Basie.

Goodman was an energetic entrepreneur of swing, but also one of its finest improvisers. His solos are packed with tone changes, tremolo, delays, and blue notes.

Jay McShann
KANSAS CITY MEMORIES

Date recorded 1941 – 1943
Label Brunswick
Musicians Jay McShann Orchestra featuring Jay McShann *piano,* Bernard Anderson, Orville Minor, Harold Bruce, "Geepy" *trumpet,* Lawrence Anderson *trombone,* Charlie Parker, John Jackson *alto sax,* Bob Mabane, Paul Quinichette, "Stoogy" Gelz *tenor sax,* Gene Ramey *bass,* Gus Johnson, Harold West *drums,* Walter Brown, Al Hibbler *vocal*
Tracks The Jumpin' Blues ❑ Hootie Blues ❑ Dexter Blues ❑ Confessin' the Blues ❑ Sepian Bounce ❑ Swingmatism ❑ Say Forward, I'll March ❑ Get Me on Your Mind
Appraisal An accomplished Basie-type Kansas City band, though Walter Brown's blues vocals sag. Its altoist is the young Charlie Parker, then in Lester Young mode.

Bebop

TRULY NEW MOVEMENTS rarely attract commerce until the fuss has died down. Bebop, which took swing and turbocharged it, was a subculture at first, rejected by many older jazz musicians and listeners. Its ideas would have been disseminated on record earlier had it not been for the American Federation of Musicians' recording ban from 1942 to 1944, so the new style was close to four years old before the general public got to know of it. When it did, the urgent message of Charlie Parker, Dizzy Gillespie, Thelonious Monk, Kenny Clarke, and others spread like wildfire. Small independent record labels, like New York's Blue Note, sprang up to catch the fast-evaporating trails of these cometlike virtuosos. Some still insisted that bebop was the end of jazz.

J. J. Johnson
THE EMINENT JAY JAY JOHNSON
Date recorded 1952 – 1954
Label Blue Note (British edition on Vogue)
Musicians J. J. Johnson *trombone*, Wynton Kelly *piano*, Charlie Mingus *bass*, Kenny Clarke *drums*, "Sabu" *congas*
Tracks Jay ❑ Time after Time ❑ Old Devil Moon ❑ Too Marvelous for Words ❑ It's You or No One ❑ Coffee Pot
Appraisal J. J. Johnson was *the* bop trombonist, a musician of great melodic invention and clarity at any tempo. There are some animated exchanges here with a fine pianist, Wynton Kelly.

Al Haig
JAZZ WILL O'THE WISP
Date recorded March 13, 1954
Label Esoteric
Musicians Al Haig *piano*, Bill Crow *bass*, Lee Abrams *drums*
Tracks Autumn in New York ❑ Isn't It Romantic ❑ They Can't Take that Away from Me ❑ Royal Garden Blues ❑ Don't Blame Me ❑ Moonlight in Vermont ❑ If I Should Lose You ❑ April in Paris ❑ All God's Chillun Got Rhythm ❑ Body and Soul ❑ Gone with the Wind ❑ My Old Flame ❑ On the Alamo
Appraisal Stan Getz and Charlie Parker both named Al Haig as their personal keyboard favorite, and on this fine session of part unaccompanied standards, part trio music, the reasons are obvious. Haig's restrained perfectionism and harmonic ingenuity create a string of gems, making his neglect from the 1950s to the 1970s hard to fathom.

Sonny Stitt
STITT'S BITS
Date recorded 1950
Label Prestige (British issue on Esquire)
Musicians Sonny Stitt *tenor sax*, Bill Massey *trumpet*, Matthew Gee *trombone*, Gene Ammons *baritone sax*, Kenny Drew, Duke Jordan, Junior Mance *piano*, Tommy Potter, Gene Wright *bass*, Art Blakey, Wesley Landers *drums*
Tracks Nevertheless ❑ Count Every Star ❑ Nice Work If You Can Get It ❑ There Will Never Be Another You ❑ Blazin' ❑ Mean to Me ❑ Avalon ❑ After You've Gone ❑ Stairway to the Stars ❑ 'Swonderful ❑ Jeepers Creepers ❑ Our Very Own
Appraisal Always unfairly in Parker's shadow, Stitt was a tireless, muscular, hard-swinging improviser whose independent imagination is better displayed on tenor than alto. Art Blakey is superb on drums.

Charlie Parker
THE COMPLETE DEAN BENEDETTI RECORDINGS
Date recorded 1947 – 1948
Label Mosaic
Musicians featuring Charlie Parker *alto sax*, Miles Davis, Howard McGhee *trumpet*, Thelonious Monk, Duke Jordan *piano*, Max Roach *drums*
Tracks More than 250 live takes on ten LPs (or seven CDs)
Appraisal An archive more than a compilation, this exhaustive charting of Bird in flight consists of many live recordings caught by amateur musician and fan Benedetti's primitive acetate disk machine. But for serious Parker students they are invaluable, including an unusual encounter with Thelonious Monk and revelations of how Bird would approach the same tune on successive nights. Sound quality, inevitably, is poor.

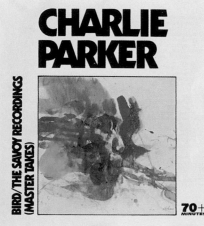

Charlie Parker
BIRD/THE SAVOY RECORDINGS (MASTER TAKES)

Date recorded 1944 – 1948
Label Savoy
Musicians Charlie Parker *alto & tenor sax*, Miles Davis, Dizzy Gillespie *trumpet, piano*, Clyde Hart, Sadik Hakim, Bud Powell, John Lewis, Duke Jordan *piano*, Tiny Grimes *guitar, vocal*, Curly Russell, Tommy Potter, Nelson Boyd *bass*, Jimmy Butts *bass, vocal*, Max Roach, Harold "Doc" West *drums*
Tracks Tiny's Tempo ❑ Red Cross ❑ Warming Up a Riff ❑ Billie's Bounce ❑ Now's the Time ❑ Thriving on a Riff ❑ Koko ❑ Donna Lee ❑ Chasin' the Bird ❑ Cheryl ❑ Milestones ❑ Little Willie Leaps ❑ Half Nelson ❑ Another Hair-Do ❑ Bluebird ❑ Klaunstance ❑ Bird Gets the Worm ❑ Barbados ❑ Ah-Leu-Cha ❑ Constellation ❑ Parker's Mood ❑ Perhaps ❑ Marmaduke ❑ Steeple Chase ❑ Merry-Go-Round
Appraisal Parker's most remarkable recordings were in the mid-1940s for the Savoy and Dial labels. His clear execution, imperious sound, and the variety of his lines create bop classics here, like "Billie's Bounce" and "Now's the Time." An uneven but distinctive Miles Davis and some excellent Bud Powell, Duke Jordan, and Max Roach complete a dazzling picture.

Bud Powell
THE AMAZING BUD POWELL

Date recorded 1949 – 1953
Label Blue Note
Musicians Bud Powell *piano*, Fats Navarro *trumpet*, Sonny Rollins *tenor sax*, Tommy Potter, Curly Russell, George Duvivier *bass*, Max Roach, Roy Haynes, Arthur Taylor *drums*
Tracks Un Poco Loco (3 takes) ❑ Dance of the Infidels ❑ 52nd Street Theme ❑ It Could Happen to You (2 takes) ❑ A Night in Tunisia (2 takes) ❑ Wail ❑ Ornithology (2 takes) ❑ Bouncing with Bud ❑ Parisian Thoroughfare ❑ Reets and I ❑ Autumn in New York ❑ I Want to be Happy ❑ Sure Thing ❑ Polka Dots and Moonbeams ❑ Glass Enclosure ❑ Collard Greens and Black-Eye Peas ❑ Over the Rainbow ❑ Audrey ❑ You Go to My Head
Appraisal Here Bud Powell the quintessential bop pianist is in powerful company, with a youthful Fats Navarro and Sonny Rollins. For all his storming technique, Powell's music was always on a knife edge of strength and poignant vulnerability, and the other musicians, particularly trumpeter Fats Navarro, tune in to his extremes. This disk captures some of Powell's most formidable works, notably "Un Poco Loco" — which reveals his probing improviser's mind over three separate takes — the bop anthem "Ornithology," and an evocative "Parisian Thoroughfare."

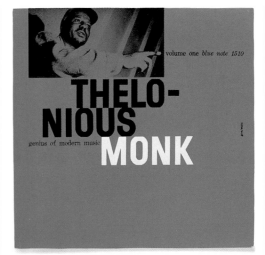

Thelonious Monk
GENIUS OF MODERN MUSIC

Date recorded October – November 1947
Label Blue Note
Musicians Thelonious Monk *piano*, George Taitt, Idresse Suliman, Kenny Dorham *trumpet*, Sahib Shihab, Danny Quebec West, Lou Donaldson *alto sax*, Billy Smith, Lucky Thompson *tenor sax*, Robert Paige, Gene Ramey, John Simmons, Nelson Boyd, Al McKibbon *bass*, Art Blakey, Shadow Wilson, Max Roach *drums*, Milt Jackson *vibes*
Tracks 'Round About Midnight ❑ Off Minor ❑ Ruby My Dear ❑ I Mean You ❑ April in Paris ❑ In Walked Bud ❑ Thelonious ❑ Epistrophy ❑ Misterioso ❑ Well You Needn't ❑ Introspection ❑ Humph ❑ Carolina Moon ❑ Hornin' In ❑ Skippy ❑ Let's Cool One ❑ Suburban Eyes ❑ Evonce ❑ Straight No Chaser ❑ Four in One ❑ Nice Work ❑ Monk's Mood ❑ Who Knows ❑ Ask Me Now
Appraisal Monk's willful genius was rarely caught as well as on Blue Notes from the forties and fifties. These were his first recordings as leader, when many of his most enduringly personal compositions were written and some erratic but eventful partnerships with other musicians occurred. However elbowing and dissonant Monk's music seems, it is always implacably logical, and his remarkable thematic variety here is rivaled only by the seamlessness with which writing and improvising entwine.

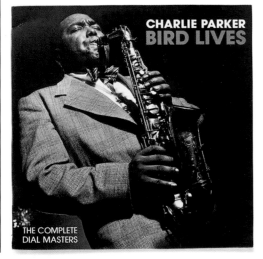

Charlie Parker
BIRD LIVES – THE COMPLETE DIAL MASTERS

Date recorded 1946 – 1947
Label Spotlite
Musicians featuring Charlie Parker *alto sax*, Dizzy Gillespie, Howard McGhee, Miles Davis *trumpet*, J. J. Johnson *trombone*, Wardell Gray *tenor sax*, George Handy, Duke Jordan *piano*, Tommy Potter *bass*, Max Roach *drums*, Milt Jackson *vibes*, Earl Coleman *vocal*
Tracks Diggin' Diz ❑ Moose the Mooche ❑ Yardbird Suite ❑ Ornithology ❑ A Night in Tunisia ❑ Max Is Making Wax ❑ Loverman ❑ The Gypsy ❑ Bebop ❑ This Is Always ❑ Dark Shadows ❑ Bird's Nest ❑ Hot Blues ❑ Cool Blues ❑ Relaxing at Camarillo ❑ Cheers ❑ Carvin' the Bird ❑ Stupendous ❑ Dexterity ❑ Bongo Bop ❑ Dewey Square ❑ The Hymn ❑ Bird of Paradise ❑ Embraceable You ❑ Bird Feathers ❑ Klactoveed-sedstene ❑ Scrapple from the Apple ❑ My Old Flame ❑ Out of Nowhere ❑ Don't Blame Me ❑ Drifting on a Reed ❑ Quasimodo ❑ Charlie's Wig ❑ Bongo Beep ❑ Crazeology ❑ How Deep Is the Ocean
Appraisal Charlie Parker signed to Los Angeles-based Dial records in 1946 and cut some of his most scorching performances for it. His speed of thought and execution and juggling with accent placing on "Ornithology" are all the more remarkable for not being exceptional by his standards, since "Yardbird Suite," "A Night in Tunisia," and many other takes reveal the same reflexive sense of form. Rivals to the Louis Armstrong Hot Fives and Sevens for small-group brilliance, these takes are among the great classics of jazz.

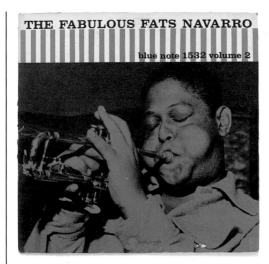

THE FABULOUS FATS NAVARRO

blue note 1532 volume 2

Fats Navarro
THE FABULOUS FATS NAVARRO

Date recorded 1947 – 1949
Label Blue Note
Musicians Fats Navarro, Howard McGhee *trumpet*,
Ernie Henry *alto sax*, Sonny Rollins, Charlie Rouse,
Wardell Gray, Allen Eager *tenor sax*, Bud Powell, Tadd
Dameron *piano*, Milt Jackson *piano*, *vibes*, Nelson Boyd,
Tommy Potter, Curly Russell *bass*, Shadow Wilson,
Roy Haynes, Kenny Clarke *drums*, Chano Pozo *bongos*
Tracks Our Delight (2 takes) ❑ The Squirrel (2 takes)
❑ The Chase (2 takes) ❑ Wail ❑ Bouncing with Bud (2
takes) ❑ Double Talk (2 takes) ❑ Dameronia (2 takes) ❑
Lady Bird (2 takes) ❑ Jahbero (2 takes) ❑ Symphonette
(2 takes) ❑ Dance of the Infidels ❑ The Skunk
❑ Boperation
Appraisal One of the most intelligent and original of
bebop trumpeters, the short-lived Fats Navarro made
his solos sound like full-scale compositions. His
deft phrasing and lovely sound illuminate "The Chase"
and "Lady Bird."

Ol' man Rebop

dizzy gillespie and his orchestra

"HIS MASTER'S VOICE"
LONG PLAY 33⅓ R.P.M. RECORD

PHOTO: MELODY MAKER

Dizzy Gillespie and his Orchestra
OL' MAN REBOP

Gillespie was bop's master
trumpeter and master showman. The
Cab Calloway Band taught him
theatricality and his brass technique
was stunning.

Date recorded 1946 – 1949
Label HMV
Musicians Dizzy Gillespie *trumpet*, Dave Burns, Elmon
Wright, Matthew McKay, Ray Orr, Lammar Wright
Jr., Ernest Bailey, Willie Cook, Bennie Harris *trumpet*,
Taswell Baird, William Shepherd, Ted Kelly, André
Duryea, Sam Hurt, Jesse Tarrant *trombone*, Howard
Johnson, John Brown, Ernest Henry *alto sax*, James
Moody, Joe Gayles, Don Byas, George Nicholas,
William Evans *tenor sax*, Cecil Payne, Alfred Gibson
baritone sax, John Lewis, Al Haig, James Forman Jr.
piano, Milt Jackson *vibes*, John Collins, Bill De Arango
guitar, Al McKibbon, Ray Brown *bass*, Joe Harris, J. C.
Heard, Kenny Clarke, Teddy Stewart *drums*, Lucien
Rose, Chano Pozo *bongos*, Vincent Guerra *congas*
Tracks Ow! ❑ Stay on It ❑ Manteca ❑ Oop-Pop-a-Da ❑
Anthropology ❑ Algo Bueno ❑ Katy ❑ Two Bass Hit ❑
Swedish Suite ❑ Ol' Man Rebop
Appraisal Although the harmonic agility of bebop
made it predominantly a small-group music, Dizzy
Gillespie adapted its methods to a big band format and
added extra excitement with Afro-Cuban rhythms.
These late 1940s takes include the ferocious "Manteca"
and reveal how a technically remarkable ensemble
negotiated the ski runs of bop melody.

James Moody's Band
MOODY'S WORKSHOP

Date recorded 1954 – 1955
Label Prestige (British edition on XTRA)
Musicians James Moody *tenor & alto sax*, Dave Burns *trumpet*, William Shepherd *trombone*, Pee Wee Moore *baritone sax*, John Lathan *bass*, Eddie Jefferson *vocal*,
Tracks Keepin' Up with Jonesy ❑ Workshop ❑ I'm Gone ❑ A Hundred Years from Today ❑ Jack Raggs ❑ Mambo with Moody ❑ Over the Rainbow ❑ Blues in the Closet ❑ Moody's Mood for Blues ❑ Nobody Knows ❑ It Might as Well be Spring
Appraisal Gillespie sideman Moody displayed a more humane and conversational approach to chord playing than many boppers. Vocalist Eddie Jefferson inspired the popular "vocalese" exploits (putting lyrics to horn solos) of King Pleasure.

Charley Christian/Dizzy Gillespie
THE HARLEM JAZZ SCENE

Date recorded May 1941
Label Esoteric
Musicians including Charlie Christian *guitar*, Dizzy Gillespie, Joe Guy *trumpet*, Don Byas *tenor sax*, Kenny Kersey *piano*, Thelonious Monk *piano*, Kenny Clarke *drums*, Nick Fenton *bass*
Tracks Swing to Bop ❑ Stompin' at the Savoy ❑ Up on Teddy's Hill ❑ Guy's Got to Go ❑ Lips Flips ❑ Stardust – Kerouac
Appraisal First low-fidelity stirrings of bop at Minton's Playhouse and Monroe's Uptown House: a live jam for virtuoso Christian, a Dizzy Gillespie shifting from swing, and revolutionary drummer Clarke.

Various artists
THE BE-BOP ERA

Date recorded 1946 – 1950
Label RCA Victor
Musicians featuring Coleman Hawkins *leader, tenor sax*, Illinois Jacquet *leader, tenor sax*, Lucky Thompson *leader, tenor sax*, Charlie Ventura *leader, tenor sax*, Dizzy Gillespie *leader, trumpet, vocal*, Count Basie *leader, piano*, Kenny Clarke *leader, drums*; Miles Davis, Fats Navarro, Kenny Dorham, Joe Newman, Russell Jacquet, Neal Hefti, Conte Candoli, Harry Edison, David Burns, Elmon Wright, Matthew McKay, Ray Orr, Lammar Wright, Ernest Bailey, Willie Cook, Bennie Harris *trumpet,* J. J. Johnson, Benny Green, Kai Winding, Dickie Wells, Taswell Baird, Ted Kelly, André Duryea, Sam Hurt, Jesse Tarrant *trombone,* Charlie Parker, Pete Brown, Georgie Auld, Howard Johnson, John Brown, Ernie Henry *alto sax*, Benny Carter, Gene Ammons, James Moody, Don Byas, Robert Lawson, Boots Mussulli *sax*, Allen Eager, Joe Gayles, George Nicholas, Yusef Lateef *tenor sax,* Leo Parker, Ernie Caceres, Cecil Payne, Alfred Gibson *baritone sax*, Sonny Stitt, Buddy DeFranco *clarinet*, Ray Abramson, Eddy DeVertetill *reeds,* Lennie Tristano, John Lewis, Bud Powell, Jimmy Henry Jones, Sir Charles Thompson, Dodo Marmarosa, Dan McKenna, James Foreman Jr. *piano,* Al McKibbon, Al Lucas, Red Mitchell, Al Hall, Red Callender, Eddie Safranski, Ray Brown *bass,* Mary Osborne, John Collins, Barney Kessel, Freddie Green, Billy Bauer *guitar,* Milt Jackson *vibes,* Shelly Manne, Shadow Wilson, Jack Mills, Ed Shaughnessy, Gus Johnson, Joe Harris, Kenneth Spearman, Teddy Steward *drums,* Chano Pozo *bongos,* Vincent Guerra *congas,* Joe Carroll *vocal*
Tracks Allen's Alley ❑ Mutton Leg ❑ Boppin' the Blues ❑ Epistrophy ❑ 52nd Street Theme ❑ Oop-Bop Sh-Bam ❑ Royal Roost ❑ Ha ❑ Overtime ❑ Victory Ball ❑ Rat Race ❑ Ow! ❑ Oop-Pop-A-Da ❑ Stay On It ❑ Cool Breeze ❑ Jump Did-Le Ba
Appraisal Although bebop was rejected as unmusical and commercial suicide by many musicians in its early years, by the mid 1940s attitudes were changing. Apart from bebop fundamentalists like Kenny Clarke and Dizzy Gillespie, Coleman Hawkins (always an intelligent listener) recognized links with his chord-based improvising style and made early bop recordings. Charlie Ventura led a popular Bop for the People band in the late 1940s and played a swing variation colored by bop. By the end of the decade, most swing musicians had adopted some of its ideas.

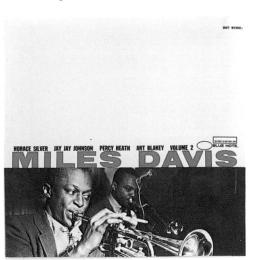

Miles Davis
MILES DAVIS VOLUME 2

Date recorded April 20, 1953
Label Blue Note
Musicians Miles Davis *trumpet*, J. J. Johnson *trombone*, Jimmy Heath *tenor sax*, Gil Coggins *piano*, Percy Heath *bass*, Art Blakey *drums*
Tracks Kelo (2 takes) ❑ Enigma (2 takes) ❑ Ray's Idea (2 takes) ❑ Tempus Fugit (2 takes) ❑ C.T.A. (2 takes) ❑ I Waited for You
Appraisal By 1950, Miles Davis was working in an intimate bop-shaped world of his own. These beautiful improvisations are often considered his best.

The Quintet
JAZZ AT MASSEY HALL

Date recorded 1953
Label Debut
Musicians "Charlie Chan" *alto sax*, Dizzy Gillespie *trumpet*, Bud Powell *piano*, Charles Mingus *bass*, Max Roach *drums*
Tracks Perdido ❑ Salt Peanuts ❑ All the Things You Are ❑ Wee ❑ Hot House ❑ A Night in Tunisia
Appraisal Contractual problems made Charlie Parker work under an alias on this dramatic live partnership between the bop leaders, with a rare outing in the idiom for Mingus, whose tape recorder caught the historic set.

Cool jazz

THE BEBOP REVOLUTION, with its fast-lane, live-for-now intensity and practitioners obsessed with avoiding or inverting the familiar, had been absorbed by the early 1950s. It still remained powerful but was mirrored by a softer, paler reflection — cool jazz. Some musicians, mostly white, had taken devices from classical music and imported them into jazz in the 1940s. Mutations of these ideas eventually inspired Miles Davis, whose oblique, muted trumpet style was a perfect solo voice, and the formation of his 1948 nine-piece band led to the recording *Birth of the Cool*. If cool was laid-back, it was not unemotional — some of its relatives, like the white West Coast school which included trumpeters Chet Baker and Shorty Rogers and saxophonist Gerry Mulligan, were marked by a boplike robustness. Record companies opened up on the West Coast to catch the new movement — notably Richard Bock's Pacific Jazz, which recorded the Mulligan/Baker band.

Chet Baker
CHET BAKER & CREW

Date recorded 1956
Label Pacific Jazz (British edition on Vogue)
Musicians Chet Baker *trumpet*, Phil Urso *tenor sax*, Bobby Timmons *piano*, Jimmy Bond *bass*, Peter Littman *drums*, Bill Loughborough *chromatic tympani*
Tracks To Mickey's Memory ❑ Slightly Above Moderate ❑ Halema ❑ Revelation ❑ Something for Liza ❑ Lucius Lu ❑ Worrying the Life out of Me ❑ Medium Rock
Appraisal Baker's first record two years after narcotics arrests shows the bruised tenderness of his sound startlingly intact. Urso provides freewheeling tenor.

Lee Konitz
VERY COOL

Date recorded 1955 or 1957
Label Columbia
Musicians Lee Konitz *alto sax*, Don Ferrara *trumpet*, Sal Mosca *piano*, Peter Ind *bass*, Shadow Wilson *drums*
Tracks Sunflower ❑ Stairway to the Stars ❑ Movin' Around ❑ Kary's Trance ❑ Crazy She Calls Me ❑ Billie's Bounce
Appraisal Much of Lee Konitz's best work was from the late 1950s, and this album is devoted to both group improvisation and the leader's growing sensitivity to simplicity and the expressiveness of tone.

Jimmy Giuffre
THE JIMMY GIUFFRE 3

Date recorded 1956
Label Atlantic (British edition on London)
Musicians Jimmy Giuffre *clarinet, tenor & baritone sax*, Jim Hall *guitar*, Ralph Pena *bass*
Tracks Gotta Dance ❑ Two Kinds of Blues ❑ The Song Is You ❑ Crazy She Calls Me ❑ Voodoo ❑ My All ❑ That's the Way It Is ❑ Crawdad Suite ❑ The Train and the River
Appraisal An emphatic, reflexive group improvisation from the 1950s around Giuffre's graceful folksy ideas. Giuffre's theme "The Train and the River" became a cool jazz anthem following the movie *Jazz on a Summer's Day*.

The Modern Jazz Quartet
ONE NEVER KNOWS

Date recorded 1957
Label Atlantic (British edition on London)
Musicians John Lewis *piano*, Milt Jackson *vibraharp*, Percy Heath *bass*, Connie Kay *drums*
Tracks The Golden Striker ❑ One Never Knows ❑ The Rose Truc ❑ Cortege ❑ Venice ❑ Three Windows
Appraisal Although cool is thought of as a white movement, Miles Davis and the M.J.Q.'s John Lewis were its most innovatory adherents, and Lewis's delicate "chamber jazz" group, with its brilliant vibraharpist Milt Jackson, became massively popular. This is one of its finest albums, showing how much powerful emotion can be evoked by understatement.

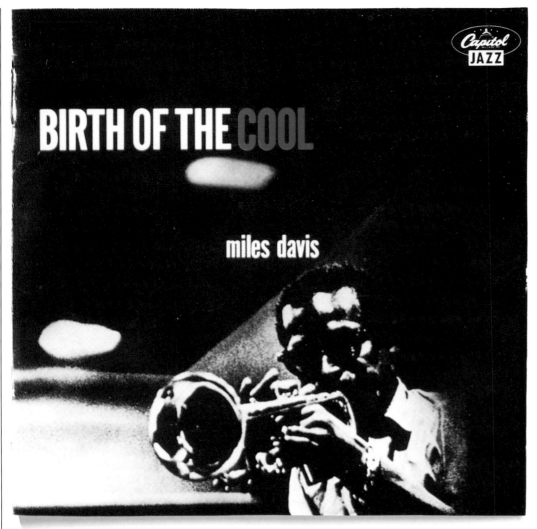

Shorty Rogers
THE SWINGING MR. ROGERS

Date recorded 1955
Label Atlantic (British edition on London)
Musicians Shorty Rogers *trumpet*, Jimmy Giuffre *clarinet, tenor & baritone sax*, Pete Jolly *piano*, Curtis Counce *bass*, Shelly Manne *drums*
Tracks Isn't It Romantic ❑ Trickleydidlier ❑ Oh Play that Thing ❑ Not Really the Blues ❑ Martians Go Home ❑ My Heart Stood Still ❑ Michele's Meditation ❑ That's What I'm Talkin' 'Bout
Appraisal A punchy trumpeter who always made cool jazz swing, Rogers is heard here with a mid-1950s quintet on a repertoire in which his sense of shape as an improviser and as a composer are indistinguishable from one another.

Miles Davis
BIRTH OF THE COOL

Date recorded 1949 – 1950
Label Capitol
Musicians Miles Davis *leader, trumpet*, Gil Evans *arranger*, Kai Winding, J. J. Johnson *trombone*, Lee Konitz *alto sax*, Gerry Mulligan *baritone sax*, Junior Collins, Sandy Siegelstein, Gunther Schuller *French horn*, John Barber *tuba*, Al Haig, John Lewis *piano*, Joe Shulman, Nelson Boyd, Al McKibbon *bass*, Max Roach, Kenny Clarke *drums*, Kenny Hagood *vocal*
Tracks Move ❑ Jeru ❑ Moon Dreams ❑ Venus de Milo ❑ Budo ❑ Deception ❑ Godchild ❑ Boplicity ❑ Rocker ❑ Israel ❑ Rouge ❑ Darn that Dream
Appraisal Davis led the Birth of the Cool band for only two weeks of live shows. These later recordings capture a flowing and contemplative sound quite different from bop's freneticism. Lee Konitz's fragile alto sound and Gerry Mulligan's velvety baritone are crucial to it, as is Gil Evans's use of unusual instrumentation.

Gerry Mulligan/Chet Baker
MULLIGAN/BAKER

Date recorded 1951, 1952, 1965
Label Prestige
Musicians Gerry Mulligan *baritone sax*, Chet Baker *trumpet, flügelhorn*, Jerry Hurwitz, Nick Travis *trumpet*, Ollie Wilson *trombone*, Allen Eager, George Coleman *tenor sax*, Max McElroy *baritone sax*, George Wallington, Kirk Lightsey *piano*, Phil Leshin, Carson Smith, Herman Wright *bass*, Chico Hamilton, Walter Bolden, Roy Brooks *drums*, Gail Madden *maracas*
Tracks Carioca ❑ Line for Lyons ❑ Moonlight in Vermont ❑ Bark for Barksdale ❑ Turnstile ❑ Lady Is a Tramp ❑ My Funny Valentine ❑ Funhouse ❑ Ide's Side ❑ Roundhouse ❑ Kaper ❑ Bweebida Bobbida ❑ Mullenium ❑ Limelight ❑ Mulligan's Too ❑ So Easy ❑ Go-Go ❑ Bevan Beeps ❑ Rearin' Back
Appraisal The pianoless early fifties Mulligan/Baker bands were the sound of cool West Coast music for many, Baker's offhand lyricism weaving around the deep-throated sound of Mulligan's baritone. This later compilation covers a lengthy period of the trumpeter's troubled career.

Gerry Mulligan/Paul Desmond
BLUES IN TIME

Date recorded August 1, 27, 1957
Label Verve
Musicians Gerry Mulligan *baritone sax*, Paul Desmond *alto sax*, David Bailey *drums*, Joe Benjamin *bass*
Tracks Blues in Time ❑ Body and Soul ❑ Stand Still ❑ Line for Lyons ❑ Wintersong ❑ Battle Hymn of the Republican ❑ Fall Out
Appraisal This is the first meeting between Mulligan and the buttery-toned Paul Desmond at 2am after Mulligan's recording with Stan Getz and Oscar Peterson. The session has a spontaneous feel and ideal contrast between the gliding alto and rugged baritone.

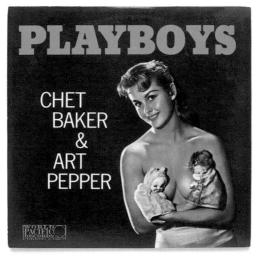

Chet Baker/Art Pepper
PLAYBOYS

Date recorded October 31, 1956
Label Pacific Jazz
Musicians Chet Baker *trumpet*, Art Pepper *alto sax*, Phil Urso *tenor sax*, Carl Perkins *piano*, Curtis Counce *bass*, Lawrence Marable *drums*
Tracks For Minors Only ❑ Minor-Yours ❑ Resonant Emotions ❑ Tynan Tyme ❑ Picture of Heath ❑ For Miles and Miles ❑ C.T.A.
Appraisal A fine band recorded in Los Angeles and featuring two of the most distinctive soloists on the West Coast: the alternately brittle and graceful Pepper and the romantic Baker on tunes written and arranged by saxophonist Jimmy Heath.

The Jimmy Giuffre 3
THESIS

Date recorded August 7 – 8, 1961
Label Verve
Musicians Jimmy Giuffre *clarinet*, Paul Bley *piano*, Steve Swallow *bass*
Tracks Ictus ❑ That's True That's True ❑ Sonic ❑ Whirrrr ❑ Carla ❑ Goodbye ❑ Musician ❑ Flight ❑ The Gamut
Appraisal One of the most underrated of great jazz trios. This meeting of Giuffre's murmuring clarinet, Bley's ambiguous chording, and Swallow's bold bass interjections is a masterpiece of collective improvisation that has not become dated one bit.

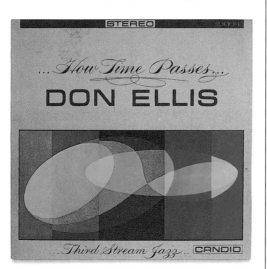

Don Ellis
HOW TIME PASSES

Date recorded October 4 – 5, 1960
Label Candid
Musicians Don Ellis *trumpet*, Jaki Byard *alto sax*, *piano*, Ron Carter *bass*, Charlie Persip *drums*
Tracks How Time Passes ❑ Sallie ❑ A Simplex One ❑ Waste ❑ Improvisational Suite
Appraisal Some cool schoolwork was inspired by nonimprovisational academic music like that of Schönberg and Stockhausen, a line of formal, rather abstract jazz dubbed Third Stream. Here the musicians, particularly the adventurous and athletic Ellis, deal ingeniously with the demands of structures rarely used in jazz, like Schönberg's twelve-tone row.

Warne Marsh
NE PLUS ULTRA

Date recorded September – October 1969
Label Revelation
Musicians Warne Marsh *tenor sax*, Gary Foster *alto sax*, Dave Parlato *bass*, John Tirabasso *drums*
Tracks You Stepped Out of a Dream ❑ Lennie's Pennies ❑ 317 E. 32nd ❑ Subconscious-Lee ❑ Touch and Go
Appraisal Like Lennie Tristano's piano figures, Warne Marsh's solos unfurl long lines of understated insistence with spontaneous melody-spinning of a sustained originality that puts him in the top league. Marsh's squawky tone and ascetic coolness make him an acquired taste but worth the effort.

Jimmy Giuffre
FREE FALL

Date recorded 1964
Label Columbia
Musicians Jimmy Giuffre *clarinet*, Paul Bley *piano*, Steve Swallow *bass*
Tracks Propulsion ❑ Threewe ❑ Ornothoids ❑ Dichotomy ❑ Man Alone ❑ Spasmodic ❑ Yggdrasill ❑ Divided Man ❑ Primordial Call ❑ The Five Ways
Appraisal Giuffre called bop harmonies vertical prisons, and this third album by the trio featuring Paul Bley and Steve Swallow is the freest and superficially the least inviting. But it is also the most powerfully realized collective interplay between these three imaginative performers.

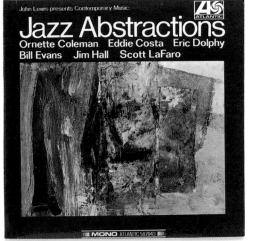

John Lewis/Various Artists
JAZZ ABSTRACTIONS

Date recorded 1960
Label Atlantic
Musicians Ornette Coleman *alto sax*, Eric Dolphy *flute,
bass clarinet, alto sax*, Robert DiDomenica *flute*, Bill Evans
piano, Eddie Costa *vibes*, Jim Hall *guitar*, Charles Libove,
Roland Vamos *violin*, Harry Zaratzian, Alfred Brown
viola, Joseph Tekula *cello*, Scott LaFaro, Alvin Brehm,
George Duvivier *bass*, Sticks Evans *drums*
Tracks Abstraction ❑ Piece for Guitar and Strings ❑
Variants on a Theme of John Lewis (Django) ❑ Variants
on a Theme of Thelonious Monk (Criss-Cross)
Appraisal Strongly conservatory-influenced Third
Stream jazz, composed by Gunther Schuller and Jim Hall.
Sober, but often fascinating, particularly for Ornette
Coleman's sweeping variations on Gunther Schuller's
"Abstraction" and the Monk theme.

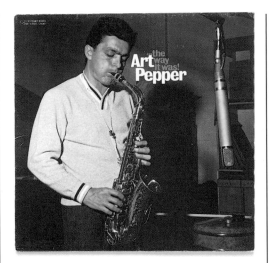

Art Pepper
THE WAY IT WAS!

Date recorded 1956 – 1960
Label Contemporary
Musicians Art Pepper *alto sax*, Warne Marsh *tenor
sax*, Ronnie Ball, Red Garland, Dolo Coker, Wynton
Kelly *piano*, Ben Tucker, Paul Chambers, Jimmy Bond
bass, Gary Frommer, Philly Joe Jones, Frank Butler,
Jimmie Cobb *drums*
Tracks I Can't Believe That You're in Love with Me
❑ All the Things You Are ❑ What's New ❑ Tickle Toe
❑ The Man I Love ❑ Autumn Leaves ❑ The Way You
Look Tonight
Appraisal West Coast altoist Pepper mixes bop
speediness with a wounded sound and fragmented
phrasing all his own. He's paired here with one of the
underrated great exponents of long-line, cool school
improvising, tenorist Warne Marsh.

Dave Brubeck was loved
by the public for blending
jazz and classical devices,
often disliked by
critics in an era
when mixed-
idioms were
distrusted. He had
a 1950s pop hit
with "Take Five."

The Dave Brubeck Quartet
TIME OUT

Date recorded 1959
Label CBS
Musicians Dave Brubeck *piano*, Paul Desmond *alto sax*,
Eugene Wright *bass*, Joe Morello *drums*
Tracks Blue Rondo à la Turk ❑ Strange Meadow Lark
❑ Take Five ❑ Three to Get Ready ❑ Kathy's Waltz ❑
Everybody's Jumpin' ❑ Pick Up Sticks
Appraisal An essential album for all music lovers in
the 1960s, distinctive for its rare time signatures,
classical forms, and often underrated group dynamism.

Hard bop

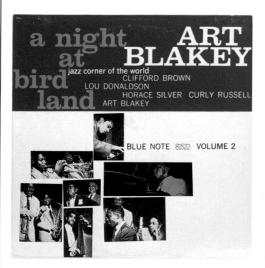

If COOL JAZZ was the antidote to bebop's hyperactivity, hard bop was the foil to cool's fragility. As rock and roll erupted during the mid-1950s, many of the players who had grown up with bop sought a return to the earthier roots of jazz — gospel music, marches, work songs, and blues. Drummers Max Roach and Art Blakey, pianist Horace Silver, trumpeter Clifford Brown, and saxophonists Cannonball Adderley and John Coltrane leaned toward a rugged, more explicitly emotional version of bebop, dubbed "hard bop." The newly invented long-playing record and better recording techniques encouraged extended solos and acceptable live recordings from clubs that intensified the atmosphere of exhilaration and spontaneity. The mix still works. The dance-jazz boom of the 1980s in Britain and elsewhere was fueled by recycled hard bop disks of thirty years earlier, and veterans like drum star Art Blakey found themselves playing to new audiences young enough to be their grandchildren.

Thelonious Monk/John Coltrane
MONK/TRANE

Date recorded 1957–58
Label Milestone
Musicians Thelonious Monk *piano*, John Coltrane, Coleman Hawkins *tenor sax*, Ray Copeland *trumpet*, Gigi Gryce *alto sax*, Wilbur Ware *bass*, Art Blakey, Shadow Wilson *drums*
Tracks Ruby My Dear ❑ Tinkle, Tinkle ❑ Nutty ❑ Well You Needn't ❑ Off Minor (2 takes) ❑ Epistrophy (2 takes) ❑ Crepescule with Nellie ❑ Abide with Me ❑ Monk's Mood ❑ Blues for Tomorrow
Appraisal Coltrane accepted Monk's idiosyncratic lead entirely. The later Hawkins/Copeland/Gryce band is riveting in an intensely personal "Abide with Me."

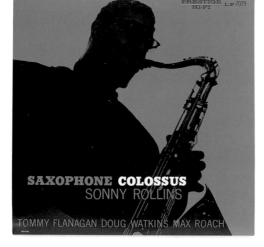

Art Blakey
A NIGHT AT BIRDLAND

Date recorded February 21, 1954
Label Blue Note
Musicians Art Blakey *drums*, Clifford Brown *trumpet*, Lou Donaldson *alto sax*, Horace Silver *piano*, Curly Russell *bass*
Tracks Split Kick ❑ Once in a While ❑ Quicksilver ❑ A Night in Tunisia ❑ The Way You Look Tonight ❑ Mayreh ❑ Wee-Dot ❑ If I Had You ❑ Quicksilver ❑ Now's the Time ❑ Confirmation
Appraisal Blakey's band before becoming the Jazz Messengers shows the energy of hard bop. As with most modern altoists in 1954, Donaldson's Parker allegiances are obvious, but Brown's horn epitomizes deft grace.

Sonny Rollins
SAXOPHONE COLOSSUS

Date recorded June 22, 1956
Label Prestige
Musicians Sonny Rollins *tenor sax*, Tommy Flanagan *piano*, Doug Watkins *bass*, Max Roach *drums*
Tracks St. Thomas ❑ You Don't Know What Love Is ❑ Strode Rode ❑ Moritat ❑ Blue Seven
Appraisal One of Sonny Rollins's most trenchant recordings, cut during a particularly creative period. "St. Thomas" is a clattering calypso and "Moritat" typically laconic. The baleful "Blue Seven" made the disk a triumph: its fragmented melodic ideas, searching deliberate development, and shifts of intensity produce one of the great improvised jazz performances.

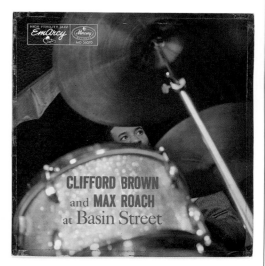

Clifford Brown/Max Roach
AT BASIN STREET

Date recorded January – February 1956
Label Mercury (British edition on EmArcy)
Musicians Clifford Brown *trumpet*, Max Roach *drums*, Sonny Rollins *tenor sax*, George Morrow *bass*, Richie Powell *piano*
Tracks What Is This Thing Called Love ❑ Love Is a Many Splendored Thing ❑ I'll Remember April ❑ Powell's Prances ❑ Time ❑ The Scene Is Clean ❑ Gertrude's Bounce
Appraisal The empathetic Rollins-Brown partnership at its most inventive, made more arresting by the stalking intelligence of Roach's drumming. Brown tragically died in a road accident later in the year.

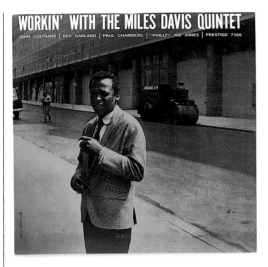

Miles Davis
WORKIN' WITH THE MILES DAVIS QUINTET

Date recorded May, October, 1956
Label Prestige
Musicians Miles Davis *trumpet*, John Coltrane *tenor sax*, Red Garland *piano,* Paul Chambers *bass*, Philly Joe Jones *drums*
Tracks It Never Entered My Mind ❑ Four ❑ In Your Own Sweet Way ❑ The Theme (take 1) ❑ Trane's Blues ❑ Ahmad's Blues ❑ Half Nelson ❑ The Theme (take 2)
Appraisal One of five superb 1956 Prestige sessions pitching the sensuous, ambiguous Davis against a youthfully bellicose Coltrane. An all-time great band.

Thelonious Monk
BRILLIANT CORNERS

Date recorded December 1956
Label Riverside
Musicians Thelonious Monk *piano*, Clark Terry *trumpet*, Ernie Henry *alto sax*, Sonny Rollins *tenor sax*, Oscar Pettiford, Paul Chambers *bass*, Max Roach *drums*, *tympany*
Tracks Brilliant Corners ❑ Ba-lue Boliva Ba-lues-are ❑ Pannonica ❑ I Surrender, Dear ❑ Bemsha Swing
Appraisal Hard to play along with, Monk's compositions resolved in odd places with treacherous spaces: even Rollins wasn't entirely at home with them. The title track splices several takes, but the material and improvisation show Monk and jazz at their willful best.

Cannonball Adderley
SOMETHIN' ELSE

Date recorded 1958
Label Blue Note
Musicians Cannonball Adderley *alto & soprano sax*, Miles Davis *trumpet*, Hank Jones *piano*, Sam Jones *bass*, Art Blakey *drums*
Tracks Autumn Leaves ❑ Love for Sale ❑ Somethin' Else ❑ One for Daddy ❑ Dancing in the Dark ❑ Alison's Uncle
Appraisal A distinctive disciple of Charlie Parker, Cannonball Adderley was a model hard bopper in his mingling of contemporary 1950s jazz with the rousing blues and dance music of Eddie Vinson and Louis Jordan. This is one of the best known of all Adderley sessions and even includes a rare Miles Davis guest appearance, in which the trumpeter delivers some distilled, oblique, and telling observations.

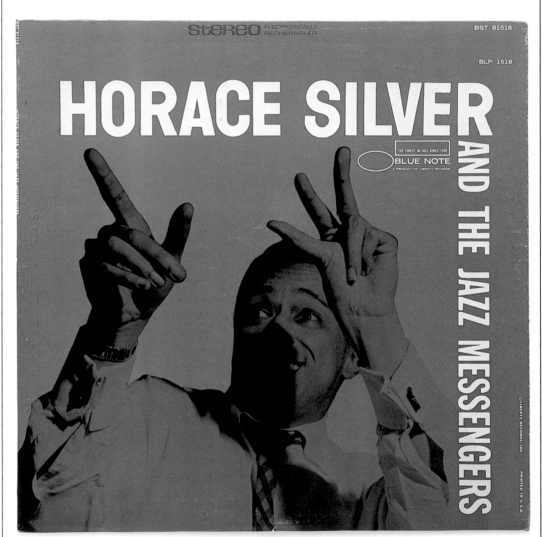

Horace Silver
HORACE SILVER AND THE JAZZ MESSENGERS

Date recorded November 13, 1954
Label Blue Note
Musicians Horace Silver *piano*, Kenny Dorham *trumpet*, Hank Mobley *tenor*, Doug Watkins *bass*, Art Blakey *drums*
Tracks Room 608 ❑ Creepin' In ❑ Stop Time ❑ To Whom It May Concern ❑ Hippy ❑ The Preacher ❑ Hankerin' ❑ Doodlin'
Appraisal The first official Jazz Messengers session, under Silver's name. Blakey's eruptions stir a volatile mix, and Silver's proximity to rhythm and blues is clear.

Johnny Griffin
LITTLE GIANT

Date recorded 1958 – 1962
Label Milestone
Musicians Donald Byrd, Blue Mitchell *trumpet*,
Julian Priester *trombone*, Pepper Adams *baritone sax*,
Kenny Drew, Wynton Kelly, Barry Harris *piano*,
Wilbur Ware, Sam Jones, Ron Carter *bass*, Philly Joe
Jones, Albert "Tootie" Heath, Ben Riley *drums*
Tracks Catharsis ❑ What's New ❑ Hot Sausage ❑
Woodyn' You ❑ Where's Your Overcoat, Boy? ❑ Little
John ❑ 63rd Street Theme ❑ Playmates ❑ The Message
❑ The Kerry Dancers ❑ Black Is the Color of My True
Love's Hair ❑ Green Grow the Rushes ❑ The
Londonderry Air
Appraisal Griffin played fast and furious saxophone
with fresh phrasing and often in great company.

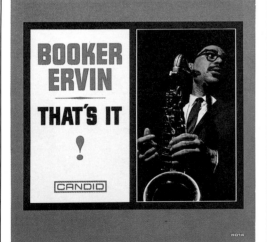

Booker Ervin
THAT'S IT!

Date recorded January 6, 1961
Label Candid
Musicians Booker Ervin *tenor sax*, Felix Krull *piano*,
George Tucker *bass*, Al Harewood *drums*
Tracks Mojo ❑ Uranus ❑ Poinciana ❑ Speak Low ❑
Booker's Blues ❑ Boo
Appraisal Soulful, dramatic set by Texan Ervin, with
an inimitably gruff, cajoling sound. "Felix Krull" is the
excellent Horace Parlan, renamed for contractual reasons.

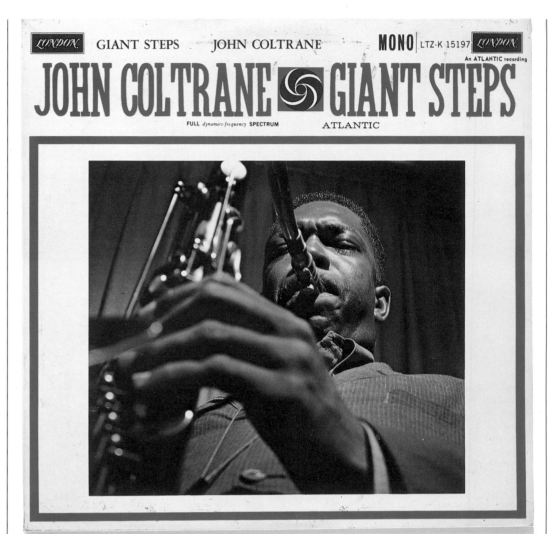

John Coltrane
GIANT STEPS

Date recorded 1959
Label Atlantic (British edition on London)
Musicians John Coltrane *tenor sax*, Tommy Flanagan,
Wynton Kelly *piano*, Paul Chambers *bass*, Art Taylor,
Jimmy Cobb *drums*
Tracks Giant Steps ❑ Cousin Mary ❑ Countdown ❑
Spiral ❑ Syeeda's Song Flute ❑ Naima ❑ Mr. P. C.
Appraisal One of Coltrane's best and best-known
albums, his music on a borderline between tough, bluesy
hard bop ("Mr. P. C.") and the
improvisational density of his study of
modes, packed into the breakneck
framework of the title track. The
sidemen are all in the hard bop mold.

Coltrane was already
one of the most
formidable saxophonists
in jazz at this point,
pushing music ahead.

Elmo Hope
WITH JIMMY BOND
AND FRANK BUTLER

Date recorded February 1959
Label Contemporary (British edition on Vocalion)
Musicians Elmo Hope *piano*, Jimmy Bond *bass*, Frank Butler *drums*
Tracks B.'s a Plenty ❏ Barfly ❏ Eejah ❏ Boa ❏ Something for Kenny ❏ Like Someone in Love ❏ Minor Bertha ❏ Tranquility
Appraisal Hope was a brilliant Bud Powellish pianist and a distinctive composer, but his reputation never matched his talent. Thelonious Monk's influence is also audible in the twitchy tempo of "Boa." A bold artist, here promising much.

Freddie Hubbard
HUB-TONES

Date recorded October 1962
Label Blue Note
Musicians Freddie Hubbard *trumpet*, James Spaulding *alto sax*, *flute*, Herbie Hancock *piano*, Reginald Workman *bass*, Clifford Jarvis *drums*
Tracks You're My Everything ❏ Prophet Jennings ❏ Hub-Tones ❏ Lament for Booker ❏ For Spee's Sake
Appraisal Freddie Hubbard was hailed as Clifford Brown's successor: a hard bop virtuoso with a polished sound, elegant phrasing, and real originality. This session sizzles throughout. Hubbard is in powerful form, and his partnership with the neglected James Spaulding, as well as some fine tunes, makes it a collector's piece.

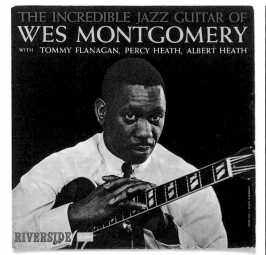

Wes Montgomery
THE INCREDIBLE JAZZ GUITAR
OF WES MONTGOMERY

Date recorded January 26, 28, 1960
Label Riverside
Musicians Wes Montgomery *guitar*, Tommy Flanagan *piano*, Percy Heath *bass*, Albert Heath *drums*
Tracks Airegin ❏ D-Natural Blues ❏ Polka Dots and Moonbeams ❏ Four on Six ❏ West Coast Blues ❏ In Your Own Sweet Way ❏ Mister Walker ❏ Gone with the Wind
Appraisal The late Wes Montgomery influenced innumerable guitarists — and still does — with his soft sound, swing, and avoidance of cliché. This brisk bop set was one of his most forthright, before commerical priorities overcame his improvising talents.

Harold Land
THE FOX

Date recorded August 1959
Label Hifijazz
Musicians Harold Land *tenor sax*, Dupree Bolton *trumpet*, Elmo Hope *piano*, Herbie Lewis *bass*, Frank Butler *drums*
Tracks The Fox ❏ Mirror-Mind Rose ❏ One Second, Please ❏ Sims A-Plenty ❏ Little Chris ❏ One Down
Appraisal Another hard bop classic. Land, like a dolorous Sonny Rollins, is beautifully complemented by an on-form Elmo Hope. The title track suggests the Clifford Brown-Max Roach band.

Dexter Gordon
OUR MAN IN PARIS

Date recorded May 23, 1963
Label Blue Note
Musicians Dexter Gordon *tenor sax*, Bud Powell *piano*, Pierre Michelot *bass*, Kenny Clarke *drums*
Tracks Scrapple from the Apple ❏ Willow Weep for Me ❏ Broadway ❏ Stairway to the Stars ❏ A Night in Tunisia
Appraisal An indisputable hard bop landmark from the man who hit notes as if sculpting in marble. The superbly conceived solo on "A Night in Tunisia" is a standout of the session.

Tina Brooks
TRUE BLUE

Date recorded June 1960
Label Blue Note
Musicians Tina Brooks *tenor sax*, Freddie Hubbard *trumpet*, Duke Jordan *piano*, Sam Jones *bass*, Art Taylor *drums*
Tracks Good Old Soul ❏ Up Tight's Creek ❏ Theme for Don ❏ True Blue ❏ Miss Hazel ❏ Nothing Ever Changes My Love for You
Appraisal Lighter than most hard bop tenorists, and less orthodox in materials, the underrated Brooks made this fine album toward the end of the era.

Early funk

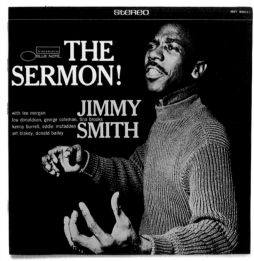

THE BIG SOUL-BAND
JOHNNY GRIFFIN ORCHESTRA — ARRANGEMENTS BY NORMAN SIMMONS

The vibrant and large-scale sound heard here is one that achieves much of its dynamic and deeply-moving newness by reaching back to the roots and soul of jazz. It makes excitingly emotion-charged modern use of such fundamentals as spirituals, blues, and gospel-imbued jazz. This is also big music; the rich, burstingly full sound of brass and reed sections. For the very first time, a truly big-band sound has been dramatically merged with the soulful earthiness of the stirring new jazz of the 1960s — music that combines down-home funk with the aggressive surge of the big city.
This startling and unique album features the JOHNNY GRIFFIN ORCHESTRA in arrangements by NORMAN SIMMONS. It spotlights the amazingly full-throated tenor saxophone "preaching" of Johnny Griffin, playing as never before in front of the fervent, larger-than-life sounds built by Norman Simmons, a young arranger whose brilliant future begins right here.

RIVERSIDE

FUNK AND ELECTRIC lineups are usually thought of as inseparable but, although guitars, electric pianos, and awesome percussion featured in the crossover and fusion music of the late 1960s and 1970s, the style had its roots in the most fundamental propositions of black music, and many of the jazz musicians who took up fusion had already played its acoustic prototype in hard bop and soul jazz a decade earlier. Hard bop was rarely far from the wail and stomp of rhythm and blues — pianist Horace Silver had composed a tune called "Opus de Funk" as early as 1954. Cool music and the more ascetic refinements of bebop had turned bluesier jazz musicians toward more heated, direct messages, and the rise of rock and roll speeded up the process. Much of the soul jazz movement was traceable to the black churches and gospel music, particularly the churning incantations of the Hammond organists. Some of it, like the music of the Crusaders, came from the Midwest, which had been pumping blues into jazz from the beginning.

Johnny Griffin Orchestra
THE BIG SOUL-BAND

Date recorded 1960
Label Riverside
Musicians Johnny Griffin *tenor sax*, Clark Terry, Bob Bryant *trumpet*, Julian Priester, Matthew Gee *trombone*, Pat Patrick, Frank Strozier *alto sax*, Edwin Williams *tenor sax*, Charlie Davis *baritone sax*, Bobby Timmons *piano, celeste*, Harold Mabern *piano*, Bob Cranshaw, Vic Sproles *bass*, Charlie Persip *drums*
Tracks Wade in the Water ❑ Panic Room Blues ❑ Nobody Knows the Trouble I've Seen ❑ Meditation ❑ Holla ❑ So Tired ❑ Deep River ❑ Jubilation
Appraisal Griffin, the "Little Giant," was a superfast hard bopper. The soul cult led to this raunchy big band in a Ray Charles mold, with some of Griffin's best playing.

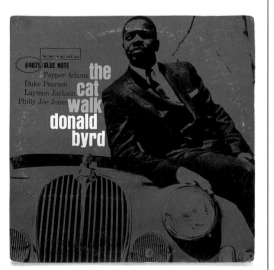

Jimmy Smith
THE SERMON!

Date recorded 1958
Label Blue Note
Musicians Jimmy Smith *organ*, Lee Morgan *trumpet*, Lou Donaldson, George Coleman *alto sax*, Tina Brooks *tenor sax*, Kenny Burrell, Eddie McFadden *guitar*, Art Blakey, Donald Bailey *drums*
Tracks The Sermon ❑ J.O.S. ❑ Flamingo
Appraisal The Hammond organ supremo's music is full of storming bass lines, explosive chords, and slashing runs. This is an epic example of how a gifted musician may need only one song if it's good enough.

Donald Byrd
THE CAT WALK

Date recorded May 2, 1961
Label Blue Note
Musicians Donald Byrd *trumpet*, Pepper Adams *baritone sax*, Duke Pearson *piano*, Laymon Jackson *bass*, Philly Joe Jones *drums*
Tracks Say You're Mine ❑ Hello Bright Sunflower ❑ Each Time I Think of You ❑ Duke's Mixture ❑ The Cat Walk ❑ Cute
Appraisal Just before Byrd's absorption in fusion, an excellent collaboration with gravelly Pepper Adams shows his hard, confident attack and unswerving swing.

The Cannonball Adderley Quintet
MERCY, MERCY, MERCY!

Date recorded 1967
Label Capitol
Musicians Cannonball Adderley *alto sax*, Nat Adderley *cornet*, Joe Zawinul *electric piano*, Vic Gatsby *bass*, Roy McCurdy *drums*
Tracks Fun ❑ Games ❑ Mercy, Mercy, Mercy ❑ Sticks ❑ Hipadelphia ❑ Sack o' Woe
Appraisal The Adderley quintet was at the forefront of soul jazz, first with ex-Jazz Messenger Bobby Timmons on keyboards, then Joe Zawinul, composer of the title track. The backbeat and roots are strong.

THE SIDEWINDER
JOE HENDERSON   BARRY HARRIS   BOB CRENSHAW   BILLY HIGGINS
LEE MORGAN

4157 BLUE NOTE

THE FINEST IN JAZZ SINCE 1939

Lee Morgan
THE SIDEWINDER

Date recorded December 21, 1964
Label Blue Note
Musicians Lee Morgan *trumpet*, Joe Henderson *tenor sax*, Barry Harris *piano*, Bob Cranshaw *bass*, Billy Higgins *drums*
Tracks Totem Pole ❑ Boy, What a Night ❑ Hocus-Pocus ❑ The Sidewinder ❑ Gary's Notebook
Appraisal The mid-tempo title groove was a hit in Morgan's lifetime, then posthumously in the 1980s. The faster, jazzier "Boy What a Night" is memorable for a serpentine melody line, Higgins's scalding cymbal, and Henderson's tenor solo. Morgan's solo on "Totem Pole" is the overlooked standout of the set.

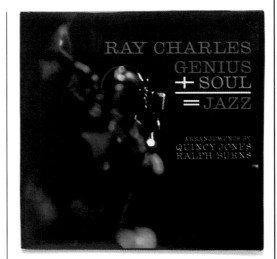

Ray Charles
GENIUS + SOUL = JAZZ

Date recorded 1961
Label Impulse
Musicians Ray Charles *organ, vocal*, Quincy Jones, Ralph Burns *arranger*, Clark Terry, Phillip Guilbeau, Joe Newman, Thad Jones, Eugene Young, Joe Wilder, John Frosk, Jimmy Nottingham *trumpet*, Urbie Green, Henry Coker, Al Grey, Jimmy Cleveland, Keg Johnson, George Matthews *trombone*, Frank Wess, Marshal Royal, George Dorsey, Earle Warren *alto sax*, Frank Foster, Billy Mitchell, Budd Johnson, Seldon Powell *tenor sax*, Charlie Fowlkes, Haywood Henry *baritone sax*, Freddy Green, Sam Herman *guitar*, Eddy Jones, Joe Benjamin *bass*, Sonny Payne, Roy Haynes *drums*
Tracks From the Heart ❑ I've Got News for You ❑ Moanin' ❑ Let's Go ❑ One Mint Julep ❑ I'm Gonna Move to the Outskirts of Town ❑ Stompin' Room Only ❑ Mister C. ❑ Strike Up the Band ❑ Birth of the Blues
Appraisal One of the greatest catalysts of popular interest in soul music, and a strong hard bop pianist, Ray Charles was set in front of most of the Count Basie band for this driving 1961 session. Although Charles sings on only two tracks, what he sings about is embodied in all the others.

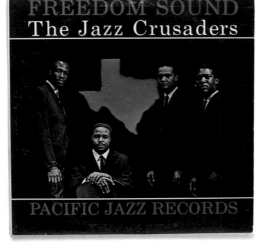

Bobby Timmons
THIS HERE IS BOBBY TIMMONS

Date recorded 1960
Label Riverside
Musicians Bobby Timmons *piano*, Sam Jones *bass*, Jimmy Cobb *drums*
Tracks This Here ❑ Moanin' ❑ Lush Life ❑ The Party's Over ❑ Prelude to a Kiss ❑ Dat Dere ❑ My Funny Valentine ❑ Come Rain or Come Shine ❑ Joy Ride
Appraisal Timmons was the most explicitly and unwaveringly church-rooted pianist of the movement, and this disk features the genre's classic, "Moanin'."

The Jazz Crusaders
FREEDOM SOUND

Date recorded 1961
Label Pacific Jazz
Musicians Wilton Felder *tenor sax*, Wayne Henderson *trombone*, Joe Sample *piano*, Roy Gaines *guitar*, Stix Hooper *drums*, Jimmy Bond *bass*
Tracks The Geek ❑ M.J.S. Funk ❑ That's It ❑ Freedom Sound ❑ Theme from Exodus ❑ Coon
Appraisal Wilton Felder's big, far-horizons tenor sound and Stix Hooper's bustling drums made the Crusaders a byword for jazz funk for a quarter century. This early version with a classic title track shows why.

Mainstream

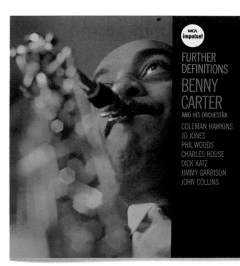

BY THE MID 1950s the prewar youth-cult music — swing — sounded like history. Bebop was not for mass audiences, but it had credibility, and it was still new. Rock and roll was even newer and had already begun to carry the postwar youth generation away. Yet a raft of older players in the 1950s was convinced that the music they felt so deeply and played so well could not simply decline and die, even if their contemporaries like Lester Young and Billie Holiday were about to. They may have been out of the headlines, but given a chance, the swing stars still produced performances brimming with all the old prebop virtues of relaxed, loping rhythms, conversational solos, accessible, songlike themes, and a lot of blues, and the mixture began to find a new audience. Count Basie's vivacious music was fundamental to the arrival of "mainstream" jazz. So was the emergence of younger solo stars carrying the swing torch, like cornet player Ruby Braff and later the young tenor Scott Hamilton.

Coleman Hawkins
THE HAWK FLIES HIGH

Date recorded March 12, 15, 1957
Label Riverside
Musicians Coleman Hawkins *tenor sax*, Idrees Sulieman *trumpet*, J. J. Johnson *trombone*, Hank Jones *piano*, Barry Galbraith *guitar*, Oscar Pettiford *bass*, Jo Jones *drums*
Tracks Chant ❑ Juicy Fruit ❑ Think Deep ❑ Laura ❑ Blue Lights ❑ Sancticity
Appraisal Hawkins was too implacably talented, and too astute, to fade away. This session couples his juggernaut sound to a mixed swing/bop band that includes the Basie drum whirlwind Jo Jones.

Benny Carter
FURTHER DEFINITIONS

Date recorded November 13, 15, 1961
Label Impulse
Musicians Benny Carter, Phil Woods *alto sax*, Coleman Hawkins, Charlie Rouse *tenor sax*, Dick Katz *piano*, Johnny Collins *guitar*, Jimmy Garrison *bass*, Jo Jones *drums*
Tracks Honeysuckle Rose ❑ The Midnight Sun Will Never Set ❑ Crazy Rhythm ❑ Blue Star ❑ Cotton Tail ❑ Body and Soul ❑ Cherry ❑ Doozy
Appraisal One of the great altoists, Carter is also an inspired composer and arranger. This classic recording includes a superb remake of Coleman Hawkins's 1939 "Body and Soul" solo.

Ruby Braff
HEAR ME TALKIN'!

Date recorded October – November 1967
Label Black Lion/Polydor
Musicians Ruby Braff *cornet*, Alex Welsh *trumpet*, Roy Williams *trombone*, Buddy Tate, Al Gay *tenor sax*, Johnny Barnes *baritone sax*, George Wein, Fred Hunt *piano*, Jim Douglas *guitar*, Jack Lesberg, Ron Rae *bass*, Don Lamond, Lennie Hastings *drums*
Tracks You've Changed ❑ Hear Me Talkin' to Ya ❑ Don't Blame Me ❑ No One Else But You ❑ Nobody Knows You (When You're Down and Out) ❑ Buddy Bolden's Blues ❑ Mean to Me ❑ Where's Freddy?
Appraisal Bop-generation, but into swing, Braff has a beautiful sound, and is in ideal company here.

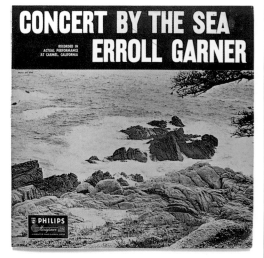

Erroll Garner
CONCERT BY THE SEA

Date recorded 1956
Label Columbia (British edition on Philips)
Musicians Erroll Garner *piano*, Eddie Calhoun *bass*, Denzel Best *drums*
Tracks I'll Remember April ❑ Teach Me Tonight ❑ Mambo Carmel ❑ Autumn Leaves ❑ It's All Right with Me ❑ Red Top ❑ April in Paris ❑ They Can't Take That Away from Me ❑ How Could You Do a Thing Like That to Me ❑ Where or When ❑ Erroll's Theme
Appraisal The definition of an "orchestral" jazz pianist. A churning, dramatic performer of multilayered variations, Garner had his biggest hit with this famous record.

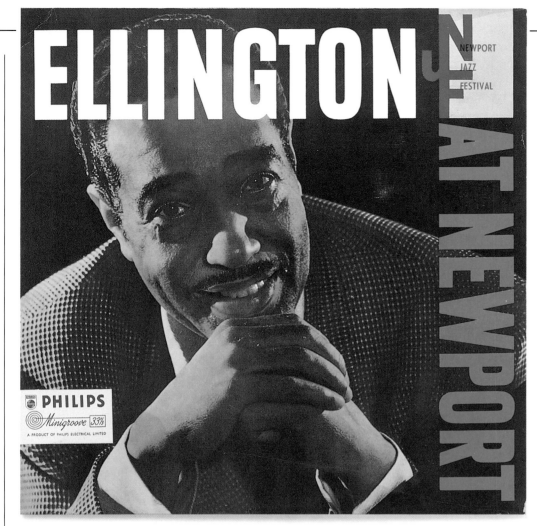

Zoot Sims
ONE TO BLOW ON

Date recorded January 11, 18, 1956
Label Meteor
Musicians Zoot Sims *tenor sax*, Bob Brookmeyer *trombone*, John Williams *piano*, Milt Hinton *bass*, Gus Johnson *drums*
Tracks September in the Rain ❑ Down at the Loft ❑ Ghost of a Chance ❑ Not So Deep ❑ Them There Eyes ❑ Our Pad ❑ Dark Clouds ❑ One to Blow On
Appraisal The warm, fluid sound of Zoot Sims, like a more rugged Lester Young, flowed through the world's jazz clubs from the 1940s to the 1980s. This is a typical example of his relaxed and consistent work.

Duke Ellington
ELLINGTON AT NEWPORT

Date recorded July 7, 1956
Label CBS (British edition on Philips)
Musicians Duke Ellington *piano*, Willie Cook, Ray Nance, Clark Terry, Cat Anderson *trumpet*, John Sanders, Quentin Jackson, Britt Woodman *trombone*, Russell Procope, Johnny Hodges *alto sax*, Paul Gonsalves, Jimmy Hamilton *tenor sax*, Harry Carney *baritone sax*, Jimmy Woode *bass*, Sam Woodyard *drums*

Tracks Newport Jazz Festival Suite: Festival Junction, Blues to Be There, Newport Up ❑ Jeep's Blues ❑ Diminuendo and Crescendo in Blue
Appraisal At a classic performance during the 1956 Newport Festival, the Ellington band stole the show and returned to the headlines when Paul Gonsalves played 27 blazing choruses in succession in "Diminuendo and Crescendo in Blue."

The Oscar Peterson Trio
NIGHT TRAIN

Date recorded December 15 – 16, 1962
Label Verve
Musicians Oscar Peterson *piano*, Ray Brown *bass,* Ed Thigpen *drums*
Tracks C. Jam Blues ❑ Night Train ❑ Georgia on My Mind ❑ Bags' Groove ❑ Moten Swing ❑ Easy Does It ❑ Honey Dripper ❑ Things Ain't What They Used to Be ❑ I Got It Bad and That Ain't Good ❑ Band Call ❑ Hymn to Freedom
Appraisal An immensely popular mainstream pianist, Peterson's only fault was that his technique could overwhelm his material. It does not happen here on his best and most emotional album.

Count Basie Orchestra
THE ATOMIC MR. BASIE

Date recorded October 21 – 22, 1957
Label Columbia
Musicians Count Basie *piano*, Neal Hefti *arranger*, Joe Newman, Thad Jones, Wendell Culley, Eugene "Snooky" Young *trumpet*, Benny Powell, Henry Coker, Al Grey *trombone*, M. Royal, Frank Wess *alto sax*, Eddie Davis, Frank Foster *tenor sax*, Charlie Fowlkes *baritone sax*, Freddie Green *guitar*, Eddie Jones *bass*, Sonny Payne *drums*
Tracks The Kid from Red Bank ❑ Duet ❑ After Supper ❑ Flight of the Foo Birds ❑ Double-O ❑ Teddy the Toad ❑ Whirly-Bird ❑ Midnite Blue ❑ Splanky ❑ Fantail ❑ Lil' Darlin'
Appraisal Basie's "new" band of the early 1950s — smoother than previous ones but emitting even more heat and using superb arrangements. This magnificent session was probably the Count's best postwar disk. Check the sleeve!

Postwar vocals

SWING INSTRUMENTALISTS dubbed female singers "chirpers" or "canaries" — glamorous box-office necessities not out front for musical reasons unless they were Billie Holiday. When swing ran out of fuel, bebop musicians rejected its commercial values but offered little refuge to singers in their intense new small-group idiom, built around fast-moving saxes and brass. So in the 1950s and 1960s, singers who had come up in front of the big bands either went to the top as jazz-influenced pop stars like Frank Sinatra or remained entertainers in supper clubs and hotels. A very few were adaptable enough to straddle jazz and pop, like Ella Fitzgerald with her *Song Book* disks for Norman Granz's Verve label in the 1950s, or some bebop-oriented singers with their witty, sophisticated, saxophonelike phrasing. But the essence of jazz vocals in this era, as in the one before, lay not in mimicking horns but in the personal, idiosyncratic, spontaneous transformation of songs and the recognition of the subtle, expressive, and unique qualities of the human voice.

Ella Fitzgerald
SINGS THE GEORGE AND IRA GERSHWIN SONG BOOK VOL. 5

Date recorded 1959
Label Verve (British edition on HMV)
Musicians Ella Fitzgerald *vocal*, orchestra arranged and conducted by Nelson Riddle
Tracks They Can't Take That Away from Me ❑ Embraceable You ❑ I Can't Be Bothered Now ❑ Boy! What Love Has Done to Me! ❑ Fascinating Rhythm ❑ Funny Face ❑ Lorelei ❑ Oh, So Nice ❑ Let's Kiss and Make Up ❑ I Got Rhythm
Appraisal This five-volume set of fifty-three songs is the elegant best of Fitzgerald's *Song Book* projects.

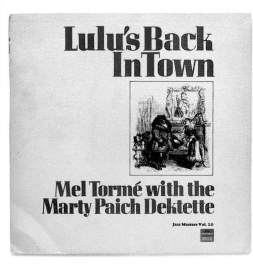

Mel Tormé
LULU'S BACK IN TOWN

Date recorded January 20, 1956
Label Polydor
Musicians featuring Mel Tormé *vocal*, Marty Paich *piano*, *arranger*, Pete Candoli, Don Fagerquist *trumpet*, Bob Enevoldsen *valve trombone*, Bud Shank *alto sax*, Bob Cooper, Jack Montrose *tenor sax*, Red Mitchell *bass*, Mel Lewis *drums*
Tracks include Lulu's Back in Town ❑ When the Sun Comes Out ❑ Fascinating Rhythm ❑ The Carioca ❑ The Lady Is a Tramp ❑ I Like to Recognize the Tune ❑ Keepin' Myself for You ❑ Lullaby of Birdland ❑ When April Comes Again ❑ Sing for Your Supper
Appraisal Paich's delightful arrangements cushion Tormé's silky voice, peppered with odd inflections.

Lambert, Hendricks and Ross
SING A SONG OF BASIE

Date recorded August – November 1957
Label Impulse
Musicians Dave Lambert, Jon Hendricks, Annie Ross *vocal*, Nat Pierce *piano*, Freddie Green *guitar*, Eddie Jones *bass*, Sonny Payne *drums*
Tracks Everyday ❑ It's Sand, Man! ❑ Two for the Blues ❑ One o'Clock Jump ❑ Little Pony ❑ Down for Double ❑ Fiesta in Blue ❑ Down for the Count ❑ Blues Backstage ❑ Avenue C
Appraisal Celebrated "vocalese" (vocal covers of instrumentals) trio with Annie Ross's superb timing driving her tribute to Buck Clayton's trumpet on "Fiesta in Blue."

Leon Thomas
SPIRITS KNOWN AND UNKNOWN

Date recorded October 21 – 22, 1969
Label Flying Dutchman
Musicians Leon Thomas *vocal*, *percussion*, James Spaulding *alto sax*, *flute*, Little Rock *tenor sax*, Lonnie Liston Smith Jr. *piano*, Richard Davis, Cecil McBee *bass*, Roy Haynes *drums*, Richard Landrum *bongos*
Tracks The Creator Has a Master Plan (Peace) ❑ One ❑ Echoes ❑ Song for My Father ❑ Damn Nam (Ain't Goin' to Vietnam) ❑ Malcolm's Gone ❑ Let the Rain Fall on Me
Appraisal Deep, powerful, skillful swing and blues-inspired singer who became influenced by free music, African vocals, and 1960s rock. Black pride and Vietnam are themes in this extension of vocal styles.

Sheila Jordan
PORTRAIT OF SHEILA

Date recorded September, October, 1962
Label Blue Note
Musicians Sheila Jordan *vocal*, Barry Galbraith *guitar*, Steve Swallow *bass*, Denzil Best *drums*
Tracks Falling in Love with Love ❑ If You Could See Me Now ❑ Am I Blue ❑ Dat Dere ❑ When the World Was Young ❑ Let's Face the Music and Dance ❑ Laugh, Clown, Laugh ❑ Who Can I Turn To? ❑ Baltimore Oriole ❑ I'm a Fool to Want You ❑ Hum Drum Blues ❑ Willow Weep for Me
Appraisal Best disk by Charlie Parker's favorite bop singer, the imaginative, intimate Jordan.

Betty Carter
LOOK WHAT I GOT!

Date recorded 1988
Label PolyGram
Musicians Betty Carter *vocal*, Don Braden *tenor sax*, Benny Green, Stephen Scott *piano*, Michael Bowie, Ira Coleman *bass*, Winard Harper, Lewis Nash, Troy Davis *drums*
Tracks Look What I Got ❑ That Sunday, That Summer ❑ The Man I Love ❑ All I Got ❑ Just Like the Movies ❑ Imagination ❑ Mr. Gentleman ❑ Make It Last ❑ The Good Life
Appraisal One of the greatest jazz singers alive. Hypnotic and tantalizing, Betty Carter makes listeners wait for resolutions and illuminates lyrics, as this essential recording shows.

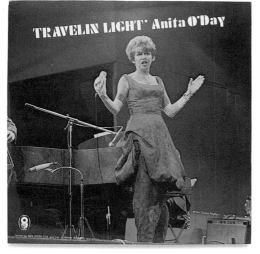

Anita O'Day
TRAVELIN' LIGHT

Date recorded 1961
Label World
Musicians Anita O'Day *vocal*, Barney Kessel *leader*, *guitar*, Don Fagerquist, Al Porcino, Ray Triscari, John Anderson, Jr., Jack Sheldon *trumpet*, Stu Williamson, Frank Rosolino, Dick Nash, L. MacCreary *trombone*, Ben Webster *tenor sax*, Joe Maini, Chuck Gentry *sax*, Rus Freeman, Jimmy Rowles *piano*, Al Viola *guitar*, Buddy Clark *bass*, Mel Lewis *drums*, Larry Bunker *percussion*
Tracks Travelin' Light ❑ The Moon Looks Down and Laughs ❑ Don't Explain ❑ You Forgot to Remember ❑ Some Other Spring ❑ What a Little Moonlight Can Do ❑ Miss Brown to You ❑ God Bless the Child ❑ If the Moon Turns Green ❑ I Hear Music ❑ Lover Come Back to Me ❑ Crazy He Calls Me
Appraisal O'Day's quirky and self-possessed performance in the well-known jazz movie *Jazz on a Summer's Day* revealed a superb vocal improviser to a wider world. This early session features a fine band and a Billie Holiday repertoire, dominated by O'Day's restless swing and instrumentlike delivery.

Sarah Vaughan
SASSY SINGS

Date recorded 1946 – 1947
Label SAGA
Musicians featuring Sarah Vaughan *vocal,* George Treadwell, Ernett Perry, Roger Jones, Freddie Webster, Neal Hefti, Sonny Rich *trumpet*, Ed Burke, Dick Harris, Donald Coles *trombone*, Rupert Cole, Scoville Brown *alto sax*, Bud Johnson, Lowell Hastings, Charlie Ventura *tenor sax*, Eddie De Verteuill, Cecil Payne *baritone sax*, Bud Powell, Teddy Wilson *piano,* Al McKibbon *bass*, Cozy Cole, Kenny Clarke *drums*
Tracks I Cover the Waterfront ❑ Tenderly ❑ Time and Again ❑ You're Blasé ❑ I Can't Get Started ❑ September Song ❑ My Kinda Love ❑ If You Could See Me Now ❑ What a Difference a Day Made ❑ You're Not the Kind ❑ Motherless Child ❑ The One I Love
Appraisal Vaughan came up with the Billy Eckstine band, and these were among her first attempts to go her own way in the late 1940s. The jazz content is not always high, but the hitching of the massive engine of her operatic voice to an idiom influenced by bop reveals her immense potential.

Carmen McRae
TORCHY!

Date recorded 1955
Label Memoir
Musicians Carmen McRae *vocal*, orchestras conducted and arranged by Jack Pleis and Ralph Burns, with Joe Wilder *trumpet*, Al Klink *tenor sax*, Andy Ackers *piano,* Danny Perri *guitar*
Tracks Last Night When We Were Young ❑ Speak Low (When You Speak, Love) ❑ But Beautiful ❑ If You'd Stay the Way I Dream about You ❑ Midnight Sun ❑ My Future Just Passed ❑ Yesterdays ❑ We'll Be Together Again ❑ I'm a Dreamer (Aren't We All) ❑ Good Morning, Heartache ❑ Star Eyes ❑ I Don't Stand a Ghost of a Chance with You
Appraisal There's a snarling edge to McRae's singing at its best that gives her work a worldly rigor quite unrelated to the assumptions about women singers that led to the "canary" tag. Ironic, rugged, witty, and swinging, McRae has recently resurfaced as an uncompromising jazz singer after some unchallenging years. This was one of her best sessions from the period of her first break, when all the qualities now regenerated in her began to bloom.

Free jazz

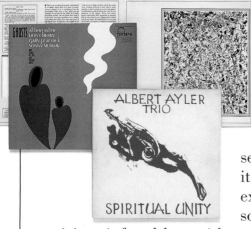

IF BEBOP HAD a strange way of talking, it still used the grammar of the jazz that had gone before. Free music was different. Some versions appeared to abandon everything at once — standard tunes, recognizable chord patterns, even the seductiveness of swing. But bebop had come to seem like a trap to many creative players, its fast runs sounding to them like exercises. In the search for new jazz sounds and new shapes for melody, some musicians infused bop with contemporary classical music, some with the cries of prejazz field hollers and blues. The rise of the civil rights movement intensified the urge toward a fierce, emotional African-American music uncompromised by music business pragmatism. These attitudes and the worldwide rock boom led to record industry disenchantment with new jazz; seeking autonomy, many free musicians launched their own independent labels.

"...One of the most important albums since...1949-1950..."
NAT HENTOFF in Harper's Magazine
RCA VICTOR

George Russell
THE JAZZ WORKSHOP

Date recorded March – December 1956
Label RCA Victor
Musicians George Russell *composer*, Art Farmer *trumpet*, Hal McKusick *alto sax*, Bill Evans *piano*, Barry Galbraith *guitar*, Milt Hilton, Teddy Kotick *bass*, Joe Harris, Paul Motian, Osie Johnson *drums*
Tracks Ye Hypocrite, Ye Beelzebub ❑ Jack's Blues ❑ Livingstone I Presume ❑ Ezz-thetic ❑ Night Sound ❑ Round Johnny Rondo ❑ Witch Hunt ❑ Concerto for Billy the Kid ❑ Fellow Delegates ❑ The Sad Sergeant ❑ Knights of the Steamtable ❑ Ballad of Hix Blewitt
Appraisal Crucial early session of progressive music by one of the most influential theoreticians in jazz.

Ornette Coleman
SOMETHING ELSE!

Date recorded February – March 1958
Label Contemporary
Musicians Ornette Coleman *alto sax*, Don Cherry *trumpet*, Walter Norris *piano*, Don Payne *bass*, Billy Higgins *drums*
Tracks Invisible ❑ The Blessing ❑ Jayne ❑ Chippie ❑ The Disguise ❑ Angel Voice ❑ Alpha ❑ When Will the Blues Leave? ❑ The Sphinx
Appraisal The disk that raised the curtain on free jazz. Tentative exploration of Coleman's revolution (it retains a pianist's harmonies) it still highlights the saxophonist's beautiful thematic sense and immediate empathy with Cherry and Higgins.

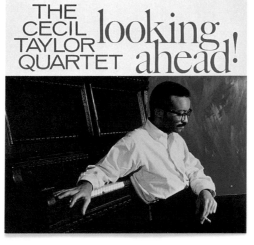

The Cecil Taylor Quartet
LOOKING AHEAD!

Date recorded June 9, 1958
Label Contemporary
Musicians Cecil Taylor *piano*, Earl Griffith *vibraharp*, Buell Neidlinger *bass*, Dennis Charles *drums*
Tracks Luyah! The Glorious Step ❑ African Violets ❑ Of What ❑ Wallering ❑ Toll ❑ Excursion on a Wobbly Rail
Appraisal Taylor's blinding technique is so intense that the conjunction of modern classical and jazz piano devices blurs. But his percussiveness and his robust affection for Duke Ellington and Thelonious Monk ("Excursion on a Wobbly Rail") make this key session both respectful of jazz and visionary in scope.

The Charlie Mingus Jazz Workshop
PITHECANTHROPUS ERECTUS

Date recorded 1956
Label Atlantic (British edition on London)
Musicians Charlie Mingus *bass*, Jackie McLean *alto sax*, J. R. Monterose *tenor sax*, Mal Waldron *piano*, Willie Jones *drums*
Tracks Pithecanthropus Erectus ❑ A Foggy Day ❑ Profile of Jackie ❑ Love Chant
Appraisal Mingus pushed soloists toward the outer reaches of hard bop bordering on abstract improvisation but kept gospel and blues pulsing through his music. Like Ellington or Morton, Mingus uses this famous session to tell a story but anticipates within it the collective free playing of the 1960s.

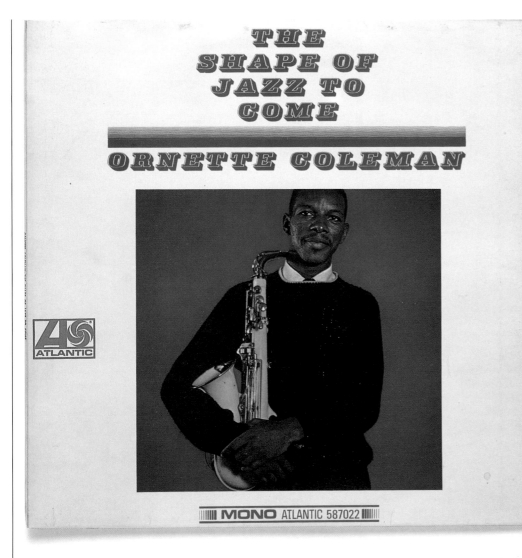

Sun Ra
ANGELS AND DEMONS AT PLAY

Date recorded 1955 – 1957
Label Saturn
Musicians Sun Ra and his Myth Science Arkestra featuring Sun Ra *piano, organ, electronic piano*, Nate Pryor *trombone*, John Gilmore *tenor sax, solar bells*, Pat Patrick *baritone & alto sax, flute*, Marshall Allen *alto sax, flute*, Ronald Boykins, Wilburn Green *bass*, Robert Barry *drums*, Jim Hearndon *tympani, timbali*
Tracks Tiny Pyramids ❑ Between Two Worlds ❑ Music from the World Tomorrow ❑ Angels and Demons at Play ❑ Urnack ❑ Medicine for a Nightmare ❑ A Call for All Demons ❑ Demon's Lullaby
Appraisal Idiosyncratic bandleader, synthesizer pioneer, and music theater maestro, Sun Ra developed from a background in swing ensemble sounds and hard bop but by the mid 1950s was close to free jazz. This forward-looking, entertaining disk splices such elements as Latin dance and atonality.

Ornette Coleman
THE SHAPE OF JAZZ TO COME

Date recorded May 1959
Label Atlantic
Musicians Ornette Coleman *alto sax*, Donald Cherry *cornet*, Charlie Haden *bass*, Billy Higgins *drums*
Tracks Lonely Woman ❑ Eventually ❑ Peace ❑ Focus on Sanity ❑ Congeniality ❑ Chronology
Appraisal One of the all-time great jazz sessions, made the year after Coleman first broke through with his most congenial quartet. Although a chord-playing instrument is absent here, and there are no repeating harmonic patterns in the accompaniment, the logic and coherence of Coleman's solos and the speed and sensitivity with which the musicians coax and cajole each other make this so musical that the fuss it first occasioned seems hard to account for. The leader's yearningly bluesy compositions "Lonely Woman" and "Peace" are among the loveliest in jazz.

Lennie Tristano/Tadd Dameron
CROSSCURRENTS

Date recorded 1949
Label Affinity
Musicians Lennie Tristano Sextet: Lennie Tristano *piano*, Lee Konitz *alto sax*, Warne Marsh *tenor sax*, Billy Bauer *guitar*, Arnold Fishkin *bass*, Harold Granowsky, Denzil Best *drums*
Tadd Dameron Orchestra: Tadd Dameron *piano*, Fats Navarro, Miles Davis *trumpet*, Kai Winding, J. J. Johnson *trombone*, Sahib Shihab *alto sax*, Dexter Gordon, Benjamin Lundy *tenor sax*, Cecil Payne *baritone sax*, John Collins *guitar*, Carley Russell *bass*, Kenny Clarke *drums*, Diego Iborra *bongos*, Vidal Bolado *congas*, Rae Pearl, Kay Penton *vocal*
Tracks Wow ❑ Crosscurrent ❑ Yesterdays ❑ Marionette ❑ Sax of a Kind ❑ Intuition ❑ Digression ❑ Sid's Delight ❑ Casbah ❑ John's Delight ❑ What's New ❑ Heaven's Doors Are Open Wide ❑ Focus
Appraisal Ornette Coleman may have been the most influential and widely acknowledged of free jazz catalysts, but iron-willed pianist and composer Lennie Tristano was investigating a music that broke conventional bar lines, evened out bebop's usual jangling rhythm sections, and in the tentative investigations of free collective improvising with his sextet, pointed toward Mingus's and Coleman's advances to come.

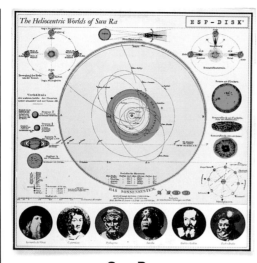

Sun Ra
THE HELIOCENTRIC WORLDS OF SUN RA

Date recorded 1965
Label ESP
Musicians Sun Ra *piano, tuned bongos*, Walter Miller *trumpet*, Marshall Allen *alto sax, piccolo, flute*, John Gilmore *tenor sax*, Pat Patrick *baritone sax*, Robert Cummings *bass clarinet*, Ronnie Boykins *bass*, Roger Blank *percussion*
Tracks The Sun Myth ❑ A House of Beauty ❑ Cosmic Chaos
Appraisal By 1965 Sun Ra with his Solar Arkestra had moved from regular melody to building sustained sounds on each other and mingling rich ensemble texture and free improvisation. "You never heard such sounds in your life," proclaims the sleeve notes.

Joe Harriott Quintet
FREE FORM

Date recorded 1960
Label Jazzland
Musicians Joe Harriott *alto sax*, "Shake" Keane *trumpet, flügelhorn*, Pat Smythe *piano*, Coleridge Goode *bass*, Phil Seamen *drums*
Tracks Formation ❑ Coda ❑ Abstract ❑ Impression ❑ Parallel ❑ Straight Lines ❑ Calypso Sketches ❑ Tempo
Appraisal One of the most original British jazz disks of the 1960s, winning a rare *Down Beat* accolade for European music. Jamaican altoist Harriott explores an intense collective free music independently of Ornette Coleman. Phil Seamen, a drummer of remarkably relaxed swing, greatly assists the general fluency.

Art Ensemble of Chicago
PEOPLE IN SORROW

Date recorded July 7, 1969
Label Nessa
Musicians Lester Bowie *trumpet, flügelhorn, percussion*, Roscoe Mitchell *soprano, alto & bass sax, clarinet, flute, percussion*, Joseph Jarman *alto sax, bassoon, oboe, flute, percussion*, Malachi Favors *bass, zither, percussion*
Tracks People in Sorrow (part 1) ❑ People in Sorrow (part 2)
Appraisal Brilliant early session from a fertile Chicago scene. A single collage atmospherically intensifying with complex percussion and abrasively tender horns.

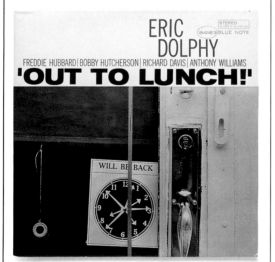

Eric Dolphy
OUT TO LUNCH!

Date recorded 1964
Label Blue Note
Musicians Eric Dolphy *alto sax, flute, bass clarinet*, Freddie Hubbard *trumpet*, Bobby Hutcherson *vibes*, Richard Davis *bass*, Anthony Williams *drums*
Tracks Hat and Beard ❑ Something Sweet, Something Tender ❑ Gazzelloni ❑ Out to Lunch ❑ Straight Up and Down
Appraisal As an original thinker and great multi-instrumentalist, intertwining harshness with delicacy, Dolphy had too short a career. This is his finest record.

Don Cherry
SYMPHONY FOR IMPROVISERS

Date recorded September, 19 1966
Label Blue Note
Musicians Don Cherry *cornet*, Gato Barbieri, Pharoah Sanders *tenor sax, piccolo*, Karl Berger *piano, vibes*, Henry Grimes, J.-F. Jenny Clark *bass*, Ed Blackwell *drums*
Tracks Symphony for Improvisers ❑ Nu Creative Love ❑ What's Not Serious ❑ Infant Happiness ❑ Manhattan Cry ❑ Lunatic ❑ Sparkle Plenty ❑ Om Nu
Appraisal Cherry's tight, bubbling sound and ease with idioms inside jazz and out are on show with this inventive group including a young Pharoah Sanders.

Ornette Coleman Double Quartet
FREE JAZZ

Date recorded 1960
Label Atlantic
Musicians Ornette Coleman *alto sax*, Donald Cherry *pocket trumpet*, Freddie Hubbard *trumpet*, Eric Dolphy *bass clarinet*, Scott LaFaro, Charlie Haden *bass*, Billy Higgins, Ed Blackwell *drums*
Tracks Free Jazz (part 1) ❑ Free Jazz (part 2)
Appraisal Archetypal free jazz disk, with a Jackson Pollock painting on the sleeve. Wild and raucous, it pitches together two quartets of different persuasions, one relaxed with freedom, one nearer hard bop.

Ascension
John Coltrane

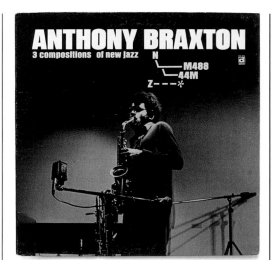

Anthony Braxton
THREE COMPOSITIONS
OF NEW JAZZ

Date recorded 1968
Label Delmark
Musicians Leo Smith *trumpet, mellophone, xylophone, bottles, kazoo,* Anthony Braxton *alto & soprano sax, clarinet, flute, musette, accordion, bells, snare drum, mixer,* Leroy Jenkins *violin, viola, harmonica, bass drum, recorder, cymbals, slide whistle,* Richard Abrahams *piano, cello, alto clarinet*
Tracks (track titles shown as graphic symbols) ⬚ The Bell
Appraisal The sixties Chicago scene's most complete virtuoso, still pushing jazz forward in the 1990s. This driving set was his debut. Check the track titles!

John Coltrane
ASCENSION

Date recorded June 28, 1965
Label Impulse
Musicians John Coltrane *tenor sax,* Freddie Hubbard, Dewey Johnson *trumpet,* Marion Brown, John Tchicai *alto sax,* Pharoah Sanders, Archie Shepp *tenor sax,* McCoy Tyner *piano,* Art Davis, Jimmy Garrison *bass,* Elvin Jones *drums*
Tracks Ascension (part 1) ⬚ Ascension (part 2)
Appraisal Coltrane's reaction to Coleman's *Free Jazz,* a fierce, thrashing exercise in dissonance for an expanded band that influenced the sound of bigger free jazz groups all over the world. It defined what came to be known as "highenergy" playing.

Elvin Jones, Coltrane's drummer in the free jazz era, brought percussion to a turbulent intensity of rhythm upon rhythm that matched the more ambiguous music. He remains the doyen of polyrhythms for young players.

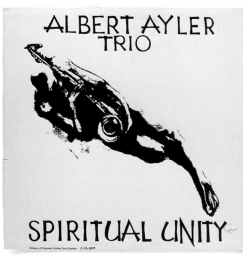

Albert Ayler Trio
SPIRITUAL UNITY

Date recorded July 10, 1964
Label ESP
Musicians Albert Ayler *sax,* Gary Peacock *bass,* Sunny Murray *drums*
Tracks Ghosts (first variation) ⬚ The Wizard ⬚ Spirits ⬚ Ghosts (second variation)
Appraisal Ayler's sax was one of the most soulful wails in jazz, and his early sessions were often spine-tingling in their intensity. "Ghosts (second variation)" is probably his finest performance, and Sunny Murray's seething cymbal sound is perfect support.

Post-bop big bands

Aᴄ̴ꜰᴛᴇʀ ᴘᴏꜱᴛᴡᴀʀ economics and the rise of bop pulled the dance floor out from under them, big bands were revived in the 1950s by revitalized Basie and Ellington ensembles. But the swing market had gone. Instead, the lessons of *Birth of the Cool* suggested a big-group jazz in which instruments reflected each other's light rather than traded shouted riffs, as they had in the 1930s Savoy Ballroom. Big bands now drew on materials from new jazz, and sometimes rock, and borrowed from European classical music if this unleashed new sound combinations without caging improvisers. *Birth of the Cool* arranger Gil Evans and his opposite, Charles Mingus — both influenced by Ellington — were at the forefront. Others, like Stan Kenton, drew on modern classical music or, like Charlie Haden and Carla Bley, on Ornette Coleman and the "New Thing."

The Gil Evans Orchestra
OUT OF THE COOL

Date recorded 1960
Label Impulse
Musicians Gil Evans *piano, arranger*, John Coles, Phil Sunkel *trumpet*, Jimmy Knepper, Keg Johnson *trombone*, Tony Studd *bass trombone*, Bill Barber *tuba*, Budd Johnson *tenor & soprano sax*, Eddie Caine, Ray Beckenstein *alto sax, flute, piccolo*, Bob Tricarico *bassoon, flute, piccolo*, Ray Crawford *guitar*, Ron Carter *bass*, Elvin Jones, Charlie Persip *percussion*
Tracks La Nevada ❑ Where Flamingos Fly ❑ Bilbao ❑ Stratusphunk ❑ Sunken Treasure
Appraisal The subtle Evans at his best: dramatic, mysterious, as original as any ensemble jazz of the era.

Carla Bley
ESCALATOR OVER THE HILL

Date recorded 1968 – 1971
Label J.C.O.A./Virgin
Musicians featuring Carla Bley *keyboards*, Don Cherry, Michael Mantler *trumpet*, Roswell Rudd *trombone*, Jimmy Lyons *alto sax*, Gato Barbieri *tenor sax*, John McLaughlin *guitar*, Charlie Haden, Jack Bruce *bass*, Paul Motian *drums, percussion*, Linda Ronstadt *vocals*
Tracks include Hotel Overture ❑ This is Here ❑ Like Animals ❑ Escalator Over the Hill ❑ Stay Awake ❑ Businessmen ❑ Why ❑ Detective Writer Daughter ❑ Over Her Head ❑ Little Pony Soldier ❑ Oh Say Can You Do? ❑ A.I.R. ❑ Rawalpindi Blues
Appraisal Ambitiously scored operalike work for big band augmented by powerful performances from guests like John McLaughlin, Jack Bruce, Don Cherry, and the country singer Linda Ronstadt. Carla Bley's Gil Evans-influenced sound is inimitable.

Charlie Haden
LIBERATION MUSIC ORCHESTRA

Date recorded 1969
Label CBS
Musicians Charlie Haden *bass*, Michael Mantler *trumpet*, Don Cherry *cornet*, Roswell Rudd *trombone*, Bob Northern *French horn*, Howard Johnson *tuba*, Dewey Redman *tenor & alto sax*, Gato Barbieri *tenor sax*, *clarinet*, Perry Robinson *clarinet*, Carla Bley *organ*, *piano*, Sam Brown *guitar*, *Tanganyikan guitar*, *thumb piano*, Paul Motian, Andrew Cyrille *drums, percussion*
Tracks The Introduction ❑ Song of the United Front ❑ El Quinto Regimento ❑ Los Quatro Generales ❑ The Ending of the First Side ❑ Song for Che ❑ War Orphans ❑ Interlude ❑ Circus 68, 69 ❑ We Shall Overcome
Appraisal Features moving accounts of Spanish Civil War songs and Ornette Coleman originals. Carla Bley's work here with Haden inspired *Escalator Over the Hill*.

The Don Ellis Orchestra
ELECTRIC BATH

Date recorded 1968
Label CBS
Musicians Don Ellis, Glenn Stuart, Alan Weight, Ed Warren, Bob Harmon *trumpet*, Ron Myers, Dave Sanchez, Terry Woodson *trombone*, Ruben Leon, Joe Roccisano *alto & soprano sax, flute*, Ira Schulman *tenor sax, flute, piccolo, clarinet*, Ron Starr *tenor sax, flute, clarinet*, John Magruder *baritone sax, flute, bass clarinet*, Mike Lang *piano, clavinet, Fender piano*, Ray Neapolitan *bass, sitar*, Frank De La Rosa, Dave Parlato *bass*, Steve Bohannon *drums*, Chino Valdes *conga, bongos*, Mark Stevens *timbales, vibes, percussion*, Alan Estes *percussion*
Tracks Indian Lady ❑ Alone ❑ Turkish Bath ❑ Open Beauty ❑ New Horizons
Appraisal Underrated jazz orchestra triumph of the 1960s. Pulsating sounds and iridescent textures in a splash of jazz color and new music experiments.

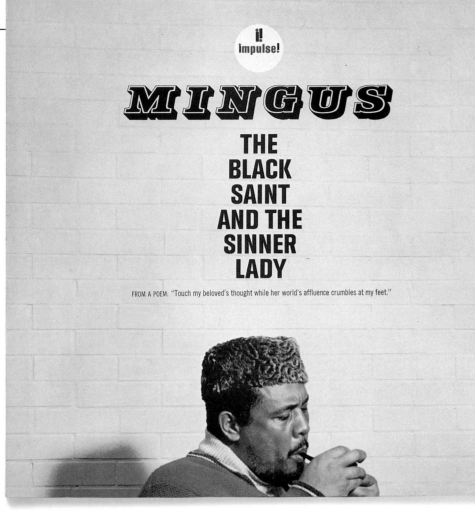

MINGUS

THE BLACK SAINT AND THE SINNER LADY

FROM A POEM: "Touch my beloved's thought while her world's affluence crumbles at my feet."

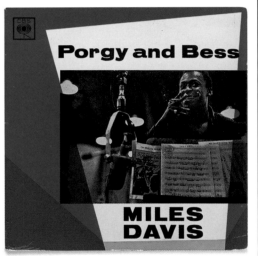

Charles Mingus, giant of string bass, conceived much of his music in workshops, composing on the run. Mingus's music reflected his volatile temperament, but his work — although rougher in texture — is comparable to Duke Ellington's.

Porgy and Bess

MILES DAVIS

Charles Mingus
THE BLACK SAINT AND THE SINNER LADY

Date recorded January 20, 1963
Label Impulse
Musicians Charles Mingus *bass, piano*, Rolf Ericson, Richard Williams *trumpet*, Quentin Jackson *trombone*, Don Butterfield *tuba, contrabass trombone*, Charles Mariano *alto sax*, Dick Hafer *tenor sax, flute*, Jerome Richardson *soprano sax, flute*, Jaki Byard *piano*, Jay Berliner *guitar*, Dannie Richmond *drums*

Tracks Track A – Solo Dance ❑ Track B – Duet Solo Dancers ❑ Track C – Group Dancers ❑ Mode D – Trio and Group Dancers ❑ Mode E – Single Solos and Group Dance ❑ Mode F – Group and Solo Dance
Appraisal Mingus took almost every ensemble device and revitalized it with new rhythmic insights, large-scale settings, and multiple textures. This session with its haunting themes is one of his finest.

Stan Kenton
NEW CONCEPTS OF ARTISTRY IN RHYTHM

Date recorded September 1952
Label Capitol
Musicians Stan Kenton *piano*, Conte Candoli, Buddy Childers, Maynard Ferguson, Don Dennis, Ruben McFall *trumpet*, Bob Fitzpatrick, Keith Moon, Frank Rosolino, Bill Russo *trombone*, George Roberts *bass trombone*, Lee Konitz, Vinnie Dean *alto sax*, Richie Kamuca, Bill Holman *tenor sax*, Bob Gioga *baritone sax*, Sal Salvador *guitar*, Don Bagley *bass*, Stan Levey *drums*, Derek Walton *conga*, Kay Brown *vocal*
Tracks Prologue ❑ Portrait of a Count ❑ Young Blood ❑ Frank Seaking ❑ 23°N-82°W ❑ Taboo ❑ Lonesome Train ❑ Invention for Guitar and Trumpet ❑ My Lady ❑ Swing House ❑ Improvisation ❑ You Go to My Head
Appraisal A distinctive Kenton disk of "progressive" music, mixing dissonance, Euro-classicism, and jazz.

Miles Davis
PORGY AND BESS

Date recorded July – August 1958
Label CBS
Musicians Miles Davis *trumpet, flügelhorn,* Gil Evans *arranger*, Louis Mucci, Ernie Royal, John Coles, Bernie Glow *trumpet*, Jimmy Cleveland, Joseph Bennett, Dick Hickson, Frank Rehak *trombone*, John "Bill" Barber *tuba*, Julian "Cannonball" Adderley, Danny Banks *sax*, Willie Ruff, Julius B. Watkins, Gunther Schuller *French horn*, Phil Bodner, Romeo Penque, Jerome Richardson *flute*, Paul Chambers *bass*, Philly Joe Jones, Jimmy Cobb *drums*
Tracks The Buzzard Song ❑ Bess You Is My Woman Now ❑ Gone ❑ Gone, Gone, Gone ❑ Summertime ❑ Bess, Oh Where's My Bess ❑ Prayer (Oh Doctor Jesus) ❑ Fishermen, Strawberry and Devil Crab ❑ My Man's Gone Now ❑ It Ain't Necessarily So ❑ Here Come de Honey Man ❑ I Loves You, Porgy ❑ There's a Boat That's Leaving Soon for New York
Appraisal Gil Evans designed some concertolike pieces for Miles Davis's moody trumpet. This famous work toughens and deepens the Gershwin originals.

Modal jazz

THE RIGID CYCLES of chords in bebop meant that even the most ecstatic solo had to keep touching very explicit bases and musicians could sound like they were trying to pack a life's work into a single night. By the early 1950s, many jazz artists were seeking other foundations for improvisation. Composer and ex-drummer George Russell wrote *Lydian Chromatic Concept of Tonal Organization*, describing how scales of varying starting points and intervals, each with a particular flavor — called modes — could underscore solos rather than the notes of chords. Bebop solos moved like pinballs, ricocheting off each new chord at sharp angles, but modal solos were shaped in gentler curves since the supporting framework changed less often. The result was a meditative, trancelike music. Modalism offered a more accessible alternative to free music in loosening jazz structure, although many players chose to use combinations of old and new forms.

John Coltrane
A LOVE SUPREME

Date recorded December 1964
Label Impulse
Musicians John Coltrane *tenor sax*, McCoy Tyner *piano*, Jimmy Garrison *bass*, Elvin Jones *drums*
Tracks Acknowledgment ❏ Resolution ❏ Pursuance ❏ Psalm
Appraisal Modal music taken as far as it goes, with a raw fierceness in Coltrane's sound, suggestive of Baptist preaching and field hollers. A great session on the borders of modal and free music, from the wildness of "Pursuance" to the tranquil power of "Psalm."

McCoy Tyner
THE REAL MCCOY

Date recorded 1967
Label Blue Note
Musicians McCoy Tyner *piano*, Joe Henderson *tenor sax*, Ron Carter *bass*, Elvin Jones *drums*
Tracks Passion Dance ❏ Contemplation ❏ Four by Five ❏ Search for Peace ❏ Blues on the Corner
Appraisal Although it was made in a fallow time for him, this is one of Tyner's great albums. With a superb band, he works close to the territory he occupied with Coltrane, but with less single-minded ferocity. The pianist's unflagging intensity around scale structures, the originality of Henderson, and material that is highly varied, make this a classic.

Herbie Hancock
MAIDEN VOYAGE

Date recorded 1965
Label Blue Note
Musicians Herbie Hancock *piano*, Freddie Hubbard *trumpet*, George Coleman *tenor sax*, Ron Carter *bass*, Anthony Williams *drums*
Tracks Maiden Voyage ❏ The Eye of the Hurricane ❏ Little One ❏ Survival of the Fittest ❏ Dolphin Dance
Appraisal Virtuoso pianist Hancock arrived in jazz when modalism was already underway, and his music outside the Miles Davis band mixed modes, funky chords, and superb compositions. Two of Hancock's most gracefully mobile pieces are here, the title track and "Dolphin Dance."

John Coltrane
MY FAVORITE THINGS

Date recorded 1960
Label Atlantic
Musicians John Coltrane *soprano & tenor sax*, McCoy Tyner *piano*, Steve Davis *bass*, Elvin Jones *drums*
Tracks My Favorite Things ❏ Everytime We Say Goodbye ❏ Summertime ❏ But Not for Me
Appraisal One of the most popular and imitated of modal improvisations, the title track from this album is developed not by following the Rodgers and Hammerstein chords, but by Tyner substituting a two-chord vamp over which Coltrane solos in an alternated mode and major scale. This session indicated scope for extended, trancelike improvising.

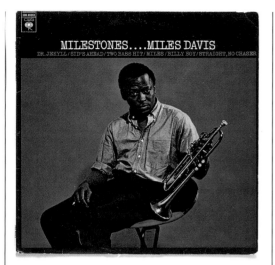

Miles Davis
MILESTONES

Date recorded 1958
Label CBS
Musicians Miles Davis *trumpet*, Julian "Cannonball" Adderley *alto sax*, John Coltrane *tenor sax*, Red Garland *piano*, Paul Chambers *bass*, Philly Joe Jones *drums*
Tracks Dr. Jekyll ❑ Sid's Ahead ❑ Two Bass Hit ❑ Milestones ❑ Billy Boy ❑ Straight, No Chaser
Appraisal *Kind of Blue* may be the best-known piece of early Miles modalism, but the lightly swinging "Milestones" — based around two scales — preceded it and immediately made jazz improvising seem leaner, airier, and more athletic.

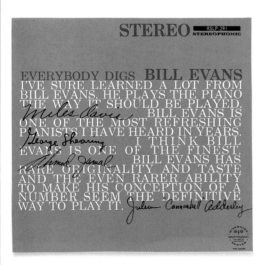

Bill Evans Trio
EVERYBODY DIGS BILL EVANS

Date recorded 1958
Label Riverside
Musicians Bill Evans *piano*, Sam Jones *bass*, Philly Joe Jones *drums*
Tracks Minority ❑ Young and Foolish ❑ Lucky to Be Me ❑ Night and Day ❑ Epilogue ❑ Tenderly ❑ Peace Piece ❑ What Is There to Say? ❑ Oleo ❑ Epilogue
Appraisal Evans, one of the most lyrical, romantic, understated, and influential pianists in jazz, with some of the music that laid the foundations for *Kind of Blue*. "Peace Piece," a delectable ballad composed in midsession, is based on the modes that became "Flamenco Sketches" on the Miles Davis classic album.

Pharoah Sanders
JEWELS OF THOUGHT

Date recorded 1969
Label Impulse
Musicians Pharoah Sanders *tenor sax, contrabass clarinet, reed flute, African thumb piano, orchestra chimes, percussion*, Lonnie Smith *piano, African flute & thumb piano, percussion*, Cecil McBee, Richard Davies *bass, percussion*, Idris Muhammad *drums, percussion*, Roy Haynes *drums*, Leon Thomas *vocal, percussion*
Tracks Hum-Allah-Hum-Allah-Hum Allah ❑ Sun in Aquarius (part 1) ❑ Sun in Aquarius (part 2)
Appraisal Sanders followed Coltrane and Albert Ayler in the 1960s, his saxophone sound emitting a fearsome, flamethrower energy, his methods based on the late Coltrane style, his pieces seething with African references, echoed by the remarkable yodeling style vocals of Leon Thomas. A highly prized disk for the first track, also known as "Prince of Peace."

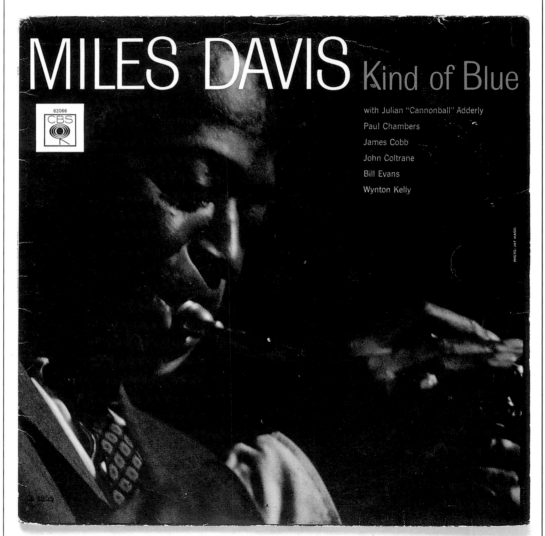

Miles Davis
KIND OF BLUE

Date recorded March – April 1959
Label CBS
Musicians Miles Davis *trumpet*, Julian Adderley *alto sax*, John Coltrane *tenor sax*, Bill Evans, Wyn Kelly *piano*, Paul Chambers *bass*, James Cobb *drums*
Tracks So What ❑ Freddie Freeloader ❑ Blue in Green ❑ All Blues ❑ Flamenco Sketches
Appraisal One of the most hypnotic and timeless jazz records ever, this modal classic featured great soloists in the first flood of exploring a new form.

Latin jazz

AFRICAN RHYTHMS went underground in the Americas in many places and many ways. Voodoo dances, ancestor worship, and work songs met both opposition and accommodation in communities run by Americans, Spanish, Portuguese, French, or English and resurfaced changed but still recognizable. Jazz beats often travel in threes, but in Latin America — particularly in Cuba and Brazil — dance rhythms operate in grouped pairs of notes in which the emphases fall irregularly (BA-ba, ba-BA, ba-ba, BA-ba). This Latin feel crept into some 1930s jazz but became widespread on record after Dizzy Gillespie hired the sensational Cuban drummer Chano Pozo in 1947. Jazz with that Latin shimmer has been popular ever since, booming in the 1960s with the jazz samba cult and dramatically coloring the rhythms of fusion in the following decade.

Tito Puente
IN PUERTO RICO

Date recorded unknown
Label Tico
Musicians featuring Tito Puente *percussion, vibes, arranger* with orchestra
Tracks Pa Borinquen ❑ El Paso ❑ Quisiera Olividarte ❑ Cancion de la Serrania ❑ Vega Baja ❑ El Que Usted Conoce ❑ Babarabatiri ❑ Morena ❑ Romance del Campesino
Appraisal Tito Puente organized his first band in the 1940s and plays with the authenticity of the priest of the *santeria* faith he also is. This live set captures the ecstatic feel of salsa influenced by jazz.

Poncho Sanchez
SONANDO

Date recorded August 1982
Label Concord Picante
Musicians Poncho Sanchez *congas, percussion,* Steven Huffsteter *trumpet,* Mark Levine *trombone,* Gary Foster *alto sax, flute,* Dick Mitchell *tenor sax, flute,* Charlie Otwell *piano,* Tony Banda *bass,* Ramon Banda *timbales, drums,* Luis Conte *percussion,* Jose Perico Hernandez *vocal*
Tracks A Night in Tunisia ❑ Sonando ❑ The Summer Knows ❑ Con Tres Tambores Bata un Quinto y un Tumbador ❑ Este Son ❑ Almendra ❑ Sueño ❑ Cal's Pals ❑ Peruchín
Appraisal Originally with Cal Tjader, Sanchez's first disk as leader features a mambo version of "A Night in Tunisia" alongside cha-chas, boleros, and salsa tunes.

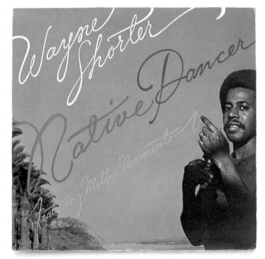

Wayne Shorter
NATIVE DANCER

Date recorded 1975
Label Columbia
Musicians featuring Wayne Shorter *tenor & soprano sax,* Milton Nascimento *vocal,* Herbie Hancock, Wagner Tiso *keyboards,* David Amaro *guitar,* Roberto Silva *drums,* Airto Moreira *percussion*
Tracks Ponta de Areia ❑ Beauty and the Beast ❑ Tarde ❑ Miracle of the Fishes ❑ Diana ❑ From the Lonely Afternoons ❑ Ana Maria ❑ Lilia ❑ Joanna's Theme
Appraisal Milton Nascimento's light, airy vocals and magical melodic compositions meet Shorter's unusual phrasing and faintly baleful tenor sound on this deceptively straight-sounding samba session: a watershed in the fusion of Brazilian music and jazz.

Hermeto Pascoal
SLAVES MASS

Date recorded 1976
Label Warner Bros
Musicians Hermeto Pascoal *keyboards, soprano sax, flutes, guitar, vocal,* Raoul de Souza *trombone, vocal,* David Amaro *guitar,* Ron Carter, Alphonso Johnson *bass,* Chester Thompson *drums,* Airto Moreira *drums, percussion,* Flora Purim, Hugo Fattoruso, Laudir de Olivera, Airto Moreira *vocal*
Tracks Mixing Pot ❑ Slaves Mass ❑ Little Cry for Him ❑ Cannon ❑ Just Listen ❑ That Waltz ❑ Cherry Jam
Appraisal Brazilian multi-instrumentalist Pascoal is an avid sound experimenter: this disk features grunts of piglets alongside his protegé Moreira. Great influence on 1970s fusion players, including Miles Davis.

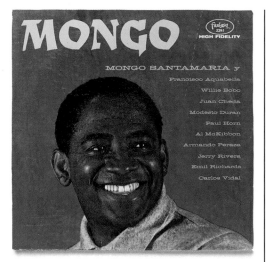

Chick Corea
RETURN TO FOREVER

Date recorded February 2 – 3, 1972
Label ECM
Musicians Chick Corea *electric piano*, Joe Farrell *flutes, soprano sax*, Stan Clarke *bass*, Airto Moreira *drums*, Flora Purim *vocal, percussion*
Tracks Return to Forever ❑ Crystal Silence ❑ What Game Shall We Play Today ❑ Sometime Ago-la Fiesta
Appraisal The first, and best, Return to Forever with Flora Purim's guileless, soaring vocals and Corea's glittering piano figures dancing together over a softly surging Afro-Brazilian beat laid down by Moreira.

Machito
THE WORLD'S GREATEST
LATIN BAND

Date recorded 1988
Label GNP Crescendo
Musicians Machito *vocal, leader*; orchestra featuring Jimmy Zito *trumpet*, Aaron Sachs *sax*, Graciella *vocal*
Tracks El Columpio ❑ Tenderly ❑ Ayer lo vi Llorar ❑ Mi Otoño ❑ Todo Es ❑ Bernie's Tune ❑ Jamaicuba ❑ Moonlight in Vermont ❑ Alma con Alma ❑ Almendra ❑ Pent-up House
Appraisal Machito's was one of the first Latin bands to absorb and reflect bop, and it had a furious swing. The repertoire here reflects its influences.

Mongo Santamaria
MONGO

Date recorded May 1959
Label Fantasy
Musicians Mongo Santamaria *drums*, Francisco Aquabella *drums arranger*, Jose "Chombo" Silva *tenor sax*, Paul Horn *flute*, Vince Guaraldi *piano*, Cal Tjader *vibes*, Emil Richards *marimba*, Al McKibbon *bass*, Armando Peraza, Willie Bobo, Juan Cheda, Carlos Vidal *percussion*, Jose Gamboa *vocal, tres*
Tracks Afro Blue ❑ Che-que-re-que-che-que ❑ Rezo ❑ Ayenye ❑ Onyaye ❑ Bata ❑ Meta ❑ Rhumba ❑ Chano Pozo ❑ Los Conguitos ❑ Monte Adentro ❑ Imaribayo ❑ Mazacote
Appraisal After Chano Pozo, Mongo Santamaria was the next major Latin jazz star, influencing Chick Corea and many others. Cal Tjader, vibes dance-floor idol, plays here, and the great "Chombo" Silva, but the rich tapestry of percussion is the real frontline. "Mazacote" stands out.

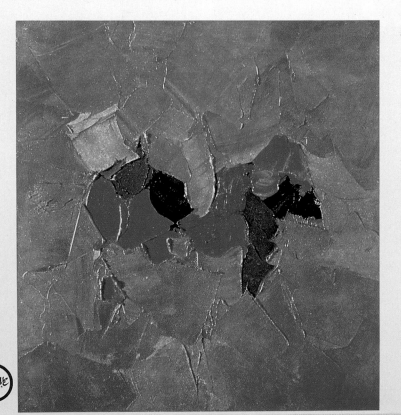

Stan Getz/Charlie Byrd
JAZZ SAMBA

Date recorded February 13, 1962
Label Verve
Musicians Stan Getz *tenor sax*, Charlie Byrd *guitar*, Gene Byrd *bass, guitar*, Keter Betts *bass*, Buddy Deppenschmidt, Bill Reichenbach *drums*
Tracks Desafinado ❑ Samba Dees Days ❑ O Pato ❑ Samba Triste ❑ Samba de Uma Nota Só ❑ E Luxo So ❑ Baia
Appraisal With the jazz samba boom of the early 1960s, Latin jazz met the cool school. The dominant voice in it was the pale, fragile sound of Stan Getz's Lester Young-inspired saxophone: one of the most affecting and eagerly imitated saxophone voices from the 1950s to the 1970s. "Desafinado" was a pop hit, as was the follow-up "Girl from Ipanema" with singer Astrud Gilberto. Although these pieces have sometimes been denigrated by comparison with noisier and more muscular versions of Latin jazz that followed, Getz's playing is no less imaginative for being restrained, and the themes are delightful. Only the rhythm section misses the buzz of Latin music, opting for a minimalist cool school shuffle.

Fusion

ROCK SPRANG from the same roots as jazz forty years before it, but by the 1960s' jazz seemed firmly in the back seat of popular music. Not that there weren't phenomenal musicians — Miles Davis, John Coltrane, Thelonious Monk, Charles Mingus, Ornette Coleman, and countless others — still making timeless music in their own way. But big audiences had gone, and rock by 1965 was becoming increasingly subtle, complex, and in some hands improvisational. Major record labels grew restless about their jazz artists and encouraged them to experiment with hybrids of jazz and rock. But these changes didn't entirely stem from accounting departments. Those musicians unconvinced that the "high-energy" free-improvised music of the 1960s had truly restored vitality to jazz heard the fire and drive they were looking for in rock and soul and absorbed their sounds, some having major chart hits.

Herbie Mann
MEMPHIS UNDERGROUND

Date recorded 1969
Label Atlantic
Musicians Herbie Mann *flute*, Bobby Emmons, Bobby Wood *keyboards*, Larry Coryell, Sonny Sharrock, Reggie Young *guitar*, Tommy Cogbill, Mike Leech, Miroslav Vitous *bass*, Roy Ayers *vibes*, Gene Christman *drums*
Tracks Memphis Underground ❑ New Orleans ❑ Hold On I'm Comin' ❑ Chain of Fools ❑ Battle Hymn of the Republic
Appraisal Crucial, clamorous fusion set with flute and vibes, which is still cooking 25 years later.

Herbie Hancock
HEAD HUNTERS

Date recorded 1973
Label CBS
Musicians Herbie Hancock *Fender Rhodes, Hohner D6 clavinet, Arp Odyssey & Soloist synthesizers, pipes*, Bennie Maupin *soprano & tenor sax, bass clarinet, alto flute*, Paul Jackson *bass, marimbula*, Harvey Mason *drums*, Bill Summers *congas, shekere, balafon, agogo, cabasa, hindewho, tambourine, log drum, surdo, gankoqui, beer bottle*
Tracks Chameleon ❑ Watermelon Man ❑ Sly ❑ Vein Melter
Appraisal Sales-busting 1970s jazz album, founded on little improvising but instant-recall tunes like the much covered "Chameleon," electric bass riffs to rattle the windows, deep wah-wah, and showers of percussion.

Dreams
DREAMS

Date recorded 1970
Label CBS
Musicians Randy Brecker *trumpet, flügelhorn*, Barry Rogers *trombone, Wagner tuba*, Michael Brecker *tenor sax, flute*, Jeff Kent *keyboards, guitar, vocal*, John Abercrombie *lead guitar*, Doug Lubahn *bass, vocal*, Billy Cobham *drums, percussion*, Edward Vernon *vocal*
Tracks Devil Lady ❑ 15 Miles to Provo ❑ The Maryanne ❑ Holli Be Home ❑ Try Me ❑ Dream Suite ❑ New York
Appraisal A founding fusion band, the inventive and influential Dreams was established by the Brecker brothers and Billy Cobham, all three musicians drawn to rhythm and blues and soul, as much as jazz.

The Mahavishnu Orchestra
THE INNER MOUNTING FLAME

Date recorded 1971
Label CBS
Musicians John McLaughlin *guitar*, Jan Hammer *piano*, Rick Laird *bass*, Billy Cobham *drums*, Jerry Goodman *violin*
Tracks Meetings of the Spirit ❑ Dawn ❑ The Noonward Race ❑ A Lotus on Irish Streams ❑ Vital Transformation ❑ The Dance of Maya ❑ You Know You Know ❑ Awakening
Appraisal British guitarist McLaughlin came out of rhythm and blues and into the Miles Davis band, then formed this thunderous quintet featuring Cobham's riotously funky drumming, Goodman's country-flavored violin, and references to Indian music. This is the first and best Mahavishnu disk.

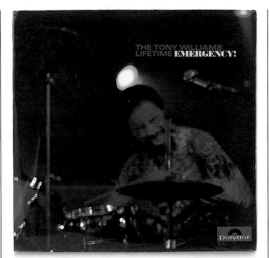

The Tony Williams Lifetime
EMERGENCY!

Date recorded 1969
Label Polydor
Musicians Tony Williams *drums*, Larry Young *organ*, John McLaughlin *guitar*
Tracks Emergency ❑ Beyond Games ❑ Where ❑ Vashkar ❑ Via the Spectrum Road ❑ Spectrum ❑ Sangria for Three ❑ Something Spiritual
Appraisal One of the most advanced jazz drummers, Williams formed this fierce, uncompromising fusion band after leaving Miles Davis.

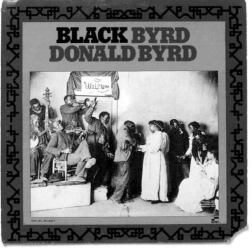

Donald Byrd
BLACK BYRD

Date recorded 1973
Label Blue Note
Musicians featuring Donald Byrd *trumpet*, Larry Mizell *producer*, *arranger*
Tracks Flight Time ❑ Black Byrd ❑ Love's So Far Away ❑ Mr. Thomas ❑ Sky High ❑ Slop Jar Blues ❑ Where Are We Going?
Appraisal Hard bop trumpeter Donald Byrd's funky reaction to Motown, gospel, and James Brown with the hallmark of the influential Mizell brothers. Going for grooves more than improvising, it rivals *Head Hunters*.

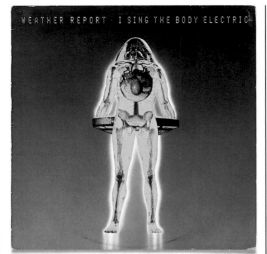

Weather Report
I SING THE BODY ELECTRIC

Date recorded 1971 – 1972
Label CBS
Musicians Wilmer Wise *D & piccolo trumpet*, Andrew White *English horn*, Wayne Shorter *reeds*, Hubert Laws Jr. *flute*, Josef Zawinul *electric & acoustic keyboard*, Ralph Towner *12-string guitar*, Miroslav Vitous *bass*, Eric Gravatt *drums*, Dom Um Romao *percussion*, Yolande Bavan, Joshie Armstrong, Chapman Roberts *vocal*
Tracks Unknown Soldier ❑ The Moors ❑ Crystal ❑ Second Sunday in August ❑ Medley: Vertical Invader, T.H., Dr. Honoris Causa ❑ Surucucu ❑ Directions
Appraisal Weather Report revolutionized the use of electric instruments in jazz and the evolution of a vivacious fusion ensemble style entwining solos and scores. This was their second record, and features the talents of Miroslav Vitous and Dom Um Romao.

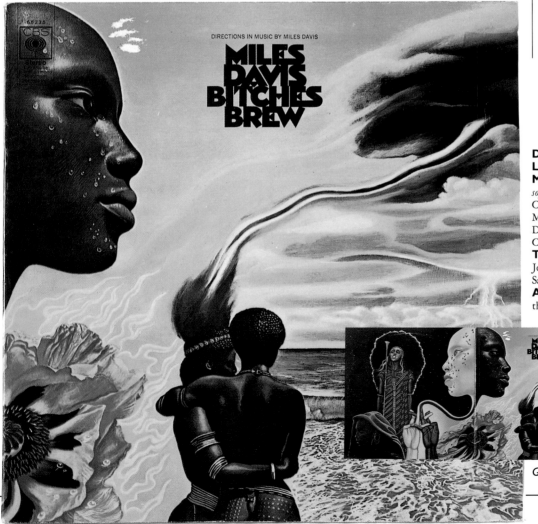

Gatefold sleeve

Miles Davis
BITCHES BREW

Date recorded 1969
Label CBS
Musicians Miles Davis *trumpet*, Wayne Shorter *soprano sax*, Bennie Maupin *bass clarinet*, Chick Corea, Joe Zawinul, Larry Young *electric piano*, John McLaughlin *electric guitar*, Harvey Brooks *Fender bass*, Dave Holland *bass*, Lenny White, Jack DeJohnette, Charles Alias *drums*, Jim Riley *percussion*
Tracks Pharoah's Dance ❑ Bitches Brew ❑ Spanish Key ❑ John McLaughlin ❑ Miles Runs the Voodoo Down ❑ Sanctuary
Appraisal The most influential of all fusion records of the late sixties, and one that begins to use studio editing as creatively as any other technique. Davis blurs the distinction between front lines and rhythm sections even further, turning the whole band into a restless, spacy generator of funky rhythmic textures, through which soloists loom and vanish like ghosts. Still eerie and compelling and bursting with life.

In the tradition

AROUND THE BEGINNING of the 1980s, acoustic jazz traditions neglected for close to fifteen years came triumphantly back. Veteran bebop giants resigned to a life on the road, scraping a living from scattered groups of jazz enthusiasts with long memories, found their names in lights again — and even on major record company contracts. Young ones flowered alongside, eagerly absorbing their autumn sunlight. Hard bop, with its punchy rhythms, catchy tunes, and robust soloing, came back into favor — as did methods and styles previously abandoned too soon, like the 1960s acoustic music of Miles Davis. Young virtuosos poured out of music colleges, particularly Berklee in Boston, to be snapped up by the major record labels. Motivated by a renewed love of jazz, confident in advanced and often highly trained techniques, and living in a period in which self-expression had ceased to be self-evidently virtuous, young musicians rekindled the experience of hearing earlier jazz styles played live as their pioneers passed on.

The Harper Brothers
REMEMBRANCE

Date recorded September 1989
Label PolyGram
Musicians Philip Harper *trumpet*, Winard Harper *drums*, Justin Robinson *alto sax*, Stephen Scott *piano*, Kiyoshi Kitagawa *bass*
Tracks Introduction by Barbara Hackett ❏ Hodge Podge ❏ In a Way She Goes ❏ Remembrance ❏ Somewhere in the Night ❏ CB ❏ Keynote Doctrine ❏ Kiss Me Right ❏ Always Know ❏ Don't Go to Strangers ❏ Umi ❏ Yang
Appraisal Plenty of young musicians in the 1980s had the notes, but not so many had the feel. The Harper Brothers, devoted to Art Blakey, recaptured much of the ecstatic energy of hard bop.

Dexter Gordon
HOMECOMING

Date recorded November 11 – 12, 1976
Label CBS
Musicians Dexter Gordon *tenor sax*, Woody Shaw *trumpet, flügelhorn*, Ronnie Matthews *piano*, Stafford James *bass*, Louis Hayes *drums*
Tracks Gingerbread Boy ❏ Little Red's Fantasy ❏ Fenja ❏ In Case You Haven't Heard ❏ It's You or No One ❏ Let's Get Down ❏ Round Midnight ❏ Backstairs
Appraisal When hard bop boss of bosses Gordon returned to the States from voluntary exile, he unintentionally kindled the neo-bop movement with this disk.

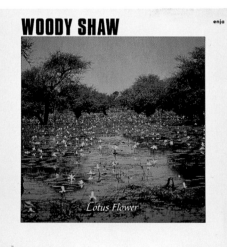

Woody Shaw
LOTUS FLOWER

Date recorded January 7, 1982
Label Enja
Musicians Woody Shaw *trumpet*, Steve Turre *trombone, percussion*, Mulgrew Miller *piano*, Stafford James *bass*, Tony Reedus *drums*
Tracks Eastern Joy Dance ❏ Game ❏ Lotus Flower ❏ Rahsaan's Run ❏ Song of Songs
Appraisal A short-lived trumpet star of the 1970s and 1980s with a magnificent band. Good material, great group interplay and fine soloing — Shaw bold but clear, Turre explicit at any tempo.

Joe Henderson
THE STATE OF THE TENOR

Date recorded November 14 – 16, 1985
Label Blue Note
Musicians Joe Henderson *tenor sax*, Ron Carter *bass*, Al Foster *drums*
Tracks Boo Boo's Birthday ❏ Cheryl ❏ Y Ya la Quiero ❏ Soulville ❏ Portrait ❏ The Bead Game
Appraisal Like a younger Sonny Rollins, Henderson proved sheer spontaneous melodic genius to be still at the heart of jazz. These live Village Vanguard sessions show how Henderson in the 1980s accumulated the worldwide awe in which he is held today.

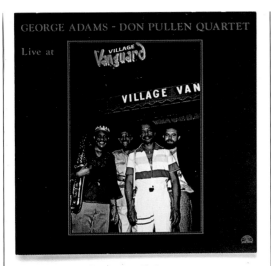

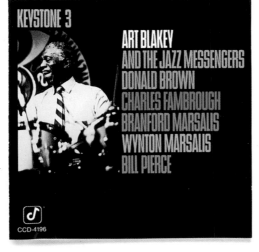

George Adams
Don Pullen Quartet
LIVE AT VILLAGE VANGUARD
Date recorded August 19, 1983
Label Soul Note
Musicians Don Pullen *piano*, George Adams *tenor sax*, Cameron Brown *bass*, Dannie Richmond *drums*
Tracks The Necessary Blues (Thank You Very Much, Mr. Monk) ❑ Solitude ❑ Intentions ❑ Diane
Appraisal From 1977 to 1989, this descendant of Charles Mingus's groups dynamically occupied a territory somewhere between free jazz and hard bop, as this fine set proves.

Art Blakey and the Jazz
Messengers
KEYSTONE 3
Date recorded January 1982
Label Concord
Musicians Art Blakey *drums,* Donald Brown *piano,* Charles Fambrough *bass,* Branford Marsalis *alto sax,* Wynton Marsalis *trumpet,* Bill Pierce *tenor sax*
Tracks In Walked Bud ❑ In a Sentimental Mood ❑ Fuller Love ❑ Waterfalls ❑ A la Mode
Appraisal Blakey was a hero of the bebop revival, and the boiling energy of the Messengers is well caught on this live set, featuring the Marsalises.

The Dirty Dozen Brass Band
OPEN UP (WHATCHA GONNA DO FOR THE REST OF YOUR LIFE?)
Date recorded January – April 1991
Label Columbia
Musicians Gregory Davis *trumpet, finger cymbals,* Efrem Towns *trumpet,* Charles Joseph *trombone, tambourine, vocal,* Kirk Joseph *sousaphone, vocal,* Roger Lewis *soprano & baritone sax,* Kevin Harris *tenor sax, vocal, cowbell, ride cymbal,* Raymond Weber *drums,* Lionel Batiste *snare drum, cowbell, bass drum, high hat cymbal,* Jenell Marshall *bass drum, claves, snare drum*
Tracks Use Your Brain ❑ Open Up (Whatcha Gonna Do for the Rest of Your Life?) ❑ The Lost Souls of Southern Louisiana ❑ Deorc Sceadu (Dark Shadow) ❑ Dominique ❑ Charlie Dozen ❑ Song for Lady M. ❑ Remember When ❑ Darker Shadows ❑ Eyomzi
Appraisal Not all the new jazz generation turned to bop. Some went further back, to the street parades and marches. This exhilarating New Orleans outfit covers all that in this storming session, with bop, the hottest funk, gospel, and Cajun music thrown in. Compositional duties are shared by the band members.

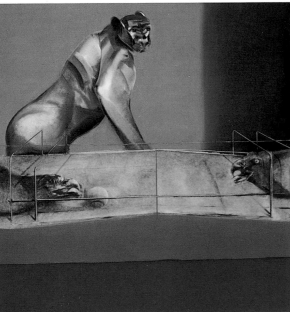

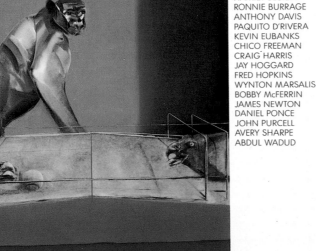

A CONCERT OF **THE**
NEW MUSIC
PLAYED BY
SEVENTEEN
EXCEPTIONAL
YOUNG MUSICIANS
THE KOOL JAZZ FESTIVAL
JUNE 30, 1982

YOUNG LIONS

JOHN BLAKE
HAMIET BLUIETT
RONNIE BURRAGE
ANTHONY DAVIS
PAQUITO D'RIVERA
KEVIN EUBANKS
CHICO FREEMAN
CRAIG HARRIS
JAY HOGGARD
FRED HOPKINS
WYNTON MARSALIS
BOBBY McFERRIN
JAMES NEWTON
DANIEL PONCE
JOHN PURCELL
AVERY SHARPE
ABDUL WADUD

ELEKTRA *Musician*

Various Artists
THE YOUNG LIONS
Date recorded June 30, 1982
Label Elektra
Musicians Bobby McFerrin *vocal,* Wynton Marsalis *trumpet,* Paquito D'Rivera *alto sax,* John Purcell *alto sax, clarinet, English horn, oboe, flute,* Chico Freeman *tenor sax, bass clarinet,* Hamiet Bluiett *baritone sax,* Craig Harris *trombone,* James Newton *flute,* John Blake *violin,* Abdul Wadud *cello,* Jay Hoggard *vibes, marimba, balafon,* Anthony Davis *piano,* Kevin Eubanks *guitar, acoustic guitar,* Avery Sharpe, Fred Hopkins *bass,* Ronnie Burrage *drums,* Daniel Ponce *percussion*
Tracks B. 'N' W. ❑ Mariel ❑ Thank You ❑ Maiden Dance ❑ What Ever Happened to the Dream Deferred ❑ Breakin' ❑ Nigerian Sunset ❑ F. M. W. ❑ Pleasant Memories ❑ Endless Flight
Appraisal Celebrated concert from the 1982 Kool Jazz Festival, putting seventeen younger musicians in various combinations. The show demonstrated how secure techniques were and how enthusiastically African and Latin music were being mixed. It had most of the flavor of the jazz to come in the 1980s.

Chick Corea
AKOUSTIC BAND

Date recorded 1989
Label GRP
Musicians Chick Corea *piano*, John Patitucci *bass*, Dave Weckl *drums*
Tracks Bessie's Blues ❑ My One and Only Love ❑ Sophisticated Lady ❑ Autumn Leaves ❑ T. B. C. (Terminal Baggage Claim) ❑ Morning Sprite ❑ Circles ❑ Spain
Appraisal The ripe, eloquent lyricism of Corea in a crisp trio, one of the most consistent albums from an artist occasionally diverted from his real talents.

Diane Schuur
IN TRIBUTE

Date recorded 1992
Label GRP
Musicians Diane Schuur *vocal*, *piano*, full orchestra under the direction of Alan Broadbent
Tracks Them There Eyes ❑ The Man I Love ❑ God Bless the Child ❑ Sweet Georgia Brown ❑ Guess I'll Hang My Tears Out to Dry ❑ 'Round Midnight ❑ How High the Moon ❑ Body and Soul ❑ Black Coffee ❑ Love for Sale ❑ Sophisticated Lady ❑ The Best Is Yet to Come ❑ Ev'ry Time We Say Goodbye
Appraisal Gospel-derived singer of strength and vitality, although sometimes undermined by bland material and grandiose schemes. This tribute to twelve jazz singers shows her best side, remaking some classic songs in her own distinctive way.

Wynton Marsalis
STANDARD TIME

Date recorded May – September 1986
Label CBS
Musicians Wynton Marsalis *trumpet*, Marcus Roberts "J. Master" *piano*, Robert Leslie Hurst III *bass*, Jeff "Tain" Watts *drums*
Tracks Caravan ❑ April in Paris ❑ Cherokee (2 takes) ❑ Goodbye ❑ New Orleans ❑ Soon All Will Know ❑ Foggy Day ❑ The Song Is You ❑ Memories of You ❑ In the Afterglow ❑ Autumn Leaves

Appraisal Marsalis dominated the 1980s jazz renaissance with his pearly sound, dazzling speed, and depth of knowledge. In the company of ideally flexible, responsive partners, here he explores twelve classic songs, including a fast, chortling "Caravan" and a softly scampering muted solo on "Cherokee." A high point of 1980s jazz discography, this was the halfway stage of Marsalis's journey into the music's history.

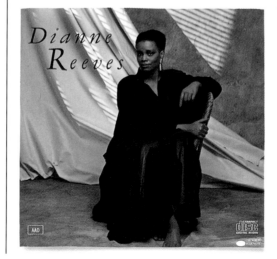

Dianne Reeves
DIANNE REEVES

Date recorded 1987
Label Blue Note
Musicians Dianne Reeves *vocal*, Freddie Hubbard *flügelhorn*, Justo Almario *tenor sax*, Herbie Hancock *keyboards*, George Duke *piano*, *Synclavier*, *TX 816*, Jorge del Barrio *Synclavier strings*, Billy Childs *piano*, Paul Jackson *guitar*, Stanley Clarke, Tony Dumas, Freddie Washington *bass*, Tony Williams, Rickey Lawson, Ralph Penland, Leon "Ndugu" Chancler *drums*, Paulinho da Costa, Airto Moreira *percussion*
Tracks Sky Islands ❑ I'm OK ❑ Better Days ❑ Harvest Time ❑ Never Said (Chan's Song) ❑ Yesterdays ❑ I've Got It Bad and That Ain't Good ❑ That's All
Appraisal Potential new Sarah Vaughan, an operatic vocalist performing many styles, with giants Herbie Hancock and funk jazz supremo George Duke.

Geri Allen
ETUDES

Date recorded 1987
Label Soul Note
Musicians Geri Allen *piano*, Charlie Haden *bass*, Paul Motian *percussion*
Tracks Lonely Woman ❑ Dolphy's Dance ❑ Sandino ❑ Fiasco ❑ Etude II ❑ Blues in Motion ❑ Silence ❑ Shuffle Montgomery ❑ Etude I
Appraisal "Dolphy's Dance" and Ornette Coleman's "Lonely Woman" reveal a stunning pianist with a low-key intensity derived from Bill Evans and Paul Bley but a sense of shape all her own. Charlie Haden and Paul Motian shadow every step.

Cassandra Wilson
BLUE SKIES

Date recorded February 1988
Label JMT
Musicians Cassandra Wilson *vocal*, Mulgrew Miller *piano*, Lonnie Plaxico *bass*, Terri Lyne Carrington *drums*
Tracks Shall We Dance ❑ Polka Dots and Moonbeams ❑ I've Grown Accustomed to His Face ❑ I Didn't Know What Time It Was ❑ I'm Old Fashioned ❑ Sweet Lorraine ❑ My One and Only Love ❑ Autumn Nocturne ❑ Blue Skies
Appraisal A mixture of muscular soul and funk with ambitious, Betty Carter-like phrasing, the M-Base singer pays her respects to the jazz tradition here.

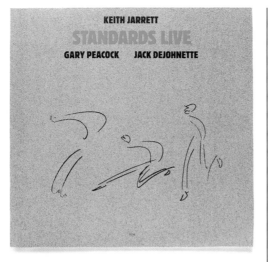

Keith Jarrett/Gary Peacock/
Jack DeJohnette
STANDARDS LIVE

Date recorded July 2, 1985
Label ECM
Musicians Keith Jarrett *piano*, Gary Peacock *bass*, Jack DeJohnette *drums, cymbals*
Tracks Stella by Starlight ❑ The Wrong Blues ❑ Falling in Love With Love ❑ Too Young to Go Steady ❑ The Way You Look Tonight ❑ The Old Country
Appraisal Some 1980s jazz revivalism just sounded overawed, but Jarrett's utterly personal development of the Bill Evans trio's methods brims with life. His two partners are crucial ingredients.

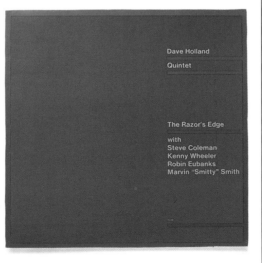

Dave Holland Quintet
THE RAZOR'S EDGE

Date recorded February 1987
Label ECM
Musicians Dave Holland *bass*, Kenny Wheeler *flügelhorn, trumpet, cornet*, Steve Coleman *alto sax*, Robin Eubanks *trombone*, Marvin "Smitty" Smith *drums*
Tracks Brother Ty ❑ Vedana ❑ The Razor's Edge ❑ Blues for C. M. ❑ Vortex ❑ 5 Four Six ❑ Wights Waits for Weights ❑ Figit Time
Appraisal Deft, quick-witted, sophisticated neo-bop from the bell-toned bassist, influenced by Charles Mingus in sound and ensemble ideas, with a band of young stars stretching the jazz envelope. This session was one of the quintet's best blends of writing and improvisation, freewheeling but taut.

29th Street Saxophone Quartet
LIVE

Date recorded July 1988
Label Red
Musicians Ed Jackson, Bobby Watson *alto sax*, Rich Rothenberg *tenor sax*, Jim Hartog *baritone sax*
Tracks The Originator ❑ Pannonica ❑ 'B.' on the Break ❑ Claudia's Car ❑ Night Dreamer ❑ New Moon ❑ The Halcyon ❑ My Little Suede Shoes
Appraisal Of several all-sax bands appearing in the 1970s and 1980s, the 29th Street was one of the most inventive. This live show catches them at their most energetically conversational.

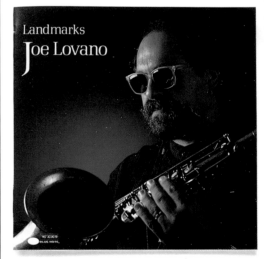

Joe Lovano
LANDMARKS

Date recorded August 13 – 14, 1990
Label Blue Note
Musicians Joe Lovano *tenor sax*, Ken Werner *piano*, Joe Abercrombie *guitar*, Marc Johnson *bass*, Bill Stewart *drums*
Tracks The Owl and the Fox ❑ Primal Dance ❑ Emperor Jones ❑ Landmarks Along the Way ❑ Street Talk ❑ Here and Now ❑ I Love Music ❑ Where Hawks Fly ❑ Thanksgiving ❑ Dig This
Appraisal Guitarist John Scofield's band reintroduced a skillful, neglected improviser in Lovano, blending Lester Young's subtlety and Coltrane's urgency with melodic unpredictability suggesting Ornette Coleman and Monk. A disk of the decade.

Club jazz

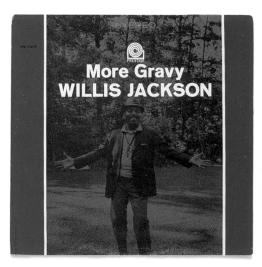

JAZZ GREW UP alongside dance: in the 1930s, even Ellington would have lost face if he couldn't keep lindy-hoppers jumping in Harlem ballrooms. In the 1980s, jazz returned to the dance floor. New black music, particularly hip hop and rap, grafted jazz themes to funk backbeats. Distinctions between deejay, performer, and producer broke down. Deejays, like Gilles Peterson, who compiled this selection of records, started to spin an eclectic mix of 1950s and 1960s soul jazz with Latin standards, rare groove funk, and contemporary rap. Producers and musicians sampled classic jazz fragments, rediscovering obscure gems, and young funk and rap musicians dug into the jazz past — the slogan being "You got to hear Blue Note to dig Def Jam"; bop virtuosos played over dance grooves; and jazz giants found their 30-year-old disks in essentials lists. If the most adventurous improvisations did not always fit in, club jazz testifies to the music's timeless energy.

Willis Jackson
MORE GRAVY

Date recorded 1964
Label Prestige
Musicians Willis Jackson *tenor sax*, Frank Robinson *trumpet*, Carl Wilson *organ*, Pat Azzara *guitar*, Sam Jones *bass*, Joe Hadrick *drums*
Tracks Pool Shark ❏ Somewhere Along the Way ❏ Stuffin' ❏ Nuther'n like Thuther'n ❏ More Gravy ❏ Fiddlin'
Appraisal "Gator" Jackson: limited, punchy soul jazz tenorist with organ bands. "Nuther'n like Thuther'n" with a "Watermelon Man" groove ignites dancers.

Airto Moreira
SAMBA DE FLORA

Date recorded 1988
Label Montuno
Musicians featuring Airto Moreira *drums, percussion, vocal, flute*, Flora Purim *vocal*, Jeff Elliott *trumpet*, Raul de Souza *trombone*, David Tolegian, Joe Farrell *reeds*, Jorge Dalto, Kei Akagi *keyboards*, Frank Colon *berimbau*, Alphonso Johnson, Michael Shapiro, Randy Tico, Keith Jones *bass*, Tony Moreno *drums*, Angel Maldonado, Giovanni Hidalgo, Don Alias, Laudir de Oliveira, Frank Colon, Luiz Muñoz *percussion*
Tracks Parana ❏ Samba de Flora ❏ La Puerta ❏ Dedos ❏ Yanah Amina ❏ El Fiasco ❏ Mulambo ❏ Latin Woman
Appraisal Few percussionists generate more heat, and the band is like a percussion choir. The gliding, sensuous title carries hands-in-the-air clubgoers to Brazil.

Art Ensemble of Chicago
LES STANCES A SOPHIE

Date recorded July 22, 1970
Label Nessa
Musicians Lester Bowie *trumpet, flügelhorn, percussion*, Roscoe Mitchell *soprano, alto & bass sax, clarinet, flute, percussion*, Joseph Jarman *tenor, alto & soprano sax, flute, percussion*, Malachi Favors *acoustic & electric bass, percussion*, Fontella Bass *vocal, piano*
Tracks Theme de Yoyo ❏ Theme de Celine ❏ Variations sur un Theme de Monteverdi ❏ Proverbes (2 takes) ❏ Theme Amour Universel ❏ Theme Libre
Appraisal Proves that if the vibes are right, dancers can thrive on free-form horns and approximate ensemble playing. A melee of squabbling sax and clattering percussion over a funk beat for soul singer Fontella Bass to deliver the erotic "Theme de Yoyo."

Public Enemy
FEAR OF A BLACK PLANET

Date recorded 1989
Label Def Jam
Musicians featuring Chuck D, Flavor Flav, Professor Griff, Terminator X, Ice Cube, Big Daddy Kane
Tracks Brothers Gonna Work It Out ❏ 911 Is a Joke ❏ Welcome to the Terrordome ❏ Meet the G that Killed Me ❏ Pollywanacraka ❏ Anti-Nigger Machine ❏ Burn Hollywood Burn ❏ Power to the People ❏ Who Stole the Soul ❏ Fear of a Black Planet ❏ Revolutionary Generation ❏ Can't Do Nuttin' ❏ Reggie Jax ❏ B Side Wins Again ❏ War at 33⅓ ❏ Fight the Power
Appraisal An influence on jazz today and tomorrow: rough, uncompromising rap from a band as rooted on the mean streets as Airto is in the Brazilian sun. "Fight the Power" — declamatory, political — is the tune.

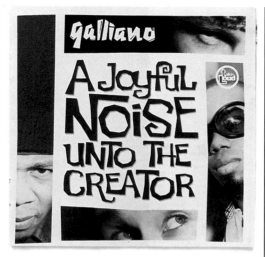

Funk Incorporated
CHICKEN LICKIN'

Date recorded 1972
Label Prestige
Musicians Eugene Barr *tenor sax*, Bobby Watley *organ, vocal*, Steve Weakley *guitar*, Jimmy Munford *drums, vocal*, Cecil Hunt *conga*
Tracks Chicken Lickin' ❑ Running Away ❑ They Trying to Get Me ❑ The Better Half ❑ Let's Make Peace and Stop the War ❑ Jung Bung
Appraisal Hot, bluesy Crusaders-style sound and a blasting recipe from the tenor/organ formula, with wailing guitar on the steaming "The Better Half."

Gang Starr
JAZZ THING

Date recorded 1990
Label CBS
Musicians Gang Starr: DJ Premier, Guru *vocal, samples*, Kenny Kirkland *piano*, Robert Hurst *bass*, Branford Marsalis *producer, sax*
Tracks Jazz Thing ❑ Instrumental
Appraisal The cutting edge of jazz rap in 1990: rap outfit Gang Starr meets neo-bop musicians. The tune pledges allegiance to the Blue Note classics and was featured in Spike Lee's jazz movie *Mo' Better Blues*.

Galliano
A JOYFUL NOISE UNTO THE CREATOR

Date recorded 1992
Label Talkin Loud
Musicians featuring Rob Gallagher, Constantine Weir *vocal*, Mick Talbot *keyboards*, Ernie McKone *bass*, Crispin Taylor *drums*, Crispin Robinson, Michael Snaith *percussion*, Valerie Etienne, Carleen Anderson, Omar *vocal*
Tracks Grounation (part 1) ❑ Jus' Reach ❑ Skunk Funk ❑ Earth Boots ❑ Phantom ❑ Jazz! ❑ New World Order ❑ So Much Confusion ❑ Totally Together ❑ Golden Flower ❑ Prince of Peace ❑ Grounation (part 2)
Appraisal British dance floor jazz from urban rap poets and funkateers with influences in New York, Jamaica, Africa, and Latin America. "Prince of Peace," originally by Pharoah Sanders and Leon Thomas, has become a classic, mingling silky soulfulness and garrulous rap.

Pharoah Sanders
JOURNEY TO THE ONE

Date recorded 1980
Label Theresa
Musicians Pharoah Sanders *tenor sax, tambura, sleigh bells*, Eddie Henderson *flügelhorn*, John Hicks, Joe Bonner *piano, electric piano*, Mark Isham *Oberheim synthesizer*, Carl Lockett, Chris Hayes *guitar*, Yoko Ito Gates *koto*, Paul Arslanian *harmonium, wind chimes*, Bedria Sanders *harmonium*, James Pomerantz *sitar*, Ray Drummond, John Julks *bass*, Idris Muhammad, Randy Merrit *drums*, Phil Ford *tabla*, Babatunde *shekere, congas*, Vicki Randle, Ngoh Spencer, Donna Dickerson, Bobby McFerrin, Claudette Allen *vocal*
Tracks Greetings to Idris ❑ Doktor Pitt ❑ Kazuco (Peace Child) ❑ After the Rain ❑ Soledad ❑ You've Got to Have Freedom ❑ Yemenja ❑ Easy to Remember ❑ Think About the One ❑ Bedria
Appraisal When Pharoah Sanders joined Coltrane in the 1960s, the hoarse, impassioned cry of his tenor would never have seemed destined for the dance floor. But in the late 1970s he hooked that spine-tingling sound to a danceable beat, and the combination of singable tunes and a timbre light years away from smooth funk tenor proved irresistible, as the anthem "You've Got to Have Freedom" proves. The spacey "Think About the One" exudes a more reflective magic.

Freebop & funk

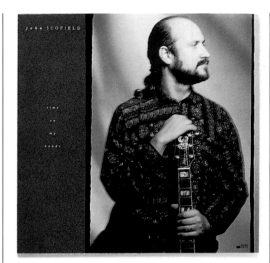

THE FUSION MUSIC OF THE 1960S AND 1970S swept separatism out of jazz. Purist prejudices about the marketplace appeal of pop music could not survive the creative onslaught of Jimi Hendrix, James Brown, Maceo Parker, Stevie Wonder, and Sly Stone — names from rock and soul that began to be mentioned as often as those of Charlie Parker, Miles Davis, Sonny Rollins, or John Coltrane, whenever young jazz musicians quoted their influences. Early fusion was often an ungainly hybrid. It had energy, spectacle, and impact, but in all but the best hands it frequently sacrificed the lightness and flow of the jazz beat, and it cramped improvisers. By the 1980s a new generation of players had learned lessons from this. Instead of grafting rock techniques onto jazz style, or vice versa, young musicians were emerging who had gradually learned these idioms together. Some were close to the avant-garde, but jazz meant to all of them a music of today, and tomorrow.

John Scofield
TIME ON MY HANDS

Date recorded November 19 – 21, 1989
Label Blue Note
Musicians John Scofield *guitar*, Joe Lovano *sax*, Charlie Haden *bass*, Jack DeJohnette *drums*
Tracks Wabash III ❏ Since You Asked ❏ So Sue Me ❏ Let's Say We Did ❏ Flower Power ❏ Stranger to the Light ❏ Nocturnal Mission ❏ Farmacology
Appraisal Bluesy, hard-driving, ex-Miles Davis guitarist's best album, influenced by Charles Mingus's writing, jazz guitar history, and rock and roll.

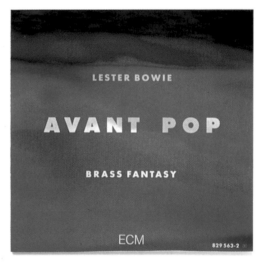

Tuck and Patti
LOVE WARRIORS

Date recorded 1989
Label Windham Hill Jazz
Musicians Tuck Andress *guitar*, Patti Cathcart *vocal*
Tracks Love Warriors ❏ Honey Pie ❏ They Can't Take That Away from Me ❏ Hold Out, Hold Up and Hold On ❏ Cantador (Like a Lover) ❏ On a Clear Day ❏ Europa ❏ Castles Made of Sand/Little Wing ❏ Glory Glory ❏ If It's Magic.
Appraisal Since Tuck Andress is virtually a band on his own, and Patti Cathcart a gospel choir, a duo with their talents never seems shorthanded. But they wear their technical prowess lightly and devote it to a tightly arranged, deceptively relaxed sounding mix of jazz standards, rock ballads, gospel, and the blues.

Lester Bowie's Brass Fantasy
AVANT POP

Date recorded March 1986
Label ECM
Musicians Lester Bowie, Stanton Davis, Malachi Thompson, Rasul Siddik *trumpet*, Steve Turre, Frank Lacy *trombone*, Vincent Chancey *French horn*, Bob Stewart *tuba*, Phillip Wilson *drums*
Tracks The Emperor ❏ Saving All My Love for You ❏ B. Funk ❏ Blueberry Hill ❏ Crazy ❏ Macho ❏ No Shit ❏ Oh, What a Night
Appraisal Art Ensemble trumpeter Bowie with a superb band including garrulous trombone star Steve Turre and the flowing blues and jazz drummer Phillip Wilson. Exhilarating, affectionate, shouting music, heavily based on 1950s rock material.

Bobby McFerrin
BOBBY MCFERRIN

Date recorded 1982
Label Elektra
Musicians Bobby McFerrin, Phoebe Snow *vocal*, Victor Feldman *keyboards*, Peter Maunu, Steve Erquiaga, Ken Karsh, Joe Caro *guitar*, Larry Klein, Stu Feldman, John Siegler, Randy Jackson *bass*, John Guerin, James Preston, Frank Vilardi, H. B. Bennett *drums*, Kenneth Nash *percussion*
Tracks Dance with Me ❏ Feline ❏ You've Really Got a Hold on Me ❏ Moondance ❏ All Feets Can Dance ❏ Sightless Bird ❏ Peace ❏ Jubilee ❏ Hallucinations ❏ Chicken
Appraisal A new breed of vocalist, McFerrin can mimic almost any instrument and can also rekindle almost any song. This disk bridges jazz and pop.

Michael Brecker
MICHAEL BRECKER
Date recorded 1987
Label Impulse
Musicians Michael Brecker *sax*, Kenny Kirkland *piano*, Pat Metheny *guitar*, Charlie Haden *bass*, Jack DeJohnette *piano, drums*
Tracks Sea Glass ❑ Syzygy ❑ Choices ❑ Nothing Personal ❑ The Cost of Living ❑ Original Rays
Appraisal One of the most revered of contemporary saxophonists, Brecker made this leadership debut of heavily jazz-angled fusion at the age of 38.

Tania Maria
COME WITH ME
Date recorded August 1982
Label Concord Picante
Musicians Tania Maria *piano, keyboards, vocal*, Eddie Duran, Jose Neto *guitar*, Lincoln Goines, John Peña *bass*, Portinho *drums, percussion*, Steve Thornton *percussion*
Tracks Sangria ❑ Embraceable You ❑ Lost in Amazonia ❑ Come with Me ❑ Sementes, Graines and Seeds ❑ Nêga ❑ Euzinha ❑ It's All Over Now
Appraisal Exuberant, energetic Latin jazz singer and pianist whose career took off internationally in the 1980s. Bebop's melody lines and Latin music's percussive chatter influence her equally, and this best-selling album features her popular, scat-like "Sangria", and the danceable title track.

Marisa Monte
MAIS
Date recorded September – November 1990
Label World Pacific
Musicians Marisa Monte *vocal*, John Zorn *alto sax*, Marty Ehrlich *tenor sax*, Bernie Worrell, Ryuichi Sakamoto *keyboards*, Arto Lindsay *guitar, vocal*, Marc Ribot, Perinho Santana, Robertinho Do Recife *guitar, violin*, Melvin Gibbs, Richardo Feijao *bass*, Romero Lubambo *violin, assovio*, Carol Emmanuel *harp*, Dougie Bowne *drums*, Prince Vasconcelos De Bois, Gigante Brazil *drums, percussion, vocal*, Armando Marcal *cuica*, Nana Vasconcelos, Cyro Baptista, Armando Marcal *percussion*, **Pastoras Da Velha Guarda De Portela** (Dona Doca, Dona Surica, Dona Eunice), Criancada *vocal*
Tracks Beija Eu ❑ Go Back to Your Home ❑ I Still Remember ❑ At Night in Bed ❑ Rosa ❑ Butterfly ❑ Soap It Up — The Washer Woman's Lament ❑ I Don't Live on Your Street ❑ Daily ❑ I Know ❑ Everything Halfway ❑ Mustapha
Appraisal Opera-trained singer, samba drummer, and TV star from Rio in an eclectic set that incorporates samba reggae — "Soap It Up" features women from the Portela samba school — co-produced by the David Byrne collaborator Arto Lindsay. Latin percussion is the boiling undercurrent, with the brilliant Nana Vasconcelos and Armando Marcal dominating it.

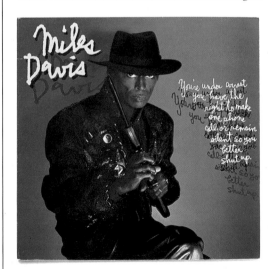

Gil Scott-Heron/Brian Jackson
FROM SOUTH AFRICA TO SOUTH CAROLINA

Date recorded 1975
Label Arista
Musicians Gil Scott-Heron *vocal, electric piano*, Brian Jackson *keyboards, flute, synthesizer*, Bilal Sunni Ali *harmonica, flute, sax*, Danny Bowens *bass*, Bob Adams *drums*, Barnett Williams *percussion*, Adenola *congas*, Charlie Saunders *congas, Chinese drum*, Victor Brown *vocal, bells, tambourine*
Tracks Johannesburg ❑ A Toast to the People ❑ The Summer of '42 ❑ Beginnings (First Minute of a New Day) ❑ South Carolina (Barnwell) ❑ Essex ❑ Fell Together ❑ A Lovely Day
Appraisal Influential singer-songwriter Gil Scott-Heron produced music to dance to, with jazz music's alertness and flow and powerful, poetic, and often angry lyrics. In the 1970s, Scott-Heron frequently collaborated with pianist Jackson, and this session includes his anthemic antiapartheid song "Johannesburg," as well as the evocative "Beginnings."

Miles Davis
YOU'RE UNDER ARREST
Date recorded 1985
Label CBS
Musicians Miles Davis *trumpet, vocal, synthesizer*, Bob Berg *soprano & tenor sax*, Robert Irving III *synthesizers, clavinet, celeste*, John Scofield, John McLaughlin *guitar*, Darryl Jones *bass*, Al Foster, Vince Wilburn, Jr. *drums*, Steve Thornton *percussion, vocal*, James Prindiville *handcuffs*, Sting, Marek Olko *vocal*
Tracks One Phone Call/Street Scenes ❑ Human Nature ❑ M.D.1/Something's on Your Mind/M.D.2 ❑ Ms. Morrisine ❑ Katia Prelude ❑ Katia ❑ Time After Time ❑ You're Under Arrest ❑ Medley: Jean Pierre/You're Under Arrest/Then There Were None
Appraisal Davis's playing in the 1980s was aimed more carefully at FM airplay and used more pop material — this set includes the Jacksons's "Human Nature" and Cyndi Lauper's "Time After Time" — but he was still capable of saying more in a single note than many musicians can in twenty.

Jack DeJohnette's Special Edition
ALBUM ALBUM

Date recorded June 1984
Label ECM
Musicians Jack DeJohnette *drums, keyboards*, Howard Johnson *tuba, baritone sax*, John Purcell *alto & soprano sax*, David Murray *tenor sax*, Rufus Reid *bass*
Tracks Ahmad the Terrible ❑ Monk's Mood ❑ Festival ❑ New Orleans Strut ❑ Third World Anthem ❑ Zoot Suite
Appraisal Great session by a leading fusion band. Jack DeJohnette was not just a percussion master, but one of the most creative leaders of the 1980s. Early jazz, funk, and bop, pungently combined.

Pat Metheny
SONG X

Date recorded December 12 – 14, 1985
Label Geffen
Musicians Pat Metheny *guitar, guitar synthesizer*, Ornette Coleman *alto sax, violin*, Charlie Haden *bass*, Jack DeJohnette *drums*, Denardo Coleman *drums, percussion*
Tracks Song X ❑ Mob Job ❑ Endangered Species ❑ Video Games ❑ Kathelin Gray ❑ Trigonometry ❑ Song X Duo ❑ Long Time No See
Appraisal This collaboration with free jazz alto saxophone guru Ornette Coleman surprised some Pat Metheny fans. But the renowned fusion-guitar romantic showed the richness and depth of his affections, imagination, and skill.

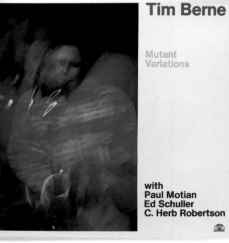

Tony Williams
ANGEL STREET

Date recorded April 4 – 6, 1988
Label Blue Note
Musicians Tony Williams *drums*, Wallace Roney *trumpet*, Billy Pierce *tenor & soprano sax*, Mulgrew Miller *piano*, Charnett Moffet *bass*
Tracks Angel Street ❑ Touch Me ❑ Red Mask ❑ Kiss Me ❑ Dreamland ❑ Only with You ❑ Pee Wee ❑ Thrill Me ❑ Obsession
Appraisal One of the most creative of post-bop drummers returned in the 1980s to the style of the Miles Davis band in the mid-1960s and set it alight all over again. His complex and canny themes were a crucial ingredient here.

The Bill Frisell Band
LOOKOUT FOR HOPE

Date recorded March 1987
Label ECM
Musicians Bill Frisell *guitar, banjo*, Kermit Driscoll *bass*, Hank Roberts *cello, vocal*, Joey Baron *drums*
Tracks Lookout for Hope ❑ Little Brother Bobby ❑ Hang Dog ❑ Remedios the Beauty ❑ Lonesome ❑ Melody for Jack ❑ Hackensack ❑ Little Bigger ❑ The Animal Race ❑ Alien Prints
Appraisal Although he has studied bop, Frisell does not sound like any other guitarist, since he mingles Hendrix, the jazz tradition, film music, country rock and many other ingredients. No pastiche, this recording is a genuine fusion of influences.

John Zorn
SPY VS SPY

Date recorded August 18, 19, 1988
Label Elektra
Musicians John Zorn, Tim Berne *alto sax*, Mark Dresser *bass*, Joey Baron, Michael Vatcher *drums*
Tracks W.R.U. ❑ Chronology ❑ Word for Bird ❑ Good Old Days ❑ The Disguise ❑ Enfant ❑ Rejoicing ❑ Blues Connotation ❑ C. & D. ❑ Chippie ❑ Peace Warriors ❑ Ecars ❑ Feet Music ❑ Broadway Blues ❑ Space Church ❑ Zig Zag ❑ Mob Job
Appraisal Zorn can play bop saxophone, but free improvisation, Disney soundtracks, and surrealism color all his work, including this breathless, flailing tribute to Ornette Coleman.

Tim Berne
MUTANT VARIATIONS

Date recorded March 5, 6, 1983
Label Soul Note
Musicians Tim Berne *alto sax*, Clarence Herb Robertson *pocket trumpet, trumpet, cornet, flügelhorn*, Ed Schuller *bass*, Paul Motian *percussion*
Tracks Icicles ❑ Homage ❑ Clear ❑ The Tin Ear ❑ An Evening on Marvin Street
Appraisal Strong session from a sax experimentalist on the borders of post-bop jazz, with remnants of 1960s free jazz and tightly defined structures. Berne devotedly avoids the obvious and develops ideas in a series of radical compositions that encourage his soloists to avoid it, too.

Gary Thomas
THE KOLD KAGE

Date recorded March – June 1991
Label JMT
Musicians Gary Thomas *tenor sax, flute, synthesizers, rap,* Mulgrew Miller, Tim Murphy, Anthony Perkins, Michael Caine *piano, synthesizers,* Kevin Eubanks, Paul Bollenback *guitar,* Anthony Cox *bass,* Dennis Chambers *drums,* Steve Moss *percussion,* Joe Wesson *rap*
Tracks Threshold ❏ Gate of Faces ❏ Intellect ❏ Infernal Machine ❏ The Divide ❏ Peace of the Korridor ❏ First Strike ❏ Beyond the Fall of Night ❏ The Kold Kage ❏ Kulture Bandits
Appraisal Muscular, large, and loud post-bop tenor player on intense and streetwise funk/jazz rap session.

Greg Osby
SEASON OF RENEWAL

Date recorded July 1989
Label JMT
Musicians Greg Osby *alto & soprano sax,* Edward Simon, Renee Rosnes *keyboards,* Kevin Eubanks, Kevin McNeal *guitar synthesizer,* Lonnie Plaxico *bass,* Paul Samuels *drums,* Steve Thornton *percussion,* Cassandra Wilson, Amina Claudine Myers *vocal*
Tracks Sapphire ❏ Enchantment ❏ For the Cause ❏ Life's Truth ❏ Dialogue X ❏ Season of Renewal ❏ Mischief Makers ❏ Word ❏ Constant Structure ❏ Eye Witness ❏ Spirit Hour
Appraisal The legacy of bop in contemporary jazz funk and rap is strong in the fast, complex Osby.

Steve Coleman and Five Elements
ON THE EDGE OF TOMORROW

Date recorded January 1986
Label JMT
Musicians Steve Coleman *alto sax, vocal,* Graham Haynes *trumpet,* Geri Allen *synthesizer,* Kelvyn Bell *guitar, vocal,* Kevin Bruce Harris *bass,* Marvin "Smitty" Smith, Mark Johnson *drums, percussion,* Cassandra Wilson *vocal*
Tracks Fire Revisited ❏ Fat Lay Back ❏ I'm Going Home ❏ It Is Time ❏ Metaphysical Phunktion ❏ (In Order to Form) A More Perfect Union ❏ Little One I'll Miss You ❏ T-T-Tim ❏ Nine to Five ❏ Stone Bone (Can't Go Wrong) ❏ Almost There ❏ Change the Guard
Appraisal Despite the funk rhythms that propel most of the music under his leadership, alto saxophonist Steve Coleman insists that his music has jazz at its core, and he remains one of the finest saxophone improvisers on the international scene. Coleman's experiments have still to resolve the merger of street music and intricate improvising. A star assembly of New York newcomers appears here.

Alto virtuoso Steve Coleman can sweep through orthodox sax techniques but seeks to build bridges between jazz and creative pop. He is a leading light in New York's progressive M-Base movement.

Worldbeat

RADIO, THE RECORD INDUSTRY, and the power-house American economy drove the word about jazz far beyond the States, and performers all over the world were playing the music of African-Americans by the 1930s. Most stood in the shadows of American heroes at first. But the past two decades have seen a startling change. In Europe, musicians have drawn on their own experiences and local folk forms, reinvigorating Celtic or Nordic songs with the surging pulses and distinctive timbres of jazz. In the former Soviet Union and Eastern Europe, jazz became an underground music of protest and independence. In North Africa, regional modal forms began to carry improvised melody lines drawn from jazz and blues. In South Africa, Duke Ellington merged with township dance music, while Japan and Australia have post-bop sax stars. The essential message of jazz — a music that enables performers to discover themselves through their unique histories — has embraced the globe.

John Surman
ROAD TO SAINT IVES

Date recorded April 1990
Label ECM
Musicians John Surman *bass clarinet, soprano & baritone sax, keyboards, percussion*
Tracks Polperro ❑ Tintagel ❑ Trethevy Quoit ❑ Rame Head ❑ Mevagissey ❑ Lostwithiel ❑ Perranporth ❑ Bodmin Moor ❑ Kelly Bray ❑ Piperspool ❑ Marazion ❑ Bedruthan Steps
Appraisal A major European jazz artist, Surman plays highly personal work linking Coltrane, English folk song, and church music. This atmospheric session is dedicated to his origins in southwest England.

Bireli Lagrene Ensemble
ROUTES TO DJANGO

Date recorded May 29 – 30, 1980
Label Jazzpoint
Musicians Bireli Lagrene *guitar*, Bernd Marquart *trumpet*, Jörg Reiter *piano*, Wolfgang Lackerschmid *vibes*, Gaiti Lagrene, Tschirglo Loeffler *guitar*, Schmido Kling *violin*, Jan Jankeje *bass*,
Tracks Bireli Swing 1979 ❑ All of Me ❑ My Melancholy Baby ❑ Boxer Boogie ❑ I've Found a New Baby ❑ Latches ❑ Night and Day
Appraisal Young gypsy guitarist Lagrene appeared to be the new Django Reinhardt of the 1980s. His records have been uneven, but this disk avoids bland fusion formulas and concentrates on some cliff-hanging improvising in an updated, post-bop Django manner.

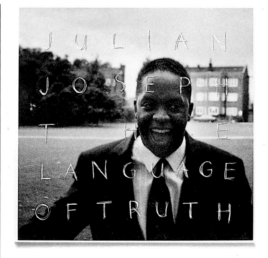

Julian Joseph
THE LANGUAGE OF TRUTH

Date recorded 1991
Label East West
Musicians Julian Joseph *piano, keyboards*, Jean Toussaint *tenor & soprano sax*, Alec Dankworth *bass*, Mark Mondesir *drums*, Sharon Musgrave, Dee Lewis *vocal*
Tracks Miss Simmons ❑ The Language of Truth ❑ Don't Chisel the Shisel ❑ Art of the Calm ❑ The Wash House ❑ The Other Side of Town ❑ The High Priestess ❑ The Magical One ❑ Brothers of the Bottom Row (Version 3) ❑ Tyrannosaurus Rex ❑ Ode to the Time Our Memories Forgot
Appraisal Fine British pianist in the Herbie Hancock acoustic tradition, with an effortlessly dynamic quartet. The execution is often thrilling.

Willem Breuker Kollektief
DE KLAP OP DE VUURPIJL

Date recorded December 31, 1985
Label BVHAAST
Musicians Willem Breuker *soprano & alto sax*, Boy Raaymakers, Andy Altenfelder *trumpet*, Chris Abelen, Bernard Hunnekink *trombone*, André Goudbeek *alto sax*, Peter Barkema *tenor sax*, Henk de Jonge *piano, synthesizer*, Arjen Gorter *bass*, Robby Verdurmen *drums*
Tracks The Little Ramblers ❑ Duke Edward/Misère ❑ El Tren Blindado ❑ Casablanca Suite ❑ Anabelle
Appraisal Dutch composer/improviser Breuker's performances are unforgettable musically and theatrically — swerving between reminiscences of Ellington and Kurt Weill, sometimes moving, sometimes hilarious.

courtney pine *to the eyes of creation*

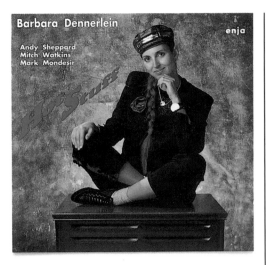

Barbara Dennerlein
HOT STUFF

Date recorded June 6 – 8, 1990
Label Enja
Musicians Barbara Dennerlein *Hammond organ, foot pedal bass, synthesizer,* Andy Sheppard *tenor sax,* Mitch Watkins *guitar,* Mark Mondesir *drums*
Tracks Hot Stuff ❑ Wow! ❑ Top Secret ❑ Birthday Blues ❑ Polar Lights ❑ Killer Joe ❑ My Invitation ❑ Seven Steps to Heaven ❑ Toscanian Sunset
Appraisal German organ queen Dennerlein mixes it with fiery young British sidemen, revitalizing the funky Hammond tradition.

Courtney Pine
TO THE EYES OF CREATION

Date recorded 1992
Label Island
Musicians Courtney Pine *soprano & tenor sax, bass clarinet, alto flute, piano, Yamaha WX7, keyboard bass, JD 800, Hammond B3 organ, Korg ML, Prophet VS, wave-station, Kurzweil 250, tamboura, drum sample d-sine, percussion,* Dennis Rollins *trombone,* Keith Waite *wooden flute, shakeres,* Julian Joseph *piano, Hammond B3 organ, wavestation,* Bheki Mseleku *piano,* Tony Rémy, Cameron Pierre *guitar,* Wayne Batchelor, Gary Crosby *bass,* Mark Mondesir, Peter Lewinson, Brian Abrahams *drums,* Frank Tontoh *drums, tambourine,* Thomas Dyani *percussion,* Mamadi Kamara *tenor talking drum, bata, thebi lipere, congo drum, cowbells, woodblocks,* Cleveland Watkiss, Juliet Roberts, Linda Muriel, Lois Farakhan *vocal*
Tracks The Healing Song ❑ Zaire ❑ Country Dance ❑ Psalm ❑ Eastern Standard Time ❑ X-Caliber ❑ The Meditation of Contemplation ❑ Life Goes Around ❑ The Ark of Mark ❑ Children Hold On ❑ Cleopatra's Needle ❑ Redemption Song ❑ The Holy Grail (parts 1 – 3)
Appraisal Pine's most focused and integrated work, fusing music from Africa, the Caribbean, America, and Europe, and uniting soul singers, reggae rhythms, and a powerful flavor of two of his abiding heroes, John Coltrane and Bob Marley.

Courtney Pine dominated the resurgence of British jazz in the 1980s, encouraging the growing confidence of young West Indian and Asian musicians.

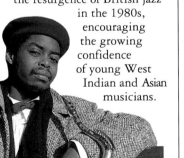

Andy Sheppard
SOFT ON THE INSIDE

Date recorded November 6 – 9, 1989
Label Antilles
Musicians Andy Sheppard *tenor sax,* Claude Deppa *trumpet,* Kevin Robinson *flügelhorn,* Gary Valente *trombone,* Chris Biscoe *alto sax,* Pete Hurt *bass clarinet,* Dave Buxton *piano,* Steve Lodder *synthesizer,* Orphy Robinson *vibes,* Pete Maxfield *bass,* Mano Ventura *guitar,* Ernst Reisjeger *cello,* Han Bennink, Simon Gore *drums,* Mamadi Kamara *percussion*
Tracks Soft on the Inside ❑ Rebecca's Silk Stockings ❑ Carla Carla Carla Carla ❑ Adventures in the Rave Trade, Part One (Smoking), Part Two (Burning)
Appraisal Latin, African, and US jazz mixed with edge-of-beyond Euro-improvising on a big band debut.

Mike Gibbs
THE ONLY CHROME WATERFALL ORCHESTRA

Date recorded 1975
Label Bronze
Musicians Mike Gibbs *keyboards*, Charlie Mariano *alto & soprano sax, flute, nadhaswaram*, Philip Catherine *guitar*, Steve Swallow *bass, electric piano*, Bob Moses *drums, percussion*, Jumma Santos *percussion*
Tracks To Lady Mac: In Retrospect ❑ Nairam ❑ Blackgang ❑ Antique ❑ Undergrowth ❑ Tunnel of Love ❑ Unfinished Sympathy
Appraisal Zimbabwe-born composer influenced by Gil Evans, Olivier Messiaen, and rock. This session features eclectic ex-Mingus saxophonist Charlie Mariano.

Jan Garbarek/Keith Jarrett
BELONGING

Date recorded April 24 – 25, 1974
Label ECM
Musicians Jan Garbarek *tenor & soprano sax*, Keith Jarrett *piano*, Palle Danielsson *bass*, Jon Christensen *drums*
Tracks Spiral Dance ❑ Blossom ❑ 'Long as You Know You're Living Yours ❑ Belonging ❑ The Windup ❑ Solstice
Appraisal Superstar pianist Jarrett was a willing experimenter with European musicians in the 1970s, and this ensemble featuring a jazzier and less isolated Jan Garbarek was one of his most evocative and original, both for the horn playing and for the unusually forthright and full-blooded piano playing.

Pinski Zoo
RARE BREEDS

Date recorded January – February 1988
Label JCR
Musicians Jan Kopinski *tenor, soprano & alto sax*, Steve Iliffe *keyboards*, Karl Wesley Bingham *bass*, Tim Bullock, Frank Tonto, Steve Harris *drums*
Tracks No Release ❑ Back Down the Mountain ❑ Nathan's Song ❑ Blueprint ❑ New Lunacy ❑ Body Moves ❑ Awkward Friends ❑ Duel in the Sun ❑ Deep Scratch ❑ Sweet Automatic (2 takes) ❑ Sun Duel
Appraisal Unusual fusion band from northern England on the disk that won *Wire* magazine's 1988 Top British Group. Energetic, pugnacious grooves from mutant disco to Miles Davis, with an Albert Aylerish tenor.

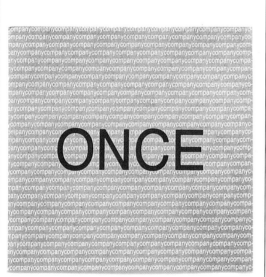

Company
ONCE

Date recorded May 12 – 17, 1987
Label Incus
Musicians Lee Konitz *alto & soprano sax, drums*, Richard Teitelbaum *keyboards*, Derek Bailey *guitar*, Carlos Zingaro *violin*, Tristan Honsinger *cello*, Barre Phillips *bass*, Steve Noble *percussion, bugle, saw*
Tracks Sextet ❑ Duo ❑ Trio I ❑ Trio II ❑ Quartet
Appraisal This ever-changing European free-playing ensemble abandons regular tonality, tunes, and tempo, yet has its alternative virtuosity and austere strength. It is joined here by cool school altoist Lee Konitz.

Keith Tippett
MUJICIAN

Date recorded December 3 – 4, 1981
Label FMP
Musicians Keith Tippett *piano*
Tracks All Time, All Time ❑ I've Got the Map, I'm Coming Home ❑ I Hear Your Voice Again
Appraisal First of a trilogy of astonishing solo piano improvisations by a British pianist sometimes showing his allegiance to Cecil Taylor, but with a textural inventiveness that often makes it hard to believe no electronics are involved.

The Paul Bley Quartet
THE PAUL BLEY QUARTET

Date recorded November 1987
Label ECM
Musicians Paul Bley *piano*, John Surman *soprano sax, bass clarinet*, Bill Frisell *guitar*, Paul Motian *drums*
Tracks Interplay ❑ Heat ❑ After Dark ❑ One in Four ❑ Triste
Appraisal Ex-Mingus, Giuffre, and Ornette Coleman partner, Bley is one of the most subtle, dramatic, and harmonically inventive of modern pianists. Although low-key and fitfully dissonant, this is an album of selfless collective interplay from four virtuoso leaders.

The Globe Unity Orchestra
INTERGALACTIC BLOW

Date recorded June 4, 1982
Label JAPO/ECM
Musicians Toshinori Kondo, Kenny Wheeler *trumpet*, Günter Christmann, Albert Mangelsdorff, George Lewis *trombone*, Bob Stewart *tuba*, Evan Parker *soprano & tenor sax*, Gerd Dudek *flute, soprano & tenor sax*, Ernst-Ludwig Petrowsky *flute, alto & baritone sax*, Alexander von Schlippenbach *piano*, Alan Silva *bass*, Paul Lovens *drums*
Tracks Quasar ❏ Phase A ❏ Phase B ❏ Mond im Skorpion
Appraisal Wild, frantic, ambitious, and often funny European free-improvisers orchestra, in the forefront of jazz structural advances since 1966.

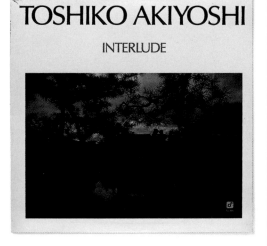

Toshiko Akiyoshi
INTERLUDE

Date recorded February 1987
Label Concord
Musicians Toshiko Akiyoshi *piano*, Dennis Irwin *bass*, Eddie Marshall *drums*
Tracks Interlude ❏ I Know Who Loves You ❏ Blue and Sentimental ❏ I Ain't Gonna Ask No More ❏ Pagliacci ❏ Solitude ❏ So in Love ❏ You Stepped Out of a Dream
Appraisal Toshiko Akiyoshi is a talented piano player — originally in the style of Bud Powell, but with a more ethereal and reflective quality — and an even better composer. For forty years she has been one of the most creative jazz artists to emerge from Japan. Oscar Peterson's interest in Akiyoshi's music took her to the States in the 1950s, and her work reflects African-American traditions more than Asian ones. This set dates from 1987, after she had built an American reputation based on both piano work and big band scores. The drummer Eddie Marshall demonstrates why he has been an Akiyoshi regular since the 1960s, shadowing and buoying up the leader constantly. "You Stepped Out of a Dream" is a lovely account of this standard by the pianist.

Loose Tubes
OPEN LETTER

Date recorded December 1987
Label EG
Musicians Chris Batchelor *trumpet*, Lance Kelly *trumpet, flügelhorn*, Dave DeFries *trumpet, flügelhorn, percussion*, John Eacott *trumpet, flugelhorn, bugle, clay trumpet*, Richard Pywell *alto & tenor trombone*, John Harborne *tenor trombone, flügelbone*, Steve Day *tenor trombone, euphonium*, Ashley Slater *bass trombone, tuba*, Dave Powell *tuba*, Iain Ballamy *alto & soprano sax, flute*, Steve Buckley *alto & soprano sax, penny whistle*, Mark Lockheart *tenor & soprano sax*, Tim Whitehead *tenor sax*, Julian Argüelles *baritone & soprano sax*, Dai Pritchard *clarinet, bass clarinet*, Eddie Parker *flute, bass flute*, Django Bates *keyboards, tenor horn*, John Parricelli *guitar*, Steve Berry *bass*, Steve Argüelles *drums, percussion*, Thebe Lipere *percussion*
Tracks Sweet Williams ❏ Children's Game ❏ Stickle-backs ❏ Blue ❏ The Last Word ❏ Ⓐ ❏ Accepting Suites from Strangers ❏ Open Letter to Dudu Pukwana
Appraisal Skilled and exuberant 1980s British big band, with its African-influenced final album. Warm, quirky, thematically original music from an open-minded outfit.

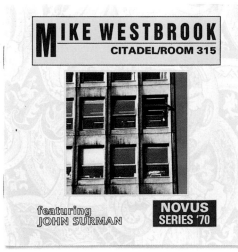

Stan Tracey
UNDER MILK WOOD

Date recorded May 8, 1965
Label Steam
Musicians Stan Tracey *piano*, Bobby Wellins *tenor sax*, Jeff Clyne *double bass*, Jackie Dougan *drums*
Tracks Cockle Row ❏ Starless and Bible Black ❏ I Lost My Step in Nantucket ❏ No Good Boyo ❏ Pen-pals ❏ Llareggub ❏ Under Milk Wood ❏ A. M. Mayhem
Appraisal From the more tentative days of European jazz, this captivating suite comes from two strong individualists — the cantankerous, percussive Tracey and the romantic Wellins.

Mike Westbrook
CITADEL/ROOM 315

Date recorded March 1974
Label RCA
Musicians John Surman *soprano & baritone sax, bass clarinet*, Henry Lowther *trumpet, flügelhorn*, Malcolm Griffiths *trombone*, Geoff Perkins *bass trombone*, Kenny Wheeler *flügelhorn*, Alan Wakeman *tenor & soprano sax, clarinet*, Mike Page *bass clarinet*, Dave MacRae *keyboards*, Brian Godding *guitar*, Chris Laurence *bass*, Alan Jackson *drums*
Tracks Overture ❏ Construction ❏ Pistache ❏ View from the Drawbridge ❏ Love and Understanding ❏ Tender Love ❏ Bebop de Rigueur ❏ Pastorale ❏ Sleep-walker Awaking in Sunlight ❏ Outgoing Song ❏ Finale
Appraisal Westbrook and his musicians took Europe by storm in the 1960s, blending Ellingtonesque richness with the roughness of Coltrane's *Ascension*. Ellington is in evidence on this disk, but so is rock music. Featured solo artist is soaring, scorching John Surman on saxes.

Vagif Mustafa-Zadeh
ASPIRATION

Date recorded 1978
Label East Wind Records
Musicians Vagif Mustafa-Zadeh *piano*, Tamaz Kurashvili *bass*, Vladimir Boldyrev *drums*, Elza Mustafa-Zadeh *vocal*
Tracks Persistence ❑ Aspiration ❑ In the Garden ❑ Dark Eyebrows ❑ The Hottest Day in Baku ❑ Concert No. 2 ❑ Autumn Leaves ❑ Bemsha Swing
Appraisal The late Azerbaidjani pianist, blending a reflective Bill Evans piano style with modal folk music rooted in the Islamic culture of his region.

Zakir Hussain
MAKING MUSIC

Date recorded December 1986
Label ECM
Musicians Zakir Hussain *tabla, percussion, vocal*, Jan Garbarek *tenor & soprano sax*, Hariprasad Chaurasia *flute*, John McLaughlin *acoustic guitar*
Tracks Making Music ❑ Zakir ❑ Water Girl ❑ Toni ❑ Anisa ❑ Sunjog ❑ You and Me ❑ Sabah
Appraisal Indian classic tabla player who heard Charlie Parker as a child and was a member of John McLaughlin's Indo-jazz band Shakti. This is one of the most fruitful of all "world jazz" collaborations.

Various Russian Artists
THE 80s DOCUMENT

Date recorded 1980s
Label Leo
Musicians featuring **Dearly Departed**; Vyacheslav Guyvoronsky *trumpet*, Vladimir Volkov *bass*; Valentina Goncharova, *strings, vocal, drums, flute*; Valentina Ponomareva *vocal*; **Arkhangelsk**; Datevik Hovhannessian *vocal*; **Orkestrion**; Petras Vysniauskas *alto & soprano sax*, Kestutis Lusas *keyboards*; Anatoly Vapirov *reeds*, Sergey Kuryokhin *piano, percussion*; **Tri-O**; Vladimir Chekasin *clarinet, alto sax, vocal, percussion, guitar*, Sergey Kuryokhin *piano, vocal, percussion, flute*, Boris Grebenshchikov *guitar, vocal, percussion*; **Homo Liber**; **Sakurov/Dronov**; **Sergey Kuryokhin Trio**; **Moscow Improvising Trio**; **Makarov New Improvised Music Trio**; **Ganelin Trio**
Tracks Composition of Russian Love Songs ❑ Skamba Gita, Jazz Raga, Five Netsuke ❑ Ocean ❑ Above the Sun, Below the Moon ❑ Concerto for Voice ❑ 1987, Tsaritson, Abyss ❑ In Memoriam ❑ Thracian Duos, Portraits ❑ Mirage, Transformation of Matters ❑ Exercise ❑ St. Petersbourg, Homage to Velemir Khlebnikov, Old Ballade ❑ Big Explosion ❑ First Recordings ❑ Natural Selection, Conspiracy, Cogito ❑ Incomplete Tendencies of Meta-reality ❑ Solo and Duo in Blue, Something Is Happening in the Seascape, Simultamente, Old Bottles
Appraisal Massive, sprawling, sometimes repetitive and unhelpfully presented package, but a fascinating survey of the underground Russian jazz and new music scene of the pre-glasnost era.

Rabih Abou-Khalil
NAFAS

Date recorded February 1988
Label ECM
Musicians Rabih Abou-Khalil *oud*, Selim Kusur *nay, vocal*, Glen Velez *frame drums*, Setrak Sarkissian *darabukka*
Tracks Awakening ❑ Window ❑ Gaval Dance ❑ The Return I ❑ The Return II ❑ Incantation ❑ Waiting ❑ Amal Hayati ❑ Nafas ❑ Nandi
Appraisal Lebanese improvising virtuoso of the eleven-string oud who has worked with jazz musicians like Charlie Mariano and Sonny Fortune. Abou-Khalil understands jazz, and it colors his powerful, ethereal music. Selim Kusur's bamboo flute lends atmosphere.

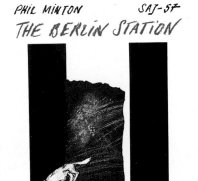

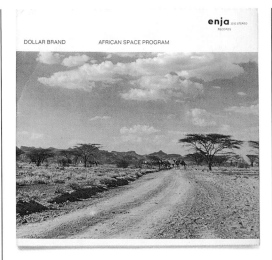

Phil Minton
THE BERLIN STATION

Date recorded 1984 – 1986
Label FMP
Musicians Phil Minton *vocal*, Peter Brötzmann *sax*, Michel Waisvisz *synthesizer*, Tony Oxley, Hugh Davies *electronics*, Ernst Reiyseger *cello*, Sven-Åke Johansson *percussion, accordion, vocal*
Tracks The Berlin Station ❏ Das Raspeln und Zischen der Nacht ❏ Lost Trainers ❏ On Metal ❏ The Slug ❏ Sweet Suite
Appraisal Minton is one of Europe's leading vocalists, handling either songs or abstract free jazz sound effects. This rugged set features the latter.

Dollar Brand
AFRICAN SPACE PROGRAM

Date recorded November 7, 1973
Label Enja
Musicians Cecil Bridgewater, Enrico Rava, Charles Sullivan *trumpet*, Kiani Zawadi *trombone*, John Stubblefield *tenor sax*, Hamiet Bluiett *baritone sax*, Sonny Fortune, Carlos Ward *flute, alto sax*, Roland Alexander *harmonica, tenor sax*, Cecil McBee *bass*, Roy Brooks *percussion*
Tracks Tintiyana (parts 1 and 2) ❏ Jabulani – Easter Joy
Appraisal Dollar Brand, now Abdullah Ibrahim, is one of the most celebrated musicians to have emerged from the South African jazz scene since the 1960s. In exile for many years, and significantly influenced by both Thelonious Monk and Duke Ellington (who introduced him to the States), Ibrahim nevertheless preserves the reverberating feel of African drums, vocal sounds, and church music in his work, which has a lyrical dignity unusual in jazz. This is a rare big band session, strongly suggestive of Ellington, built around Ibrahim's compelling composition "Tintiyana" and featuring the moving saxophone of Carlos Ward.

Salif Keita
AMEN

Date recorded 1991
Label Mango
Musicians Salif Keita *vocal*, Ron Mesa *trumpet*, Raymond Brown, Gary Bias, Reggie Young *horn*, Wayne Shorter *tenor & soprano sax*, Joe Zawinul *keyboards, arranger*, Cheik Tidiane Seck *keyboards*, Korg Pepe *accordion*, Kante Manfila, Jeff Baillard, Carlos Santana, Mamadou Doumbia *guitar*, Etienne M'Bappe *bass*, Keletigui Diabate *balafon*, Paco Sery *drums*, Souleymanne Doumbia, Bill Summers *percussion*, Djene Doumbouya, Djanka Diabate, Assitan Dembele, Nayanka Bell, Assitan Keita *vocal*
Tracks Yele n Na ❏ Waraya ❏ Tono ❏ Kuma ❏ Nyanafin ❏ Karifa ❏ N B' I Fe ❏ Lony
Appraisal Malian superstar Salif Keita's dazzling voice fuses with jazz. In a radical mix of continents, West African and Caribbean musicians record in Paris with veteran fusion heroes Joe Zawinul, arranger and producer, Wayne Shorter on saxes, percussionist Bill Summers, and the great 1970s guitarist Carlos Santana. Keita's work confirms that the "world music" movement may change its vocabulary but not its spirit of adventure.

Sadao Watanabe
CALIFORNIA SHOWER

Date recorded March 1978
Label JVC
Musicians Sadao Watanabe *alto & sopranino sax, flute*, Oscar Brashear *trumpet*, George Bohanon *trombone*, Ernie Watts *tenor sax*, Dave Grousin *piano, Fender Rhodes*, Lee Ritenour *guitar*, Chuck Rainey *bass*, Harvey Mason *drums*, Paulinho Da Costa *congas, percussion*
Tracks California Shower ❏ Duo-Creatics ❏ Desert Ride ❏ Seventh High ❏ Turning Pages of Wind ❏ Ngoma Party ❏ My Country
Appraisal Leading Japanese saxophonist on an early album featuring assorted American fusioneers. Watanabe's delicious tone shines through.

Chris McGregor
BROTHERHOOD OF BREATH

Date recorded 1970 – 1971
Label RCA
Musicians Chris McGregor *piano, xylophone*, Harry Beckett *trumpet*, Mongezi Feza *pocket trumpet, Indian flute*, Mark Charig *cornet*, Malcolm Griffiths, Nick Evans *trombone*, Dudu Pukwana *alto sax*, Mike Osborne *alto sax, clarinet*, Ronnie Beer *tenor sax, Indian flute*, Alan Skidmore *tenor & soprano sax*, John Surman *baritone & soprano sax*, Harry Miller *bass*, Louis Moholo *drums, percussion*
Tracks Mra ❏ Davashe's Dream ❏ The Bride ❏ Andromeda ❏ Night Poem ❏ Union Special
Appraisal Another Ellington-influenced South African composer. Debut of a remarkable, still-functioning orchestra, featuring the ferociously rapturous alto sound of the late Dudu Pukwana and Louis Moholo's whiplash drums.

Index

A

A Love Supreme, 40, 120, 136
Abou-Khalil, Rabih, 210
Abrams, Muhal Richard, 43
Acid Jazz label, 47
Adams, George, 49, 197
Adderley, Julian "Cannonball," 39, 41, 175, 178
Africa, 11, 12, 29, 31, 126, 127, 142
Akiyoshi, Toshiko, 209
Allen, Geri, 49, 81, 199
Allen, Henry "Red," 19, 57, 159
alto saxophone, 65
American Federation of Musicians, 28, 141
amplification, 55, 89
Armstrong, Louis, 14, 15, 17, 23, 24-5, 26, 29, 30, 34, 40, 46
   biography, 96-7
   improvising, 132, 135
   recordings, 35, 155
   scat, 19, 54,
   style, 18-19, 27, 57
   with King Oliver, 20, 21
arrangement, 137-9
Art Ensemble of Chicago, 41, 43, 186, 200
Asia, 127
Association for the Advancement of Creative Musicians (A.A.C.M.), 41, 43
Atkins, Charles "Cholly," 142, 143
"Austin High School gang," 21, 26
Ayers, Roy, 44, 49
Ayler, Albert, 40, 41, 136, 187

B

Baker, Chet, 34, 37, 170, 171, 172
Baker, Josephine, 143
Baldwin, James, 42
ballet, 144, 145
Bang, Billy, 84
baritone saxophones, 65
Basie, William "Count," 23, 30, 31, 34
   arranging 137-9
   biography, 108
   recordings, 163, 164, 169, 181, 197
   style, 26, 27, 35, 81
bass, 88-90
bass clarinet, 62
bass drum, 71
bass guitar, 88
bassoon, 68-9
Bates, Django, 50

Beatles, 40
bebop
   drumming, 73, 131
   harmony, 132
   history, 28, 29, 30-3, 38, 49
   improvisation, 135
   piano, 82
   recordings, 166-9
Bechet, Sidney, 17, 18, 19, 26
   biography, 99
   improvising, 18, 135
   recordings, 20, 25, 156
   style, 62, 64, 65
Beiderbecke, Bix, 18, 19, 21, 22, 25, 57, 98
   recordings, 159
Benson, George, 45, 46
Berigan, Bunny, 27
berimbau, 74, 75, 77
Berne, Tim, 204
Berry Brothers, 143
big bands, 22
   recordings, 188-9
Bigard, Barney, 19, 22, 62
Birth of the Cool, 29, 36, 37, 45, 171
Bitches Brew, 41, 45, 195
"Black and Tan Fantasy," 19
black bottom, 142, 143, 146
Black Jazz label, 46, 49
Black Panther Party, 41
Black Swan label, 23
Blackbyrds, 45
Blackwell, Ed, 43
Blake, Eubie, 18, 41
Blake, John, 84
Blakey, Art, 7, 47, 48
   biography, 117
   recordings, 174, 175, 197
   style, 38, 49, 70
Blanton, Jimmy, 28, 88
Bley, Carla, 40, 43, 47, 188
Bley, Paul, 208
Blood, Sweat and Tears, 44
Blue Note label, 29, 38, 141
blue note scales, 129
blues, 10, 126
   chords, 133
   history, 12-13, 29
   piano, 82
   recordings, 150-1
"Blues for Pablo," 138-9
Bluiett, Hamiet, 65
Bojangles, 22, 143
Bolden, Charles "Buddy," 14, 16, 17, 38, 57, 140
Bond, Graham, 44
boogie, 82
bop see bebop
bossa nova, 44
Bowie, Lester, 202
Brackeen, Joanne, 49
Braff, Ruby, 34, 50, 180

brass bands, 16, 17, 127
Braxton, Anthony, 43, 46, 137, 187
Brazil, 126, 131, 142, 144
breathing, circular, 66
Brecker, Mike, 44, 47, 49, 64, 65, 203
Brecker, Randy, 44
Bridgewater, Dee Dee, 54
Brooks, Tina, 177
Brotzmann, Peter, 43
Brown, Clifford, 33, 35, 38, 57, 174
Brown, James, 40, 44
Brown, Lawrence, 138-9
Brown, Ray, 88
Brubeck, Dave, 37, 173
Bruce, Jack, 44, 45
Brunies, George, 18, 60
bugle, 16
Burton, Gary, 44, 78, 79
Byrd, Charlie, 193
Byrd, Donald, 44-5, 178, 195

C

cabaret tax, 28
cakewalk, 13, 142
call-and-response, 10, 12, 127
Calloway, Cab, 22, 23, 25
Camilo, Michel, 81
candomblé, 75, 142
Carn, Jean, 54
Carnegie Hall, New York, 23, 165
Carney, Harry, 19, 62, 138-9
Carter, Benny, 180
Carter, Betty, 46, 51, 54, 183
Carter, Ron, 43, 45
Casa Loma Orchestra, 26
cello, 84, 85
Central America, 126
Chambers, Paul, 39
Charles, Ray, 39, 44, 179
Charles, Teddy, 78
Charleston, 143
Cherry, Don, 43, 47, 58, 186
Chicago jazz, 19, 20-1
   recordings, 158-9
chords, 132-3
Christian, Charlie, 27, 28, 86, 169
circular breathing, 66
civil rights movement, 35, 42-3
clarinet, 62-3
Clarke, Kenny, 28, 31, 32, 36, 49, 70
Clarke, Stanley, 88, 90
classical dance, 144, 145
Clayton, Buck, 27
Clef label, 141
clefs, 128
club dance, 146-7
club jazz, recordings, 200-1

Cole, Cozy, 70
Cole, Nat King, 45
Coleman, Ornette
   biography, 122
   recordings, 43, 47, 173, 184, 185, 186, 191, 204
   style, 35, 40, 41, 42, 44, 64, 65
Coleman, Steve, 47, 51, 64, 205
Coles, Charles "Honi," 142, 143
Coltrane, John, 31, 35, 43, 44,
   biography, 120-1
   improvising, 39, 133, 135
   modes, 40, 42
   recordings, 174, 175, 176, 187, 190
   style, 41, 64, 65, 66, 133
Columbia Records, 25, 44
Commodore label, 141
compact discs, 47
Company, 208
composition, 137-9
computers, sampling, 91
   see also synthesizers
Condon, Eddie, 21, 158
conga drum, 74
Cooke, Doc, 154
cool jazz
   history, 33, 36-7, 38
   recordings, 170-3
Cooper, Lindsay, 68-9
Corea, Armando "Chick," 45, 46, 51, 80, 81, 193, 198
cornet, 56, 97, 98
Coryell, Larry, 44
Cotton Club, New York, 19, 22, 25, 143
Cox, Ida, 160
Creole Band, 21
Creoles, 14, 16, 17, 127
Cuba, 14, 29, 40, 126, 131, 142, 144
Cubop, 29, 33
cuica, 74
cymbals, 71, 130, 131

D

Dameron, Tadd, 185
dance, 142-7
Dankworth, Alec, 88-91
Darrell, Robert Donaldson, 19
Davis, Miles, 29, 32-3, 35, 38, 39, 46 50, 51
   biography, 114-15
   modes, 42, 128, 129, 133
   recordings, 35, 41, 47, 91, 133, 137,
   solos, 7, 40, 138-9
   style, 29, 36-7, 43, 44, 45, 57, 59
Decca Records, 40
DeJohnette, Jack, 47, 70, 72, 199, 204

Dennerlein, Barbara, 207
Deppa, Claude, 56-9
Depression, 19, 22, 25, 27, 141
Desmond, Paul, 36, 64, 65, 172
Dial label, 141
Dickerson, Walt, 78
digital keyboards, 83
Dirty Dozen Brass Band, 50, 197
disc jockeys (deejays), 23, 39, 49, 91, 144
discos, 46, 144
Dixieland revival, 40
Dodds, Johnny, 62, 157
Dodds, Warren "Baby," 70
Dolphy, Eric, 40, 62, 68, 186
dominant chords, 132
Dorian scale, 129, 133
Dorsey, Jimmy, 22, 23, 26, 27, 62
Dorsey, Tommy, 22, 26, 27, 30, 60
double bass, 88-90
Dreams, 194
drums, 70-3
  cuica, 74
  history, 131
  notation, 130
  snare, 71, 130, 131
  tabla, 74
  talking, 74, 76
duple time, 130

E

Eastwood, Clint, 47, 49
Eckstine, Billy, 29, 33, 54, 160
Edison, Thomas Alva, 140
Eldridge, Roy, 30, 32, 57
Ellington, Duke, 18, 31, 36, 41
  biography, 100-1
  composing, 34, 132, 137-9
  Cotton Club, 19, 22, 25
  Newport, 35
  recordings, 163, 181
  style, 22, 26, 27, 81
Ellis, Don, 172, 188
embouchure
  clarinet, 63
  saxophone, 66
  trombone, 61
  trumpet, 57
Ervin, Booker, 176
Europe, 127
Evans, Bill, 35, 42, 46, 49, 81, 191
Evans, Gil, 29, 36, 40, 42, 45, 137-9, 188
Evans, Herschel, 27

F

Farlow, Tal, 86
Farrell, Joe, 39
Fender, Leo, 88

Fender Rhodes, 80
fingering
  double-bass, 89
  saxophone, 67
  woodwind, 69
Fisk Jubilee Singers, 12, 14
Fitzgerald, Ella, 34, 51, 54, 161, 182
Fitzgerald, F. Scott, 10, 18, 19, 48
flamenco, 127
flügelhorn, 56-7, 138
flute, 68-9
Flying Dutchman label, 49
Foster, Pops, 88
Franklin, Aretha, 41
free jazz
  history, 41, 42-3, 51
  improvisation, 136
  recordings, 184-7
freebop and funk, recordings, 202-5
Frisell, Bill, 86, 204
funk, 39, 44, 178
  recordings, 178-9, 202-5
Funk Incorporated, 201
fusion
  dance, 147
  drumming, 73, 131
  history, 44-5, 50
  recordings, 194-5

G

Galliano, 201
Gang Starr, 91, 201
Garbarek, Jan, 43, 47, 49, 64, 208
Garland, Red, 39
Garner, Erroll, 81, 180
Garrison, Jimmy, 43
Gennett label, 141, 154
Gershwin, George, 24
Getz, Stan, 29, 36, 40, 44, 193
"Ghosts," 136
Giant Steps, 35, 176
Gibbs, Mike, 208
Gibbs, Terry, 78
Gillespie, Dizzy, 23, 35
  biography, 112-13
  Cuban influence, 29, 33, 144
  recordings, 33, 168, 169
  style, 28, 31, 32, 34, 57
Giuffre, Jimmy, 62, 63, 170, 172
Globe Unity Orchestra, 209
Goldkette, Jean, 19, 26
gongs, 75, 77
Goodman, Benny, 21, 22, 23, 32
  recordings, 165
  style, 62
  swing, 26-7, 34, 143
Gordon, Dexter, 33, 37, 38, 46, 48, 49, 64
  recordings, 177, 196
gospel music, 12
Grappelli, Stephane, 22, 84
Gray, Wardell, 38

Green, Freddie, 86
Greer, Sonny, 18
Griffin, Johnny, 48, 176, 178
Grofé, Ferde, 24, 26
guitars, 86-7
  bass, 88
  fretboard, 128
Gurtu, Trilok, 74

H

Haden, Charlie, 41, 43, 88, 188
Haig, Al, 166
Haiti, 126, 142
Haley, Bill, 34
Hall, Jim, 44, 86
Hamilton, Scott, 46, 50
Hammond, John, 22, 26, 27
Hammond organs, 35, 39, 80
Hampton, Lionel, 27, 28, 78, 79, 165
Hancock, Herbie, 39, 40, 43, 45, 47
  recordings, 39, 46, 190
  style, 44, 80, 81, 82
Handy, W.C., 13, 14, 129
hard bop, 38-9
  recordings, 174-7
Hargrove, Roy, 50
Harlem Hamfats, 158
Harlem Renaissance, 25, 143
Harmon mutes, 35, 59
harmonics
  bass, 90
  guitar, 87
  saxophone, 67
harmony, 132-3
Harper Brothers, 50, 196
Harriott, Joe, 43, 186
Harris, Bill, 60
Harrison, Jimmy, 60
Hart, Clyde, 30
Hawes, Hampton, 37, 38
Hawkins, Coleman, 19, 26, 27, 31, 38
  biography, 102-3
  improvising, 135
  involvement with bebop, 28, 30, 33
  recordings, 23, 28, 43, 163, 169, 180
  style, 15, 64
Haynes, Roy, 49
Henderson, Fletcher, 19, 22, 27, 156
  bandleader, 18, 24, 26
Henderson, Joe, 48, 49, 196
Hendrix, Jimi, 41, 44, 45, 86
Herman, Woody, 29, 33, 36, 164
Hill, Teddy, 31
Hines, Earl, 19, 26, 28, 33, 81, 155, 158
hip hop, 51, 144
history, 10-51
Hodges, Johnny, 64, 138-9
Holiday, Billie, 22, 27, 35, 51, 54
  biography, 104-5
  recordings, 23, 160, 161
Holland, Dave, 46, 49, 199
Holmes, Richard "Groove," 39

Hope, Elmo, 177
Hot Fives, 19
"hot music," 14
Hot Sevens, 19
"How Come You Do Me Like You Do," 135
Hubbard, Freddie, 38, 46, 49, 177
Hughes, Langston, 42
Hughes, Spike, 19
Hussain, Zakir, 210
Hutcherson, Bobby, 78

I

Ibrahim, Abdullah (Dollar Brand), 211
"I'm a Ding Dong Daddy," 135
improvisation, 21, 134-6
independent labels, 23
intervals, 132
Islam, 29, 32

J

"Ja Da," 134
Jackson, Brian, 203
Jackson, Milt, 34, 37, 38, 78
Jackson, Willis, 200
Jamaica, 126
Jarreau, Al, 54
Jarrett, Keith, 46, 123
  style, 49, 81
  recordings, 49, 199, 208
Jazz at the Philharmonic (J.A.T.P.), 29, 103
Jazz Composers Guild, 40
Jazz Composers Orchestra Association (J.C.O.A.), 40, 41, 43
Jazz Crusaders, 179
Jazz Exchange, 144
Jazz Messengers, 34, 35, 38, 49, 197
jazz samba, 40, 131, 193
Jegede, Tunde, 85
Jenkins, Leroy, 84
Johnson, Bunk, 17, 28, 33, 152
Johnson, J. J., 60, 166
Johnson, James P., 19, 25, 81, recordings, 143, 153
Johnson, Walter, 70
Jones, Elvin, 40, 43, 70, 130
Jones, Jo, 27, 30, 31, 70
Jones, LeRoi (Amiri Baraka), 41
Jones, Philly Joe, 39
Jones, Ricky Lee, 54
Joplin, Scott, 15, 46, 94
  recordings, 153
Jordan, Louis, 29
Jordan, Sheila, 183
Jordan, Stanley, 87
Joseph, Julian, 50, 80, 81, 82-3, 206
juke boxes, 23

K

Kansas City, 18, 22, 23, 27
Keita, Salif, 211
Kenton, Stan, 29, 34, 36, 37, 189
Keppard, Freddie, 15, 17, 154
Kerouac, Jack, 35
Kessell, Barney, 86
keyboards, 80-3, 128
Kind of Blue, 7, 35, 42, 133, 191
King, Dr. Martin Luther, 40, 41
Kirby, John, 88
Kirk, Andy, 27
Kirk, Rahsaan Roland, 41, 66, 68, 69
Konitz, Lee, 34, 36, 64, 170
Kool Jazz Festival, 47, 197
kora, 85
Krupa, Gene, 21, 27, 70
Kuhn, Steve, 49

L

Lacy, Steve, 65
Ladnier, Tommy, 26, 134
LaFaro, Scott, 88
Lagrene, Bireli, 206
Laine, "Papa" Jack, 15
Lambert, Hendricks & Ross, 54, 182
Land, Harold, 37, 177
Lane, William Henry "Master
  Juba," 142
Lang, Eddie, 158
Lateef, Yusef, 40, 44, 68
Latin jazz, 131, 144
  recordings, 192-3
Lauper, Cyndi, 50
Leadbetter, Huddie "Leadbelly,"
  25, 150
Lewis, John, 34, 37, 42, 137
Lewis, Ramsey, 39
Lifetime, 45, 46
Lincoln Gardens, Chicago, 21
lindy hop, 143, 144
"lining out," 12, 127
Lion, Alfred, 29, 38
Lockwood, Didier, 84
Loose Tubes, 50, 209
Lovano, Joe, 199
Lunceford, Jimmie, 22, 27
*Lydian Chromatic Concept of Tonal
Organization*, 34, 39, 133, 190

M

M-Base, 47, 51
McCandless, Paul, 68
McCann, Les, 39
McFerrin, Bobby, 47, 51, 54, 202

McGregor, Chris, 211
McGriff, Jimmy, 44
McKinney, William, 26
McKinney's Cotton Pickers, 162
McLaughlin, John, 44, 45, 46, 86
McLean, Jackie, 35
McPartland, Jimmy, 21
McRae, Carmen, 54, 183
McShann, Jay, 30, 165
Machito, 33, 74, 193
Mahavishnu Orchestra, 46, 194
mainstream jazz, recordings, 180-1
major scales, 129, 132
Malcolm X, 41, 42
mambo, 29, 144, 146
Mangelsdorff, Albert, 60
Manhattan Transfer, 54
Mann, Herbie, 68, 194
Manne, Shelly, 70
Mantler, Mike, 40, 41, 43
maracas, 77
marching bands, 15, 16, 17
Mares, Paul, 18
Maria, Tania, 203
Mariano, Charlie, 68
marimba, 79
Marsalis, Branford, 49
Marsalis, Wynton, 47, 48, 49-50, 57
  recordings, 198
Marsh, Warne, 34, 36, 172
melody, 128-9
Metheny, Pat, 44, 45, 46, 49, 86
  recordings, 47, 91, 204
microphones, 23, 55, 141
Middle East, 127
Miley, "Bubber," 19, 25, 59, 137
Miller, Glenn, 27, 32
Mingus, Charles, 34, 40, 50
  biography, 109
  composer, 35, 42, 137
  recordings, 184, 189
  style, 88
  workshops, 35, 38, 39
minor scales, 129, 132
minstrelsy, 13, 15, 142
Minton, Phil, 211
Minton's Playhouse, New York, 28, 31
Mississippi riverboats, 15, 21
Mitchell, Joni, 109
Mizell, Fonce, Larry, 44
Modern Jazz Quartet, 34, 37, 170
modes
  harmony, 133
  history, 40
  improvisation, 136
  recordings, 190-1
  scales, 129
Moncur, Grachan, 60
Mondesir, Mark, 70-3
Monk, Thelonious, 29, 30, 35, 38, 129
  biography, 116
  composer, 28, 137
  recordings, 166, 167, 174, 175
  style, 31, 81
Monte, Marisa, 203
Montgomery, Monk, 88
Montgomery, Wes, 44, 86, 177

Moody, James, 169
Moog synthesizers, 44, 81, 83
Moore, Brew, 36
Moreira, Airto, 47, 74, 75, 200
Morello, Joe, 37, 70
Morgan, Frank, 37
Morgan, Lee, 35, 38, 39, 41, 179
Morton, Jelly Roll, 13, 19, 21, 27, 74
  biography, 95
  composer, 137
  New Orleans, 16-17
  recordings, 18, 152, 155, 157
  style, 14, 20, 81
Moten, Bennie, 18, 23, 27, 156
Motian, Paul, 70
Motown style, drumming, 73
Mulligan, Gerry, 34, 36, 37, 171, 172
Murphy, Mark, 49
Murphy, Paul, 39
Mustafa-Zadeh, Vagif, 210
mutes
  trombone, 61
  trumpet, 35, 59
  violin, 84-5

N

nagaswaram, 68
Nanton, Tricky Sam, 60, 61, 137
National Broadcasting Company, 19
Navarro, Fats, 33, 168
New Orleans
  drumming, 131
  history, 10, 14-15, 16-17, 21, 24, 126
  improvisation, 134
  recordings, 154-5
New Orleans Rhythm Kings
  (N.O.R.K.), 18, 19, 21
New York, 24-5, 30
  recordings, 158-9
Newport Jazz Festival, 35, 181
Nicholas Brothers, 143
Nichols, Red, 26
Noone, Jimmy, 62
North America, 12, 126
Norvo, Red, 78
notation, 137
  drum, 130
note values, 130,

O

oboe, 68-9
O'Day, Anita, 54, 183
Okeh label, 18, 140, 141
Oliver, Joe "King," 15, 17, 25, 57, 59
  Creole Band, 18, 20-1
  recordings, 154
  style, 57, 59
Onyx, New York, 28, 30
Original Dixieland Jazz Band

(O.D.J.B.), 15, 20, 21, 24,
  recordings, 10, 17, 140, 154
Ory, Kid, 15, 18, 21, 60, 157
Osby, Greg, 47, 51, 64, 205

P

Pacific label, 141
Page, Walter, 88, 90
Panassie, Hugues, 19
"Panassie Stomp," 138-9
Paramount label, 141
Paris Jazz Festival, 29, 32-3
Parker, Charlie, 22, 23, 34, 36, 42, 49
  bebop, 29, 30-1
  biography, 110-11
  improviser, 31-2, 38, 132, 135
  recordings, 33, 141, 165, 166, 167, 169
  style, 28, 64, 65
Parker, Eddie, 69
Parker, Evan, 43, 64
Pascoal, Hermeto, 192
Pastorius, Jaco, 88
Peacock, Gary, 199
Pepper, Art, 36, 37, 46, 64, 65
  recordings, 172, 173
percussion, 74-7
Peterson, Gilles, 39, 200
Peterson, Oscar, 181
Petrucianni, Michel, 81
Pettiford, Oscar, 88
phonographs, 140
piano, 80-3
  bebop, 82
  boogie, 82
  keyboards, 128
  pedals, 83
  stride, 13, 19, 82
Pine, Courtney, 47, 50, 207
Pinski Zoo, 208
pocket trumpet, 58
Ponty, Jean-Luc, 41, 84
Powell, Bud, 28, 81, 167
Pozo, Chano, 29, 74, 144
Presley, Elvis, 35, 38, 46, 143
Prestige label, 141
Prohibition, 18, 21, 22, 25
Public Enemy, 200
Puente, Tito, 74, 192
Pullen, Don, 49, 197
Purim, Flora, 47, 91

R

Ra, Sun, 41, 42, 185, 186
"race" labels, 13, 25, 140-1, 160
radio, 18, 21, 22, 23, 27
ragtime, 126
  history, 13, 15
  recordings, 152-3
rap, 91, 200, 201

Rainey, Ma, 13, 54, 151
Rebello, Jason, 83
recordings, 15, 22, 91, 140-1
  bebop, 32-3
  classic, 149-211
  compact discs, 47
  electrical, 19
  independent labels, 23, 46
  microgroove long-players, 34
  reissues, 47, 149
  78 rpm discs, 23
  stereo, 35
  "vinyl" discs, 34
Red Hot Peppers, 19, 95
Redman, Dewey, 43
Redman, Don, 24, 26, 132
reeds
  bassoon, 69
  oboe, 69
  saxophone, 65
Reeves, Dianne, 198
Reinhardt, Django, 22, 86, 164
religious music, 126, 127
Rémy, Tony, 86-7
Return to Forever, 45
rhythm, 130-1
Rice, Tom, 13
Rich, Buddy, 70, 72
Richardson, Jerome, 68
Richmond, Dannie, 49
ride cymbal, 71
rim shots, drumming, 72
Riverside label, 141
Roach, Max, 34, 35, 36, 38, 174
  recordings, 28, 33, 40, 43
  style, 32, 70
Roberts, Luckyeth, 19, 25, 81
Robinson, Bill "Bojangles," 22, 143
Robinson, Orphy, 78
rock and roll, 34, 38, 144
Rogers, Shorty, 37, 171
Rollini, Adrian, 78
Rollins, Sonny, 33, 38, 39, 49
  biography, 118-19
  recordings, 35, 43, 167, 174
  style, 6, 64, 65, 66, 67
Roney, Wallace, 50
"Round Midnight," 129
Royal Roost, New York, 29
Rudd, Roswell, 60
Rushen, Patrice, 45
Russell, George, 34, 39, 136, 184
  composer, 42, 133, 137
Russell, Luis, 19, 26, 156
Russell, Pee Wee, 62

St. Cyr, Johnny, 19
sampling, 91
Sanborn, David, 51
Sanchez, Poncho, 192
Sanders, Pharoah, 41, 47, 66, 191, 201

Santamaria, Mongo, 74, 193
Savoy Ballroom, New York, 22, 26, 142
Savoy label, 141
Sax, Adolphe, 64
saxophone, 18, 64-7, 134
scales, 128, 129, 132
scat, 19, 54, 55, 96
Schuur, Diane, 198
Scofield, John, 44, 47, 50, 86, 202
Scott-Heron, Gil, 46, 203
Seifert, Zbigniew, 84
shakers, 77
Shank, Bud, 68
Shankar, L., 84
Sharrock, Sonny, 86
Shaw, Artie, 23, 32, 62, 162
Shaw, Marlena, 54
Shaw, Woody, 49, 196
shekere, 75
Shepp, Archie, 41, 42, 43
Sheppard, Andy, 50, 64, 66-7, 207
Shihab, Sahib, 68, 69
Shorter, Wayne, 43, 45, 51, 64, 65
  recordings, 46, 192
show dance, 145
"The Sidewinder," 39, 41, 179
Silver, Horace, 34, 38, 44, 48, 175
  recordings, 39, 178
simdrums, 70
Simeon, Omer, 62
Sims, Zoot, 181
Sinatra, Frank, 34
singing, 54-5
Singleton, Zutty, 70
slap-tonguing, 67
slapping, 67, 90
slavery, 11, 12, 142
Smith, Bessie, 18, 19, 54
  recordings, 25, 140, 160
Smith, Jimmy, 35, 39, 44, 178
Smith, Mamie, 15, 18, 140
Smith, Stuff, 84, 85
Smith, Willie "The Lion," 81
snare drums, 71, 130, 131
"So What," 7, 129, 133
Sonning Award, 47
Sony Walkman, 47
soprano clarinet, 62
soprano saxophone, 18, 65
soul jazz, 39
South America, 126
"spasm" bands, 14
Stearns, Marshall, 31
stereo recordings, 35
Stitt, Sonny, 33, 166
Stockhausen, Karlheinz, 43, 44
Stone, Sly, 41, 44, 45
Storyville, New Orleans, 16-17, 21, 142
Strata East label, 46, 49
Strayhorn, Billy, 23
stride piano, 82
  history, 13, 19
  recordings, 152-3
stringed instruments, 84-5
subdominant chords, 132

Surman, John, 43, 63, 65, 66-7, 206
Swallow, Steve, 88
swing
  dance, 147
  drumming, 131
  harmony, 132
  history, 22, 23, 26-7, 28, 29, 32
  recordings, 162-5
  rhythm, 130
synthesizers
  Moog, 44, 81, 83
  Roland D-50, 81
  sampling, 91
  wind, 65
"Sweet Georgia Brown," 129

T

tabla, 74
talking drums, 74, 76
tambourine, 75
Tate, Buddy, 21
Tatum, Art, 23, 30, 80, 81, 135
  recordings, 153
Tavernier, Bertrand, 49, 106
Taylor, Cecil, 43, 51, 81,
  recordings, 35, 41, 184
Teagarden, Jack, 60
tenor saxophone, 64
"territory bands," 22, 26
Thomas, Gary, 51, 205
Thomas, Leon, 54, 55, 182
Thornhill, Claude, 36, 137
Threadgill, Henry, 65
Three Deuces, Chicago, 23
Three Deuces, New York, 30, 33
time, 130
Timmons, Bobby, 38, 39, 179
Tin Pan Alley, 24
Tio, Lorenzo, 17, 62
Tippett, Keith, 208
Tjader, Cal, 78
tonguing, 57, 61
Tormé, Mel, 182
Tough, Dave, 70
Toussaint, Jean, 67
Tracey, Stan, 209
triads, 132
A Tribe Called Quest, 91
Trinidad, 126
triple time, 130
Tristano, Lennie, 34, 36, 37, 81, 185
trombone, 60-1
Trumbauer, Frankie, 19, 25
trumpet, 56-9
Tuck and Patti, 202
Tucker, Earl "Snakehips," 143
Turpin, Tom, 13
12-bar blues, 133
29th Street Saxophone Quartet, 199
Tyner, McCoy, 40, 43, 49, 81
  recordings, 190

U V

Urban Species, 91
valves, trumpet, 58
Van Halen, Eddie, 87
Van Derrick, Johnny, 84-5
Vasconcelos, Nana, 74-7
Vaughan, Sarah, 51, 54, 183
Venuti, Joe, 84, 85, 158
vibraphone, 78-9
violin, 84, 85
Virgi, Fayyaz, 60-1
voice, 54-5

W

walking bass line, 90
Wall Street Crash (1929), 19, 22, 25
Waller, Fats, 22, 25, 31, 80, 81
  recordings, 141, 152, 162
Watanabe, Sadao, 211
Waters, Ethel, 18, 54, 161
Watkiss, Cleveland, 54-5
Watts, Jeff "Tain," 70
Weather Report, 39, 45, 46, 50-1, 195
Webb, Chick, 22, 26, 164
Weber, Eberhard, 85, 88
Webster, Ben, 27, 28
Wess, Frank, 68
West Coast jazz, 34
Westbrook, Mike, 41, 209
"What a Wonderful World," 135
Whiteman, Paul, 18, 19, 24, 25, 26, 48, 137
Willem Breuker Kollektief, 206
Williams, Clarence, 13, 18, 38, 155
Williams, Mary Lou, 29
Williams, Tony, 40, 43, 45, 46, 70, 195, 204
Williamson, Steve, 49
Wilson, Cassandra, 47, 51, 199
Wilson, Teddy, 22, 23, 27, 81
Wolverines, 18
Wonder, Stevie, 55
woodblocks, 74, 77
woodwind instruments, 68-9
work songs, 12, 54
worldbeat, recordings, 206-11
Wray, Sheron, 145

Y Z

Young, Lester, 22, 27, 30, 31, 35, 38
  biography, 106-7
  recordings, 164
  style, 23, 36, 64
Zawinul, Joe, 39, 41, 45, 46, 80
Zorn, John, 47, 51, 204

Acknowledgments

John Fordham Special thanks to Fred and Leo Fordham and Ros Asquith for being rejuvenating reminders that, consuming as jazz is, there is life outside it. Grateful thanks also to Val Wilmer, who set the ball rolling in my direction, to Daphne Razazan, who speeded it up; and to Susannah Marriott, this project's editor, thanks for being unfailingly patient, hip and enthusiastic.

Dorling Kindersley would like to thank Eddie Brannan for jazz and picture research; Helen Gatward, Tanya Hines, Diana Craig, and Alexa Stace for editorial assistance; Rowena Feeny, Karen Mackley, and Noel Barnes for typesetting; Sarah Ashun, Nick Goodall, Gary Ombler, Jonathan Buckley for photographic assistance; Jo Leevers for proofreading and research; Jo Edwards and Helga Evans for research; Hilary Bird for the index.

Special thanks to Sonny and Lucille Rollins, Gilles Peterson, Val Wilmer, Max and Nick Jones, Ronald Atkins, James Joseph, and Graham Lock for all their advice and expertise, and Carroll Pinkham at Serious Speakout for untiring help in organizing musicians.

Thanks to all the musicians and dancers: Cleveland Watkiss, Claude Deppa, Fayyaz Virgi, Jimmy Giuffre, John Surman, Jean Toussaint, Andy Sheppard, Eddie Parker, Lindsay Cooper, Mark Mondesir, Nana Vasconcelos, Orphy Robinson, Julian Joseph, Jason Rebello, Tunde Jegede, Johnny Van Derrick, Tony Rémy, Alec Dankworth, Urban Species, and Paul Borg; Sheron Wray, Melanie Joseph, Lorraine Le Blanc, Nikki Woollaston, Irven Lewis from Brothers in Jazz, and Legs.

Neil Ardley and Brian Priestley for advice on the Techniques section, and for selecting and transcribing examples; John Marshall for advising on rhythm and providing drum notation examples; Julian Joseph for transcribing the bebop example page 82. John Harle, George Haslam, Robyn Archer, and Chris Hodgkins for advice on the Instruments section.

Paul Wilson at the National Sound Archive for advice and information; Dr. Bruce Boyd Raeburn at the William Ransom Hogan Jazz Archive at Tulane University, and Don Marquis, Jazz Curator at the Louisiana State Museum, New Orleans, for all their advice, help, and for making us so welcome.

All those who loaned records and artifacts for photography: The Jazz Collection, Louisiana State Museum, Val Wilmer, Gilles Peterson, Max Jones, Ronald Atkins, Graham Lock; Soul Jazz, especially Stuart Baker, Simon Adams, Chrissie Murray, Victor Shonfield, John Crosby, Katrina Payne, Paul Carter, James Joseph; Honest Jon's, especially Alan Scholefield, Mr. Bongo, Ray's Jazz, Mole Jazz, Asman James; and all the companies that loaned sleeves: Fantasy, New Note, Mosaic, EMI, Harmonia Mundi, Island, Polygram, Warner Bros. Steinway & Sons for piano 80-3, Bill Lewington Ltd. for mouthpieces and reed 64, Ray Man for nagaswaram 68, Impact Percussion for vibes 78-9, Paul Clarvis for Gretsch Birdland drumkit 28, Ken Jones at the National Jazz Foundation Archive for magazine 49, Acid Jazz for t-shirt 47, Harrods for John Smedley black turtleneck 146, The Hat Shop, Covent Garden, for porkpie hat on jacket. *Down Beat* cover with permission 34; *Time* cover 49 © 1990 Time Inc. reprinted by permission; Ian Swift flyers 49 designed by Swifty Typografix.

Illustration
Stephen Bull 56, 58, 61, 62, 65, 68, 84, 86, 88. Amy Lewis 126-7; 15cl, cr; 18 b,cr; 19c, cr; 23 bl, br; 29 b x 2; 34; 40. Sarah McMenemy 18c, 23, 28-9. Stephen Michael 82, 128-36, 138-9. Lynda Payne 54, 57, 63, 64.

Photographs
Key t = top, c = center, b = bottom, l = left, r = right
All photography by the DK studio: Tim Ridley, Andy Crawford, Steve Gorton, and Sarah Ashun; and Dave King. Additional photography by Geoff Dann, Philip Gatward, Phillip Dowell, Matthew Chattle, and Paul Goff.
Val Wilmer, 20b, 42, 43, 45t, 96, 97, 99, 101t, 102, 121, 122b, 123 br, 128tr, 157b *Timecharts* 15 – 1917t • 23 – 1939c • 28 – 1942t, 1943c • 35 – 1957t, c; 1958b • 40-1 – 1961c; 1963t; 1964 t, c; 1965t, cl/136b; 1966c; 1968t, 1969c • 46 – 1970t, 1972c
James J. Kriegmann/Val Wilmer Collection, *Timechart* 29 – 1949t
Eric Jelly (photography 33)/Val Wilmer Collection, *Timechart* 35 – 1958t
Daniel Filipacchi courtesy of Val Wilmer 106b
David Redfern, 39, 44, 50, 118, 120, 132tr, 187bl, 189tr *Timecharts* 34-5 – 1951r, 1954c, 1955c, 1956t, 1958c, 1959t • 40-1 – 1961c; 1962t, 1963c/109, 1965cr, 1966t, 1967t, 1969t • 46-7 – 1972t; 1976c, b; 1982t, c; 1984c
Bob Willoughby/Redferns, 115, 173b *Timechart* 34 – 1952c, 1953t
Chuck Stewart/Redferns, 176br
J. Krebs/Redferns, 123t A. Putler/Redferns, 45b *Timechart* 46 – 1974c
Gems/Redferns, *Timechart* 46 – 1974t
Stephen Morley/Redferns, *Timechart* 46

– 1978c Mick Hutson/Redferns, *Timechart* 47 – 1984t Tim Hall/Redferns, *Timechart* 47 – 1986t Beryl Bryden/Redferns, *Timechart* 34 – 1953b
William Gottlieb/Redferns, 27, 30, 33b, 107, 116, 168b *Timecharts* 22-3 – 1934b; 1935t, c; 1939t/103t/jacket • 28-9 – 1940tl, c; 1942c; 1944t, c; 1945c/92; 1946t/113b/jacket; 1947t •34 – 1950t, 1951c
Max Jones Files/Redferns, 31b, *Timecharts* 14-15 – 1903t, 1907t • 19 – 1926c, b • 23 – 1936t • 29 – 1944bl, 1947c
Max Jones Files, 17b, 100, 104b, 105 *Timecharts* 14-15 – 1909t, 1915t, 1919t •18-19 – 1920t, c; 1925c, b; 1927t; 1928t; 1929t/95b • 22 – 1933c/104tl Max Jones/Sinclair Triall collection, 14 –1900t
Tim Motion, 5c/112, 114tl, 117, 119, 123bl *Timechart* 46-7 – 1970b, 1978t
Frank Driggs Collection, 8-9, 25r, 108t, 142t *Timecharts* 15 – 1913t, 1919b • 18 – 1921b, 1922t, 1924c/24 • 23 – 1936c • 28-9 – 1940b, 1941t, 1945t Greg Kerr/ Frank Driggs Collection, *Timechart* 29 – 1948t Charles B. Nadell/Frank Driggs Collection, *Timechart* 28 – 1940tr Popsie Randolph/Frank Driggs Collection, 36
The Bettmann Archive, 25t, 26b, 32-3, 94, 140bl, 141t, 143 *Timecharts* 18 – 1924b • 22-3 – 1930c; 1932c, b; 1934t
The Bettmann Archive/Hulton Deutsch Collection, 10t, 11, 12b, 13b, 21, 26t, 98t, 104 tr, 110, 134tr, 165b *Timecharts* 14-15 – 1907b, 1911c, 1915b • 18 – 1921t, 1923c, 1925t • 23 – 1932t, 1933t, 1937t, 1938c • 34-5 – 1954t, 1959c
Hulton-Deutsch Collection, 12t, 20t, 139 *Timechart* 14 – 1905c
Francis Wolff, courtesy of Mosaic Images, 38t, 136t
Archives Jazz Memories Francis Paudras, 31 *Timecharts* 18 – 1923t • 22-3 – 1938t Herman Leonard Archives Jazz Memories 111, *Timechart* 35 – 1955t Magnum Photos Miles Davis jacket Guy Le Querrec/Magnum Photos, *Timecharts* 34 – 1953c • 40 – 1960t
Chris Clunn, *Timechart* 47 – 1988c
Nick White, 2, 6, 130tr, 207bl *Timechart* 46-7 – 1978b, 1980t, 1982b, 1984b, 1988t
Andy Crawford, 114tr
Bruce Rae, 48
Gert De Ruyter, 51
Mary Evans Picture Library, 16b
Peter Newark's Western Americana, *Timechart* 15 – 1911b
The Advertising Archives 140t, 141b
William Ransom Hogan Jazz Archive, 10b, 17t, 125, 142b *Timecharts* 14-15 – 1900b, 1905b, 1909c, 1913b • 28 – 1944br
Solid State Logic Limited, mixing desk 91
AKAI Professionale AKAI S1000 91
Saydisc Records, Pianola Jazz 153
BMG Records (UK) Ltd., 205b
Record sleeves
reproduced with kind permission from: Atlantic Recording Corporation; Biograph^R Records Inc. 16 River St., Chatham, NY 12037, USA; Blue Note Records, a division of Capitol Records Inc.; BVHAAST; Black Lion and Candid courtesy Candid Productions Ltd.; Capitol Records Inc.; World Pacific, Pacific Jazz courtesy of Capitol Records Inc.; Castle Copyrights Ltd.; Affinity, Esquire, Tico courtesy of Charly Holdings Inc.; Circle from the catalog of Solo-Art Records 1206 Decatur Street, NO, LA 70116, USA; Concord Jazz Inc.; Concord Picante, a Div. of Concord Jazz Inc.; Red courtesy of Crepuscule;

Delmark Records; Savoy Jazz courtesy of Denon/Nippon Columbia Co. Ltd.; ECM Records; EMI Records; East West Records; album cover artwork approved on behalf of Elektra Entertainment; Enja Records; Everest Record Group; Saturn, Theresa courtesy of Evidence Records; FMP, Germany; Debut, Contemporary, Jazzland, Milestone, Pablo, Prestige, Riverside, courtesy of Fantasy Inc.; Leo Records courtesy of producer Leo Feigin; GNP Crescendo Record Co. Inc., Hollywood, California, USA; Mike Gibbs; Incus 14 Downs Rd., London E5 8D5 UK; Jazzpoint, Soul Note courtesy of Harmonia Mundi UK Ltd.; Island and Mango courtesy of Island Records Ltd.; MCA Records Inc.; Meteor courtesy of The Magnum Music Group; Montuno; Mosaic Records 35 Melrose Pl., Stamford, CT06902, USA; Nessa courtesy of Chuck Nessa; Motown courtesy of Polygram International Ltd.; RCA, RCA Victor, Bluebird © 1959, 1962, 1965, 1966, 1967, 1968, 1971, 1974, 1981, 1982, 1989 BMG Music; SAGA Continuation Ltd.; Sony S² and Sony Music Entertainment; Smithsonian Institution Press, Smithsonian/Folkways; Spotlite Jazz Sawbridgeworth, Herts CM219JJ, UK; Steam; Talkin Loud/Phonogram Ltd.; TKO Records Ltd. and its subsidiary Ember Records; VeraBra Music Group; Miracle courtesy of Victor Musical Industries, Inc.; Virgin EG Records Ltd.; Warner Bros., ©1977, 1993 Warner Bros. Records Inc.; ESP-DISK and Village with permission of ZYX-MUSIC GmbH, Germany.

Musical extracts
"Round Midnight," "So What" and "Panassie Stomp" reproduced by permission of Warner Chappell Music Ltd./ International Music Publications Ltd. "A Love Supreme" used by kind permission of Island Music Ltd., Media House, 334-336 King Street, London W6 ORA, UK "Sweet Georgia Brown" (Ben Bernie, Kenneth Casey, Maceo Pinkard) © 1925 Warner Bros. Inc. (Renewed). All Rights Reserved. Used by Permission and 33.33% Redwood Music Ltd. (Carlin) "Blues for Pablo" by permission of Solar Plexus Music (BMI) "Ghosts" by permission of Syndicore "Composition No. 107" by Anthony Braxton by permission of Synthesis Music.

Quotes
Black Nationalism and the Revolution in Music, Frank Kovsky ©1970 Pathfinder Press, reprinted by permission
Black Dance 1680 - Today with kind permission from Dance Books
Down Beat quotes pages 30, 41 reprinted with permission
Bird Lives! by Ross Russell by permission of Quartet Books
The Sound of Surprise by Whitney Balliett, *The Story of Jazz* by Marshall Stearns, *The Jazz Tradition* by Martin Williams with kind permission of Oxford University Press, Inc.

Sleeve artwork/design
Marshall Arisman for painting *Witness*, 1981 on *Young Lions*; **GIANT** for Loose Tubes *Open Letter*; **Shoot that Tiger!** for art direction and design Sidney Bechet *The Bluebird Sessions*; **Swifty Typografix** for Galliano *A Joyful Noise unto the Creator*; **Kate Westbrook** for *Citadel/Room 315*; **Joe Boyd** for Chris McGregor *Brotherhood of Breath*.